ALSO BY CARL SAFINA

Voyage of the Turtle

Eye of the Albatross

Song for the Blue Ocean

THE VIEW FROM LAZY POINT

THE VIEW FROM
LAZY POINT

A Natural Year in an Unnatural World

CARL SAFINA

with Drawings by Trudy Nicholson

Maps by Jon Luoma

A JOHN MACRAE BOOK

HENRY HOLT AND COMPANY   NEW YORK

Henry Holt and Company, LLC
Publishers since 1866
175 Fifth Avenue
New York, New York 10010
www.henryholt.com

Henry Holt® and ▊® are registered trademarks of
Henry Holt and Company, LLC.

Copyright © 2011 by Carl Safina
All rights reserved.
Distributed in Canada by H. B. Fenn and Company Ltd.

Library of Congress Cataloging-in-Publication Data

Safina, Carl, 1955–
  The view from Lazy Point: a natural year in an unnatural world / Carl Safina.—1st ed.
    p.   cm.
  "A John Macrae Book."
  ISBN 978-0-8050-9040-6
  1. Coastal ecology.   2. Marine ecology.   3. Human ecology—Philosophy.   I. Title.
  QH541.5.C65S35 2010
  508—dc22   2009040108

Henry Holt books are available for special promotions and
premiums. For details contact: Director, Special Markets.

First Edition 2010

Illustrations by Trudy Nicholson
Maps by Jon Luoma
Designed by Kelly S. Too

Printed in the United States of America
3   5   7   9   10   8   6   4   2

For Jack

"We'll talk soon!"

Only connect! That was the whole of her sermon. . . . Live in fragments no longer. Only connect.

—E. M. FORSTER, *Howards End*

I arise in the morning torn between a desire to save the world and a desire to savor the world. That makes it hard to plan the day.

—E. B. WHITE

CONTENTS

THE VIEW FROM LAZY POINT

PRELUDE

I slide a fishing rod into my kayak as birds begin gathering over our bay. They know what's coming. So do I. On many summer afternoons, packs of surfacing Bluefish chase up small fish, drawing excited flocks of diving terns. The terns carry those little fish a few miles to hungry youngsters waiting eagerly on small, unpeopled islands. As it has been for millennia, so it is this very moment.

Having long studied—and sautéed—this aspect of our neighborhood both formally and at leisure, applying both statistical models and garlic as appropriate, I can report that this relationship—prey fish, terns, Bluefish, and me—shows scant sign of failing anytime soon.

The future is by no means doomed. I'm continually struck by how much beauty and vitality the world still holds.

But beauty and vitality isn't the whole story either. In the panic among the fishes and in the frenzying terns, it's also evident that nature has neither sentiment nor mercy. What it does have is life, truth, and logic. And it strives for what it cannot have: an end to danger, an assurance of longevity, a moment's peace, and a comfortable death. It's like us all, because we are natural. What anyone needs to know about mercy, one can learn by watching nature strive, seeing people struggle, and realizing what a compassionate mind could add to the picture. So I'm also struck that we who have named ourselves "wise humans"—*Homo sapiens*—haven't quite realized that nature, civilization, peace, and human dignity are all facets of the same gemstone, and that abrasion of one tarnishes the whole.

My neighbor's cottage is right on the bay, and where I launch my kayak I find him wading waist-deep with a spade, digging sea-worms for bait. Bob hopes to slide a few porgies into his frying pan by sundown. I ask how the worm digging's going. Squinting against shards of summer light jabbing upward from the water, he says, "S-l-o-w. Even the worms are getting scarcer." He'd earlier commented on the dearth of clams. Just a few years ago we could wade out right here and, using merely our feet to detect buried clams, emerge in an hour lugging four dozen. The hour now yields perhaps half a dozen. Nothing too mysterious; a few too many people from elsewhere, having raked over their spots, found our spot. The whole world has a pretty similar story to tell.

But I don't pretend to speak for the sea-worms or the clams. The voiceless among us got on for hundreds of millions of years without hearing from me.

It's true that a lot was gone by the time I got here, and that worms are waning and clams are counting down. But, there's quite a lot left. Maybe not a lot of clams (though I've found a couple of decent pockets in the harbor, and my neighbor Dennis generously clued me to a heavy set over in—well, I probably shouldn't say), but I mean in general, a lot remains. And some of what had gone has returned. You'll see. As watching those terns and fish and the activities of my human neighbors continually reminds me, the world still brims with the living.

Yet here's the paradox: In the cycle of seasons and the waves of migrating fishes and birds that come and go along my home coast, I still find sanity, solace, and delight, more than a few fresh meals, and the power and resilience of living things; the wider lens of distant horizons, however, reveals people and nature up against trends serious enough to rattle civilization in this century.

This is a chronicle of a year spent partly along local shores, partly exploring the world from polar regions of the Arctic, across the tropics, down into the Antarctic, and home again. In some ways, this could be any year; in some ways, it couldn't be any other.

The world still sings. Yet the warnings are wise. We have lost much, and we're risking much more. Some risks, we see coming. But there are also certainties hurtling our way that we fail to notice. The dinosaurs failed to anticipate the meteoroid that extinguished them. But dinosaurs didn't create their own calamity. Many others don't deserve the calamities we're creating.

We're borrowing heavily from people not yet born. Meanwhile, the framework with which we run our lives and our world—our philosophy, ethics, religion, and economics—can't seem to detect the risks we're running. How could they? They're ancient and medieval institutions, out of sync with what we've learned in the last century about how the world really works.

So, how to proceed? I've come to see that the geometry of human progress is an expanding circle of compassion. And that nature and human dignity require each other. And I believe that—if the word "sacred" means anything at all—the world exists as the one truly sacred place. Simple things, right?

As we walk the shores and launch our travels, several axes of possibility—evidence, ignorance, indifference, and compassion—will form the north, south, east, and west upon which we'll plot our course.

Amagansett, Long Island
June 2010

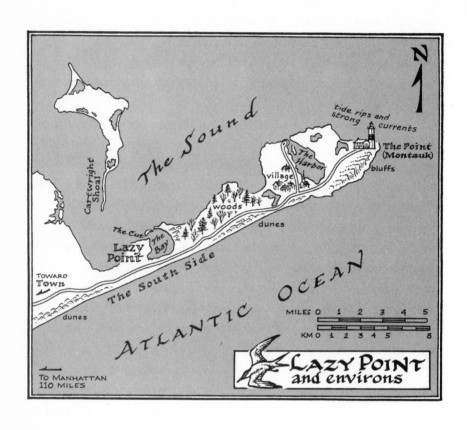

N

The Sound

tide rips and
strong   currents

The Point
(Montauk)

Cartwright
Shoal

The Harbor

village

bluffs

woods

The Cut

dunes

Lazy
Point

The Bay

TOWARD
TOWN

The South Side

ATLANTIC OCEAN

dunes

MILES 0   1   2   3   4   5

KM 0   1   2   3   4   5   8

LAZY POINT
and environs

To Manhattan
110 Miles

THE VIEW FROM LAZY POINT

My dog, Kenzie, a fifty-pound black wolf—more or less—goes loping along the shore as is her custom, energetically invested in the obvious truth that all adventure lies at the tip of one's nose. The familiar is always also the exotic, and if you can detect the scent and follow it, it'll take you far. And soon, as always, she's way ahead.

Today we woke to glass-calm water. The Sound is stretched taut to the far points of land. Out across the open water, the sea melds with hazy air and blends skyward without horizon. On a morning this placid and beautiful, dying and going to heaven wouldn't be worth it.

A few years ago, I became the "owner" of a beach cottage that had fallen into such disrepair that I could afford it. One can own an apartment or a condo or a suburban home, but when a place is already old, and if it sits amid dune grass and wild Beach Plums, and a box turtle comes confidently seeking the blackberries it has known about for decades, you feel—at least I feel—like the property has many owners and I'm just the newest tenant.

As much as I admire Henry Beston's classic *The Outermost House*, this is not a story about getting a little place out past the edge of the world and finding one's self in the solitude and the peace. This story is, though, partly about going home, about immersing in rhythms that come naturally. As a kid I'd stalk shallow waters with a net in my hand, captivated by shadows of tiny sand-colored fishes fanning away from me. Despite added detail and time, I'm still the minnow-chasing boy.

But this story's also partly about a kind of heartbreak for a world that remains so vitally unaware of how imperiled it is. The more I sense the miracle, the more intense appears the tragedy. The only way to feel better, then, is to appreciate less, which would of course feel worse. Let's put a positive spin on it and say that for now the miracle is winning.

So this story is also about the tension created when those things mistakenly called "the real world"—though they are entirely artificial—continually intrude on the *real* real world. In a *real* place, the mysteries of ages pile thick with enduring truths and complex beauties.

And that's why I was looking for a house. I'd hoped to find a home in a certain fishing village. Well, the fishing village was turning into a resort, with prices to match. The next town was long since unaffordable, too. So one day I ended up down a road through a marsh popular with mosquitoes, looking at a dilapidated summer cottage with no windows and a square hole in the roof with no skylight. It was bright—and certainly airy—but humidity posed a problem. Some of the inner walls had been torn from the studs, freeing a bloom of insulation and leaving exposed wires in a puddle under the skylight hole. Better houses have been demolished. I wisely dismissed that house as a wreck, out of the question.

I walked across the street, over the dune, and got a glimpse of the water. A five-minute beach walk took me to where a broad, shallow bay communicates with the Sound through a deep, fast-flowing channel about as wide as I might be able to cast a heavy lure. Even in the late winter, when I first laid eyes on it, I could see that this channel would be fishy in springtime. The house said I'd be crazy. The place said I was home.

It's called Lazy Point. I've been told the name derives from ne'er-do-well baymen who'd come to squat on worthless land. Whether or not that's true, I don't much care; I like the name.

In summer the place is idyllic; it can make anyone lazy. But in winter it takes effort to get comfortable with the gales. I once read that the incessant howl of wind on the prairie could drive settlers mad. I couldn't really understand how—until my first winter alone at Lazy Point.

The cottages sit on a flat peninsula of scrubby pines between the

Sound and the bay. That fishy channel I mentioned; I call it "the Cut." Along the bay's south shore runs the railroad, then the main road—two lanes—then high dunes, then the sandy ocean beach that continues on for miles. In winter it's deserted and I have it to myself. We call the ocean beach "the south side." And beyond the ocean: more ocean to the blue horizon, beyond that to the edge of the continental shelf—under six hundred feet of water—and then the deep sea, the Gulf Stream, and the rest of the world. You can feel it.

The harbor village is about five miles east; another six miles and you get to Montauk Point, a defiantly reared-up, jutting jaw of land—exposed to the open ocean on the south, and exposed on the north to the full-face force of all nor'easters. Forming the break between New England and the Mid-Atlantic, it's the southernmost rocky beach on the entire East Coast. We call this extremity simply "the Point."

None other than Walt Whitman enjoyed the exact same spot: "The eastern end of Long Island, and the Peconic bay region, I knew quite well—sail'd more than once around Shelter Island, and down to Montauk—spent many an hour on Turtle hill by the old light-house, on the extreme point, looking out over the ceaseless roll of the Atlantic. I used to like to go down there and fraternize with the blue-fishers, or the annual squads of sea-bass takers." Well, a century-plus later, "the blue-fishers and bass-takers" includes me.

With its headland, lighthouse, bluffs, buffeting breezes, surging tides, and crashing waves, this is a place of real power. All the energy draws and holds great numbers of seabirds and other ocean life. It is a great cauldron of vitality.

In the circle of a year you may see around here everything ranging from Arctic seals whose summer home is Canadian pack ice to tropical reef fishes that have ridden up from the Caribbean in flickering tongues of warm water. Some, like the terns that often lead me to dinner, breed here. Others, like harlequin-costumed Ruddy Turnstones, migrate right on through. Sometimes, thousands of miles from home, I run into migrants I'd last seen here at home.

They all remind me that the world is both much bigger than Lazy Point and yet surprisingly small. "I have traveled a great deal in Concord," reported Henry David Thoreau. And how much greater might he have thought his travels if he'd lived at Lazy Point instead. The coast and its migrants bring to Lazy Point a much bigger picture than any map of the place suggests. I sometimes tell friends it's possible to see the whole world in the view from Lazy Point.

COAST OF CHARACTERS

We've had no ice on the Sound this winter, and this morning portends more warmth, well above freezing. By now, late January, the days are already noticeably longer and the light has changed. It's a little stronger, a little brighter.

Though the beach is lovely, the air remains raw, with a damp south wind. Kenzie's dark shape is loping along far ahead, zigzagging the beach. The tide, already low, is still ebbing. Pebbles are mounded at the upper boundary of the wave wash; above them, near the swipe of highest tides, lies a line of slipper shells. Six decades ago, my neighbor J.P. tells me—and he's got photos—this beach was all sand, no pebbly stretches. A generation ago, the beach was windrowed with jingle shells. Kids, hippies, and young mothers (some people seemed all three at once) liked to string them into little driftwood mobiles to hang in windows and breezeways. Now slipper shells reign. It never occurred to anyone that counting shells on a beach could be science, so there's no data on how jingles have nearly vanished. Only the neighbors speak of it; only the neighbors know.

A large time-blackened oyster shell, newly uncovered by the collusion of wind and water, speaks of when they grew wild in abundance, and big. Every walk is a product of the present and a relic of the past. And on a very recent clamshell I recognize the perfect, tiny borehole of the predatory snail that was its assassin. Three round, translucent pebbles catch my eye; they fit snugly across my palm—not that I need more pebbles. Then again, Isaac Newton himself said, "I do not know what I may appear to the world, but to myself I seem to have been only like a boy playing on the seashore and diverting myself in now and then finding a smoother pebble or a prettier shell than ordinary, while the great ocean of truth lay all undiscovered before me." Well, exactly. So I'll grant myself the pretty stones.

The Sound reflects both the light of morning and the calls of sea ducks. I cup my ears and hear the Long-tailed Ducks' *ah—oh-da-leep*. Their call means it's winter—*and* it means I'm home. When I'm on a different coast, Long-tailed Ducks often make me feel at home. Among the gifts of the sea is a wonderfully portable sense of place. Portable because one ocean washes all shores. Like these migrants themselves, my sense of home goes where they go.

Scanning with binoculars, I locate those elegantly streamered Long-tails. The morning light is falling across their pied heads, putting a gleam on their whites and setting their pink bill tips aglow. I swivel my gaze across the water, past several Common Loons in their soft-gray winter pajamas. Red-breasted Mergansers, heads war-bonneted with ragged crests, sit scattered across the Sound. On the shore across the Cut, three Harbor Seals are resting with their bodies grace-

fully bowed, heads and rear flippers up off the sand, air-cooling themselves.

Their beauty alone is inspiring. But what in the journey of their ancient lineage led one kind to develop a black-and-white head, another a cap of ragged plumes? How does one's DNA begin building a Bufflehead and another's start assembling a seal—when cells are so similar? Each kind is an engraved invitation posted on an unlocked door that opens to a mansion bigger than human time. Step inside, and you can easily spend a lifetime.

Mysteries notwithstanding, this daily morning walk is how I take the pulse of the place, and my own. It's a good spot in which to wake up.

The sun here comes out of the sea and returns to the sea—a trick that's hard to pull off if you don't live on an island or some narrow bit of land with its neck stuck out. As Earth revolves around that disk of sun, you can watch dawn and sunset migrate across the horizon a little each day.

On a coast ruled by a wandering sun and twelve moons that pull the tides like the reins on a horse, a year means something. Seasonality here isn't just a four-season, common-time march. The rhythm of the year here beats to the pulse of a perpetual series of migrations, rivers of life along the leading line of coast. Fishes and birds mainly, but also migrating butterflies, dragonflies, whales, sea turtles, even tree frogs and toads and salamanders, whose migrations take them merely from woodland to wetland and back. Each kind moves to its own drum. Getting tuned in to the migrants' urgent energies turns "four seasons" into a much more complex idea of what life does, what life is, of where life begins and goes.

Time has been called an arrow, but here time's directionality assumes the circularity of the sky, the ocean's horizon-in-the-round. Circular time. This is perhaps time as an animal perceives it, each day replayed with all the major elements the same and every detail different. It's a pinwheel in which each petal creates the one behind it, goes once around and then falls, as all petals eventually do. Time and tide. Ebb and flow. Many a metaphor starts in water. As did life itself.

Life—Earth's trademark enterprise—starts with plants and algae capturing energy from sunlight and using solar power to turn carbon dioxide and water into sugar. Then they use the sugar they've created as fuel for turning the nutrients in soil and water into cells, and for powering growth, reproduction, repair, and defense. Whether at sea or on land, plants, and countless trillions of single-celled algae drifting in the ocean create the planet's basic living matter. They're the world's "power plants." Their exhaust gas is the oxygen that animals breathe. Basically all of life on Earth is the story of plants making and animals taking.

"Follow the money" explains a lot in politics and in nature, although nature's currency is energy. Almost all of it comes streaming to the treasury in gold bars of sunlight (some deep-sea creatures also use volcanic energy from the seafloor). The natural economy is flowing energy. World history is not the story of politics, wars, ideologies, or religions. It's the story of energy flow, beginning with a fraction of the sun's radiance falling on a lifeless planet coated with water.

When an unusually fragile new ape began using fire to harness the energy in plants it could not eat—such as wood—to initiate digestion (by cooking), ward off predators, and provide warmth, and when it learned that by assisting the reproduction of plants and animals it could garner more food, its radical new ability to channel energy flow changed the story of life on Earth.

Animals eat plants, so, ultimately, we are all grass, pretty much. Now, the astonishing thing is *how much of the grass* we are. Each time a plant of the land or coastal sea uses the sunlight's energy to make a sugar molecule or add a cell, chances are about four out of ten that the cell will become food—or be eaten by an animal that will become food—for a human. In other words, we now take roughly 40 percent of the life that the land produces; we take a similar proportion of what the coastal seas produce. For one midsized creature that collectively weighs just half a percent of the animal mass on Earth, that is a staggering proportion. It redefines "dominion." We dominate.

Maybe it's time to redefine our goals. If the human population again doubles, as some project, could we commandeer *80 percent* of life?

More conservatively, the United Nations expects the population to grow to over nine billion people by the middle of this century. That's two more Chinas. We'd have to expand agriculture onto new land, and that means using more water—but water supplies are shrinking. Since all growth must be based on what plants make using sunlight, continuous growth of the human enterprise for more than a few decades may not be possible. By midcentury it would take about two Planet Earths to provide enough to meet projected demand (add another half-Earth if everyone wants to live like Americans). In accounting terms, we're running a deficit, eating into our principal, liquidating our natural capital assets. Something's getting ready to break.

Population growth adds about seventy million people to the world each year, twice as many as live in California. Meanwhile, since 1970 populations of fishes, amphibians, mammals, reptiles, and birds have declined about 30 percent worldwide. Species are going extinct about one thousand times faster than the geologically "recent" average; the last extinction wave this severe snuffed the dinosaurs. We're pumping freshwater faster than rain falls, catching fish faster than they spawn. Roughly 40 percent of tropical coral reefs are rapidly deteriorating; none are considered safe. Forests are shrinking by about an acre per second. Compared to the day thirteen colonies on the sunrise side of a wilderness continent asserted independence as the United States, the planet's atmosphere is quite different. Ozone: thinner. Carbon dioxide: denser by a third and concentrating further. Synthetic fertilizers have doubled the global nitrogen flow to living systems, washing down rivers and, since the 1970s, creating hundreds of oxygen-starved seafloor "dead zones." Americans—only 5 percent of the world population—use roughly 30 percent of the world's nonrenewable energy and minerals. The Convention on Biological Diversity aims—*aimed*—to protect the diversity of living things, but its own assessment says, "Biodiversity is in decline at all levels and geographical scales," a situation "likely to continue for the foreseeable future."

Oh, well.

As a new force of nature, humans are changing the world at rates and scales previously matched mainly by geological and cosmic forces like volcanoes, ice-age cycles, and comet strikes. That's why everything from Aardvarks to zooplankton are feeling their world shifting. As are many people, who don't always know why.

I hope that someday, preferably this week, the enormity of what we're risking will dawn on us. So far it hasn't. True, without the environmental groups, much of the world would probably resemble the most polluted parts of eastern Europe, South Asia, China—. Then again, it does. Still, if not for Sisyphus's efforts, the stone would merely stay at the bottom of the hill. But that doesn't mean he's succeeding.

There are those for whom the dying of the world comes as unwelcome news. Many others seem less concerned. Yet maybe to have hope is to be hope. I hope life—I don't mean day-to-day living; I mean Life, capital L: bacteria, bugs, birds, baleen whales, and ballerinas—I hope Life will find a way to hold on, keep its shape, persist, ride it out. And I also hope we will find our way toward quelling the storm we have become.

The question: Why are we the way we are?

Around Lazy Point, driving all the goings-on are things partly apparent—sand, water, birds, weather, mudflats, clams, fishes, pines, oaks, tides, neighbors on two legs, neighbors on four—and partly cloaked: the carbon, water, and nitrogen cycles; the atmosphere; microbes; and other barely imagined figments of invisible reality that, for almost all of human history, remained wholly unknown.

Only since the mid-1800s have we started learning basic things about how the world actually works. For the longest time, people didn't even have a sense of—well, time. Until the early 1800s, Western people had essentially no concept of Earth's age, or that certain formerly living things had become extinct, or that the world pre-dated humans by more than a few biblical days. The modern study of life started, one might argue, with Charles Darwin. But even during Charles Darwin's times, science was primitive. Darwin was born in 1809. It wasn't until 1833 that William Whewell coined the word "scientist." It wasn't until 1842, six years after Darwin returned from his voyage on the *Beagle,* that the paleontologist Richard Owen coined the term "dinosaur." No whiff of early humanity was known until odd skulls were found in Belgium in

1829; and not until 1857 did Johann Carl Fuhlrott and Hermann Schaaffhausen announce that bones found in Germany's Neanderthal Valley were different from those of typical humans—and perhaps the remains of a very old human race. Darwin was an adult before scientists began debating a controversial new idea: that germs cause disease and that physicians should keep their instruments clean. In 1850s London, John Snow tried to combat cholera without the knowledge that bacteria caused it. In Darwin's lifetime scientists were still arguing over whether life continually arose spontaneously from nonliving things; in 1860 Louis Pasteur performed a series of experiments that eventually put to rest the idea of "spontaneous generation." (Now, ironically, many people have a hard time believing that at some point in the distant past the building blocks of life became organized into living things; but in the Middle Ages people routinely believed that flies, mice, and rats literally formed from meat, grain, and filth.)

Science has marched forward. But civilization's *values* remain rooted in philosophies, religious traditions, and ethical frameworks devised many centuries ago.

Even our economic system, capitalism, is half a millennium old. The first stock exchange opened in 1602, in Amsterdam. By 1637, tulip mania had caused the first speculation bubble and crash. And not a lot has changed. Virtually every business still uses the double-entry bookkeeping and accounting adopted in thirteenth-century Venice, first written down in the 1400s by a friend of Leonardo Da Vinci's, the Franciscan monk Luca Pacioli. His book *Summa de Arithmetica* established the concept that banks' main *assets* are other people's debts—and we know where that's gotten us recently.

So our daily dealings are still heavily influenced by ideas that were firmly set before anyone knew the world was round. In many ways, they reflect how we understood the world when we didn't understand the world at all.

Our economic, religious, and ethical institutions ride antique notions too narrow to freight what we've learned about how life works on our sparkle dot of diamond dust in space. These institutions resist change; to last this long, they had to. But they lack mechanisms for incorporating discoveries about how life operates. So they haven't assimilated the last century's breakthroughs: that all life is related by lineage, by flows of energy, and by cycles of water, carbon, nitrogen, and such; that resources are finite, and creatures fragile. The institutions haven't adjusted to new realizations about how we can push the planet's systems into dysfunction.

In important ways, they poorly correspond or respond to a changing world. You wouldn't treat an illness by calling a medical doctor from the Middle Ages, but we run the modern world with only premodern comprehension. Old thinking prevails. In the main, our philosophy of living, our religions, and our economics simply don't have a way of saying, "As we learn, so will we adjust."

Though we're fearless about revolutionizing technologies, we cling to concepts that no longer reflect realities. We're incredible at solving puzzles, poor at solving problems. And if the whole human enterprise has one fatal shortcoming, this is likely it.

Meanwhile, when thinking about this feels like walking in a world of wounds, the vitality of birds can be a partial antidote. This morning Kenzie and I decide to grant ourselves a treat and go to the lighthouse. We're looking for Razorbills and King Eiders on a fine Sunday morning.

The sea is still calm when we get to the Point—no whitecaps, no swells—but a light ruffling breeze is up, and the tide is streaming a broad current of water seaward. The southerly sun nicely side-lights the view eastward. And to the south, it shimmers the water and silhouettes the birds.

Of ducks, numbers reward us. Numbers uncountable. I scan with binoculars and see many floating scoters—Black, White-winged, and the endearingly skunk-headed Surf Scoter—and lots of Common Eiders. To the eye the scoters differ mainly in the amount and location of white patches on black bodies, though the differences go deeper. The scoters largely breed in the interior of Canada, mostly the *western* half, and into Alaska. They're long-distance migrants. Their summer grounds are so locked in ice in winter that, by comparison, our stinging-cold winter ocean is warm enough for them. The eiders, renowned for down, nest on the coldest coasts and up along the Arctic Ocean and Greenland. They're still going to need that down, because for all the short days and long nights and frigid storms of our local winter, they all live utterly exposed. Hard to imagine. Hunters consider these sea ducks too tough for the table. Well, look how tough they have to be to *live* out here. Free-range doesn't get much freer than this.

The floating clumps of ducks are called "rafts," and the rafts are nearly continuous for a couple of miles. I look at the edge of the flock and count about a hundred birds. Using this mental template, I apply it ten times to estimate a thousand. With this thousand-duck estimator I census the flocks and come up with a rather hefty approximation: twenty thousand sea ducks. The sheer abundance of ducks is both astonishing yet expected here at this season. It's really quite something

that these numbers still gather here, and that the sea supports them. It makes me wonder if this place could ever have harbored more birds.

It's possible. Early on, Europeans in the New World could scarcely believe their own eyes. In the 1620s, one Nicolas Denys wrote, "So great an abundance of Wild Geese, Ducks, and Brant is seen that it is not believable, and they all make so great a noise at night that one has trouble to sleep." He said, "All my people are so surfeited with game . . . they wish no more. . . . Our dogs lie beside this meat so much are they satiated with it."

In 1841, John James Audubon, in his epic work *The Birds of America,* said of the Black Scoter, "They congregate in vast multitudes." I don't know how many are in a multitude, but this morning's twenty thousand ducks is still a fair number.

Of the eider, Audubon says,

> This remarkable Duck must ever be looked upon with great interest by the student of nature. The depressed form of its body, the singular shape of its bill, the beautiful colouring of its plumage, the value of its down as an article of commerce, and the nature of its haunts, render it a very remarkable species. . . . The down of a nest rarely exceeds an ounce in weight, although, from its great elasticity, it is so bulky as to fill a hat. . . . The eggers of Labrador usually collect it in considerable quantity, but at the same time make such havoc among the birds, that at no very distant period the traffic must cease.

In 1917, in a different book similarly titled *Birds of America,* Edward Howe Forbush further commented about eiders,

> In Iceland, Norway, and some other parts of Europe the down is considered so valuable that the birds are conserved, tended, and protected, so that they become almost as tame as domesticated fowls. Nesting places are made for them in the turf or among the stones. . . . In some places the nests are so numerous that it is impossible to step among them without endangering the sitting birds. Some birds become so tame while

on the nest as to allow the inhabitants to stroke their feathers. . . . The down and eggs taken are not sufficient to interfere with the breeding of the birds, and both the birds and the inhabitants prosper in the partnership.

We do it differently in America. The coast of Labrador formerly was a great breeding ground of the Eider Duck . . . [but] eggers, fishermen, and settlers have destroyed both birds and eggs [they actually killed birds for down], until the vast Eider nurseries of the Labrador coast are little more than a memory.

As sport, sea-duck gunning has a wasteful tradition going back a century or so. Forbush commented that scoters are "not very appetizing . . . abominable. . . . [But] large numbers are killed merely for sport, and either left to lie where they fall or to drift away on the tide. . . . On some mornings . . . it sounds like a regular battle." The Bufflehead was called "a very common and well-known bird" in 1870, but by 1917, Forbush noted that "its great weakness is a fondness for decoys. . . . [Though] the flesh is usually not of a very good quality . . . its diminution on the Atlantic sea-board has been deplorably rapid."

I guess that helps answer my question about whether there were formerly more ducks.

We stand upon the flat boulders armoring the slope below the lighthouse, with green swells crashing the rocks before us. A Herring Gull gliding overhead is as beautiful as any idea perfected. Their abundance tends to render them invisible; it's to everyday miracles that we're most blind. With the scope I'm picking carefully through hundreds of birds, looking for those Razorbills and those Kings. There are, let's see: a couple of loons and a few gulls, some mergansers. A few grebes with light cheeks, so Horned Grebes. A couple of flying gannets skim the distance, bodies gleaming white and wingtips velvet black. No Razorbills and no Kings. Not yet.

The ebbing tide is sweeping the birds to our right, southward. When it pushes them past the submerged hills where they've been swimming down for mussels, snails, and such, they're in water a little too deep, about sixty feet. Somehow they know; they rise and fly a half mile or so uptide to reposition themselves for another drift over their feeding spots. This creates a conveyor belt of birds drifting right and birds flying left. In my binoculars, the flying birds seem to swarm across the sea surface, while just under them, thousands more ducks bob and dive. Ever mindful of their social status, many males are displaying, vocalizing, and chasing each other.

The best spots for winter ducks and summer fish here are the same, for the very same reason. Strong tides keep the region bathed in nutrients and plankton. Where broad bouldery hills and seafloor ridges rise to within thirty to fifty feet of the surface from water twice as deep, they squeeze the flow, concentrating the nourishment. Mussels get a banquet. The mussel-crusted hills provide food and—for fish—hiding places and ambush positions. Great schools of small fish coming to the plankton soup kitchen also get squeezed into closer quarters. Bigger fish come to hunt, and they, too, concentrate. When fishing here, we do exactly the same as the ducks, letting the tide take our boat over these submerged hills and then, when we're past them, going back upcurrent to do the drift again.

Makes sense, but I've often wondered: How can this place feed thousands of ducks day in and out, all the months of winter? My friends Chris and Augie are expert breath-hold spear fishermen, and they know the sea bottom like no one does. Chris says everyone thinks mussels set only on rocks and boulders, but he's also seen them set by the millions on bare sand flats in thirty to forty feet of water around those hills where the ducks focus. Augie says you can land on open bottom in places where the mussels are piled so thick and stacked so deep, they're springy; you can compress them with your hand. I knew there were mussels in the fishing spots because we snag them sometimes, but I never knew they grew like that. Coincidently, just a day or two after we were talking about this, my neighbor J.P. came to my house with his hands cupped around some seaweed called Irish Moss. He said it was washed up all along the beach—miles of it—and he wanted to show me the density at which baby mussels can set. At least a thousand very tiny mussels had settled on just his handful of washed-up seaweed. Well, I was duly impressed. The ducks are impressed enough to come a thousand miles for them.

• • •

In winter it's often blustery here. But today, with little wind, calmer water, and warmer air than usual, my eyes aren't tearing, and even without gloves my fingers aren't cold. Although I scan carefully through a couple thousand ducks that bob close enough for a good look in the telescope, I see none of the spectacular King Eiders. And none of the sleek black Razorbills.

The rarer birds are here in spirit, one might say. As with many things, looking for birds entails three increasing levels of skill: recognizing what you're looking at, knowing what you're seeking, and knowing where to find it. Want to see Harlequin Ducks? Go to one particular bouldery stretch of surf a few miles west of here. They're there most winters.

One of the benefits of knowing the local birds is that the mind tallies what is here as well as what is not, filling in the blanks, rounding out the scene. In any work of art, you're aware of what the artist has included. Yet what the artist has left out informs the work, making possible a picture that's a little larger than life. And that's partly why this coast of characters, so rich and so real, seems bigger than its physical dimensions.

The coast is an *edgy* place. Living on the coast presents certain stark realities and a wild, bare beauty. Continent confronts ocean. Weather intensifies. It's a place of tide and tantrum; of flirtations among fresh- and saltwaters, forests and shores; of tense negotiations with an ocean that gives much but demands more. Every year the raw rim that is this coast gets hammered and reshaped like molten bronze. This place roils with power and a sometimes terrible beauty. The coast remains youthful, daring, uncertain about tomorrow. The guessing, the risk; in a way, we're all thrill seekers here.

One night last summer, the air was so still you could actually see distant lightning reflected in the water; that's how calm it was. But soon that black downpour full of thunderbolts arrived upon ten thousand winged stallions that beat the water frothy, and my neighbor George's anemometer registered winds suddenly leaping to over fifty knots before one staggering *eighty-knot* gust blew it to pieces that lodged under his roof shingles. The handset of his phone blew across the living room, and the wall got plastered with sand driven right through his screens. Marilyn Badkin, now in her mid-seventies, saw it full force because their tiny beach shack is right on the dune. The next morning she said approvingly, "That was a fantastic storm."

Jackson Pollock, who worked just a few miles from here, famously said that his art was about the rhythm in nature. In a word, this place is *fluid*. Mountains, plains, and valleys dotted pleasantly with cows—to me, they seem uncomfortably . . . what is the word . . . *stuck*. The coast is no still life.

FEBRUARY

A Snowy Owl has its winter palace in the windswept dunes a few minutes' walk from my door. Having a Snowy in the neighborhood isn't an annual event; this bird is special. He—it's a very white bird, a male—has been here a week, and on most days I seek a brief and respectful audience. In bright sun his feathers gleam, and I often see him. He's harder to find on cloudy days, when his reflectance matches the pale swale of his sandy castle.

To animals whose food stopped breeding last summer, February makes no promises. For those of us accustomed to supermarket shelves that endlessly get restocked, it may seem like news to remind ourselves that winter is a race against time in a season getting hungrier. February becomes the deepest, sparest part of winter.

But lengthening days mean the sky is about to draw a deep breath.

The first singing Red-wing returns the world. This morning, the year's initial hit of Red-winged Blackbirds have sprinkled themselves thinly across our marshes.

You can tell if a winter morning is on the warm side even while you're still under your quilt with the windows shut tight, by whether the wrens are caroling, the crows crowing, the cardinals whistling, or the chicka-dees calling their own name. But no amount of wrens, crows, cardinals, or chickadees means spring.

One singing Red-wing means spring.

Except maybe to Kenzie, who just takes their calls in stride as we walk the marsh road.

Kenzie's opinion notwithstanding, a full month before the equinox these Red-wings have delivered vernal energy to these drab marshes, their lush and lustrous blackness showing just as finely as the scarlet shoulders they so exert themselves displaying. Just four days ago, a mid-February snowstorm whitened our pines and beaches. Patches of snow now splotch the straw-brown marsh and ice-paned creeks. But these newly arrived Red-wings have the place lit up with sound, and the sudden visual shock of rubies in black velvet on the bare branches.

With no females in sight, it is nonetheless for females they compete. Each will be judged by the piece of marsh he holds against the ambitions of other males. For his status and his real estate alone might he be loved. It's her proxy for guessing whether she'll get what she needs if she puts her eggs in his basket.

Of females, males care only that they be fertile. This value differential—he for his wealth, she for her womb (so to speak; egg layers lack wombs, of course)—stems from the fact that sperm are cheap and eggs expensive. Her bodily investment in offspring is much greater than his initially, so she wants to make sure he's got the goods to make the venture work. You see the implications playing out all over the animal kingdom, from the behavior of these birds to women letting men pay for a dinner date.

The Red-wings I'm watching are older, more experienced birds that have arrived first to claim the best territories. But in doing so, these pioneer pilgrims play a high-stakes game. Late freezes, cold rains that harden into ice storms, heavy snow: there are many ways to die early when you gamble for the benefits of being first.

If you come later you're less exposed to dangerous weather, but you likely don't breed. And in the harsh calculus of evolution, if you don't breed, you don't count. Not breeding is safer, but too much safety is a dead-end strategy. So for the chance to reproduce, much is risked.

These singing Red-wings are the first drip in the stream of life that will widen and deepen into a river of up-and-coming migrants. Over several months the stream will swell to include such varied components as hawks, woodpeckers, flounders, mackerel, herons, weakfish, warblers, striped bass, flycatchers, blackfish, butterflies, vireos, frogs, bluefish, terns, squid, skimmers, sharks, shearwaters, tuna, toads, dragonflies, porgies, petrels, and many others: sea turtles, whales, dolphins—. Of birds alone, over *three hundred* species regularly migrate through or stay to breed here. A sharp birder can see well over one hundred species in a day. This remains a place still—despite major losses—remarkably rich and alive.

The migrants' imperative is about food and sex. (What isn't?) For many, migration bridges breeding and feeding grounds thousands of miles distant. Whales that wintered south while fasting for weeks and giving birth now turn north toward summer feeding grounds that will soon swarm with fish and plankton. Sea turtles generally go southward when the north chills. They nest on warm beaches once every few years; in between, they may row clear around the ocean. Giant Bluefin Tuna and some other heavyweights also breed in warm seas, then move toward us. Only the birds do most of their breeding in the north, though some ocean-wandering birds nest in the distant South Atlantic and come here in summer when it's winter there. These include several shearwaters; the occasional South Polar Skua; and Wilson's Storm-Petrel, here by the thousands, which I've actually seen nesting in Antarctica. Either way, birds come northward as insects, small fishes, and the right plankton become available. Because insects and fish are profoundly affected by temperature, the birds that eat them are among the most migratory. Arctic Terns undertake the world's farthest migration, following food and summer from the Arctic to the Antarctic, about ten thousand miles and four months—each way. They see more daylight than any other creature. They pass here but usually far offshore, and are seldom detected.

All birds must track their food closely. Many small birds have their heaters turned up so high that they can starve in a day if they get uncoupled from their food supply. That's why these Red-wings sing: to hold down the territories that are their food banks.

There is no exact symmetry between northward and southbound migrations. In autumn, far greater numbers of birds and many fishes—adults and newly minted young following their first migrational urges—depart in great gusts of autumnal energy, the rushing peak of the year's powers, an urgent emergency, an insatiable, frenzied evacuation.

Then—you're left just standing there.

But I'm getting way ahead of our story. The coming days will deliver more Red-wings. Any misfortunes befalling the already arrived elders may mean a momentarily vacant territory—a younger bird's first chance to breed. But for now these birds on the reeds know little of what may happen to them tomorrow or next week. That is one of many things we share.

They fluff their plush black bodies and flare their scarlet shoulders and utter forth their souls. Their call is *kon-ka-reeee,* but a literal translation is "Here am I!" It's a good thing to be saying in late winter. Many a Red-wing of last fall no longer claims a presence in this world. In this most meager of months, for these survivors, as for us, the inevitable remains forestalled, for now. Their turf holder, this ecstatic statement of fact: I sing, therefore I am.

Anxious to keep its foothold and its competitive edge, each Red-wing is, of course, a living, acting, self-interested individual. Living things are generally entities capable of growth, reproduction, and repair—but an individual isn't as distinct an entity as it seems. No life is an island. We, the living, must be continually plugged into flowing energy and flowing materials. Animals such as we are like bonfires. Stop providing energy and material (food, fluid, and air), and we not only go out, we cease to exist. We're not like a motor or computer that can be restarted. We're much more networked, much more fragile, more ephemeral.

The biophysicist Harold Morowitz questions whether individuals are even real, "because they do not exist per se but only as local perturbations in this universal energy flow." He uses the analogy of a whirlpool in a river. The whirlpool does not exist as a separate entity; rather, it is made of an ever-changing collection of water molecules, facilitated by the energy of moving water. "It exists only because of the flow of water through the stream. If the flow ceases the vortex disappears," he says. In the same sense, living things like Red-wings and you and me "are transient, unstable entities with constantly changing molecules dependent on a constant flow of energy to maintain form." You don't just go with the flow—you live by it. The loss of the inbound flow is death. Death is merely life unplugged.

While an individual is a real entity in some meaningful ways, blurring the edges of our sense of self gives a more accurate picture. We're less like crisp photographs and more like impressionist paintings. Our material makeup is constantly changing. We are made individuals by our genes—which make us each a bit different—and by our unique actions, memories, and histories. But our histories are largely shared. All the creation myths that intuit a single origin for people are essentially correct. All life is of the same kind: a DNA framework and its consequent window dressing. There is one tree, one family of life, no other.

Albert Einstein went further, saying, "A human being is part of the whole, called by us the 'Universe,' a part limited in time and space. He experiences himself, his thoughts and feelings as something separate from the rest—a kind of optical delusion of his consciousness. This delusion is a kind of prison for us, restricting us to our personal desires and to affection for a few persons nearest to us. Our task must be to free ourselves from this prison."

If you still believe you are distinct from your surroundings, try reading the next three pages while holding your breath. The point is: you are not just an entity; you are an *interchange*.

A living thing is a knot of passing time, flowing material, and continuous energy. From dust, air, and water, energy assembles itself into the wood, leaves, bone, and muscle that we recognize as living. All lives depend on how energy pushes matter through plants and animals. Often the matter, like carbon, nitrogen, and water, cycles from one living thing to the next through the whole community. We are these dynamic processes in relationship to one another. We are a *relationship* to the world.

Ecology—the term was coined by the German zoologist Ernst Haeckel in 1866 from the Greek word for "household"—blurred the individual further. Ecology investigates how all living things depend on other living things, and on that flow of energy and materials. Ecology reveals a world where each individual seed, each creature, is an experiment, testing the waters with its own uniqueness, striving for a fit. But the chances of surviving to adulthood range from under 10 percent—for most mammals and birds with highly developed parental care—to as low as one in millions, for example for big fish that lay immense numbers of eggs.

How can so harsh a world brim with life? The whole thing works because nature preserves not individuals but the enterprise by which life struggles to survive and adapts to changes. In other words, individuals disappear, species disappear; what survives is the *process*. The living enterprise continues because the process continues. To keep life alive, what's important is this: preserve the process.

Ethics that focus on human interactions, morals that focus on humanity's relationship to a Creator, fall short of these things we've learned. They fail to encompass the big take-home message, so far, of a century and a half of biology and ecology: life is—more than anything else—a *process*; it creates, and depends on, *relationships* among energy, land, water, air, time, and various living things. It's not just about human-to-human interaction; it's not just about spiritual interaction. It's about *all* interaction. We're bound with the rest of life in a network, a network including not just all living things but the energy and nonliving matter that flows through the living, making and keeping all of us alive as we make *it* alive. We can keep debating ideologies and sending entreaties toward heaven. But unless we embrace the fuller reality we're in—and reality's implications—we'll face big problems.

• • •

The Red-wings call, listen, call again. One note is not music. It is what lies *between* the notes that makes the music. And what is between them is: their relationship. Relationships are the music life makes. Context creates meaning. Asking, "What is the meaning of life?" is the wrong question; it makes you look in the wrong places. The question is, "Where is the meaning in life?" The place to look is: between. Neither the Red-wings nor Kenzie need to be taught that what's crucial is that we be mindful of the relationships.

In a universe devoid of life, any life at all would be immensely meaningful. We *are* that meaning. "And what we see," says the poet Mary Oliver, "is the world that cannot cherish us, but which we cherish." As though life itself is the great, universal, unrequited love of all time. But there is even more to this. Deep mystery. We are the universe aware of itself.

We let the miracle get lost in distractions. On a planet so rich with living companions, much of humanity sentences itself to solitary confinement. Late at night I used to lie in my boat listening to radio calls from ships to families ashore. There was only one conversation, and it boils down to these words, repeated each time: "I love you and I miss you; come home safe." Companionship, relationship.

Connections make us individuals. Ironic, isn't it? The more connected, the more unique our life becomes. It's got to be part of the reason I feel that the animals expand the circle of my life. It's another reason living here feels more plugged in, more vivid.

Still February, yes, but the Red-winged Blackbirds awaken all this. Their voices anticipate that first faint springtime greening that makes it seem the whole world's inhaling.

MARCH: IN LIKE A LION

The first Northern Harrier in weeks comes slowly tilting just above the marsh reeds, its attention focused downward, intent on seizing opportunity. Harriers are at all times heavily invested in vole futures. When the short-tailed, small-eyed marsh mice are showing profits in progeny, harrier living is easy. Vole scarcity means hard times.

Binoculars inform that a patch of white in the marsh is not snow but—long legs, long neck—a Great Egret. I know its grace. It knows its hunger. With the temperature around freezing, this egret crucially needs the pond's saltwater to remain open so it can stalk small fish and begin reversing the depletion of its journey.

Pioneering Yellow-rumped Warblers, still molting toward spring brightness, are just beginning to filter in. And one lone Tree Swallow is zigging the marsh. Though I've recently seen a few bees and the year's first Mourning Cloak butterfly, being the first swallow seems a risky gambit, foodwise. But if the insects remain scarce, as they surely are in the chill today, Tree Swallows, unlike other swallows, can eat leftover Wax Myrtle berries—those waxy, perfumed "bayberries" once favored for candlemaking. The Yellow-rumped Warblers, formerly called Myrtle Warblers, can also digest wax. Bayberry wax is mainly made of saturated long-chain fatty acids. To turn wax into food, Tree Swallows and Yellow-rumped Warblers bring to bear an assemblage of adaptations, including a slower rate of food movement through the digestive tract, a back-and-forth movement of food between gizzard and intestine, and an increased bile concentration in the gall bladder and intestine. The ability to digest wax allows these two birds to spend winters farther north.

And they can return here well ahead of the dozens of other warbler species, ahead of other swallows, such as Rough-winged, Bank, and Barn Swallows, which remain flight-delayed until warm weather makes insects reliably airborne in late April and early May. So no matter how small or similar to others, species are usually specialized and distinguished in ways not at all obvious. These varied adaptations are both the outcome of past evolution and the raw material for adapting to future change.

It's probably worth pausing to mention that the biggest misconception about evolution is that it's "only" a theory. To most people, a theory is an untested hunch. But in science, a hunch is called a hypothesis. If a hypothesis is tested and confirmed repeatedly, and if all the confirmation creates a body of knowledge useful for predicting events, the knowledge is called "theory." That's very different. Imagine a girl sitting at a piano for the first time. She notices that some keys sound dissonant together, and others harmonize. Eventually, the child may know how notes will sound before she plays them; that's music theory. It's not "just" a theory. It's an understanding of music so thorough that one could compose a symphony despite being completely deaf—as Beethoven did. This predictive sense of "theory" is the same way scientists use the word. Atomic theory predicted that a series of procedures would cause a big explosion. Germ theory predicts that if surgeons wash their hands, fewer people will die of infections. Evolutionary theory can predict, for example, that excessive fishing will create genetically smaller fish. It explains why malaria and insects develop resistance to antibiotics and pesticides. Evolution is as scientifically accepted as gravity. And while we don't quite understand how gravity works, we know a lot about how evolution works.

Evolutionary theory predicts that the more diversified the living enterprise, the more it will adapt to change. The more diminished, the more trouble it will have. And changes are coming, faster than before, that will challenge all of us to adapt.

Over by the ocean, Kenzie and I find Sanderlings in flocks augmented by new migrants. They scurry along the surf's foamy thrusts, probing the wetted sand with bills they work like sewing-machine needles. Over the next few days their numbers will quadruple. Then they'll depart with their bills pointed northbound, toward the high Arctic. Some have wintered as far north as these beaches and Cape Cod, but many ventured vastly farther south, as far as southern Chile and the distal tip of South America. No one can explain that spread, but it means they'll be passing through for weeks. They, and most other sandpipers, must have the longest, thinnest foraging range of any birds. Think about it; they live mainly in the hairline crack between high tide and low, between the wipe of waves. You couldn't really draw their feeding range on a map of the continental coast; no line thin enough would be visible to the naked eye.

About four dozen of the birds suddenly rise. They flare over the gleaming surf and flutter back upon the sand. Up ahead, another group stand on one foot, bills tucked under wings, indulging in brief rest.

When I alter our path to avoid disturbing them, a young Harp Seal suddenly raises its head from the dry sand. I whistle Kenzie close until we're past those big doleful eyes. This is not the white-coated infant that seal hunters have famously killed for fashion. It's older, about four feet long, marked with large irregular spots. The killing—hundreds of thousands annually—did little to diminish their numbers; there remain several million. The seals' main threat is not coldhearted hunters but the warmth that is melting away the sea ice required by Harp Seal mothers for giving birth. Throughout human experience, extinction has usually required rarity and a downward trajectory. Now an animal can be both abundant and endangered.

I give this young seal a wide berth, so it won't waste precious calories dragging itself back into the surf. I get the feeling that most young wintering seals here are within ounces of their lives. And sure enough, half a mile down the beach I find a young Harbor Seal, dead.

When she comes to a series of high dunes, Kenzie, trotting a hundred yards ahead, glances toward me. And as soon as I turn around, she comes zooming back and continues past, loping the full mile down the beach. I know I'll find her panting at the foot of the path, waiting, because she knows we're family.

To March mud comes one of the more surprisingly risk-prone early arrivals, a strange, seldom-seen, earthworm-eating ground bird. Woodcocks began quietly slipping back into our woodlands during the last days of February. By early March many reside unseen back in their light-dappled haunts of wet bottomlands and damp meadows.

Such optimism with the calendar and climate runs a high risk of frost. I have read that a week of frozen ground or snow cover will starve hundreds of them, and it's difficult to imagine otherwise.

Driving to the lighthouse, I draw the luck of seeing two of them at the edge of a woodland along the south-facing shoulder of the road, probing the sun-warmed mud with their long, sensitive bills and finding much success. I've never before seen one—much less two—calmly foraging in broad daylight. I open the window, switch off the ignition, and watch.

Spending as much time as it does with its bill in the mud and all its foraging attention oriented downward, a Woodcock would seem particularly vulnerable to ambush assassins like Cooper's Hawks. Indeed, the pressure must be intense, because Woodcock camouflage is exquisite. A Woodcock so well matches fallen leaves that if it remains still it is practically impossible to notice. I imagine that to be born a Woodcock with one white feather is to draw a death sentence. The hazards of being small and round and needing to keep your bill in the ground are further evident in the positioning of Woodcocks' eyes. Predators' eyes focus frontally. Often-preyed-on animals have eyes on the sides of their heads (think of a rabbit). Woodcocks' eyes are positioned so far to the side that they sit toward the rear of their heads. It looks a little like their bill is attached to the wrong end of their skull, but with that bill in the earth and their eyes so far afield, they can still see well around them. Each eye has a 180-degree field of view, meaning the bird has no blind spot behind its head. Only an intense and continual process of elimination can evolve an animal to such extremes.

When the two Woodcocks I've been watching melt back into the forest, half an hour has elapsed. It occurs to me that I may never again get so good a view of them.

But many things are risked for love, and Woodcocks don't always hide. The normally invisible males parse the risks and rewards of courtship by calling attention to themselves—at dusk.

Based on nothing more than faith derived from the smell of moist earth, I believe Woodcocks must now be present in the shadows among the fallen leaves and pinecones in the woods around my home. So into a chilly sunset, I step from my cottage to the edge of a clearing in the pinewoods, where the needles and sandy soil lie moist. That damp earth, smelling like spring to me, must smell to Woodcocks like reassurance of another few days of thaw and food.

As dusk settles I hear that first *"Peent!"* More nasal than I remember it, almost an electronic buzz, it's an April Fool's joke of a voice. *"Peent!"* Suddenly there are two. Then a distant third.

"Peent!"

"Peent!" I say back.

This actually works. The next *peent* comes from a place much closer. When I again respond, I see a shadow move even nearer in the dusk-grayed heather.

"Peent!"

An airplane drags slow thunder. A dog barks. The twilight woods tinkle with the calls of unseen birds already self-secured into briar-tangled roosts. Robins are talking in bed. I've been drawn into a world more of sound than sight. Listening more intently than usual, I'm thinking the wren seems loud. Traffic from the main road, a mile away, often unnoticeable, seems likewise loud. So does the snoring surf beyond that road.

"Peent," calls the cautious shadow.

And now the act of daring and bravery I'm here to witness. Suddenly comes the strange twittering that signals Woodcock flight. I can't spot the suitor until it has risen past the trees, but then I see that odd ball of a bird with round whirring wings and that bayonet bill emerge from the skyline of branches scrawled on the western blush of dusk.

I follow with binoculars its wide-spiral display as the twitter of its whistling wings intensifies, then follow higher, till this noisy dot is almost directly overhead and its track crosses the night's first star. It continues screwing itself deeper into the sky. The twittering climaxes to a frenzied pitch and peak, as the bird arcs through one last slow overhead spiral, drops a bit without letting up the frenzied fluttering, then suddenly goes silent, as though the faucet of sound has abruptly been turned off.

I watch the bird plummeting rapidly, then slipping sideways like a falling leaf until I lose it against the trees; soon it lands again on the same stretch of open ground.

Almost immediately: "*Peent!*"

Through several such cycles, I linger. I hear other, more distant Woodcocks rise too and twitter ardor to the galaxy. Dusk pulls down the night, quieting the robins and a few chill-resistant Spring Peepers, who begin calling from a marshy pond at the woodlands' edge.

Among Lazy Point's many splendors is a sky dark enough to really fill up with stars as soon as night falls. The newspaper has reported, "Two-thirds of Americans and a fifth of the world can no longer see the Milky Way." That's not a problem here. Especially on a clear, moonless night. My binoculars are strong enough to pry apart the Pleiades star cluster, and reveal much more depth in the galaxy—many thousands more stars—than I can see by naked eye. Surely worlds lie up there? So far our navigational charts of space show only distant desert islands, of utmost hostility, with this floating vessel our shared ark, our one chance. One day this understanding, too, may give way to include other worlds. Perhaps, as we fear, better worlds. But so far, this our world includes all the life, all the love, and all the mind yet detected. So, a question arises: What ought we do?

It's an old question. Nearly twenty-five hundred years ago, Socrates realized that "we are discussing no small matter, but how we ought to live." Aristotle helped get the ball rolling twenty-three hundred years ago: "Plants exist for the sake of animals . . . animals exist for the sake of man. . . . It must be that nature has made all things specifically for the sake of man." Saint Thomas Aquinas (in the 1200s) believed that only humans have an eternal soul (implying that other animals are terminal cases with no escape from Earth), that God gave all the animals to people for our use, and that people can kill or use animals however we desire, "without any injustice." "The world is made for man, not man for the world," said Francis Bacon (around 1600). René Descartes (1600s) believed that animals lack consciousness and could be treated without concern for their well-being. He declared men "lords and possessors of nature." Immanuel Kant (1700s) believed that each moral being has the right at all times to be treated respectfully as an equally free and rational being, but that only rational beings are moral beings, and only humans are rational beings. To Sigmund Freud, "the principal task of civilization, its actual *raison d'être,* is to defend us against nature" (1927).

These thinkers drew a chalk circle around humanity and erected a firewall between us and the rest of creation. They may sound arrogant now, but their time was not our time. The scale of the human enterprise was small, the world vast. They worried that nature would destroy people—and it often did. The world—so far as they knew it—didn't need our sympathy. That humans might ever acquire power to harm the world could scarcely have crossed their minds. They thought only about creating a conceptual space for humanity and improving human interactions.

Even the animal-rights movement, though often viewed as radical, focuses only on individual animals that appear capable of suffering (so, for instance, not oysters). The obvious limitations are major. A cow can experience pain, but a *herd* can't. So conserving populations or preventing extinction lies outside animal rightists' usual considerations. Saving pigs from slaughter is a concern of animal-rights proponents. Preserving a forest, not so much; the trees aren't animals. Animal-rights activists have famously protested conservationists' plans to live-trap feral house cats in order to save endangered colonies of ground-nesting birds like terns and plovers. Apparently the cats have a right to be free, but birds have no "rights" to be spared predation by people's escaped pets. On the major issues affecting animals' future—endangered species, human poverty, human encroachment, forest destruction, ocean depletion, pollution, climate and ocean-chemistry change—giving individual animals rights offers no actual help. Animal-rights philosophy, so focused on "sentience," is itself unaware of ecological relationships and seemingly unconscious of the big picture.

Viewed by the light of what we know, much of mainstream philosophy can seem like an astonishing series of self-serving cop-outs. Essentially all of philosophy misunderstands where attention must be paid if humanity might ensure its own longevity and the continuity of the living enterprise. These are the foundations of Western self-identity and our declared relationship with the world.

The things that matter in the long run—life-supporting systems and the very cycles that produce and facilitate people, culture, living things, and the future—are the things ethicists have almost completely ignored. That is quite an achievement of Western thought!

In the main, philosophy hasn't had the world in mind. And the problem is—it shows.

The second week of March opened with the kind of deep freeze that can kill early migrants. Temperatures down to 15 degrees Fahrenheit grew shelves of shore-fast sea ice in the Sound. Biting winds drove explosive surf that recontoured the oceanside beach.

But the ides of March dawns sunny, and the air has that spring-morning light that promises later warmth. Unlike the withering cold blasts of a few nights ago, today's wind, though cool, blows southerly, pushing the tails of oncoming birds, bringing more first arrivals. On the marsh shore stands the first American Oystercatcher, wielding its wondrous crimson pry-bar bill.

Momentously, our first Osprey sails over and hovers in the stiff breeze above the pond, feathers rippling, before swooping across the marsh to

light upon its massive aerie. Its first task: defend the fortress and deflect rivals. Challengers soon appear. They can all see one another very well up there, and before long three of the big fish hawks are writing the letter *O* across the sky, negotiating airspace. Their thin chirping whistles are not what you'd expect from weapon-wearing birds with six-foot wingspans.

Over on the ocean beach, the first Piping Plover looks like a running dollop of sand. When it stops, it disappears. These tiny plovers were once perhaps the most endangered nesting bird on Long Island. A couple of decades of keeping people away from their sandy nests with nothing more than one strand of string and a little flagging tape has done much to help them. Protecting their nests with cages that are pervious to plovers but impervious to cats, coons, and foxes has helped as much, perhaps more.

dogs

From just outside the surf and above the ocean horizon, skeins of scoters are purring by, draining away toward the distant north. They continue steadily for the hour Kenzie and I are walking, about three hundred birds per hour. Winter birds are leaving, summer birds arriving, everything shifting north toward the lengthening sun.

❧

Just as I was getting used to spring, this morning delivers a dusting of snow at a startling 23 degrees. It chills the Red-wings to silence. Our hardened ponds have locked out the ducks. In a brilliantly cold blue sky, a Red-tailed Hawk circles the marsh; it knows a snow-white tablecloth is good for spotting mud-brown voles. The voles know too, and hunker tight in their highways in the bent-over grass.

I'm going to correct myself. Or at least amend something. I've said that ethics, religion, and economics reflect philosophies devised centuries ago and doesn't accord well with the last 150 years of science, and that our thinking is way behind. But not all the old thinking was narrow. To every tide, a countercurrent. A few philosophers came closer to getting it right. And in every case it's because they actually left the house to see what the world is really like.

In the mid-1700s, Gilbert White of Selborne, an English clergyman, helped establish a respect for nature as a kind of philosophical sub-theme. In the early days of systematic observation, many important men of science were clergymen. Studying God's work—the world itself—was a way to better understand the Creator. White thus introduces his purpose for writing *The Natural History of Selborne:*

> If the writer should at all appear to have induced any of his readers to pay a more ready attention to the wonders of the Creation, too frequently overlooked as common occurrences; or if he should by any means, through his researches, have lent an helping hand towards the enlargement of the boundaries of historical and topographical knowledge . . . his purpose will be fully answered. But if he should not have been successful in any of these his intentions, yet there remains this consolation behind—that these his pursuits, by keeping the body and mind employed, have, under Providence, contributed to much health and cheerfulness of spirits, even to old age.

I like that phrase "enlargement of the boundaries." It's the pattern of all human progress. Later in his book, he says,

> The most insignificant insects and reptiles are of much more conse-quence, and have much more influence in the Economy of nature, than

the incurious are aware of; and are mighty in their effect, from their minuteness, which renders them less an object of attention; and from their numbers and fecundity. Earth-worms, though in appearance a small and despicable link in the chain of nature, yet, if lost, would make a lamentable chasm. For, to say nothing of half the birds, and some quadrupeds, which are almost entirely supported by them, worms seem to be the great promoters of vegetation, which would proceed but lamely without them, by boring, perforating, and loosening the soil, and rendering it pervious to rains and the fibres of plants, by drawing straws and stalks of leaves and twigs into it; and, most of all, by throwing up such infinite numbers of lumps of earth called worm-casts, which, being their excrement, is a fine manure for grain and grass. Worms probably provide new soil for hills and slopes where the rain washes the earth away.

At that time, earthworms were believed to be pests, so his observations required the courage of the original eye. "Gardeners and farmers express their detestation of worms; the former because they render their walks unsightly . . . and the latter because, as they think, worms eat their green corn. But these men would find that the earth without worms would soon become cold, hard-bound, and void of fermentation; and consequently sterile."

David Hume, also in the 1700s, saw *sympathy* as fundamental to humanity. For him this *feeling for the other* is central to the origin of ethics. He clearly distinguished between what *is* and what *ought* to be. Rousseau saw our human self as "true" in a state of nature, but by society corrupted. "Man is born free," he wrote in 1762, "and everywhere he is in chains. One man thinks himself the master of others, but remains more a slave than they."

Wordsworth and the Romantic poets elevated love of nature:

> One impulse from a vernal wood
> May teach you more of man,
> Of moral evil and of good,
> Than all the sages can.
> —"The Tables Turned," 1798

So did New England's Transcendentalists of the 1800s, principally Emerson and Thoreau. Said the observant Emerson, "To speak truly, few adult persons can see nature. Most persons do not see the sun." "In wildness is the preservation of the world," Thoreau howled to the sky. Thoreau's prescient dictum has resonated truer and truer over the last century and a half as we've learned the price of losing what's wild, the vulnerabilities of small populations, and the miseries of people in degraded landscapes.

Charles Darwin's great incendiary insight blasted a crater in the philosophers' firewall between humans and nature, with his articulate realization that all the world is kin. "There is grandeur in this view of life," he wrote famously in 1859, "with its several powers, having been originally breathed by the Creator into a few forms or into one; and that, whilst this planet has gone cycling on according to the fixed law of gravity, from so simple a beginning endless forms most beautiful and most wonderful have been, and are being, evolved." Darwin's insights blurred lines and blended borders, placing us on a continuum of lineage and time, in an organic tree of life. Again, here was a genius realizing we're not the center of the circle, and pushing the borders outward.

Industrial pollution and the wholesale destruction of wild lands during the latter half of the 1800s prompted early perspectives on nature conservation. George Perkins Marsh, a Yankee intellect who had been a farmer, lawyer, teacher, businessman, scientist, congressman, linguist, and foreign ambassador, made the first systematic assessment of damage to the natural world. He'd observed degraded landscapes in Europe and the Middle East, where logging and farming had ruined soils. He saw that crops were most plagued by pests where people killed the birds that ate them; thus the farmer was "not only depriving his groves and his fields of their fairest ornament, but he is waging a treacherous warfare on his natural allies."

Concern about running out of natural resources like wood spawned a conservation ethic called utilitarianism. Theodore Roosevelt sent utilitarianism into the forests by appointing Gifford Pinchot head of the U.S. Forest Service. The utilitarian philosophy is "To provide the greatest good for the greatest number over the longest time." Pinchot defined forestry as "the art of handling the forest so that it will render whatever service is required of it without being impoverished or destroyed." Utilitarian thinking underestimates interrelationships of nature and processes like evolution; but still, it isn't bad strategy. Pinchot eventually clashed with his contemporary John Muir, who believed both that nature has an intrinsic right to exist and that protecting wild nature is essential for the human spirit. Twining their strands, you get something like: the world is ours to use, never ours to harm. In his 1864 book *Man and Nature; or, Physical Geography as Modified by Human Action,* Marsh had written, "Man is everywhere a disturbing agent. Wherever he plants his foot, the harmonies of nature are turned to discord." He concluded that rebuilding nature "must await great political and moral revolutions in the governments and peoples."

Right he was. Wait we do. But one doesn't wait for a revolution. One becomes it.

MARCH: OUT LIKE A LAMB

~ ~ ~

Spring begins painting the landscape with a slow blush. Red Maples are showing such a subtle glow that at first I'm not sure whether it's just the early light. But no, the blush is swelling buds. The sensual implies the sexual. This is the season of anticipation, full of vernal foreplay.

Not all migrations of middle March are long-distance or aerial. Blue-spotted Salamanders are moving out of burrows and into ponds to mate and lay eggs. They do this when the first warm enough rains wake them. For a Blue-spotted, warm enough rain is 40 degrees Fahrenheit—still pretty cold by hairless-ape standards. But for a salamander, spring rains mean a long nighttime trek for a tryst. Using navigational abilities no one understands, they mysteriously find their way around logs and boulders to small "kettlehole" ponds, then take to the water to locate mates in the dark.

As mysterious as the rite itself is that anyone even knows it happens, and where. My friend Andy—we call him the "salamander commander"—knows where. Because we are not salamanders, for us it's a fairly short walk from the road to a little woodland pond that Andy has found. Ours is a tiny, isolated population; this species' main range is much farther north, throughout the upper Midwest, New England, and southern Canada. But it's special. Andy is telling me that our local area may have the only pure, nonhybridized form of this salamander in the country. We pull on waders and step into the pond, headlamp halos casting little search beams into dark water.

Andy annually brings in kids and families game enough to brave the nocturnal chill for a glimpse at this little local mystery. Tonight he's scouting for an upcoming night walk.

In a few minutes Andy spots a salamander swimming underwater like a miniature alligator. He scoops it with a net. It's about five inches long. For an animal that spends most of its time underground, it has surprisingly large eyes. The skin is smooth and pleasant, dark blue with light flecks and spots, like old enamelware. We find another. The air is actually below freezing; the nets are getting stiff with frost. I remain amazed equally that these animals are even moving in such cold and that Andy knows the habits of such small and secretive forms of life—and can find them.

To protect the salamanders from the freezing air and to better see them, we put them into a white bucket of water. Andy says, "See, look at the color on their belly; isn't that beautiful?" Having affirmed that the salamanders are at it, in a few days he'll be back with several dozen kids and their parents. We release the pair and spend a little time looking for more, talking softly—it's so quiet here—as we slowly walk, with our attention focused through the water's surface.

Amphibians are declining in many parts of the world, with several well-documented recent extinctions of formerly abundant species. The Americas have been hard-hit, and Andy says that even locally, amphibians are declining at an "unbelievable" rate. Not so much the Spring Peepers, but these salamanders, the Wood Frogs, the Leopard Frogs, Fowler's Toad—.

What worked for amphibians for 300 million years seems suddenly to have stopped working. These soft, naked animals, so apparently vulnerable to small changes in temperature and moisture, are beset by perhaps the widest and deepest losses to hit any vertebrate class during recorded history. Since just the early 1980s, about 170 amphibian species—frogs, toads, salamanders, and the like—have gone extinct. About 2,500 of the world's 6,000 species are suffering declines. The continued existence of nearly 2,000 is formally assessed as threatened. They're losing ground not just in developed areas where people drain wetlands and eat certain amphibians but also in wilderness, including Yellowstone National Park. The reasons appear varied: a deadly fungus that may have been spread around the world by African Clawed Frogs sold as pets and formerly used for pregnancy testing in hospitals; chemicals from common weed killers proven to cause frog deformities and death; climate changes that are warming, drying, and otherwise altering their habitats; increased ultra-violet radiation formerly deflected by the ozone layer and now known to interfere with growth and immune function and to kill outright; and chemical pesticides, metals, and estrogens in human wastewater that disrupt their sex hormones. Atrazine, perhaps the most commonly used herbicide in the world, seems to interfere with tadpoles becoming adults and to convert testosterone to estrogen, also disrupting sexual development. While the causes are many and varied, the amphibians' dilemma shows again that industrialization affects more than just the industrialized.

~

On the penultimate evening of March it's still too chilly to think about opening windows. I've got some music playing. But through the closed windows I hear something else, something I've been anticipating. So I open a window to let in the season's lushest, most delicious sound. It's from tiny tree frogs that come to water to go a-courting—Spring Peepers. So far, these little amphibians remain abundant. And for as long as they've been, and as long as they are, their singing makes the difference between the night of winter and the breath of spring.

Unlike earlier evenings, when a scattered few gave voice from vernal pools in the wetted woods, tonight the peepers have gathered strength enough to become a chorus. With a ringing chirp that pierces half a mile of damp woodland, their calls emanate from various ponds and wet-lands and from rainwater pools just yards above the high-tide line. After the sun melts away, with the air full of salt scent and the distant rumble of ocean surf, thousands of tiny frog "peeps" merge into a trilling cho-rus. At water's edge, they're often loud enough to vibrate in your chest.

Hearing them is easy. Seeing them takes some effort. But even after I step into the shallows as deep as my boots allow, even though I hear calls coming from the half-submerged vegetation right around me—well within the halo of my flashlight—they're all invisible. They're smaller than the tip of your thumb, colored like dead leaves. The majority of my neighbors—even many who were raised here—have never seen one. Many people assume the callers are crickets. But the sound and season are so different, one might as logically assume the moon is just the sun at night.

When I was a kid, I didn't know what they were, either. One night I discovered them, and taught myself how to find them, by just following the sound into the night-shadowed woods. The calls were coming from the grassy edge of a rain-swollen stream. I stopped and crouched. The calls stopped too; then a peep here, a peep there, until *everywhere*—. I localized one caller almost under my nose and flicked on the flashlight. He stopped, and for the life of me, I could not see anything in the flooded grass.

I froze as still as a heron. The surrounding chorus resumed full volume, but the invisible being somewhere within my light beam held his peace. Eventually, though, he couldn't stand being left out, and resumed calling.

And when that tiny movement caught my eye, I saw the littlest frog I'd ever seen, his bubble-gum throat puffed almost as big as his body, calling his heart out. That mighty sound from that tiny body appealed to my teenage sensibilities. His was a strong, clear voice, defiantly undaunted about being so small a soul in so big a world.

In recent years, with these oddly warm winters, you might hear Spring Peepers calling in any month. Even in January or February the

ponds may stay ice-free, and after a few warm days a couple of bold and hopeful peepers might rise from the mud and call for a while.

With amphibians declining worldwide, Spring Peepers remain—so far—a strong and joyous life-affirming presence. I've shared Spring Peepers with many a friend and child, taking them by the hand with boots and a flashlight, re-creating that spark of first discovery.

My appreciation of them has deepened like true love. At first, they were merely charming. Now I find the sound more soothing and delicious than ever. I gladly suffer a chilly bedroom just to open a window in spring when the peepers are at their peak, and let that exuberant, trilling chorus resonate in my chest. "We're alive," they seem to say, "and time is short." No sound in our region is so welcome and welcoming, so revivifying, as peepers in full spring chorus. Or so seemingly unlikely. Out of dust, God is said to have made one man. But here, out of mud, such *song*!

It's often said that animals live "in the present" and don't fret about the future. But all these exertions and strivings and migrations are about getting somewhere you will need to be. Mating and raising young are future-focused. DNA itself is a blueprint for something that will be built. All life recognizes time. And that *this* moment—is already gone.

Genetics and evolution might explain why you care for and protect your child. But they don't quite explain why you should protect anyone else's. If humans deserve moral consideration in face-to-face dealings, what about humans living a mile or a hundred miles away? Is there any moral difference between strangers living miles apart and days apart? Between strangers living now and strangers who will be living in a few years, a few decades? Here things begin to get interesting.

And what of those children a generation or a hundred generations down the line, whose hearts will pump by the unbroken beat of our own genes, just as much as our hearts were handed to us?

The philosophers whose thinking is imprinted in our thinking largely rejected the future. Future people posed no concern because of their "remoteness," "incapacity," "non-actuality," and "indeterminacy." Easy for those philosophers to say, but from where we sit now—local, capacitated, actual, and determined—they appear wrong on all points. Yet we indulge the same fallacy, granting ourselves the same clemencies. And that's a problem, because the future—and, with it, all those people—arrives daily.

A stranger who lives across town, or across the ocean, or in 2050, falls into the same category: people we happen not to know personally. Except that those in the future cannot be queried or respond to e-mail, cannot defend their interests, are more helpless, and are more reliant on us to consider them.

But really, what can we do for future people when we know so little about their wants and needs? Who in 1850 could have guessed that we'd want cell phones and frozen peas?

Yet people have been people for a long time, and they've all needed air, water, and food. They've created art. They've cared for their children. I'm willing to believe that this will continue to be true. The gadgets of our great-great-grandchildren and their families and friends will differ, but I'm willing to go out on a limb and guess that their lives will be about as valuable to them as ours are to us.

So, do we have justification for calling ahead and canceling the reservations of the next generations just because we want to eat their lunch? I guess it's obvious that I don't think we do. If we wholly discount the needs of those blameless innocents who will in the coming days and decades appear on our planet's surface, then the whole notion of moral responsibility to anyone loses all its value. In that case, the point of every human action and interaction becomes: to take away as much as possible and to leave, ideally, nothing.

Shouldn't we try to reduce the suffering we inflict on future generations? Don't we have strong personal utilitarian motives even now, anyway, to develop new energy sources and halt population growth, so that people will have a more reasonable chance at happiness and peace? Shouldn't we just *care*, if only because that's the kind of people we wish to be?

Maybe not. It's debatable. Anyway, these kinds of arguments always seem a little shrill. Who'd miss Yellowstone and Central Park if they'd simply been settled like all the adjacent land? Would we miss the Grand Canyon if it was merely as full of water as Lake Powell and Lake Mead, whose water-skiers happily circle where hawks once did, above now-forgotten canyons drowned behind dams? There are trade-offs. We lost a few canyons and rivers but benefit from gifts received from those same times—like antibiotics and classic movies and anesthesia and jazz. We live with what we have.

In 1850, the Passenger Pigeon was the most abundant bird in the Americas. Around that same time, a long-distance migrant bird called the Eskimo Curlew was shot by the wagonload on the plains. The prairies and their herds of Buffalo are essentially gone, both birds are extinct, and even the very remembrance of the curlew is vanishing. I feel a loss, but, honestly, does it matter? How many people miss Passenger Pigeons?

Into the 1800s, Passenger Pigeons ranged from Newfoundland through the whole forested East to Florida and west to the plains, occasionally spilling into Mexico, reaching the Pacific coast, even straying at times to Bermuda and the British Isles. The pioneering ornithologist Alexander Wilson described one Passenger Pigeon breeding colony in Kentucky around 1806 as occupying an area forty miles long and several miles wide, with densities of over one hundred nests per tree, containing many millions. In 1810, Wilson described one "almost inconceivable multitude" of pigeons that rolled overhead all during an afternoon. By multiplying flight speed by hours taken, he estimated the flock at 240 miles long, with 2.2 *billion* birds. He judged that flock's fuel needs at 17.5 million bushels of acorns daily. Others described flocks taking days to pass, darkening the sun "as by an eclipse," as "abundant as the fish" on the coast, and elsewhere "beyond number or imagination," "in innumerable hordes," and, often simply, "incredible." Audubon painted this description from Kentucky in 1827:

Few Pigeons were to be seen before sunset; but a great number of persons, with horses and wagons, guns and ammunition, had already established encampments. . . . Suddenly, there burst forth a general cry of *"Here they come!"* The noise which they made, though yet distant, reminded me of a hard gale at sea. . . . As the birds arrived, and passed over me, I felt a current of air that surprised me. Thousands were soon knocked down by polemen. The current of birds, however, still kept increasing. . . . The Pigeons, coming in by thousands, alighted everywhere, one above another, until solid masses . . . were formed on every tree, in all directions. Here and there the perches gave way . . . with a crash, and, falling to the ground, destroyed hundreds of the birds beneath, forcing down the dense groups with which every stick was loaded. It was a scene of uproar and confusion. I found it quite useless to speak, or even to shout, to those persons who were nearest me. . . . The uproar continued . . . the whole night. . . . Towards the approach of day, the noise rather subsided. . . . The howlings of the wolves now reached our ears; and the foxes, lynxes, cougars, bears, raccoons, opossums, and pole-cats were seen sneaking off from the spot, whilst Eagles and Hawks, of different species, accompanied by a crowd of Vultures, came to sup-plant them, and enjoy their share of the spoil. It was then that the authors of all this devastation began their entry amongst the dead, the dying, and the mangled. The Pigeons were picked up and piled in heaps, until each [hunter] had as many as he could possibly dispose of, when the hogs were let loose to feed on the remainder.

As early as 1672, one New England observer wrote of vast numbers of the pigeons but noted, "of late they are much diminished, the English taking them with nets." Yet even in 1878 one last great nesting colony settled in on an area in Michigan forty miles long and three to ten miles wide, "where a tremendous slaughter took place." Both the slaughter and settlers' felling of the forests that fed and bred the birds took their toll. (Yet, true to our uniquely human capacity for denial, people wondered how the birds had "disappeared"; some writers seriously speculated that they all somehow drowned in the ocean or the Great Lakes—or migrated to Australia.) The last Passenger Pigeon, named Martha, died in the Cincinnati Zoo on September 1, 1914. She was the final ambassador of her species, but the phenomenon that her species had been had already vanished from Earth.

The conservationist and writer Aldo Leopold lamented in 1949: "Trees still live who, in their youth, were shaken by a living wind. . . . We grieve because no living man will see again the onrushing phalanx of victori-ous birds, sweeping a path for spring across the March skies, chasing the defeated winter from all the woods and prairies." We grieve for a marvel squandered.

Many regions have their stories, from the shattered turtles and extinguished monk seals of the Caribbean, to swarms of salmon that formerly streamed into the Northwest's former forests and up the once-mighty Columbia, to the vast sea-thundering herds of giant tunas I saw, to—.

But okay; let's not get overwound. We can live well without them, so this reasonable question often arises: Does losing them "matter"?

Hell yes, it *matters*. Don't let anyone suggest it doesn't *matter* because people can live without them. People can—and most do—live perfectly well without computers, refrigerators, the Winter Olympics, plumbing, libraries, concert halls, museums, and ibuprofen. Whether things are worthwhile for survival or whether they help make survival worthwhile are two quite different things. Whether we "need" them, is a dull and uninteresting question. Need? We never needed to *lose* our living endowment, our inheritance. Less recklessness by people in the past would have maintained them all, in rich abundance. People in the future will probably level the same charges at us.

Charles Darwin, always insightful, recognized that "the simplest reason would tell each individual that he ought to extend his social instincts and sympathies to the men of all nations and races . . . our sympathies becoming more tender and more widely diffused until they are extended to all sentient beings."

Aldo Leopold marked this wider perimeter of kinship with his softly stated revolution, which he called "the land ethic." In his own words (published posthumously in *A Sand County Almanac* in 1949), "The land ethic simply enlarges the boundaries of the community to include soils, waters, plants, and animals." But here is the revolution: "A land ethic changes the role of *Homo sapiens* from conqueror of the land-community to plain member and citizen of it." In all the history of philosophy and ethical thought, no one had ever quite come out and said we are part of the world. Imagine.

Leopold said the problem stems from treating land as mere property. His analogy is slavery: people were once held as property; now land is held as property.

The right of private property is central to Western philosophy and Western political traditions and laws. It is also central to many environmental problems. John Locke, writing in the 1600s, believed that land was originally owned by God and that when a man "mixes his labor" with land, he comes to own it.

But what if the labor harms the land? Land stays, after all, and men pass. Does a man really own a thousand-year-old tree because he has just cut it down, or is he a thief who has severed history and taken a little of the future? Locke believed ownership is justified as long as it doesn't violate the liberty of others to also get "as much and as good." This is possible only as long as there are thousand-year-old trees enough for all, land enough for all—still imaginable in Locke's sparsely populated time. Times change.

To Bacon's assertion that "the world is made for man," Leopold answered, "Granting that the earth is for man—there is still a question: what man? Did not the cliff dwellers who tilled and irrigated these our valleys think that they were the pinnacle of creation—that these valleys were made for them? Undoubtedly, and then the Pueblos? Yes. And then the Spaniards? Not only thought so, but said so. And now we Americans? Ours beyond a doubt!" He seemed to be saying that only by saving the world *from* us can we save it *for* us.

Leopold wrote, "All ethics so far evolved rest upon a single premise: that the individual is a member of a community of interdependent parts." For him, our community went far beyond people, beyond even wildlife and plants, into the very soil and water and life-supporting systems, all part of our community.

That resonates with me because I know the feeling. And I especially feel it here at Lazy Point.

Each time people like Copernicus, Darwin, and Leopold widened the circle—moving us further from the center of the universe, the center of time, the apex of creation—we got a better, more realistic view of who we are. I find the improved understanding immensely satisfying. Others paid heavily, like Bruno (burned to death by the Catholic church) and Galileo (banned by same for saying that Earth moves). It's said that freedom doesn't come free. Neither does the ability to think.

Expanded views make us more civilized. But being civilized gets us only so far. In the twentieth century's wars, civilized people killed about

150 million civilized people. And this century hasn't gotten off to a smooth start. Just as we went from hunter-gatherers to agriculturalists to civilized societies, now we must take the next great leap: from merely civilized to humanized.

The geometry of human progress is an expanding circle of compassion. Every advance in thinking has shown that our relationships extend further than we thought. Every hideous perversion has emphasized differences. Humanized people seek, more than anything else, peace. Tolerance strengthens peace. But as the world becomes more crowded, global tolerance remains elusive, perhaps partly because we feel forced to hold our ground.

Two decades after Aldo Leopold died, Garrett Hardin's "The Tragedy of the Commons" (1968) showed that it is not enough to be a plain citizen; we must each be actively committed to the common good—and that's a taller order. Hardin used the metaphor of common grazing land to show how "each man is locked into a system that compels him to increase his herd without limit—in a world that is limited. Ruin is the destination toward which all men rush, each pursuing his own best interest in a society that believes in the freedom of the commons. Freedom in a commons brings ruin to all. . . . The individual benefits as an individual from his ability to deny the truth even though society as a whole, of which he is a part, suffers." Hardin pointed out that limits to individual "freedoms" are not limits to *freedom;* they are public defenses against those individuals' social pathologies and excesses that limit most other people's freedoms. Freedom to wave your arm stops at my nose.

The tragedy of the commons is one symptom of the main problem: that customs became institutionalized habits while humanity still didn't have a clue about the forces that drive the world. And old habits—and ignorance—die hard.

Before the U.S. Congress passed the Clean Air Act, the Clean Water Act, and the Endangered Species Act of the early 1970s, polluting public air and water was not considered ethically wrong. (This is partly a lingering symptom of the classic philosophers' having had no way to know, and little reason to ponder, how connected and fully networked the living world is.) Before these laws, only individuals who could prove they were harmed could seek compensation, and only after the fact. No one could sue a company or the government on behalf of safeguarding public health or interests. Animals and plants—even large populations and whole species— were largely out of luck. The modern burst of environmental laws better recognized the public's interests—and fundamentally shifted the burden of proof from an individual who was harmed to those causing harm.

Acting like new philosophies brought on by new realities, these laws altered the moral landscape. Especially the Endangered Species Act. In all the preceding march of time, nothing in nature or the human mind had accorded species anything like a right to exist. That was a major advance. But the Endangered Species Act steps in only after harm is done and a species is in trouble. It sets a floor—mere existence—and not a standard. It's not the Abundant Species Act or the Healthy Habitat Act. In contrast, the Clean Water Act sets a standard, not a floor. It requires that we maintain all waters in "swimmable and fishable" condition. The act aspires to healthy, viable waters capable of supporting wildlife and people. It aims high. It has vision. It lets people engage earlier. As a result, many waters in the United States now flow greatly improved.

At least the U.S. has its Endangered Species Act; the vast majority of countries know no such laws, and the few that do usually lack the means to enforce them. No one can appeal to the World Court to save Mountain Gorillas or Bluefin Tuna. And global wildlife and fisheries treaties are loose nets full of loopholes big enough to let whales fall through.

Special though they are, these laws have critics—like some ranchers asserting that "property rights" should let them do anything they want to their land (recall Aldo Leopold's slavery analogy) and fishers demanding access to everywhere all the time. (Numerous "freedom to fish" bills continually swim around Congress, though scientists keep showing that some ocean areas should become reserves.) These people want to reassert exactly those "rights"—to harm public assets for personal gain—that compelled the public to defend itself in the first place. Such people assert, basically, that if we, the public, wish to defend ourselves from them, we should pay them for losing the opportunity to destroy something they did not create.

One can fully own a manufactured thing—a toaster, say, or a pair of shoes. But in what reasonable sense can one fully "own" and have "rights" to do whatever we want to land, water, air, and forests, which are among the most valuable assets in humanity's basic endowments? To say, in the march of eons, that we own these things into which we suddenly, fleetingly appear and from which we will soon vanish is like a newborn laying claim to the maternity ward, or a candle asserting ownership of the cake; we might as well declare that, having been handed a ticket to ride, we've bought the train. Let's be serious.

And let's be clear. No one speaks of limiting "freedom" for the sake of our environment, our health, or our children's future. When the many protect themselves from the greed or tyranny of a few, freedom increases. "Thou shalt not steal" and "Thou shalt not kill" are not attacks on individual "freedoms."

⤜

On a Friday in the final week of March, the air is suddenly so warm that I leave my jacket behind at the front door. The sun is up earlier; so am I. It's cool enough to see my breath, but after a light predawn rain, steamy water vapor is rising off the road in the sun shafts of morning.

Salamanders and frogs are not the only animals who'd been hibernating. A groggy-looking chipmunk is sitting on a log. In the woods, spring has touched the chickadees; they've dissolved their safety-in-numbers foraging flocks of winter and reassorted themselves back on territorial real estate. And no more *chick-a-dee* ("Where's everybody?"). From these respective turfs they're singing their thin, sweet two-note descending *dee-dee* breeding song ("I'm here").

Out on the Sound, several hundred Bufflehead ducks pepper the water's surface. Such numbers mean they are massed and on the move. I'm seeing not only the most but pretty much the last of them this year. Meanwhile, the first ragged lines of cormorants are rowing northeast overhead, cleaving a sky path up the coast.

But the most unexpected thing in the sky is a fish—in the grip of a circling Osprey. For the female who has just arrived, our male hovers high, calling, then dives through the air and rises again, performing an aerial dance reenacting the art of catching food, the fish his stage prop, turning sky into theater, proving his worth as a provider. Like her, I, too, admire his chocolate back and creamy undersides, the stiff beats of his strong wings, and his fishing prowess.

When I was in my early teens, I knew these birds only by the huge stick nests they left behind. Virtually all the Ospreys in our region had died. Stricken by pesticides that made their eggshells thin and brittle, they'd gone nearly extinct throughout the East. The ghost nests haunted me. I could not believe we'd lost—and I had just missed seeing—a creature who could build such a structure. I felt cursed with having been born too late for the things I love.

When several local bird lovers sued the government in the late 1960s to stop the wholesale spraying of DDT and other pesticides that were causing the birds' eggs to fail, they had no idea they'd win. In the process they largely invented the modern environmental movement, with its focus on law, courts, and large species whose fortunes signal the health of whole habitats.

I saw my first Osprey when I was fifteen, and despite being compulsively addicted to shorelines, I didn't see my second one for six years. Now there are four active nests within a mile of Lazy Point. These decades later, the Ospreys' recovery is a big change for the better. They're a lesson in healing and in the power of acting over cursing. I enjoy them much more now that they're common than when a glimpse of one was so rare I'd worry it might be my last.

Overhead, the big hawk's tightly clutched fish looks like a sleek slab of chrome, not brown-and-white and oval like a flounder. It's likely an Atlantic Menhaden, Hickory Shad, or Alewife. In former times, arriving Ospreys mainly made their living catching Winter Flounders, but now that winter isn't what it was, Winter Flounders aren't what they once were. A professor tells me that our water's getting too warm for them to breed successfully, and that this fish, once superabundant, seems poised for departure from our region.

When I was young, March simply meant: flounders. By the third month the meager sun could warm the shallow water just enough to tune a Winter Flounder's mind to a worm on the mud. But we paid our dues with red

hands and cold noses; no March days ever seemed more raw than those
when, aged fifteen or so, we'd ridden our bicycles ten miles to the draw-
bridge to ambush a few flounders on the creek's ebbing tide.

When April came we felt—sitting on the sunny dock in Oyster Bay,
with yellow daffodils and greening lawns on the far shore—that we'd
earned the warmth. By then spring's flounders were in full swing.

We'd gently lift, lift our sunken bait until we'd lured a flounder's
attention, then wait, wait until that nibble became a tug. Effort, perse-
verance, patience, success. A good lesson and a good meal.

I saw my first flounder as a small child of perhaps five. I was entranced
by the utter outer weirdness of a fish that lay on the bottom on one white
side that faced down, had one mottled camouflaged side that faced up—
and had both eyes on one side of its head. A flounder would look at
Picasso's cubist figures and say, "Couldn't he come up with anything
original?"

Flounders (and other flatfishes, like halibut and soles) hatch into

normally swimming juveniles, like other fishes. After a short while, the fish stops swimming upright. It settles to the bottom, like a fluttering flag that's been lowered and spread on the ground. Most fish lying on their side are dying, but for flounders it's normal. The side that's down loses its pigment and becomes essentially the pearly "belly," though it's actually one whole side. Then, true weirdness: one eye migrates around the head until half its face—the down side—is eyeless, while the up side—the Picasso side—has two eyes. Imagine that you lay down on your side on your mattress and when you woke you had actually become the mattress, with both your eyes where one ear was, looking at the ceiling. That's a flounder's life.

When I was in my teens, you could catch flounders in spring from every dock, bridge, or pier and many a stretch of shore. Once, in unusually clear water, I watched my bait fall to the bottom, only to see what seemed like the entire seafloor suddenly move toward it. The bottom seemed tiled with baby flounders. No one ever heard of coming back from flounder fishing empty-handed. The question was never "Did you catch?"; it was always "How many?" "How big?" and "Do we have a lemon and enough butter?"

One of our favorite spots for hefty "snowshoe" flounders was the blackened planks of an erstwhile waterfront restaurant's outdoor deck—burned for the insurance money, people whispered. The charred planks jutted out over a channel. We weren't allowed there, of course—too dangerous. It certainly proved a dangerous place for flounders, because we were there often.

If you had a boat and could position in the best passes to intercept migrating fish at the height of spring, you caught hundreds. It was called "flounder pounding," and it took its toll. In those days no one ever did anything to attract flounders. They just came to you. Now people throw cracked mussels and chopped clams or stir the bottom in an attempt to pull a few flatfish toward their hooks. But catches, like the fish themselves, are thin. Few people even try.

We may make from our acquaintance with the flounder more than just dinner and the usual lesson of fishing excess and diminishment. Its worst foe in our region is not the sizzling pan but power plant and tailpipe; warming water has robbed our region's Winter Flounders of the temperatures in which they thrive.

What would be gross disfigurement for most any other animal is normal for a flounder, and we don't judge flounders the less for it. We appreciate the flounder in its context. Flounders teach a wider range in which to sense the beautiful. Granting that latitude to people is called tolerance. Flounders can see from only one side of their head, but they take in the whole view. Too often we see only half the view. For some reason, we are fascinated by the unusual in nature but insist on conformity among people.

We may yet learn a thing or two from flounders. Among those things is that the effects of change can be subtle, yet operating all around us.

While all that moves is heading north toward spring, we'll be going south, to the Caribbean, to see some of those subtle changes—and to gain a wider view. Honestly, I'm always disappointed to have to leave and miss the flow of any season. The real voyage of discovery consists not in seeking new landscapes but in having new eyes, said Marcel Proust. And T. S. Eliot famously wrote that the end of all our exploring will be to arrive where we started and know the place for the first time. But seeing new landscapes—and seascapes—does improve one's vision. And so Kenzie watches dolefully as the familiar duffel bags come out of the closet and I fill them with short pants and T-shirts, and my mask and snorkel. Sorry, Kenzie, you have to stay.

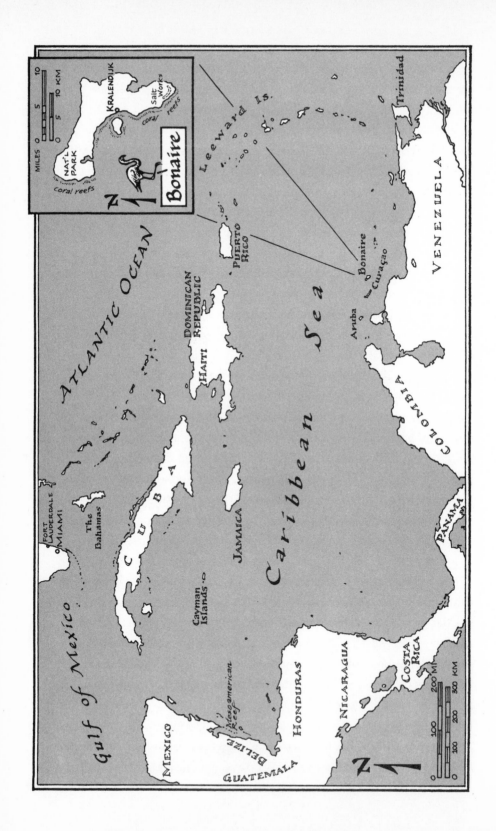

TRAVELS SOLAR: CORAL GARDENS OF GOOD AND EVIL—BELIZE AND BONAIRE

≈≈≈

Looking like a helium-filled peach, the moon floats free of the horizon. I slip into warm black water and begin swimming. When the ocean's motion begins massaging my progress and a swell rolls over my snorkel, I know I've reached the channel slope. I flick on my light. Its halo ushers me among the hulking shapes and shadows of massive Elkhorn Corals.

The seafloor is a field of their broken skeletons overgrown with seaweeds. But many living—or partly alive—coral colonies also stand here. The hope: that these survivors might be disease-resistant, signaling possible recovery from the epidemics.

Squid jet past my light beam; night is their time, too. The reflective eye of a smallish Nurse Shark reminds me that there may in such dark water lurk much larger sharks, though certainly far fewer than in the past.

As porch lights attract moths, my beam soon swarms with frenzied mysids and polychaetes and glass-clear larval fishes that whirl and spin too fast for me to closely examine them.

I'm actually searching for something I've never seen. I'm inspecting the corals' tiny polyps for signs of pregnant swellings. The moon cue is right, but I've been told it doesn't happen every year. I dive, and the polyps look—though it's subtle—bulgy and lighter colored.

My light beam begins filling with minute pink balls wafting from the polyps. Suddenly the reef is a fantasy ballroom, a blizzard, and I can hardly see. This blizzard falls *upward*. Soon the sea's underside is coated

with drifting pink grains of bundled eggs and sperm. At the dark surface, the smell of them is thick and erotic, the smells of oils and sex.

～

In the morning, a couple of very tired scientists are still poring over microscopic new corals. They show me single egg cells, a four-cell blastula, and an embryo with sixteen cells. These are the first unfolding stages of the same set of instructions that will enable these creatures to build the most massive structures created by living things, rock formations visible from space: coral reefs. As the embryos in the lab become swimming larvae, the researchers will test where they decide to settle down to begin growing into what we think of as "coral."

A stone's throw away from the island lab on Carrie Bow Cay, Caribbean waves lap an exposed bank of coral rubble and limestone stretching away to the north and south. Running from Mexico's Yucatán along Belize, Guatemala, and Honduras, the Mesoamerican Reef is the world's second longest, after Australia's Great Barrier.

• • •

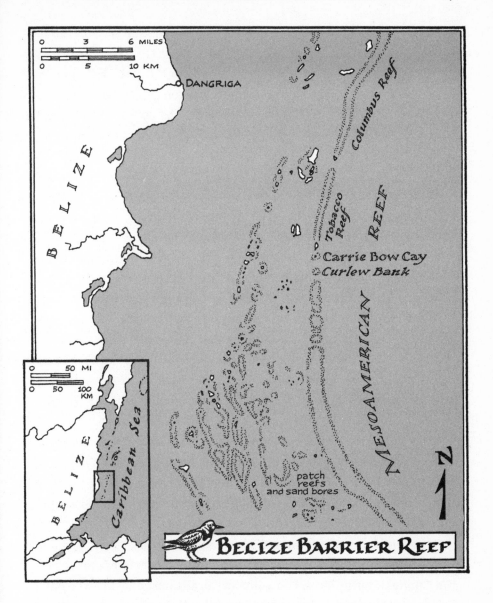

Wiry and athletic, Susie Arnold grew up on Cape Cod. Her PhD adviser, professor Bob Steneck, in his late fifties, is the kind of older professor young students have a hard time keeping up with. He has light gray-green eyes and a jaunty reddish goatee. He's not tall—about my height—but broad across the chest, and always revving. During fieldwork, Bob dives daily and works toward midnight entering his data. A few hours later, he drifts out of bed in the moonlight to log a couple hours' worth of writing and several cups of coffee before breakfast. His university tenure would let him coast, but Bob's name appeared on twenty-one published studies this year. He annually completes a dozen and a half research trips and conferences, and travels to give two dozen academic talks, for which he charges no fee. When I asked who else in his field works so hard, it seemed the question had never occurred to him.

Susie has put fifty 6-by-6-inch terra-cotta tiles out on the reef. The tiles act like blank diary pages. Coral larvae settle on a tile and start growing. So do seaweeds, sponges, and a lot of other things. Susie and Bob have tiles on other reefs in the Caribbean and across the Pacific. With these tiles they can, in a sense, read what reefs are writing across vast regions.

Often, the first pioneer on the tiles is a coralline alga called *Titanoderma*. It's just a thin, pink crust—but alive. (Coralline algae—like corals—make calcium carbonate, basically limestone.) *Titanoderma*'s talent is in getting there fast, but it gets overgrown by pretty much everything else that comes along. Other pioneers shed their outer layer, so in the cutthroat race for living space, they slough off competitors. By contrast, *Titanoderma* doesn't shed. To corals, this is a big difference.

And so, a lab experiment: Hundreds of coral larvae go into several dozen dishes with chips from three kinds of coralline algae. Where will they settle? Under a microscope I watch oblong larvae moving through the water. Avoiding corallines that shed, they probe until their senses say, "This is it." Usually they choose *Titanoderma*.

"If a coral larva selects *Titanoderma*," Susie explains, "it can stick." It won't get sloughed off. To a coral larva, all the other surfaces available—tiny sponges, bushy bryozoan colonies, algal films, and the like—are hostile territory. Coral larvae have no eyes, but we're watching them home in on *Titanoderma* by taste. With such exquisite fine-tuning, they begin their struggle for survival against nearly impossible odds.

Almost as soon as a larva attaches, its pill-shaped body flattens. Within hours calcium carbonate forms around the soft parts and it begins creating the coral's characteristic polyps. Coral larvae have no mouth. High on the to-do list: get a mouth. Soon we have an oral coral. What seemed wondrous in the night sea becomes incredible by noon. Some say science spoils the mystery. They stay mystified, and miss the miracles.

✦

With Susie steering, our boat skims across a polished sea over corals in air-clear waters. When Bob's GPS says we've arrived, we drop anchor on sand in forty feet of water, an easy swim to the reef.

We suit up and tumble overboard. As the bubbles clear, I am amazed—and this time not in a good way—to find myself in a sea of plastic bits. Everywhere I look. Their uniform size (they're all about three inches square) suggests a ship's macerator. The United Nations has banned dumping plastic at sea. The U.N. isn't here to check.

I pull my snorkel from my mouth and ask Bob if he's ever seen this kind of thing. He's as dismayed as I.

All naturalists carry the reasonable fear that anything new is the start of something unfortunate. Burdened by foreboding, we soon reach the reef. It's a series of corrugated coral ridges alternating with sandy grooves.

Living hard coral covers only 10 to 20 percent of the whole reef area. Few branching corals remain.

A tightly packed group of snappers with gray bodies and yellow fins—Schoolmasters—spontaneously rises excitedly, releasing eggs and sperm. That's normally done toward night. Last night's moon must really have their hormones juicing.

A seaweed-seeking parrotfish grinds into a coral with its fused, beak-like teeth. Each time it hits the coral, I can hear it from ten feet away. Any coral that a parrotfish ingests returns as fine sand. Enough parrotfish, over centuries, largely built the tropics' coral-sand beaches. Yes, those lovely beaches: parrotfish poop.

I'm not certain what kind of parrotfish this is. Hundreds of fishes inhabit Caribbean reefs. Like birds, many look different as juveniles and adults, males and females. Some change sex. And some even develop very different-looking dominant "supermales." Knowing one species requires being able to recognize three or four different-looking fish. It's a little like learning the alphabet; for each letter you need to recognize four

letterforms: uppercase and lowercase, script and print. But instead of twenty-six letters, there are over five hundred species in this region. That's just fish; never mind the sixty different corals, the snails, shrimps, jellies, sponges, and other animals. Or the algae.

Susie, working along a ten-meter tape, is counting baby corals. Along another tape, Bob is noting how much coral, how much algae, how much sponge, which species.

Bob points to his eye, meaning, "I want to show you something."

On my pad he writes, "More small corals here." I glance around, see them, nod. He takes my pad again, writes, "Little seaweed here—more nursery habitat." Then just a few yards away he plunges his fingers into a deep cushion of weeds and writes: "Lots of seaweed—few nooks for baby corals." He pushes away weeds at the base of several young fist-sized corals, revealing dead white coral skeleton. They're doomed.

Round us like Greek statues stand hulking wrecks of old Elkhorn colo-r.es, their broken limbs gesturing toward the sun. Staghorn fragments lie everywhere, fuzzed with seaweed. Over millennia, branching Elkhorn and Staghorn Corals built the Caribbean's high-rise reefs. Starting in the

1980s, nearly a dozen diseases no one had ever seen swept through, apparently triggered by stresses such as seaweeds, warming waters, changing ocean pH, and certain pollutants. Floor upon floor, those corals collapsed. Seaweeds took over.

In the lab, Susie's examining tiles she's brought up temporarily from the reef.

The tiles display only a film of greens, browns, blues, rusts, and crusts. But the microscope reveals an astonishing community of plants, animals, and plantlike animals—all battling for real estate. Baby sponges, bryozoans, baby urchins, minute snapping shrimp living *inside* minute sponges, copepods, amphipods, baby brittle stars—. Among this minuscule menagerie, Susie seeks corals. Suddenly she says, "Here, take a look."

A small coral comes into focus. It's about half an inch across. Susie checks the plate number and announces, "So—I first noted this one a year ago."

They certainly grow *slowly*!

She adds, "See all this fleshy seaweed on the side of the tile? This little coral's gotta deal with all this. To make it, it'll have to outgrow all this stuff." She's finding high mortality; over 90 percent of baby corals die.

Reef corals internally harbor single-celled algae that use sunlight to make sugars. They're a little like renters, paying with the sugars that the corals need for survival. A bright reef full of healthy corals reflects light into safe nooks. But if the reef gets weedy, shadows fall across crevices. Susie muses, "When you look at a reef and see a lot of seaweed and it's kind of dark? That's, like, the last thing a baby coral sees before it dies."

Besides creating deadly shade, seaweeds can carry infectious bacteria to corals or irritate coral polyps so they close—and starve.

Bob says, "None of the ways seaweeds affect corals are good; they're all different variations of bad."

Susie, gazing into the microscope, adds, "It's a tough time to be a baby coral."

Bob recently stumbled upon some photos he'd taken of his sister swimming underwater in the Caribbean in the early 1970s. The whole backdrop is corals. "You could drive a boat along and see branching coral mile after mile," he says. "Ten years later—it was all dead."

Why? Three waves of assaults: an unprecedented sea urchin–killing epidemic, those new coral diseases, and fishing.

"After they pretty much fished out groupers and snappers," Bob says, "people started targeting parrotfish."

But parrotfish turn out to be really important for reefs. Parrotfishes' fused teeth make them uniquely capable of scraping seaweed. "There was absolutely nothing else like them till the Eocene, which started about fifty-five million years ago," Bob says. There still isn't. Surgeonfish graze seaweed, too, but they nip it; parrotfish really scrape it away. Fossilized reefs show that before parrotfish, reefs were moundlike and dominated by seaweed. When parrotfish evolved, modern reefs appeared. They've been scraping seaweeds from reefs ever since. Without parrotfish, reefs would likely again become moundlike and dominated by seaweed.

Corals probably don't care whether seaweed gets removed by fish, urchins, or a guy with a brush. What matters is, the reef must be frequently scrubbed.

Fast-forward to the early 1980s. With fish depleted by overfishing, the Caribbean's Long-spined Sea Urchin, *Diadema antillarum,* assumed the role of major seaweed grazer. Urchin densities rose to ten to fifteen per square yard. But in 1983, an urchin-killing epidemic appeared off Panama, and in just months the Caribbean's urchins were covered with a death blanket.

"The urchin die-off," Bob remembers, "caused just unbelievable change. It was cataclysmic for the Caribbean because too many reefs were already overfished." Bob emphasizes the point: "The reefs needed either grazing fish or urchins. They could not withstand losing both."

Meanwhile, during the 1980s, new diseases raging throughout the Caribbean killed almost all the branching coral. With the fish populations depressed and the urchins all but gone, there were not enough grazers to suppress the seaweed that sprouted on all that dead coral, "and the reefs just flipped." What had been high-rise coral reefs became seaweed rubble mounds.

Fishing, the urchin-killing epidemic, and the new coral diseases.

These decades later, Caribbean fish remain widely depleted by overfishing, and the urchins remain down by over 90 percent.

In the 1970s, live coral covered more than half the surface of most Caribbean reefs. By the early 2000s, live coral cover had plunged to 10 percent. With enough parrotfish, young corals would have weed-free space for potential recovery. It's not possible to have both widespread overfishing and healthy coral reefs.

Where seaweed eaters get scarce, seaweed blooms. Where seaweed blooms, it kills even more coral. Expanding seaweed creates a death spiral that Bob calls "the Coral Garden of Evil." Keeping the seaweed in check creates a positive life spiral for the reef, the Garden of Good.

But even if there were enough fish, reefs now face the larger threats of changing climate and changing ocean chemistry.

In the late afternoon I watch Ruddy Turnstones picking along the tropical shoreline, working their way north toward the Arctic. Assuming they follow the coast, they'll have to pass near Lazy Point on their way. Maybe I'll see some of these same individuals in a few weeks. Ospreys are here too, but these are whiter-headed locals, not migrants. It's a distinct kick to see an Osprey catch a bright, colorful reef fish. And I hear—then see— Roseate Terns. Immaculate white adults, as well as juveniles, work the channel in small groups. In late spring the largest Roseate Tern breeding colony in the Western Hemisphere convenes on Great Gull Island, just across the sound from Lazy Point. It's quite possible that these very terns have been frequent foragers in the Cut. Seeing them here reminds me again that the familiar is always also the exotic.

We settle in, beers in hand, to watch the sun go down. Bob is color-blind, a rather cruel cosmic joke for someone dedicated to rainbowed reefs and isles of pink sands and pastel sunsets.

"Because I've worked with fossils," he says grimly, "I can envision a bleak future for coral reefs."

I see that it's not quite happy hour.

"Before the major continental breakup," he says, "the movement of Earth's plates caused extremely high volcanic activity, which streamed enormous plumes of greenhouse gases into the air. It got really

warm—and corals and a lot of other groups suffered heavy extinctions."
This "Great Dying" of 250 million years ago (not to be confused with the
much later asteroid strike that helped terminate the dinosaurs) killed about
95 percent of all life in the sea and 70 percent of all life on land. By far the
most catastrophic extinction in Earth's history, it ended the Permian
Period and began the Triassic.

Bob takes a swig of his beer and adds, "So when heat spikes in the
1990s started causing all that coral bleaching in the Pacific, and so much
coral died, I thought of the carbon dioxide and other greenhouse gases
we're putting into the air, I thought of the Permo-Triassic extinction—
and it suddenly hit me like: 'Holy shit; we're *doing* that to ourselves!'"

When the Titan Prometheus stole fire for mankind, an enraged Zeus
punished both him and man. Prometheus was bound to a rock, where,
each day, an eagle tore his liver from his immortal body. To man he sent
Pandora, who unleashed all the world's ills. This is a story older than
even the ancient Greeks imagined; it appears that "we" weren't first. An
earlier human, *Homo erectus,* appears to have controlled fire perhaps
as early as 1.5 million years ago. Origins aside, fire changed human evolution.

But humanity did not change fire until the Industrial Revolution. For
hundreds of thousands of years, using fire always meant an open flame.
Much later, inventors realized that the steam from boiling water—if
confined—had power to make things *move*. With steam engines we *harnessed* fire's power and put it to work for us. When we placed the combustion directly inside an engine, we almost literally set the world ablaze. Fire
power vastly extended our reach into the soils, the seas, the forests, and
the skies. It allowed us to literally move mountains to get at more fuel or
at minerals locked deep within the earth, to slice down gigantic trees
in a matter of minutes, or to send the nets of fishing fleets deep within
the ocean. Harnessed fire allowed construction, destruction, and trans-
port at a scale and speed unimagined before 1800.

Since first becoming human, we have mainly been burning things to
harness energy. To become fully human we'll have to fully come out of
the cave, quench the fires, and harness nonburning energy. But until

then there is this problem: burning things—like coal, gas, oil, and wood—releases carbon dioxide.

Back in 1956, Roger Revelle and Hans Suess started measuring the air's carbon dioxide to get "a clearer understanding of the probable climatic effects." And that's what they got.

There's a third more carbon dioxide in the air than at the start of the Industrial Revolution. The current concentration is higher than it's been for several million years; it's rising one hundred times faster than at any time in the past 650,000 years. The *planet* has survived much higher greenhouse gas concentrations; civilization hasn't. Our species invented agriculture about 10,000 years ago; writing and towns are about 5,000 years old. All of civilization and agriculture developed with the help of a relatively stable atmosphere, and rather stable weather. Now human-caused greenhouse gases have reversed a long, slow natural cooling.

Just to clarify, the greenhouse effect—caused mainly by the heat blanket properties of water vapor, with an assist from carbon dioxide and other so-called greenhouse gases—is natural and crucial; it prevents Earth from looking like a snowball. The concern is over how much additional heat heat-trapping gasses will trap. We now have too much of a good thing.

Stabilizing the climate requires that the world cut greenhouse gases by 80 percent by 2050. But unlike the payoff of improving, say, sewers, cutting emissions won't actually stabilize the climate for perhaps another fifty years, because the planet will continue adjusting to gas already out of the box. Doubling the atmosphere's carbon dioxide—expected by between 2050 and 2080 unless we quench the fires—would create a planetary-average warming of roughly five degrees Fahrenheit. If we let that happen, we'll hand our kids a different planet, far outside the range that any humans have ever experienced, with no return possible within any fore-seeable future generation. So it's our children's world we're mainly talking about. But some of what will happen next is starting to happen now to people, and to corals.

When Bob talks about "coral bleaching," he means the corals' loss of their internal sugar-making algae partners (called zooxanthellae) when unusually hot weather drives the seawater temperature abnormally high.

Because "zoox" give corals their color, reefs without them turn porcelain white. Prolonged "bleaching" can kill corals. It's already killed large swaths of reef. In 1980, coral bleaching was brand-new. Now it's frequent and widespread.

About half the human-produced carbon dioxide has dissolved into the ocean. We're producing it so fast, it's "backing up" near the ocean's surface. The North Atlantic is absorbing only half the carbon dioxide it did in the mid-1990s. That will warm the climate faster. By 2080, bleaching will likely hit 80 to 100 percent of the world's tropical coral reefs every year. That could be the end of them. To outrun that, corals would have to continually adapt their temperature tolerance.

But even if corals outran warming, they'd still run into the pH problem.

In seawater, carbon dioxide triggers a short series of reactions that form carbonic acid and lock up carbonate molecules. Corals, corallines like *Titanoderma,* and other creatures that make skeletons and shells of calcium carbonate need those same carbonate molecules.

Chemistry buffs, this is for you: When a molecule of carbon dioxide (CO_2) enters the ocean, it soon finds itself attracted to water (H_2O). These two molecular parents spawn carbonic acid (H_2CO_3), which then releases one hydrogen ion (H^+), leaving a molecule of bicarbonate (HCO_3^-). The concentration of those hydrogen ions is measured as pH. The more hydrogen ions, the more acid, but the *lower* the pH (a pH of 1 is a very strong acid). Because increasing hydrogen ions push seawater pH toward the acid end of the scale, this is being called "ocean acidification" (even though the ocean is still slightly alkaline). Compared to before the Industrial Revolution, the upper ocean already has about 30 percent more hydrogen ions.

The problem is that those hydrogen ions easily bind with carbonate ions (CO_3^{2-}). Using up carbonate ions deprives animals like hard corals, clams, snails, and various plankton of building material for making their calcium carbonate skeletons and shells. Carbonate scarcity slows their growth; they become fragile and, sometimes, fatally deformed. Carbonate concentrations in the upper few hundred feet of the ocean have already declined about 10 percent compared to seawater just before steam-engine times.

. . .

"To see where this is heading," warns Bob, "put a clamshell or an egg in vinegar for a day."

I did. Not good. My shell began dissolving.

"Already," Bob adds, "some corals are growing thinner, weaker walls."

And I've already talked to shellfish growers who are seeing their larval oysters dying as lower-pH seawater reaches their hatcheries.

Carbonate concentration varies regionally. It's normally highest in the tropics, lowest near the poles. It's low around the Galápagos Islands. But Indonesia's waters have plenty of dissolved calcium carbonate of the form hard corals need (that form is called aragonite, by the way). So Indonesia's corals should be okay for decades. But only decades.

Since about 1800, the atmospheric carbon dioxide concentration has risen about 35 percent, from 280 molecules per million molecules of air to about 385 (in the year 2010). It's increasing by about 2 parts per million annually. When it reaches 450 parts per million—a near certainty in the middle of this century—the aragonite concentration around Australia's Great Barrier Reef will fall below the lowest concentration now bathing any coral reef on the planet. At 500 parts of carbon dioxide, large swaths of the Pacific and Indian Oceans will fall below the minimum aragonite concentration required by hard corals. If the atmosphere's carbon dioxide hits 550 (actually expected later in this century) the aragonite concentration that coral reefs require will essentially cease to exist. So it appears that carbonate availability will drop too low for reef growth before 2100. If we keep running civilization with fire, and the carbon dioxide concentration reaches abut 560, the world's seawater will begin to dissolve shellfish and coral reefs.

At the base of the food chain, some of the most important ocean drifters use calcium carbonate. They include organisms like single-celled foraminifera and coccolithophorids, which drift the ocean in uncountable trillions, plus pteropods (silent *p*; they're related to snails) that can swarm at densities of up to 1,000 per cubic meter of water. Foraminifera shells are now a third thinner than those from before the Industrial Revolution. Trouble for them means trouble for everything that eats them. Most people haven't heard of pteropods, but they're well-known to hungry young mackerel, pollock, cod, haddock, and salmon.

Copepods are often the first animal link in the food chain. When experimenters lowered seawater pH by 0.2 units, half their copepods died within a week. The pH of the ocean's surface has already dropped by about 0.11 units. In other laboratory experiments mimicking conditions predicted between 2040 and 2100, clams, oysters, mussels, urchins, and snails all had problems growing and reproducing.

Life often finds ways, but it needs time. Adaptation becomes less likely as changes accelerate.

While some people still argue over whether warming will generally be good or bad (though it will generally be bad), there is no argument that acidification will be anything *but* bad for things people care about, like shellfish and coral reefs, and all the associated fish, turtles, seafood, tourism—.

For the early Triassic period, when the air's carbon dioxide concentration was very high, the fossil pages of the coral chapter go blank. Bob speculates that without carbonate, some may have survived "by going naked." That is, corals may have lived like anemones, with no hard parts. "It took, I mean, *millions* of years for hard corals to reappear," he says.

We sip our beer. I'm thinking. Hundreds of millions of people depend heavily on reefs for food and livelihood.

I must look a little fatigued, because Bob asks, almost innocently, "Am I piling on the bad news?" He mentions that letting grazing fish recover—especially parrotfish—would buy reefs a little time to solve our atmospheric crisis. He knows two places where fish have saved coral in trouble: Bonaire, in the Caribbean, and Palau, in the western Pacific. I tell him I'd like to see that.

As the sun sinks, the plump moon rises, spreading its silver cloak upon the sea and the shadowed clouds, the sandy curve of shore, and the white gleam of surf. Under this moon, any slender hope will have to do. I decide not to think, and to just feel the night sea breeze.

~

Bonaire, anchored off Venezuela, has wild flamingos and the best remaining coral reefs in the Caribbean. Our first dive will be from the beach. As usual, Bob and Susie are studying coral, crusting algae, and seaweed. Also as usual, Ruddy Turnstones—birds I seem to see wherever I go—are picking along the waterline.

We suit up and walk into the shallows, suck a couple of breaths to make sure our air is on, pull our diving masks down, and plunge seaward.

The remains of past Staghorn thickets were mounded on the beach. Now they carpet the shallows between patches of dazzling sand. Old-timers tell of thickets of Staghorn and Elkhorn so dense that in the 1950s people here used chains and clubs to smash paths through the coral so they could dive from shore.

I see precisely zero live Staghorn, zero live Elkhorn. Yet this is, overall, the best place in the Caribbean to experience a "healthy" reef—one that is still functioning as a coral reef and hasn't gone over to the dark side of seaweed and gloomy shadow.

Past where those thickets once grew, the seafloor slopes to a rather narrow—but nice—band of reef from about twenty to fifty feet deep. There's a decent amount of live coral, covering about a quarter of the bottom. Corals shaped like brains, plates, and soft whips.

On this island, where since 1971 it's been illegal to even possess a speargun, the fish on the reef are delightfully abundant—and tame. They don't turn tail. Yellowtail Snappers and Bar Jacks swim almost touchingly close. You can approach parrotfish easily; they're as likely to turn toward you as away. Over the slope swarm thousands of Blue and Brown *Chromis*, white-lipped Creole Fish, and platoons of Sergeant Majors. They cloud the water in schools extending halfway to the surface, nabbing invisible plankton from an imperceptibly gentle flow.

A coral reef may be the most beautiful natural system on Earth. A towering rainforest, a lakeshore by campfire light, endless tundra, the dazzle of polar ice, turquoise atolls in azure seas, crystal alpine meadows, rolling grasslands pulling down the whole horizon, any water under the influence of gravity, desert solitude, the song of the blue ocean—no natural place lacks a claim to beauty. But unlike a place that whispers intimate secrets, a coral reef parades its pageantry. It's got to be the most spectacular cabaret in nature.

Discus-shaped surgeonfishes rove the reef here in herds of several dozen. When they descend to graze, they give close buzz cuts to coral heads, nipping any soft filaments, causing ruckus enough to dust up the place with clouds of sediment. Trumpetfish follow them, hoping to pick off little swimming animals displaced from cover.

Of parrotfishes, eight kinds here are recognizable as adults: Stoplight, Queen, Striped, Redfin, Redband, Blue, Rainbow, Princess. The only juvenile I learn easily is the Queen, because Susie calls them "crackheads" for their washed-out gray-and-white appearance and the dark circles under their eyes. The parrots scrape into the reef, chipping audibly, excreting lines of fine coral sand. They're abundant. Damsels are superabundant. Everywhere they're chasing grazing fish from their little seaweed gardens. Butterfly fishes flutter by like pennants in a stiff breeze. Angelfishes—French Angels, Queen Angels, and the superb Rock Beauty—cruise along arrayed in blues and golds.

They can take your breath away, but so can mere time; our air is limited. As we're swimming shoreward, Susie peeks into a pile of Staghorn rubble and a jade octopus slyly slides from its garden. And as we cross the dazzling shallows, a fencepost-sized Great Barracuda glides effortlessly into view, very much at home. It's the first big 'cuda Bob's seen here in a while, and he nods and signs an enthusiastic "Okay."

Walking to shore, we notice two big parrotfish in water so shallow their tails break the surface. Over white sand, they stand out like watermelons in a porcelain sink. When an Osprey comes over, it *has to* see them—but it sails past. It must be full. Plenty of parrotfish, it seems to me.

But the Osprey and I know what is, not what has been, or what is coming.

A middle-aged woman who has seen a lot of sun comes over. She recognizes Bob. Turns out she's a divemaster. Nice parrotfish right there, we agree. She's worried, though, because parrotfish are being increasingly caught from shore by recent immigrants from South America. "Every day, I see them casting their nets, taking the big ones," she reports.

Bob's been counting—and he concurs; parrots are still common but are definitely suffering decline compared to past years. Parrotfish have long been protected here by the ban on spearguns, and they are vegetarians, so they usually don't take a baited hook. But: new people, new method, new problem. Old story.

Bob's also seeing more seaweed. He showed me. So far it's just a tiny fuzz, in small patches. It's not the bushy growth that turns other Caribbean reefs gloomy. Not yet. Parrotfish decline looks like the smoking gun. As elsewhere.

I came to this last best place in the Caribbean to see a reef without obvious overfishing. As usual, it seems I'm a little late.

Old-timers say there were vastly more groupers and snappers—big ones—years ago. Easy to catch on a hook, they remain fished out. Among other things, they ate damselfish. And damselfish, though they eat seaweed, effectively defend their little seaweed gardens against other grazing fish. Fewer groupers and snappers mean more damsels, which means more gardens, more seaweed. And reduced parrotfish also means more seaweed.

Bob says, "I'm hearing alarms." One, a drop in parrotfish; two, increasing seaweed. "It worries me. Every coral reef in the world where seaweed got a foothold has unraveled—no exceptions." Susie's data show that baby corals have declined by fully half in the last few years. Getting a grip on life is becoming increasingly difficult for corals, even here.

Bob loves parrotfish. The few new immigrants love them too—mainly steamed. In most of the Caribbean, fishing pressure is much harsher than here in Bonaire, and the problems worse. Throughout the Caribbean, about 60,000 small-scale fishers set nets and traps and baited hooks on, in, over, and around coral reefs, dropping 180 kinds of fishes onto the tables of fish markets and high-end resorts. In Belize, where fishing has depleted groupers and snappers, fishermen sell parrotfish as "snapper." Tourists don't know the difference; locals don't care. But it boomerangs.

In Belize I once went out with some fishermen who'd set a half-kilometer-long gill net overnight. At dawn we began hand-hauling the net, and at first, no fish appeared. After twenty minutes it was clear these guys were in for a meager catch. By the time they'd hauled the entire five hundred meters of net into the boat, they'd caught not one single fish. Not one. It was a brutal lesson: if you take all, you get nothing.

Rising tides of people accelerate the strains on food, freshwater, forests, and fish. And as a man from nearby Nicaragua who is here studying the reefs points out, "Many poor Latin American places have a dual problem: poverty is hard to solve when the Catholic church forces people to choose between birth control and God."

What can a poor person do? The Nicaraguan man added, though, that it's usually not the local community that depletes the resources; it's the *market*. But the market is just a distant community that has come to buy resources because it can't feed its own beast. The "market" is overpopulation looking for a place to shop. The market is people living elsewhere who can support themselves only by sticking their straw into other communities, other countries. The market is immigration that stays at home but arrives on your doorstep dressed as cash.

The big cities and crowded corridors of the world pull nature into the vortex of their appetites, from across town and across the planet. People inside that vortex who don't get enough may decide to leave. Emigration is just overpopulation looking for a place to eat. And so a few have arrived here, and elsewhere, bringing a taste for, say, parrotfish. Enough parrotfish for the reef may look to fishers like plenty for them, and too many people for the reef might look like just a few more people.

Bob's hearing a third alarm besides declining parrotfish and increasing seaweed: *Titanoderma* is rapidly declining. So are other crusting algae. Bonaire, with the best reefs in the Caribbean, has also had the Caribbean's highest density of *Titanoderma*, helping give coral babes a boost. In under a decade, crusting algae have shrunk from covering 20 percent of the bottom to, now, under 5 percent. Bob says warily, "You don't want to lose such an important coral starter." Bob thinks *Titanoderma's* decline might result from acidification.

But if that's true, wouldn't corals be having the same problem? "No, probably not," Bob explains. Corals use the much more common form of calcium carbonate, aragonite. Crusting algae use the scarcer form called calcite. Getting enough calcite from the seawater demands more energy. As ocean acidification makes calcium carbonate scarcer, calcite users might be the first in their neighborhood to show the strain.

Bonaire's government understands that luring crucial tourists depends on Bonaire's ability to boast the region's best reefs. But "best" doesn't mean Bonaire is immune from the region's problems. Bonaire was not spared the diseases that killed the Caribbean's branching coral and grazing urchins. It's been spared the plague of excess seaweed only because, compared to the rest of the region, it better protected its fish. But it's not *immune* to the possibility of overfishing. The reefs need fish. That's not *all* they need, but as Bob had said, keeping fish on the reef is the best time buyer against climate changes.

Until the last few years, many problems appeared to be simply a matter of people taking too much out. Rising population continues adding tension to the planet's life supports, and now the problems also include people putting too much in. Pollution has long been an issue, but carbon dioxide is a global matter.

Climate change seems to enter every equation. Who'd have thought that the same clear, natural, nontoxic gas we exhale would turn out to be history's most threatening pollutant? This is partly a symptom of how little we've understood the world. And our dearth of ways to deal with such enormous problems is a symptom of the relationship we've decided to have with the world. When it would have mattered, no one ever said, "Thou shalt not pollute." Now that it's an issue, our wisdom traditions, and our economic system, lack adequate moral language to address it and the ethical consensus to deal with it. And because we're not really in control of the vehicle we're driving, the world is entering a truly new time.

FAREWELL, WHOLE NEW TIME

The grapevine reports that to the springtime beach has come a remarkable castaway: a dead whale. To find it, I just drive into the next town, go to the beach, and look up and down the surf line. About a mile away I see what looks like a black-hulled trawler wrecked on the beach.

In the sea such a creature is impressive. But one gets mainly glimpses: the top of a head, a rolling back. Up close, as I walk alongside its massive contours, it seems surreally revealed, as though here to herald some message, some annunciation, an oracle.

This is a Fin Whale. The world's second-largest animal, Fin Whales can reach about ninety feet and an estimated eighty tons, and can live up to about a century. This one is about sixty feet long. (The closely related Blue Whale, reaching a little over one hundred feet, is the most massive animal known to have ever lived. Hunted to near extinction, it's barely hanging on in the Antarctic, recovering strongly in the eastern Pacific, and remains elsewhere very rare.)

The whale's hulk lies on its port side, marooned past the last high-tide line. The waning moon and weakening tides will leave it there for quite a while. But I know the people here won't allow this. The nearby homes are too expensive to share the beach with such a wonder; it will draw onlookers and hoi polloi such as myself. And the stench will become unpleasant. Full decomposition would likely take us through the summer. Bikinis and decaying blubber—not the image this place is marketing. Bad for business.

So I'm sure the fire department and the police will soon intervene: rope off the site; place someone officious to prevent people from doing something stupid to themselves or, maybe worse, the carcass; allow biologists to open a cavernous portal and explore, measure, assess, perhaps reveal; and eventually bury it.

But not yet. For now it lies in state with a certain fitting dignity. I circumambulate the corpse freely, unaccosted and unopposed. Under the wide sky and with the backdrop and sound track of the immense sea whence it has just come, it is both in and out of its element, natural and unnatural.

Its tar-black skin is calico-patched with pink sand abrasions from the surf swells that pushed it aground. The huge pleats of its distendable throat, looking like the lapstrake hull of a wooden vessel, run halfway down its body. Its mouth bites a bulldozer's wedge of beach sandwich. In life, this Jonah-gulping throat ballooned like a pelican's pouch, engulfing a swimming pool of water, fishes, and krill. Then its unspeakable tongue would strain water through the mouth-rimming brush of baleen, concentrating entrapped hordes into a satisfying swallow.

Living Fin Whales don't lift their tail flukes above water, yet here the tail lies in full view. Reddened with the bruise of burst blood vessels, these flukes span about twice my body length. One fluke has furrowed a gouge in the sand like the rudder of a ship run aground. On the landward side, sand has built up against it; on the seaward, the swirl of receding waves has dug a little hollow. The tailstock connects

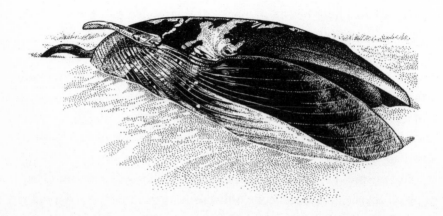

the hull-like body with the massive blades of its propelling tail. That stock seems as sturdy as a tree trunk, but the linkage bears the sleekness of motion, attenuating to a wedge above and a wedge below, like a double-edged splitting maul for shattering water as the whale swims. Or swam.

The whale's blowholes are slammed shut like deck hatches. Its left pectoral fin lies embedded in the sand; its right—about as long as I am tall—dangles high and dry. The sun throws a lifelike highlight onto its open eye. That rather tiny-looking eye is about the size of the circle you can make with your thumb and forefinger.

Blood and fluid ooze from a wound near the base of its pectoral fin, as though the percolating corpse is just another leaking tanker. Formerly, whales were the world's wells, civilization's chief source of oil, and we pumped the sea nearly dry of them. Now many wish to pump it dry of petroleum, incurring deeper risks at deeper depths (and not just in the Gulf of Mexico). We appear to have learned little of whales and nothing of oil. Japan, Norway, and Iceland cannot get beyond their blood thirst, nor we our oil addiction. The average Yank uses twice as much fossil fuel as the average Brit. Compared to 1970, we in the United States use half again as much energy, have increased our paved-road miles by half again, upped our vehicle miles driven by more than 175 percent, and increased the size of our new homes by half again. In 2007 the United States was burning over twenty million barrels of oil a day, about the same as the industrial behemoths Japan, Germany, Russia, China, and India—combined. God bless us indeed.

I notice that the whale's also got a bruise across its back and a gash near its eye, possibly from its battering grounding.

Whales die. All things die. But when a whale biologist arrives, she examines the oozing bruise and pronounces trauma; a ship has done this.

This makes it a death less easily accepted. We stand here in our encounter with an ancient being simply because the ancient being has encountered us first, and tragically.

Indeed, the entire world has encountered us. Geologists place time on Earth into great bins and drawers called eons, eras, epochs, and so forth. These mark times when the planet changed its marquee. Each time the theater of life has opened the curtain on a new act (such as the first appearance of cells, the first multicelled organisms, the first animals with shells) and each time it has brought down the house with mass extinctions, catastrophic meteors, and cycles of ice ages, it has left a playbill in the rocks. All these ages later, geologists have named and labeled the boundaries of these internested bins and boxes of time. They name the last ice ages as the Pleistocene epoch. They call the time after them, starting roughly 12,000 years ago, the Holocene, meaning "whole new time." It includes all of civilization. And "whole new time" may be an understatement.

This scene is so full of contrasts that one feels some immense transition arriving on the sea breeze. Here lies this great and awesome beast, this time-traveling messenger of travail. Several Shinnecock Indians from the nearby reservation arrive and begin singing and chanting. In earlier times, Indians pursued passing whales. Now they grieve their passing. Soon come a phalanx of schoolchildren, being herded over the dune to gawk and horse around, and a couple of dogs, which begin barking at the enormous corpse. From the beachfront mansions, to the metallic gleam and the glint off windshields of arriving cars, to the kids let loose from school, minute by minute, more and more people flood the shore. I stand regarding the whale, listening to the surf and watching the dune grass shudder. And before long, people so dominate the scene that their overwhelming numbers transform the enormous creature that has convened us from monument to amusement.

In just this way a funny thing has happened on the way to the future. In the year 2000 Nobel laureate Paul Crutzen suggested that the Holocene epoch is finished. Human domination has so changed the world as to constitute a new epoch: the new time of humans—the Anthropocene. The suggestion surprised many. Geologists are debating. Can it be so?

Has the time really come when people are *the* dominant force on the planetary surface? While people argue over the idea of the Anthropocene, to this whale it might have seemed obvious.

The sky over the ocean is laden with migrants. Cormorants that started appearing in small groups a couple of weeks ago now come in many black

ragged lines headed north and east. By the hundreds, they scribble themselves across the morning.

While Kenzie and I walk down the beach from the whale, scoters are
continually moving above the horizon. Each scarflike skein carries dozens of birds, wings blurred with the effort of flight as the flocks slither
east like sky snakes. They've spent winter not just off our lighthouse at
the Point, but in various locales from Canada down past Hatteras, and
similarly on the West Coast of the continent, too. As they've been doing
every morning for weeks, they're still passing at a rate of several hundred per hour. What uncountable legions of them must still populate
the winter coasts and summer tundra.

Half a dozen net-dragging trawlers are giving early-arriving fish and
squid a working over. The fish spent the winter in deep water, where the
trawlers have been on them, far over the horizon, about sixty miles offshore. Now they're here. Through binoculars I see dozens of gannets
diving on—herring? mackerel? No; the gannets are cratering the water
behind the boats as the fishermen shovel much of their catch—fish that
are too small, damaged, the wrong species—overboard. The abundant
waste seems at least a boon to birds.

But in the pretzel-textured logic of the post-Holocene, even the conclusion that food nourishes no longer necessarily holds. The easy junk
food from the trawlers—unlike human junk food—has only half the calories of the gannets' normal wild food. A study of Cape Gannets who'd
acquired the trash-diving habit off southern Africa found that discarded
bottom fish pack only half the nutrition of the anchovies and sardines the
gannets normally catch. That's not a problem for the adults. But chicks
need high-calorie food. Result: due to abundant food from fishing
boats, gannet chicks are starving to death. This helps explain the precipi-
tous halving of the Cape Gannet population in recent decades. Further,
gannets with chicks *tried* to eat better. They made twice as many hunting dives, and stayed underwater twice as long, as did nonbreeding adults.
They just couldn't find enough real food to keep their chicks alive. That's
because Cape Gannets are joined on their fishing grounds by people,
and people, true to form, are taking vast quantities of the sardines and
anchovies in the region.

This story is more widespread than I'd thought. Scientists have linked breeding collapses of various seabirds to fisheries targeting their prey in northern Europe. And the study's authors note that nothing's preventing the same thing from happening to our Northern Gannets, too. I've seen the gargantuan herring trawlers that rake the very same New England waters where gannets, whales, other seabirds, and tuna need those herring.

In a world of starving people, people still discard food. In a time dominated by people, seabirds starve by eating the fish people throw away. Waste like this, the inequity of haves and have-nots, overpopulation, and a world more tightly networked than it first appears, all conspire to keep many poor—people and seabirds alike.

We've seen that civilization chose for itself a distant, dismissive relationship with the world. This happened early on, before people understood that the world is round, let alone how it works. It's as though humanity had an adolescent need to project an independent identity before it really knew enough to think things through. But to be fair, a lot of that became ingrained when the world really was in many ways a threatening, scary place, especially to desert tribes and their scribes.

We've also seen that industrialization's side effects started to worry a few people much later. Some of those thinkers established a countercurrent that reconsidered our estrangement from the world. And I've noted that human progress has depended on enlarging the circle of compassion. Recognizing the value of wider compassion seems inescapable when you think about it—at least it did when Darwin and Einstein and Schweitzer thought about it. But that view doesn't yet dominate—though *we* dominate.

In all the long train of ages, inanimate nature and life have shaped each other. I love this coast because it's "real," but what does that mean nowadays? Can we distinguish real from artificial in the human-dominated Anthropocene world? The migrations, the weather—when we look closely, all bear our thumbprint. In my youth I was sometimes told to pay attention to the "real world," that place of tedium tallied in digits and zeros, where strings of zeros are pursued and prized. The mass delusion of that "real world" is the fervent belief that the ledger books capture the value and the consequences of our transactions. Yet that collective illusion is real enough to do some very concrete things—at least until real reality catches up.

If people are using the world's forests, fishes, soils, freshwater, and other resources something like 25 percent faster than the world can replace them, it means, basically, that the world would be broke if we weren't borrowing so heavily from the future. People call it "leveraging," but a new word for delusion doesn't cure the illness.

In his prescient 1848 essay "The Art of Living," John Stuart Mill foreshadowed much about what counts as progress—and what really *is* progress:

> There is room in the world, no doubt . . . for a great increase in population. . . . I confess I see very little reason for desiring it.
>
> If the earth must lose that great portion of its pleasantness which . . . the unlimited increase of wealth and population would extirpate from it, for the mere purpose of enabling it to support a larger, but not a better or happier population, I sincerely hope . . . they will be content to be stationary, long before necessity compels them to it.
>
> . . . A stationary condition of capital and population implies no stationary state of human improvement. There would be as much scope as ever for all kinds of mental culture, and moral and social progress; as much room for improving the Art of Living, and much more likelihood of its being improved. . . .
>
> All the mechanical inventions yet made have . . . enabled a greater population to live the same life of drudgery and imprisonment, and an increased number of manufacturers and others to make fortunes.

By around 1800, when the world had about one billion people, the Reverend Thomas Malthus had become alarmed at the implications of population growth. Though water remained plentiful, vast tropical and temperate forests still stood as strangers to the saw, and the oceans shimmered with fishes that had never met a strand of twine, Malthus divined trouble brewing.

Growing at just 1 percent annually, a population doubles in seventy years. The United States already has twice as many people as when I was born; Tokyo's greater metropolitan area—35 million—now has more people than all of Canada. During the twentieth century, the world population quadrupled; it's now approaching 7 billion. By 2050, we'll *add* to that more than the total human population of 1950.

How many people can this world support? It depends on how they live. If everyone gets 800 kilograms (1,760 pounds) of grains annually, like Americans, then the world can carry 2.5 billion people. Problem: we passed that number in 1950. The world could support 10 billion people living like Indians. Problem: most Indians want to live more like Americans. (It would be interesting to see a seventy-year-old American standing next to all the food—and everything else—that person had consumed in their entire life.)

Of course, before we eat our dinner, we need a refrigerator to store our food. In 1980, China produced 50,000 refrigerators; in 2004, it manufactured 30 million. We need to put the refrigerator in a house, and houses use wood. The forests of Indonesia, Burma, the Russian Far East, and Papua New Guinea will be largely gone by around 2025, and with them their birds, bugs, and Orangutans.

To buy the food, we drive to the store. The Chinese would also like to drive to the store. To have as many cars per person as the United States does, China will need 30 percent more cars than exist worldwide today. Driving them would burn 98 million barrels of oil a day (the world now produces 85 million barrels). If this can't work for China, it can't work for India—it can't work.

We need a new, nonburning energy economy, a way of reducing population, and a way of replacing the delusion of infinite growth. That's what we need.

The road to Lazy Point runs past two Osprey nests I like to check. One's on a platform atop a utility pole near an old fish factory. In former times, that factory shipped so many fish there's still a set of railroad tracks leading to the old buildings. Like somebody running with scissors, those fishermen fell on hard times of their own making. They largely emptied the Sound of the fish they processed, and starved to death from their own success. Loser takes all. It's ironic that you can starve by taking too much, but overshoot equals crash—the familiar formula.

Today there's another kind of shoot here. Right at the base of the pole, directly under the immense nest, a fashion model is posing for a photographer while two other people earn their fees by standing with arms folded, scowling importantly.

Frightened out of their nest, the birds are nearby, calling. Early in the season like this, a prolonged disturbance might cause them to lose confidence in their site's security and abandon it. I pull over next to their van, ask who is in charge, get importantly scowled at, and explain that they are right under a nest and that they are scaring these two huge birds that are zooming back and forth and calling nervously overhead. The fashionistas look up, startled. I'm as surprised that anyone could miss the two giant hawks with six-foot wingspans yelling at them from fifty feet directly overhead. The crew is actually very nice about it, explaining that they didn't know. They lose no time moving over to a nearby dune—nicer backdrop anyway, in my unprofessional opinion, with the yellow beach heather blooming—and as the birds settle back in, we all wish each other a nice day.

At the nest closest to my house, the salt-pond nest, I notice that two Ospreys now look comfortable where a few days ago up to five had appeared in contention for possession. Because there seemed to be a question of ownership, I fear our familiar male of quite a few years has not returned. He liked to spend the night perched across the road from the pond. But he hasn't been there. Old habits probably die harder than do old birds, so I'm presuming he's gone.

One male goes; another takes his place. Food availability and the number of nest sites dictate the Ospreys' population's limits. The same is true for people. But Ospreys can't make more fish for themselves. People, we're different. In the latter half of the twentieth century, humanity's food production tripled, thanks to new high-yield grain varieties, artificial pesticides and fertilizer (40 to 60 percent of the nitrogen in the human body now originates in a factory), and—pumped water.

The Green Revolution was accomplished largely by doubling the amount of irrigated land. Hundreds of millions of wells now reach into the earth like straws in a thick drink on a hot day. But as with many things, we're taking more water than we're getting.

Because much food production relies on pumping groundwater

faster than it recharges, the world has blown a big food bubble. The Green Revolution turned India—where millions once died in famines—into a food exporter. But now in parts of India, water tables are dropping more than half an inch a day. Many wells are depleted, and irrigated farmland has shrunk.

India recently stopped sending rice to Bangladesh; then India began importing rice from Australia. (But Australia's droughts dropped its rice exports 90 percent.) An Indian water official said ominously, "When the balloon bursts, untold anarchy will be the lot of rural India."

Many wells mine deep "fossil" water, vast reserves of locked-away liquid that, like oil, can be pumped dry. Where China grows half its wheat and a third of its corn, the water table drops ten feet each year. In the United States, the water has dropped more than one hundred feet under Kansas, Oklahoma, and Texas.

In many countries, women walk an average of four to five miles just for household water. By 2025, as many as two-thirds of all people will live in places suffering a scarcity of clean water. Health experts expect lack of clean water to cause more cholera, dysentery, hepatitis, and infant mortality.

Who will have water? A ton of grain represents a thousand tons of water, and grain imports become proxy for rain. The poorest countries will, of course, lose the bidding for food. We may have a hard time feeling their pain, so for us, the Hausa people of West Africa have a saying: "The stone in water does not comprehend how parched is the hill."

Engineered to end hunger, the Green Revolution failed because most of the world allowed the increased food to grow more hungry people. China, partly because of its one-child policy, has eased more hunger, faster, than anyplace ever has. Meanwhile, India's population growth largely erased its food-production increases. Now a record 1 billion people suffer malnutrition; 10 million more do so each year. A recent U.N. report titled *The State of Food Insecurity* came with a press release saying, "For millions of people, eating the minimum amount of food to live an active and healthy life is a distant dream."

Dividers: Over 2.5 billion people live on less than two dollars per day.

Nearly 1 billion people get less than 80 percent of the U.N.-recommended caloric intake; they are, technically, starving. Undernourished women annually bear 20 million underweight infants, and more than half of Indian newborns would be in intensive care if born in California. Some 1.5 billion people are overweight.

So there are two kinds of people in the world: those who want more and those who need more. And those who need more want more. One-quarter of the world's people consume more than three-quarters of the world's goods. That's not fair. But as I've already mentioned, to give everyone an American level of material living, we'd need two and a half Earths. That's not possible.

Because forests, oceans, croplands, and water supplies are all being depleted by the number of people we have now, a grim logic appears irrefutable: as we add people, either everyone will get poorer on average, or the poor will get much poorer. Or the population will be adjusted in the usual way: with shortages, bullets, and bombs.

Land, water, population growth—violence. When Rwanda's population tripled, between 1950 and the early 1990s, it became Africa's most densely populated country. Farmland and food—and tempers—grew short. In the ethnic rampage that killed 800,000 in ten days, whole families were hacked to death lest there be survivors to claim the family farm plot. Sudan's Darfur genocide was also ignited by disputes over farmland, exacerbated by drought. Sudan's population, about 10 million in 1950, is projected to hit 70 million by 2050. If it does, Sudan will likely fight a newly doubled 120 million Egyptians for Nile water—unless Ethiopia, whose population will have more than doubled to over 80 million, tries diverting the 85 percent of the Nile headwaters it controls.

Poor people don't want to stay poor. But there's a misconception that it's somehow "unfair" to poor people or, worse, racist, to let them in on the main secret of wealthy, educated, and successful people: smaller families mean larger lives.

The thing that brings fertility down fastest happens to be the same thing that brings down poverty: educating girls. Turns out, illiterate women bear three times as many children as literate women, and their children tend to stay poor. Meanwhile, each year of schooling raises a woman's earning power 10 to 20 percent. And when people are a little better off, they desire fewer children.

Good news: things are getting worse at a slower rate; the rate of population increase is easing. More than forty countries now have populations that are stable or slowly declining, including Germany, Italy, Russia, and Japan. At present trends, the world population will likely peak around midcentury (at between 8 and 11 billion). By then, something like fifty countries will likely already have fewer people than today. People can live crowded and in fear, but real human beings will always need soil, water, food, wood, air, beauty, freedom from oppression, freedom of expression, room for compassion, the company of creatures, and a future.

When the ship *Titanic* set out to cross the ocean, its proprietors believed it indestructible. So they did not equip it with enough lifeboats for all the people on board. History is sometimes destiny. Believing ourselves too clever to sink our enterprise, we're on another voyage where the lifeboat room is limited. And we're discovering that there are more passengers than the mother ship was built to handle. No known island exists, no opposite shore, no passing ships to call for rescue. Just us. Just us, and the wish—perhaps too late—that we had steered a more careful course while the band gaily played.

As we bravely enter the Anthropocene and the uncertainties of a world with us at the helm, it's worth reconsidering Thoreau's declaration "In wildness is the preservation of the world." Wild places produced the living world and its inhabitants in abundance and resilience. On the other hand, for most of human history, natural things stood poised to recycle us at any moment. Weather, beasts, famine, enemies. We can live more safely and better by enjoying those elements that have come under control, including agriculture and medicine. I wouldn't recommend a "return to nature." I like books and science. I like music. I am willing to abandon the concept of Natural. Nature is moot, anyway, because we've so thoroughly changed the world. I'm willing to abandon it—for any approach that works better.

As oceans get depleted, water tables drop, sea levels rise, and forests fall, you begin to realize that the drawdown of nature is just one side of a coin on which hundreds of millions of people face a world wherein dignity—always so elusive throughout history—now drains away with the freshwater; hope flies away like birds that no longer return. If, to paraphrase Aldo Leopold's dictum, "a thing is right when it tends to preserve the integrity, stability, and beauty" of the living community, then we've passed "right" traveling in the opposite lane. If our values change, we might use science and technology to save us. If our failed values persist, science and technology will only press our accelerator.

It seems our world-changing capabilities are just too new. For hundreds of thousands of precivilized years, and then through all the time philosophers, theologians, and economists were crafting our contract with the world, nature always seemed to be the one dishing out those famines, diseases, sharp-fanged beasts, and killer weather. Only in the twentieth century did nuclear weapons signal a clear power shift between people and fate and create the first widespread wonder about whether the world would one morning wake into a day with no tomorrow. In all the prior crystal-ball gazing and the straining to see the future, the one thing everyone assumed was that there would *be* a future. And now we're realizing one additional thing that was never wholly possible: we might ruin the world even in an era of peace. Before, no one expected we could change the weather, dissolve the world's corals, alter the chemistry of oceans and our bodies—. These things represent a radical new relationship with the world, but we haven't revised our contract.

So the matter requires a moral answer. But it's no longer the old philosophers' question of "who has moral agency." The question now is: How can we survive? Our values will have to catch up to our understanding of the world and its workings.

The appalling dislocation caused by the 1930s Great Plains Dust Bowl made it evident that conservation, economy, and community can intermesh on scales large enough to rattle nations. In 1944, while planning the founding of what would become the United Nations, President Franklin D. Roosevelt—still deep in fighting World War II—asked his secretary of state to begin preparations for a world meeting on conservation, writing:

In our meetings with other nations I have a feeling that too little attention is being paid to the subject of the conservation and use of natural resources.

I am surprised that the world knows so little about itself.

Conservation is a basis of permanent peace.

It occurs to me, therefore, that even before the United Nations meet . . . it might do much good to hold a meeting in the United States of all of the united and associated nations. . . .

I repeat again that I am more and more convinced that Conservation is a basis of permanent peace. . . .

I think the time is ripe.

How we think of problems determines where we look for the solutions. If we think the problem is that we are running out of oil, we will look for more oil. If the problem is that we waste too much, or need clean energy, we'll look for different solutions.

FDR died before the meeting was held, and its conservation agenda was abandoned. Roads not taken.

APRIL

Where did spring go? A local birder reported a Yellow Warbler on April 8—*eleven days earlier* than the previous earliest state record. But on April 9, a morning snow squall brings spring to a halt. Early blossoms bow their heads under snowy crowns. The early egrets' stark white finery is suddenly camouflage. And now the mud-brown geese stand out like raisins in sugar. In measured tones they conference about the state of nature. Snow flurries continue into late morning. But calendar-smart crows read the sun, and know better than to be fooled by weather. Flurries be damned; they continue breaking twigs and making nests. Wise is the crow who works through the snow.

Flurries turn to April showers, and by late in the day all snow is memory.

Winter's visitors continue departing as spring residents arrive. The last Harp Seals departed toward the northern ice a month ago. A young Gray Seal, its coat like mottled charcoal, comes out into the sparkling sun, gripping the sand with its nails. It's the last seal I'll see this spring. Wading birds are trading places. Great Blue Herons who've survived winter gather across the marshes in small flocks of up to about half a dozen. Dressed in bright new plumage, they'll soon leave. New waders are arriving. The salt-marsh meadows hold several Great Egrets, and a Little Blue Heron stalks the salt pond's shore. Glossy Ibis should be here soon.

Not all is pageantry. A pile of mallard feathers lies at the edge of the reeds. Life ends. Other birds will use some of this down to line their nests. Life continues.

Over the ocean, a heavy flight of gannets—their spring peak—is under way across a broad front. Each time I lift my binoculars to an "empty" section of ocean horizon and hold still, at least one gannet appears in my sights within five seconds. When small groups of them pass close, just outside the surf, they gleam with the immaculate luster of spring: body feathers dazzling white, jet black wingtips shiny, and heads airbrushed peach. This glowing vitality is their reward for withstanding winter at sea.

It's been one of those nights when gusts charge across the open water like Mongol hordes and the gale howls like wolves pounding down the door. During big storms like this, even the water in my toilet starts pulsing. By dawn we had eight inches of rain. Mid-April can still hurl fierce weather.

The wind is throwing a tantrum that has trees down and airports closed all the way to Maine. Two smaller storms have apparently combined forces: one coming across the northern United States and one coming up the coast from Florida. Our tide clock indicates incoming when I grab my binoculars and venture across the road with Kenzie to assess the tempest.

My neighbor's picnic table has found its inner driftwood and is floating on its side a hundred yards from shore, rapidly sailing toward the open Sound as though eloping with the storm.

The beach looks rearranged. Most alarmingly, what had been the gently sloping path to the Sound shore now ends in a two-foot drop. Waves have simply gobbled a wedge of sand as though lifting a beach-long slice of cake. I'm startled to see an exposed pile of boulders I hadn't even known lay buried here.

The old-timers tell stories of storms that ate chunks of our neighborhood, washing away houses and the sand they'd stood on. Of one storm in the '50s, a neighbor recalls, "I had a flounder in my living room. I guess I'd left a window open."

Our road's end shatters to fragments at the high-tide line, its blacktop crumbling as water nibbles landward over time. In one place, stumps of old cedars remain where barnacles now cover the rocks at low tide. They're remnants of long-forgotten freshwater wetlands, inundated by the sea's uprising, now battered by ocean surf.

The struggle with coastal storms is mainly about water that gets uppity. And the main reason houses fall to the tide and waters swallow wetlands is that the sea level is creeping up. If the sea level were falling, people who'd bought waterfront homes would have to keep extending their path to the beach. Instead, the surf grabs walkways and wooden stairs and hurls them down the shore. Like a toddler getting better at walking, it reaches for things it couldn't have before.

Several big insurance companies have stopped writing new home-insurance policies here. They've considered the science about storms intensified by warming ocean waters, analyzed how future storm surges may inundate homes, calculated property values, tallied recent payouts—and gotten scared. Or rather, smart. Smart enough to pull away from tidewater. Because my home's a hundred paces from the present high-tide line, I find this unsettling.

The last time our planet was completely free of polar ice, about forty million years ago (following high greenhouse-gas concentrations resulting from the intense volcanic activity of the times), the sea level was about two hundred feet higher than it is today. It's taking a lot less than that to scare my neighbors. Three neighbors on the seaward side of my road recently sold their cottages. Seeing the beach incised so deeply must surely have been on their minds.

Because the only road to our houses borders a wide marsh, exceptionally high tides can actually trap us. And in this morning's nasty weather, the marsh is gone. What had been marsh looks like open bay. The tide has annexed the road, and bay water is streaming across the pavement. In the swarming puddles I need to get through, the saltwater is deep enough to resist my car, which throws a boatlike wake as I move forward. I'll pay for this in the price of new brakes in a few weeks, when the mechanic asks, "Were you driving through *saltwater* or anything like that?"

Who else pays for the rising sea level? If you live miles inland, you likely don't drive through saltwater, you know that the sea won't flood your neighborhood, and you're probably not very concerned about the answer to that question. But the joke's on you, because the answer is: you pay. You pay to pump eroded sand back onto beaches from here to Florida. And—thank you very much—you pay most of my flood insurance. Yes, while many private insurers are too smart to write a policy on my vulnerable little beach house, you pay for my taxpayer-subsidized federal flood insurance. I appreciate it, but I wish you'd stop. Your hard-earned dollars help wealthy people build seashore McMansions where they otherwise wouldn't build, because the cost—or unavailability—of private insurance would make such risky self-aggrandizement prohibitive. Only consider the politics. People lean on their coastal congressional representatives, the congressional reps demand pork-fed subsidies, and deals are made. As a friend of mine likes to say, "Poor people have capitalism; the rich have socialism." And I have flood insurance. But I'd rather see the program axed. It's selfish for grown-ups who decide to live in high-risk, flood-prone areas to spread their own risks to everyone else. Those of us who would take our chances could still take our chances—and you wouldn't have to be involved.

But even if environmentalists succeed in eliminating the federal flood insurance subsidy, we'll all pay for the rise in the sea level eventually, because we're all netted by an increasingly globalized economy with increasingly shared risks. I suppose that's fair enough, because we all help cause the sea-level rise. If we shirk the responsibility, we simply shift the cost to someone, somewhere, someday—but what goes around usually comes back around.

So part of what's on my mind is mere sea level, but that connects to energy, economics, and how we value things. The wind has these topics swirling around in my neighborhood and in my head.

As I feared, our salt-pond Ospreys are missing in action, gone from their nest and nowhere in view. This kind of weather can make them abandon the whole season's breeding.

At the nest near the old fish factory, though, the Ospreys are home. They've weathered fashion models *and* they're weathering this storm. The male is kiting in the wind over their bowl of big sticks. I'm amazed that the whole nest hasn't blown away. The female is hunkered down, head barely visible, probably already on eggs. Lucky for her, the nest is in the lee of trees and high dunes that are weakening the blast of the tempest.

. . .

I don't mind the weather so much. But it happens to be a day I've never liked: Earth Day. It seems pathetic to mark just one day for, well, the whole world. It's as if for most people, the planet is somehow out of context. (And in an awful irony, Earth Day 2010 saw the beginning of the Gulf of Mexico oil eruption.)

Earth Day originated as a response to pollution. But more important than marking the day is when and where that response was possible. Environmental movements arose not in the most polluted places on Earth but in the most democratic. The growth of environmental activity elsewhere often paralleled the overthrow of authoritarian and military regimes and the rise of democracies. When Václav Havel became president of a newly democratic Czechoslovakia in 1989, he lamented to the Czech people, "We have laid waste to our soil and the rivers and the forests that our forefathers bequeathed to us, and we have the worst environment in the whole of Europe today." The previous repressive regime's suppression of citizen groups, the press, universities, and other potential sources of objection allowed it to pollute with impunity while people stood powerless. Nature is most abused where human rights are most abused. A country serves justice, or it doesn't. When it doesn't, it poisons air, water, and soul alike. When it does, the environment becomes a key toward unlocking justice—but free people must hold those keys.

Saving the world requires saving democracy. That requires well-informed citizens. Conservation, environment, poverty, community, education, family, health, economy—these combine to make one quest: liberty and justice for all. Whether one's special emphasis is global warming or child welfare, the cause is the same cause. And justice comes from the same place being human comes from: compassion.

The main point of a democracy—protecting the best interests of the many, and the rights of the minority, from the greed and bullying of a few—is accomplished by having "the many" run the government. The social contract is that people voluntarily give some authority to a citizen-run government that serves social order and the public interest. That was the idea.

But greed has grown into a parasitic infestation of the body politic that bleeds us weak. Just look at the multinational corporations' lobbying, the resulting flow of taxpayer subsidies, and the failure of government oversight.

Political institutions can't correct the economic forces—or even stop feeding corporations with public money—because they've been captured by them. Each year, globally, governments shell out $700 billion in subsidies that help pay people to overpump groundwater, overcut forests, overfish oceans, and overuse fuel. The world taxes itself to pay for its own destruction.

Modern corporations were essentially illegal at the founding of the United States. (The colonists had had enough of British corporations.) In the new country, corporations could form, raise public capital, and share profits with stockholders only for specified activities that benefited the public, such as constructing roads or canals. Corporate licenses were temporary. Corporations were forbidden from attempting to influence elections, lawmaking, public policy, or civic life. Imagine.

But from the beginning, corporate-minded men chafed for power, prompting Thomas Jefferson to write in 1816, "I hope we shall . . . crush in its birth the aristocracy of our moneyed corporations, which dare already to challenge our government to a trial of strength and bid defiance to the laws of our country."

For the first century after the American Revolution, legislators maintained control of the corporate chartering process. Then they essentially lost it as a series of court decisions established corporate "rights" and corporate "personhood." These have been catastrophic for democracy, with planetary implications.

We didn't need the U.S. Supreme Court to tell us that corporations have the same rights of "free speech" as real persons. Of course they do— they are much freer, in fact, than normal humans, since they can buy airtime and advertising, dose candidates with fairy dust, and mobilize paid persuaders in quantities out of the orbit of the budget of any *real* real person. Corporations have free speech. Normal humans, not so much.

Our problems are not the inevitable price of progress. They are the eventual cost of stupidity, ideology, superstition, greed—the list is short. The problems spawned are vast. They're intractable, but not because we lack know-how. They're intractable because we can't find the sense that informs the will.

That avuncular Trojan horse of greed, Ronald Reagan, largely abrogated the social contract because—as far as I can tell—he and his ilk didn't like paying taxes or being "regulated." Well, who does? But who doesn't want roads, police, education, fire protection, and jobs; who doesn't see Europe's often-superior health care, job training, child care—and its citizens' generally higher level of satisfaction with their lives and their government; who besides our enemies doesn't want America to be a great, strong, cohesive nation; and who besides the greediest doesn't realize that being great means we all pitch in? Anyone looking for a country with low taxes; no funds wasted on social programs; no government regulation of business, health, worker safety, or the environment; and no gun control might consider moving to Somalia. Anyway, Reagan said that if rich people were allowed to keep more of their money, it would "trickle down" to po' folk. A slogan that sounds like you're waiting for something to leak down someone's leg should raise a red flag. But, in practice, not just money "trickled down"; greed did. The 1980s saw the democratization of greed. Reagan and his neo-conmen replaced the ethic of "one for all and all for one" with "all for me," immortalized by the movie *Wall Street*'s Gordon Gekko, who says, "Greed is good. Greed is right. Greed works." Those lines were based on a real-life commencement speech at the University of California–Berkeley's School of Business Administration, where Ivan Boesky (who later did a prison stint for massive insider trading) told the 1986 graduates, "Greed is all right, by the way. I want you to know that. I think greed is healthy. You can be greedy and still feel good about yourself." Applause. Because everyone wanted to feel good about themselves (and get a piece of the booty), a generation embraced greed. Bill Clinton likewise got seduced by deregulation's easy feel-good, not to mention the unmentionable administrations that bookended his. The only problem was, the regulations they deregulated had been built up over a century for a very good reason: the public needs to defend itself against greedy excess. All in all, deregulation dealt a devastating blow to the social contract and the idea that we're all in America together, with both feet. The divisive partisanship, the screaming head media freak show, and the fiscal recklessness that followed were an inevitable result of the lost discipline and the lost sense of common cause. And by the time everyone realized their pockets had been fleeced, the fleecers had fled, beyond law, beyond regulation—beyond national borders. But not everyone lost out; you glimpse a winning ticket, for example, every time you read the words "Made in China."

Across the marsh, a Cooper's Hawk perches briefly in an elder, its manic hyperawareness evident in its swiveling gaze. Built for short, high-acceleration sprints and turn-on-a-dime maneuvering, it specializes in snatching flying birds in close cover. In a flash it pours itself into the cloaking vegetation, toward its next explosive ambush.

I can't resist seeing what the storm's doing on the ocean side, so I'm going to stop the car for a quick look. Just getting the car door open is a little difficult in this wind. Beating my way into the blast, I glance down the beach. Where beach had been, it's all raging surf laying siege, hurling driftwood against the dunes. Usually, ocean and land maintain more civility, but right now everything is whiteness and spume and the full-force teeth of the gale. The ocean is spitting sea foam that blows across the road in pillows.

Over the last couple of weeks I'd been concerned that during my walks with Kenzie we might be disturbing the Piping Plovers who'd arrived to set up their territories. Now those territories are inundated with pounding surf. I wonder if *any* birds can be finding much food in this weather.

But these onshore winds must be carrying millions of migrant birds up the coast, birds whose northbound trek had, until now, taken them only as far as the West Indies or Mexico or the U.S. South.

As I drive away from the beach, a streaking Cooper's Hawk blurs across the road clenching a blackbird. Not everything has had trouble catching food today.

Meanwhile, getting back briefly to the other storm: the one in which corporations inundate democracy—. Corporate globalization has been called "the most fundamental redesign of social, economic, and political arrangements since the Industrial Revolution." Corporations have swept real economic and political power away from governments. Of the hundred wealthiest countries *and* corporations listed together, more than

half are corporations. ExxonMobil is richer than 180 countries—and
there are only about 195 countries. Without the responsibilities or
costs of nationhood, corporations can innovate and produce at unprecedented speed and scale. Yet they can also undertake acts of enormous
environmental destruction and report a profit.

The behavior of corporations arises from their wide freedom of
action and their limited liability for harms caused. Further, shareholders "own" and profit by the corporation, but "limited liability" means
shareholders can lose no more than the money invested; they aren't held
responsible for anything the corporation does. If they were, stockholders
might know what companies they "own" and why. They might demand
corporate responsibility. They might invest more carefully. But because
they're not, they don't.

Further, if a corporation can make a larger profit by wrecking a community, the law says it must. Perhaps the most famous case in corporate

law was decided in the Supreme Court of Michigan in 1919 when Henry Ford got sued by the Dodge brothers. (Yes, *those* Dodge brothers.) Ford wanted to plow profits back into the company and its employees. "My ambition is to employ still more men," the *New York Times* quoted Ford as saying, "to spread the benefits of this industrial system to the greatest possible number, to help them build up their lives and their homes. To do this we are putting the greatest share of our profits back in the business." The judges posed a short question: What is a corporation for? The judges answered themselves by saying corporations are "primarily for the profit of the stockholders." Not for the benefit of employees or community. Corporate managers—regardless of personal scruples or desire to "do good"—are forced to always put profits first.

The profit-maximization imperative creates continuous pressure to dump waste in the public commons and to shift the resulting costs to the public through subsidies, tax-funded pollution cleanups, and such. Where dumping waste is illegal, corporations may be fined for violations. Such fines often become "a cost of doing business," while shareholders know that corporations never get sent to jail, and that some are "too big (to be allowed) to fail." To the extent that governmental regulations get annoying, corporate appetites engulf those too, backing and basically installing cooperative elected officials, then coercing the removal of regulatory "barriers" (formerly: "public protections").

However, we can envision how a more public-minded government might deal with risk-prone corporations. In World War II, the U.S. government seized control of certain German companies inside the United States. Obviously, it wouldn't do to have German chemical plants on American soil while we were engulfed in war with Germany. The companies were not destroyed, just controlled by the government for a while; some still exist. When U.S. automakers got into serious trouble and went into bankruptcy in 2009, the federal government stepped in to control management for a while. These weren't punitive moves exactly, but one can imagine ways in which corporations acting as bad citizens might have to do some time with, say, their stocks frozen—no trading, maybe—while a government of the people does a little potty training with the executives.

In real life as we know it, the profit-maximization imperative means that any company seeking to act responsibly incurs a competitive disadvantage. The implications are generally a cascade of catastrophes, because, essentially, all the money in the world is thus under pressure to act irresponsibly. Any other impulse must buck that tide.

The corporations' central tenet of faith, their object of worship, their grail and their gruel: growth. Growth fueled by continually unearthing new resources and cheaper labor. Growth fed by raising and fattening new consumers. Growth had historically resulted from technical progress and growing population. It became a *central pursuit* of government policy mainly after World War II.

But Planet Earth cannot grow. Not any faster than it accumulates stardust, anyway. If the economy "grows" while resources like water, forests, and fish are being depleted, it's not growth, its just blowing more bubbles. Yet because our economic system shows unconditional love for growth, it doesn't ring alarm bells over bubbles. But count on this: the bigger the bubble, the worse the burst.

The first corporate century, the twentieth, was a period of explosive growth. Despite as many as 150 million human beings killed in warfare between 1900 and Y2K, the world population quadrupled. Energy use increased sixteen-fold. The fish catch—which peaked in the late 1980s—increased thirty-five-fold. The sheer amount of stuff used annually flies in flocks of zeros that defy comprehension: 275,000,000 tons of meat, 370,000,000 tons of paper products, et cetera. Incredibly, of all the earthly materials that human hands have ever transformed, fully half of that material transformation has occurred since World War II.

"It is impossible for the world economy to grow its way out of poverty and environmental degradation," writes the resource-minded economist Herman Daly, because the economy is a "subsystem of the earth ecosystem, which is finite, non-growing, and materially closed."

And economists think the solution to our problems is more *growth*? We've been terribly misled. But more *development*—that's a different proposition. "Grow" means to increase in size by adding. "Develop" means to realize potentials, to make better. Growth is greater flow of material and energy from the natural environment through the economy or system. Growth is quantity; development, quality.

Because the world is pretty much fully tapped, growth now threatens development. In a postgrowth world, we'd measure things like community and satisfaction. We'd replace the feverish tail chase of the material with life, liberty, and the pursuit of happiness. Those come from development, not from growth. Let's not confuse the two.

❦

At first light after a mild rain has stopped, the spring's first real dawn chorus of birds wakes me so cheerfully and agreeably that I lie in the soft flannel sheets, listening to the cooing doves of the world, too soothed to move. I soak in the swooping, drooping wolf whistles of cardinals. I listen to raucous jays. White-throated Sparrows—molted into whiter throats and flashy yellow eyebrows that anticipate breeding in the motherland— repeat their rousing anthem to where they're headed: *Oh, Canada-Canada-Canada*. A couple of newly arrived Chipping Sparrows are calling from the sandy-footed pines. And a song I can't identify turns out to be from a Carolina Wren that has composed an original tune—a feat rare among wrens.

I emerge; it's cool, about fifty degrees, but the breeze is breathing from the south. In the yellow slants of early light, Kenzie and I address the Sound shore, six legs between the two of us. The air, suddenly holding its breath, produces a no-wind situation that rests the bay to mirror calmness. But the storm has left upon the ocean a heave so massive I can hear the south side surf rumbling from a couple of miles away.

It happens to be the first really golden morning we've had in a while, and warming quickly. From the tropics, delivered well ahead of their normal dates in the storm's fierce rage of air, will today and in the next few days appear Eastern Kingbirds, Scarlet Tanagers, Rose-breasted Grosbeaks, Indigo Buntings, Barn Swallows, and others. Almost incredibly, at least four Sooty Terns will be seen or found dead by birders on Long Island, and in Rhode Island and Connecticut, some of them blown well inland. Only once before has a Sooty Tern been seen in our region in springtime, and that was in late May—never in April. Its nearest breeding site is south of Florida. Its multiple appearances here bear further testimony to the strength and consequences of this storm and to the role of luck and timing—and occasional chaos—in the destiny of lives. No doubt many other wonders will arrive, and perhaps perish, exhausted and unseen.

• • •

I've been talking rather disparagingly about growth and population. I should say that growth was good, to a point. Now, if the point of growth is to give each person more, then at this stage, less means more for each. Shrinking our population by half gives each person double. Shrinking to one-fourth (the population the world had in 1900) would mean each person would have—on average, potentially—four times the freshwater, food, lumber, and so forth. Places like India and the American Plains that are running a groundwater deficit would use it at one-fourth the rate. Some places might replenish.

With over two and a half billion people living on less than two dollars a day, born into hunger, filth, infection, ignorance, oppression, violence, and no options, it seems to me that the loss of natural beauty and diversity constitutes a terrible ante paid just for coming into a world where the slices shrink faster than the pie can possibly grow. It appears irrational to think that more growth can solve anything at all. Quite the contrary; growing smaller seems the best hope for bringing justice and compassion—or even a decent meal—within reach of many people, especially in the generation coming along.

It takes neither justice nor compassion to ready a duck for breeding, but it does take new outerwear. The last of winter's Long-tailed Ducks look lustrous with new feathers. The drab-feathered loons of winter, too, have transformed into sleek breeding dress, with checkered jackets and velvety black plush heads setting off their crimson eyes. Some are flying; quite a few are floating in the bay's little swells. One surfaces with a wriggling fish. A friend of mine once tried to aid an ailing loon. Resisting rescue, it skewered his cheek. He says you can't believe how fast they are. I believe it. I keep scanning.

A big flock of Sanderlings—about two hundred—surprises me on the bay shore. Normally they stay along the ocean. And this isn't just the largest flock I've seen in a long while; it will be the last large group I'll see this season.

With each flock of sandpipers alighting to run the waves and every line of sea ducks beating north, I'm reminded that we've got another chance. These creatures inspire me. Oblivious to their fate, they do as always: strive to survive against long odds in a world of change. They teach Equanimity 101, with a vengeance.

Every adult person has experienced bodily exactly what it means to stop growing and continue developing. Who would go back to the drama and the growing pains of their teen years? So why do economists insist on pegging humanity perpetually in its awkward, temperamental, pimply, adolescent growth spurt? As a more mature and level-headed grown-up, humanity could continue developing for the rest of its life.

Development would look like: education, vocational training, democracy, human rights; better tech, better-quality goods and services; fair health care; better family time; clean air and water; clean energy; art, beauty, wildlife, civility. Rather than focusing on growth and the (increasingly unlikely) possibility of further development, we could focus on development with the (increasingly implausible) possibility of growth. That thought would never cross the mind of most economists—but focusing on improvement wouldn't be the worst thing in the world.

And I wonder if it would even be so hard. In a matter of days during the fall of 2008, the United States and other governments abandoned decades of economic doctrine to rescue a reckless financial system from global collapse. Yet, decade after decade, we make no move to stop the growth obsession that is wrecking the mother of economies, the planet itself. Economists don't seem to have noticed that the economy sits entirely within the ecology. An economy shifting from growth to development, from combustion to renewable energy, for instance, would still entail tremendous investment opportunities.

During challenging ocean conditions, certain sea jellies "de-grow." They don't just lose fat or slim down; they actually lose cells and simplify structures. When times are good, they regrow. Because they are adding new cells and regrowing structures (not just replumping), they are actually rejuvenated—*younger than they were.* On the other end of the scale, Edward Abbey long ago observed that growth for the sake of continuous growth is the strategy of cancer. Knowing what we now know, it appears that the world can't produce enough to grow our way out of poverty. But we could certainly shrink our way out. The goal of giving people more per person would be most quickly and easily accomplished fastest by having fewer people. Knowing what we know now, if I were going to pattern my economy and society on anything, I'd go with the forever-young jellyfish and ditch the cancer model.

The first Ruddy Turnstones to make it as far north as Lazy Point this year are foraging around some barnacle-encrusted rocks. Did I see any of these same individuals in the Caribbean? Probably not, but it's an appealing possibility.

The water here is clear enough to see bottom a few yards from shore. And it's late enough in the month that there should be some bass here already. I scan almost instinctively for signs of fish, thinking that the first few must have arrived by now.

On the marsh, Barn Swallows have indeed begun arriving in some numbers. Their physical elegance—their metallic-blue plumage and the streaming feathers of their deep-forked tail—and their masterfully controlled grace are always arresting, always a favorite.

Our salt-pond Ospreys again stand proudly in renewed attendance, the female at the nest, the male on a nearby pole. They, too, have weathered the storm, after all. He looks like he has some netting lightly tangled on one foot. This kind of thing kills birds, but when he shifts his weight the netting falls off. His other foot grips a small Striped Bass, confirming my suspicions: the bass are already arriving.

Over near the lighthouse, the recent storm has shoved thousands of bowling-ball-sized boulders high up on the beach, past the reach of the tides. I've been here during the crash and surge of thunderous rumbles before. Among the lobbed rocks lies a galaxy of storm-cast sea stars, uncountable multitudes, stretching out of sight down the shoreline. For the rummaging gulls, the fallen stars are bounty.

Because the ocean stays colder longer than the air, it's spring on land but still a more or less winter sea. Even though so many have passed in the last couple of weeks, several thousand sea ducks, all now molted into their finest courting plumage, pepper the ocean off the lighthouse. As always, they're feeding here, drifting in the strong tidal currents over the best foraging bottom, then lifting off in sheets to fly uptide to the beginning of the drift. This duck conveyor has been operating for months. And like some biblical miracle or mythical fable of inexhaustible abundance, the place continues to produce for them. Having braved the spray of a hundred frozen nights and weathered yesterday's storm, they will soon join the lines withdrawing northward.

Fifty feet from the high-tide line lies the shore of a small, shallow freshwater pond, into which the storm has washed seashells and a skate's carcass. I'm wondering if the pond's amphibians have perished from the brine. But in the water swim tadpoles—dozens of them. Has evolution forged a more salt-tolerant frog here? Or maybe the eight inches of rain the storm doused us with amply diluted the saltwater that washed in. Just a few paces away, surf growls. Fishing boats ply the ocean beyond. Yet I'm watching tadpoles. One can penetrate deep forest and deep ocean, but there's no such thing as deep coast. The coast is all about borders. It's all edges and angles, like Thelonius Monk music. It's bebop habitat.

It's hard to walk briskly at this time of year; the accelerating pace of unfolding spring slows my own. I repeatedly stop—to watch what's moving. Soon the torrent of migrants will completely overwhelm my ability to keep up with all the changes. But it's easy to revel in the exuberance and the sense of rebirth, renewal.

MAY

April showers have wrought May bouquets. Purple-blossomed beach peas now line the sand path to the beach. Shadbush, Beach Plum, and Wax Myrtle blooms paint the higher marsh and the wild, scruffy yards around our cottages in luxuriant broad-brushed whites, perfuming the almost-warm air. Around the marsh edges, I try not to alarm the fiddler crabs that bustle around their burrows as they spring-clean for the May Queen.

By the second week of May I've seen no swirls or splashes indicating fish along our shore. But the date suggests that a few casts would be reasonable. So toward dusk I take a rod and walk to the Cut.

The tide is ebbing nicely, creating a swift, riverine current. When the water pours from the bay into the Sound like this, fish—if there are any—concentrate in the narrow Cut, stemming the accelerated flow while waiting for any smaller fish being swept into striking range.

Nothing is showing at the surface. But maybe some fish are holding near the bottom. I choose a small lure that sinks rapidly and resembles a little fish swimming. I cast it out, reel it back.

Fishing isn't esoteric or mysterious. There're just various facts and feelings one accumulates: where to go, when, how to tell if it's worth staying; how to judge when the wind will help or hinder; knowing the local haunts and movements of different fish throughout the year; various lures and baits; which populations remain robust or depleted. All this accumulated knowledge merely facilitates informed guesswork. The most valuable thing one can learn is how much you don't know. So you try a lure you think will work; if it doesn't work, you try another.

What I most like about fishing is knowing a place well enough to find the fish. In an exotic locale, especially with a guide, fishing becomes just a matter of following instructions and then having a fish at the end of a line. Separated from my own understanding of the place, my seasons there, my kitchen, and my friends, fishing loses most of its appeal.

It's not that I don't simply enjoy catching fish; I do. There remains the sudden connection to that startling aliveness. And how else would you know what's in all that deep, dark water? But to me, home water is best. To know what's in that water before you get there, to find it where you seek it, and to conjure it into grasp; these things create a different affirmation of intimacy. It's a little like the difference between meeting a stranger and meeting someone who's waiting for you.

Fishing provides time to think, and reason not to. If you have the virtue of patience, an hour or two of casting alone is plenty of time to review all you've learned about the grand themes of life. It's time enough to realize that every generalization stands opposed by a mosaic of exceptions, and that the biggest truths are few indeed. Meanwhile, you feel the wind shift and the temperature change. You might simply decide to be present, and observe a few firm facts about the drifting clouds.

You cast again. And again. Investing your effort, trying and failing, a modicum of eventual success, and life-and-death stakes—the act becomes allegory. And precisely because it carries symbolic qualities, fishing can, in its best moments, feel like art.

Fishing in a place is a meditation on the rhythm of a tide, a season, the arc of a year, and the seasons of a life. The more repetitive, the better, because the experience is like a wheel that—by going around and around as though doing the same thing—continually covers new ground, bringing you to a very different place.

The lure comes wiggling to my rod; I cast again.

For those who don't fish, the ocean is just scenery. The beauty in fishing comes to the senses as a search for *connection* with deep-dwelling mysteries. Being at the water becomes a very different proposition when you're sending forth that inquiring, hopeful filament.

I fish to scratch the surface of those mysteries, for nearness to the beautiful, and to reassure myself that the world remains. I fish to wash off some of my grief for the peace we so squander. I fish to dip into that great and awesome pool of power that propels these epic migrations. I fish to feel—and steal—a little of that energy.

Connection creates meaning. And so fishing provides meaning— and a full stomach. Thoreau observed, "Many men go fishing all of their lives without knowing it is not fish they are after." Well, Henry, I am, indeed, after fish. My fishing has no arbitrary goal, nor the artificial scorecard of mere sports. It's not a game. A fish is a real thing. Its death is a real death.

Hunting and killing come naturally to cats and people. And to fish, too. Many things that are "in the blood" are not to be recommended. But I think a modicum of fishing justifiable for the table and for sharing with friends. Most people get all their food—every scrap of it, for the long duration of their lives—across a counter. I prefer not to imagine such a severed life.

When you're eating wild, every meal carries a narrative. If most days go forgotten into the junk heap we create of our lives, it may be because we fuel our days with things that come and go like mail addressed to someone else, instead of writing our own story.

But a day remembered is a day lived, and fishing harbors that poten- tial. So I fish to obtain stories and share them into memory. Fishing's stories often involve many of the people at my table. We share the prize we've captured. We share adventures and the storytelling impulse that's as basic to being human as tales around cave fires. This is impossible with supermarket food, which just shows up, devoid of identity, bereft of experience.

The food I seek derives from a wondrous proposition: you look out at that infinite span of water that gift-wraps the planet and you say, "Get dinner." Needles would spring willingly from haystacks before finding a fish in a whole ocean seemed reasonable. The true act of fishing is attain- ing some sense of when, where, and how to begin searching for a fish.

Weather, tides, moon phases, and seasons—in a circular, self-reinforcing way, catching a fish both provides and requires a sense of place.

The experiences build, so that each time you sweep your eyes over the horizon you think of all the prior times and what happened. As teenagers, we rigged for fishing the way Neolithic hunters prepared for the hunt, a sacred rite of great spiritual import, critical for survival. Fishing seemed a wilderness experience no matter how close to home I pursued it. We fished, brought our catch to our secret campsite in the woods, and hid our bicycles with leaves. We waited until dark to make a small fire, so no one could see our smoke rising. A bellyful of fried fish plus a whole package of cookies is a good, rounded meal for a sixteen-year-old. We fell asleep to owls, and woke to crows.

As the years layer up, you can catch a tiny, silvery, firsthand glimpse of time. Your mind relives all those evenings, friends, and meals. A string of notes on the strand of time makes life's music. I'm therefore grateful to be here, hunting my food in the water.

On this side of the Cut, a shelf of cobblestone-sized rocks forms a shallow reef a few feet deep. The rest of the channel is about twelve feet deep. Fish often position themselves on that shallow reef because the squeeze narrows their prey's escape options. So I've planted myself a little uptide, where the current sweeps my lure over the shallows. Again I cast about halfway across the channel, let the line sink to where the fish might be, and reel back the wiggling lure.

For all I appreciate about fishing, there is no hiding the fact that its basic premise is an unfair deception. It has another fundamental drawback: it's not much fun for the fish. The correct mental posture for fishing always keeps that fact in mind. Some people make a hash of it.

I continue casting and reeling back.

One autumn I lost my appetite for the killing. I was on a friend's boat and we were jigging Bluefish from a deep rip, and my heart just went out of it. This had been building for months. Then I looked over the side and saw thousands upon thousands of glittering anchovy scales just drifting loose in the tidal current, mute testimony of the violent siege and chaos beneath our hull. I realized that if the Bluefish and I could converse about appetites and predatory urges, we'd understand each other well.

The anchovies would certainly have urged me back into the fray, since every Bluefish I took meant dozens of anchovies rescued for the day. Just a few miles and two centuries away from where we drifted, Benjamin Franklin, then a vegetarian, had a similar thought:

> In my first voyage from Boston, being becalm'd off Block Island, our people set about catching cod, and hauled up a great many. Hitherto I had stuck to my resolution of not eating animal food . . . taking every fish as a kind of unprovoked murder, since none of them had, or ever could do us any injury that might justify the slaughter. All this seemed very reasonable. But I had formerly been a great lover of fish, and, when this came hot out of the frying-pan, it smelt admirably well. I balanc'd some time between principle and inclination, till I recollected that, when the fish were opened, I saw smaller fish taken out of their stomachs; then thought I, "If you eat one another, I don't see why we mayn't eat you." So I din'd upon cod very heartily. . . . So convenient a thing it is to be a reasonable creature, since it enables one to find or make a reason for everything one has a mind to do.

If Ben Franklin stopped to fish for cod off Block Island today with only the tools available then, he and his comrades would likely *all* have dined as vegetarians; cod are now scarce. But having found and made my own reasons for being here, my main quarry is the Striped Bass. Following their deep crash from overfishing in the 1980s, the Striped Bass's subsequent recovery is perhaps the world's best fisheries management success, a triumph of political discipline, a lesson in healing, and a source of solace in a world so full of holes.

In my kind of fishing, there are two varieties of disappointments. One makes a hole in dinner plans; for that, vegetables suffice. The other punctures your heart. Many of the creatures that should be in a place at an appointed time and season come no longer. Menu substitutions might work for dinner, but not for the future of the world. I have watched animals that once thrilled me—like Bluefin Tuna and mako sharks—struck to such staggering scarcity that, in my own time, fishing for them has been transformed from celebration to transgression.

The stories from *before* my time speak of a sea that so swarmed with life no one now venturing forth can really imagine it. In my time, marlin and Albacore and big sharks were prizes—but some people once avoided them. I met an old gentleman who, as a youth, ignored all the marlin he saw, so as not to miss a chance at a Swordfish. (Now we see no marlin, either.) I met a man who in his prime was so intent on Bigeye Tuna that he'd reel in his lures and run from acres of Albacore. Nowadays, a few Albacore in eight hours of trolling, eighty miles from shore, is considered "a good trip." A man formerly employed to spot Swordfish from a plane said his biggest problem was that sharks were so plentiful they made Swordfish hard to pick out. Now even the fish-spotting airplanes are gone. The stories of bygone plentitude read like fairy tales, yet they are the experiences of people still alive. Too soon they will pass into memory. And then the memories themselves will be forgotten. A few recovered species don't compensate for the lost company of great beasts.

I keep casting and retrieving for about half an hour. Nothing at all happens. Even the loafing gulls look bored.

Sunset yields to sundown, and the red west slowly deepens toward darkness. I'm about to quit when on a whim I decide to try changing lures. No fish have been showing at the surface, so I've been using deep-running lures. But when nothing is working, anything is worth trying, so I snap on a surface lure.

I watch the lure sail into the deep dusk, plop down, and spread dark ripples in the flowing tide. I start retrieving, and since there's not quite enough light to see it, I listen as I begin chugging it across the surface. Chug . . . chug . . . *poosh!* I see a black splash. The line stretches taut and the rod dips as a fish—a good one—thrashes furiously to shake the lure loose. Still attached, it catches the current and frantically beelines away.

The fish runs and stops. I reel it closer, and it runs again. Failing to free itself, the fish slowly begins losing this tug-of-war. In a few minutes a Bluefish is thrashing at my feet and I grab the line and slide it ashore. Landing a Blue is an act so familiar it seems to sum up my whole life in the moment. I admit it's not the thrill it was at fifteen, when my friend John and I would ride our bikes twelve miles to the shore in predawn darkness and cast to the sunrise. But because it was such a thrill, catching a Bluefish still feels like a genuine part of me.

This early in May, however, this Bluefish comes as a surprise. In no prior year have I caught a Bluefish before I've caught a Striped Bass. This one seems early by a couple of weeks.

The fish clamps the razor-toothed vise of its undershot jaw onto the shank of the steel hook. Exhausted and perhaps slightly dazed, it swivels its bright yellow eye but does not return my gaze. I put a foot lightly behind its head so it can't thrash and slash my hand, then reach down with pliers and pull the hook. I pick up a fist-sized stone and hit the fish decisively on its head; its fins stiffen and shiver, then twitch a bit, relax, and go still. Less an act of "mercy" than of hastening the death I've chosen to inflict, this is the aspect of fishing I find least palatable. Simply letting the fish suffocate in the air is easier for me, but more prolonged. For the fish, I'm not sure which is worse.

In two more casts I hook two more Bluefish. The motivation to catch persists longer than the actual need of food, giving rise to that most peculiar of all predatory acts: catch-and-release fishing. The problem with catch-and-release is that it's hard on fish; the hooks injure them, the handling bruises them, the exhaustion makes them vulnerable, and some die. I am past catch-and-release. I now practice kill-and-go-home. Less is more. An ample sufficiency is enough. When I feel torn between sympathy and the urge to use—as I feel when I'm fishing—the balance becomes *restraint*. Maybe restraint is just selfishness that has learned to walk upright.

As soon as I pull the third thrashing fish ashore, I hang up the lure, string up all three fish, and begin walking home in dense fog. Peepers are still calling into the spring air, now augmented by the little foghorns from Fowler's Toads.

Gutting the fish on my backyard table, I'm further surprised to discover that the Blues were eating butterfish, and large ones at that. This accounts for their preference for a big lure. Those butterfish are why they're unusually fat for spring Bluefish. (They're usually quite lean by the time they arrive here, on the north end of their journey.) And that unusual fatness, more so than the olive oil and oregano, is why they taste really, really good. While I'm watching the pan sizzle and trying to get a nice browning on the fillets, I can't resist slicing a little off and nibbling it raw with just fresh lemon. So nice. Kenzie eagerly devours some scraps with her dinner.

In savoring both the fish and my surprise at their early appearance, it occurs to me that I've also never seen a Bluefish before even the terns have arrived. Experience is worth less in a time without precedent.

～

Through this morning's thick spring fog comes the call of a bird who has just ended a long migration, the year's first Common Tern. The bird does not so much appear as materialize. It is its own annunciation, light and buoyant on the wing, precise in motion. As one Red-wing makes the spring weeks before the equinox, the first tern heralds summer with a month to go before the solstice.

Light-plumaged and black-capped, its red-and-black bill brightened for sexual attractiveness, the tern flies gracefully thirty feet or so above the shoreline's shallows, sharply alert for movement below. It parallels the shore until it reaches the Cut, turns a half circle with its forked tail flared, hovers for three beats of its slender wings, then sleeks itself and swoops into a shallow arc that wets its bill but fails to snatch a catch.

The bird calls again but receives no answer. It merges back into the fog. Being an early arriver, this is likely a senior bird. From South American wintering grounds, it may be completing a migration it has made many times; they can live for a quarter century (as I'll find out in a couple of months). My interest in terns goes back a ways, as well. I've spent

more time with terns than any other animals, first because they led me to fish, then because they led me to a doctoral dissertation, then because they led me to realize that the whole ocean was changing. In that sense, terns made me who I am. I owe them, and I thank them; they have my admiration.

Over the next few days, many more—thousands—arrive to join that vanguard bird. Their flocks soon billow into white clouds diving into schools of small fishes throughout the Sound.

The Cut is one of the most favored hunting sites for terns of three species breeding on several islands within a fifteen-mile radius; one island has perhaps ten thousand pairs and is among the world's largest colonies. That's one reason there are often hundreds of terns right around here. Terns come for the same reason the area draws the larger fish: the bay manufactures small fish by the millions, and the tidal current flowing through the narrow Cut concentrates them into a confined and vulnerable gauntlet.

The terns' season here is all about raising families. Over the weeks, their colonies go from busy towns of sexual politics to quiet communities of meditative incubation to bustling neighborhoods striving to bring off one more generation before they have to leave. In broad strokes, their nesting season is the life we all share.

The terns lay two or three speckled eggs in shallow sandy ground scrapes lined with bits of shell or grass. Then the three-week countdown to hatching becomes a race against Raccoons, foxes, introduced rats in some places, gulls, and night herons, plus beach buggies, sunbathers, and dogs. Nesting on islands is the birds' strategy for minimizing trouble from mammals, and the water barrier still helps—especially when boaters and their dogs cooperate with the "No Landing" signs (as they sometimes do).

Great Horned and Short-eared Owls and harriers pose additional threats after the terns' spotted chicks hatch. And then the birds must also cope with the near impossibility of finding food enough for all their young. Many chicks die in the three weeks between hatching and flight. Fledging and being on the wing guarantee nothing, either. At each step, the odds weigh against survival.

Catching fish by plunging is so demanding a skill for an airborne creature that—very unusually among birds—adult terns continue to help feed their flying young, sometimes for weeks. The fish they must catch are small, mobile, and live mainly out of reach. Water diffracts angled light, making fish often appear to be where they are not. No wonder young terns need time to master fishing.

Each breeding colony is a fishing port. When a few birds arrive carrying fish, others mobilize, and soon whole squadrons are in the air, traveling over the waves toward the site of the lucky strike. Terns make a good fraction of their living catching small fish driven to the surface by larger fish. For a teenager fishing along the beach, diving terns were always worth a brisk walk and a long cast; they still are.

In college I volunteered to work with a professor studying terns in their nesting colonies. From the beach, I watched as the hungry ones flew seaward past the breaking surf on strong wings, direct and determined, and disappeared beyond the ocean haze. Others, from somewhere at sea, came bombing back fast and low, bringing glistening fish for hungry chicks. Somewhere out of sight on that wide ocean, they knew exactly where to go and what to do. It would remain their mystery as long as they could go beyond the blue horizon—and I could not. I wanted to go. I wanted to know what was *out* there.

I finished college and was faced with the need to get a job and, in general (so I was told), to grow up. All the men I knew were grown-up; I couldn't see a way to avoid it. But then I discovered a remarkable social institution that allows one to defer growing up, sometimes indefinitely. It's called *graduate school.* Signing up to pursue a PhD qualified me to apply for grants, and I submitted a proposal to get a boat to study terns. It worked!

With an eighteen-foot boat named *Ternabout* I was thrilled to begin discovering what seabirds did *at sea.* I also discovered—slowly—the elegant power of science. I'd locate a feeding flock, then pilot through and past the diving birds while generating a sonar profile of the fish below. Next I'd tally individual birds' fishing success rates. I also trolled fishing lures behind the boat, so that if a fish grabbed a lure just after dark marks appeared on the sonar, I could reel it up and say what kind of predatory fish the marks represented.

This clearly beat growing up. And the prospect of building a body of work, rather than performing a job task, was much more appealing. There was something primal, too. Birds have been leading other animals to food since honeyguides somehow figured out that certain mammals, including humans, can open beehives. Hunters have watched the skies since circling vultures led early people to lion and hyena kills they might commandeer. Seabirds themselves spend a good part of their time watching for other birds that have found fish. And I was involved in their lives. I was at work in the real world.

There was growing up during those years, too. I commonly saw tuna ripping through the surface, sharks swimming along with dorsal fins out, marlin charging through balled-up schools of small fish. But each year, I saw fewer. The loss and diminishment compelled me to get involved in conservation. Out on the ocean alone, merely following curiosity and a quest for beauty, I also found a calling, and my life's work.

This was all in the waters around Long Island. Here, when terns are working over larger fish, it's usually Bluefish. Every fisherman chasing the Blues knows the obvious: that in pushing small fish to the surface, Bluefish provide a feast for terns. Every fisherman is basically wrong, but it's an easy mistake to make, and even the terns make it all the time.

When I studied them, terns always arrived from migration before Bluefish. For a couple of weeks the terns often fished in large, loose, relaxed feeding flocks. Tern feeding flocks can last hours, until the tidal conditions change and the fish schools' locations shift. The terns often patrol back and forth in easy ellipses over schools of small fish they can see but cannot reach, waiting for the chance to dive. Terns can catch fish only within a foot or so of the surface. My sonar showed that schools of small fish usually remain at middle depths, maximizing their distance from both diving birds and bottom-traveling predators. Eventually, the small fish rise to feed on swarms of near-surface plankton. Or tidal currents sweep them over a shallow sandbar. When opportunity arises, the terns seize it quickly, diving rapidly, often reappearing with a wriggling fish and swallowing while looping back to position for another plunge.

The terns had little trouble gaining the considerable energy needed to finance a clutch of two or three eggs. Males supplemented females' foraging by delivering whole little fish, highlighting the bill-to-bill transfer with a flourish and a formal display. Often, just after the male provided dinner, the two would mate. It appears that certain dating traditions were invented long before humans came up with theirs.

Each year, there comes a morning when the large, loose feeding flocks are suddenly replaced by small fluttering tornadoes of tightly packed terns hovering excitedly for a few moments, breaking up, and forming again nearby. The quiet contact calls and evenly spaced flocks of recent weeks change to loud vocal threats and outright attacks as birds collide and jostle each other for position at the focal point of the tornado, right at the water's surface. A few small fish spray from the water directly beneath the birds, and only the nearest terns get a chance for a rapid plunge. Quickly the tight pack disperses and spreads out. When a distant tern stops to hover, all the birds within hundreds of yards rush toward it. A small skipping fish vanishes in a sudden explosion from below, while several terns grab others. Approach by boat, and distinct marks appear on the sonar screen. If you're trolling, the rod suddenly starts bouncing. The Bluefish have arrived in force.

Caught between the Bluefish onslaught from below and the terns raining from above, the prey fish panic. As their schools fragment, individuals fall vulnerable to being singled out and nabbed. This *seems* a boon for terns, because the Bluefish obviously do chase up small fish that would be unavailable in deep water. But the Bluefish set the terns up for ecological betrayal.

Bluefish eat a lot, and they greatly outnumber terns. And what they don't eat seems to flee the area. So arriving Bluefish dramatically drop local prey fish densities. The relaxed and bountiful days terns enjoyed *before* the Blues arrived grow few; the small fish just aren't there in those numbers. When that happens, diving over Bluefish schools becomes the only game in town. Common Terns are often forced to chase the Blues just to make a living and raise their chicks—but their fishing success rate declines. So the relationship is a lopsided dependency in which terns first benefit but ultimately suffer. The Bluefish look like they're helping, but they can be the terns' worst competitor.

When I studied this relationship, the prey fish abundance increased through May as the small fish migrated into the area. Their abundance peaked in early June, then fell off when the Blues arrived. Food was already declining by the time tern chicks were growing rapidly; starvation of one or two siblings out of two- or three-chick broods was, and is, common.

Nowadays, Bluefish are arriving weeks earlier, as spring water temperature warms. But the terns, traveling from their South American wintering areas, base their migration on day length. They're keeping the same schedule as always. What might this mean for the birds' food supply?

Common Terns are versatile birds; a significant part of their continental population even nests inland, along large lakes. So how these coastal nesters will cope with change isn't clear. Shrinkage of this population seems possible as their major competitors for food—Bluefish—arrive earlier.

• • •

About a week after that first Common Tern came calling through the fog, a whiter tern, with a slightly more rapid wingbeat, appears at the Cut— the endangered Roseate Tern. It was a treat to see them in Belize, and I'm happy to see them come "home," as I think of it.

I've never met a tern I didn't like, but Roseates are unusually elegant. And Lazy Point happens to be the best place I know to see them from shore. Newly arrived Roseates sport a jet-black bill and longer tail stream-ers; while they're still courting, you might catch that rosy cast if the light is low and the sun angled just right. But it took me a whole season before I could tell them from Common Terns at a distance. The main thing is a subtly different wingbeat. For them, that subtlety has major implications.

A puzzle: Why are there about a hundred Common Terns for every Roseate? After all, they often mix in foraging flocks and are so closely related they occasionally interbreed. What could possibly account for their grossly disproportionate numbers? I could not imagine. So I spent a lot of time watching Common and Roseate Terns fishing. Feeding flocks formed in inlets full of tidal energy, on shallow sandbars, and in deep water over churning schools of predatory fish. Traveling to different places where they foraged, I'd stay out for several days in a new boat named *First Light*, anchoring for the night as the red sky darkened, then waking up to calling gulls.

Some of the loveliest spots I worked remain largely unchanged. The same little islands still bear cloaks of breeding terns, keeping the faith of cycles that make the world round. My favorite among their foraging sites was a slender teardrop-shaped shoal at the end of a large, nearly unin-habited island. I lived far away from it back then, but now it lies in view of my cottage, only about two miles from Lazy Point. And even without binoculars I often see that terns still find it well worth their travel.

At first it looked like Roseates caught more fish than Common Terns. Roseate Terns' slightly smaller wings mean they're a little more compact, and this seems to let them dive just a little deeper, catching some fish that Commons cannot quite reach. If anything, then, there should be more Roseates, not the other way around.

But when Bluefish are driving the prey fish, the terns' tables turn. That same slight difference in wing-loading lets Common Terns hover better. They can hold the positions required for quick, successful dives when fish suddenly surface. Because Roseates can't hover as well, they can't hold the choice spots in dense, competitive crowds of fluttering wings. Pushed to the periphery, they're seldom in the right place at the right moment to dart in when the Bluefish drive up small fish.

Because Common Terns can feed over schools of predatory fish in deep water, they forage over vast areas that Roseates can't well exploit. Roseates' best foraging sites are confined to inlet sandbars where currents and shallows concentrate prey fishes and force them within reach. In such limited places, Roseates excel; their catch rates exceed those of Commons. But the key phrase there is "limited places." This is how they coexist, and why Roseates are so rare. In the days before dredging made life better for boats, just about every inlet and harbor mouth was full of shallow bars and, probably, full of Roseate Terns.

And that's why, even though Commons so outnumber Roseates, Roseates usually outnumber Commons right in the Cut. It's still the kind of place Roseates are built for.

So to me, terns and Bluefish always seem like old friends coming home. Few people realize it, but the most satisfying part of science is the intimacy. And anyway, growing up looks overrated.

＞

The Sound is in motion. Whitecaps and the wind make it seem not a day for boats, and I've spent it comfortably indoors, working. The phone rings. It's my friend Bob, telling me he actually ventured out, and asking, "Do you want some mackerel?" Because I first got to know mackerel when their migration took a full month and their numbers seemed limitless, mere mention of mackerel sparks a flurry of childhood scenes remembered like old photographs: of fishing with my father; of tiny rented boats; of the sight of schools of fish pushing on a slick sea, and casting lures we'd shined with steel wool to make them irresistible; of catching mackerel from the shore and warming our shins and stiffened fingers with a morning fire in the sand, then enjoying mackerel for breakfast. All this and more comes to mind with one little question from Bob. "Sure," I say, and drive over, and we end up talking for two hours simply because a few mackerel have convened our first visit in months.

To each May arrives a day when the songs of migrant warblers do damage to a morning's work as the little sirens lure me out for eye candy. This is it.

Over the political and economic drudgery of the radio's early news I hear their little chants and lisplike songs, their trills and glissandos, their declarations and affirmations. I click the radio off and close my computer, reach for my binoculars, and whistle Kenzie off her bed. Outside, we have a nice, warm southerly breeze following several days of inclement weather from the north. That inclement weather held up northbound birds; that's what happens. (The birds know enough not to fight a headwind unless, say, they're trapped over the ocean in shifted weather.) So they massed up patiently, until the breeze blew their skirts up and they lifted off. And here they are, in force. For starters there's a multihued Chestnut-sided Warbler right in my rosebushes, eye level and just a few feet away, a lucky find and a rare and auspicious gift. So great in number and small in size are the birds today that in almost an hour I move barely a quarter mile from the house, looking into trees the whole time.

Warblers seem as thoroughly benign as any living thing can be. With more than fifty species on the continent—all variations on a theme, as though one plain little outline of a bird was given to an advanced art class to riff upon—American wood warblers are to my mind among the most alluring and endearing birds in the world. Except for the greenish Pine Warbler and the brush-dwelling bandit-masked Common Yellow-throat and the willow- and elder-hosteling Yellows with their *sweet-sweet-sweet* theme; and except for the bayberry-loving Yellow-rumps, with their high-contrast black-and-white and golden patches, *most* seem to prefer gleaning insects from oak blossoms. Inland, it can be hard on your neck, looking straight up the whole time. Here in our realm of salt spray and sea wind, most of the trees are scrubby, so that's an advantage. And the leaves are still small. Many of the birds have just come off the ocean and haven't yet dispersed inland and upward, another advantage.

What you do is, locate a caller and look for a bouncy little bird flitting and swooping among the drooping blossoms, or perhaps pausing just long enough for a few successive declarations. Binoculars are a must, and you need to be good at nailing your target on your first sweep of the glass. What comes into focus is pretty amazing, because without binoculars they'd just be little birds in the treetops; most people overlook them entirely.

I find a Canada Warbler (gray back, yellow belly, wears a necklace of black pearls), a Magnolia Warbler (black mask and cape, boldly black-streaked egg-yolk belly), an energetic American Redstart (unmistakable black and bright orange) eating a bright green caterpillar, Black-throated Blue Warblers, Northern Parula Warblers (blue-gray hood and wings, yellow throat, handsomely contrasting black-and-rufous breastband, olive cape), Black-and-white Warblers, plus a black warbler with white wing patches and an absolutely flaming head: the Blackburnian—truly spectacular beyond all bounds of its tiny size. Many are destined for much farther north and will be gone in a few days. That makes this a rare annual treat. If I'm traveling, I may miss the best action entirely.

In the right weather—warm fronts and tailwinds—May propels such waves of migrant birds that my ability to keep track of arrivals falls apart. *Many* kinds of warblers, diverse arrays of sparrows, sandpipers, swifts, woodpeckers, gulls, hawks, grosbeaks, hummingbirds, kingbirds, tana-gers, thrashers, orioles, flycatchers, and more hit our beaches daily and move inland or along the shorelines. They *invade* our coast. (I'm sure they'd say the same of us.) Sometimes, in the middle of a big push of migrants, the air will change direction or just go still or foggy. And then migrant birds seem to rain into the coastal vegetation until the weather changes. That's called a "fallout."

This morning, a few towns west of here, my friend Eric saw "waves of birds with literally hundreds of warblers coming in across the marsh." The seventeen species of warblers he saw on his small property included Blue-winged, Nashville, Black-throated Green, and Worm-eating Warblers, Ovenbirds, and more. Adding other birds, he tallied sixty-five species for the morning, right around his house. Later in the month the tally will swell to over 260 species of birds seen locally since New Year's Day.

Gray Catbirds, which seem to have all hit together, overnight, are meowing from the briars. A greenish vireo moving silently has spider silk wrapped around its bill, evidence of its last meal. Strikingly rufous-and-black Eastern Towhees offer their simple toast, *Drink!,* and their fuller song, *Drink your teeeee!* That and their scratching in dry leaves will again become familiar sounds. Song Sparrows pump their notices from bush tops; Barn Swallows zoom the dunes in precision flight. And ringing throughout the salt marshes are the self-titled songs of Willets. They're not the most melodic, I admit, but are exuberant, their authors easily recognizable with long, stout bills, long legs, and wing patches flashing white over the greening marsh grass. The United States is home to about eight hundred bird species, including about seventy listed as threatened or endangered. Many of the warblers and shorebirds, especially, stand greatly diminished in number compared to decades past. But despite those melancholy notes, they can still amaze and delight. Most importantly, their songs continue to insist that we remember how things are supposed to be.

Soon, broadening leaves will make seeing small birds in high trees difficult. Knowing the songs—and I'm still learning—lets one envision birds you can hear but can't see. And as always, the ability to envision what is just out of sight is more important than merely seeing what's right in front of you.

Stepping out at four-thirty A.M.—still chilly, but I decided to get in a good spring walk before work—puts me and Kenzie on the shore in time to hear a Whip-poor-will give way to a Bobwhite, and see the year's first skimmers yield night patrol to the gulls of dawn.

The rich rouge of first light seems to purge the lingering chill, and even if the effect is purely psychological, it works for me. Well before sunrise, the air over the beach and ocean has become a conveyor of loons. More loons than I ever remember seeing—all Common Loons—are streaming northeast into the red-throated dawn. Continuously, I have loons in sight. If a casual glance upward reveals none, a scan with the binoculars reveals many. They flap constantly, as if flying is always an effort. With their long necks extended and legs outstretched, their wings seem smaller than needed for so long and hefty a body. They come singly or in loose groups of up to about a dozen. Many come close over-head, their blacks lustrous, their whites luminous. By the time I leave the beach, the red sun of dawn has already mellowed to yellow, the blue sky paled, but loons are still coming. In an hour, I've seen about four hundred. Here on the flyway, they stream past in a living river, but even-tually they will fan out and sift themselves into forest lakes and tundra ponds. Their lonely tremolo will dissipate into the vast spaces of the great North, and, two by two, they will spend an all-too-brief season raising the new loons we will see southbound on the far side of summer.

Past the Cut the channel widens, letting the current drop its sand, creat-ing shoals. Over those shallows, the tide is sending a clear sheet of mov-ing water. From that quick-flowing sheet, Roseate Terns are picking off small fishes, their elegant tail streamers enhancing their grace of flight. An egret's long stilts have taken it onto the same shoal, stalking the same fishes on foot. The water is still falling. On full and new moons, low tides expose several of the bars to air, drawing Willets and American Oyster-catchers, who probe and pick over the wet, silty sand for worms, small mussels, possibly little Mud Dog Whelks, and fiddler crabs. Like them, I venture out on a part of the bar already exposed, looking for nothing in particular, a strategy that has fueled many a discovery.

Just past the main sandbar, the channel's shore takes a right-angle turn and the whole bay opens up into a pleasing vista of water and sky.

Most of the bay is also shallow, with sandbars that discourage boaters. It's the kind of place where jet-propelled watercraft excel. Fortunately, they're banned here. Thus: quiet.

Down to these bars and shores, down out of the northbound lanes of May come Arctic-bound shorebirds whose travels stand among the most epic. This morning's complement includes more of those harlequin gypsies the Ruddy Turnstones. Among them mix dark-bellied Dunlins, plus Black-bellied Plovers, whose new breeding plumage and striking black faces look painstakingly rendered in India ink. The bay shores and inches-deep shallows and mudflats also hold Least, Semipalmated, Pectoral, Solitary, and White-rumped Sandpipers, Short-billed Dowitchers, and other waders.

We should also be seeing a few Red Knots. But we're becoming Red Knot have-nots; they're going extinct. And part of their problem involves crimes against crabs. I'll explain shortly.

In the sand exposed by the dropping tide, numerous foot-wide drag tracks lead to wet pits where horseshoe crabs were digging, mating, and laying eggs last night. The shorebirds are picking around the nest pits, eagerly eating some of the several thousand peppercorn-sized eggs planted like green-tinted pearls in the sand of each pit. I decide to come back tonight and see if I can find any horseshoe crabs in the act.

Day yields. Earth turns its face to outer space, and a tide of darkness signals the start of activities to night's creatures.

I finish working, fry up some Bluefish, clean up just enough. Then Kenzie and I walk along the shore in fine moonlight. Several invisible Whip-poor-wills have again added their rhythmic triad to the night chorus. Their calls ring from the dark woods. A few remain to be heard here in the relative isolation of Lazy Point, but they're vanishing in many places, possibly because ground nesting makes them vulnerable to loose cats. The ghostly birds chant incessantly, making their haunting call, so welcome at first, seem ultimately more forlorn than any raven of Poe's. It's as though they're trying to etch themselves into memory before they're gone.

But tonight it's horseshoe crabs I seek. The night is stock-still. It remains too cool for mosquitoes, and I enjoy the quiet water, the mild air, the night chorus. When I reach the bay, the tide is within an hour or so of high. It's so calm it touches the shore like pond water. I flick on my flashlight. The water is clear. I sweep the beam, startling a few small fish, illuminating a few snails.

I walk and stalk my way along the shore. And in just a few steps I find the first consorting horseshoe crabs. A large female, with a smooth, pea-green shell about two feet long, is traveling along the bottom with a male holding on to her and two smaller males following.

The horseshoe crabs' main breeding periods straddle the full moons of May and June. It's now two days to full. They've waited a year, and waited for high tide. Their hour arrives. Roused from depth by moonlight and some kind of memory, they begin working shoreward in the dark water. In the shallows they assemble for a rite ancient beyond human imagining.

Their rounded shield of shell looks a little like a horse's hoof; a few older fishermen still call them "horsefoots." To me their shell recalls a helmet. That helmeted body trails a spikelike tail that looks like weaponry, but they use it solely to right themselves if they get overturned. Unusually strange yet strangely familiar, these "crabs" are actually more closely related to spiders. But with a crablike shell shielding crablike legs, "crab" is the only word that works. Most jointed-legged invertebrates—arthropods—are either insects, arachnids (spider types), or crustaceans like true crabs. Yet within the arthropods, horseshoe crabs are in a class by themselves, called Merostomata, meaning their mouth is at the center of their legs.

Their looks are debatable, but one can hardly argue with their track record of success. With no other defenses than this shell, they've existed for 450 million years. In other words, their same basic body plan has worked for nearly half a billion years. None of us can imagine what that kind of time even means. When horseshoe crabs were new under the sea, fish did not yet have jaws, corals were just evolving, and flowering plants, amphibians, reptiles, birds, and mammals did not exist. Hundreds of millions of years later, dinosaurs would arise, flourish, and vanish. Right around closing time we've strolled in, and they're still here.

Four horseshoe crab species survive worldwide, two off the east coast of Asia, one in the Indian Ocean, and these American Horseshoe Crabs. Sea turtles of several kinds are just about the only things that naturally prey on the adults. Yet nowadays, they're defenseless toward their new major predator: guess who.

Though the Asian species are apparently considered a delicacy during breeding season, American Horseshoe Crab eggs can reportedly cause poisoning and death. That would seem sufficient to save them. But a few years ago enterprising fishermen discovered that cracked-up egg-bearing females prove peerlessly attractive in luring eels and whelks to traps.

Dark shapes appear farther out in slightly deeper water, like an approaching armada of landing craft. Each couple of steps reveals more horseshoe crabs along the shore, and more in deeper water, males scooting along in deft pursuit of brides, and females already burdened with love. These animals are not just ancient, they're old. They've molted their shells about seventeen times before reaching adult size at around nine years of age (unmolested, they can live to about twenty years). Males ultimately emerge into adulthood with a distinguishing pair of "boxing glove" claws on their front legs, designed specifically for clinging to the shell of a female. The male rides a likely mate, and when she digs a nest and lays a clutch of eggs, the male fertilizes them with a cloud of sperm.

Right along the waterline, crabs are working at various stages of their task, some females just bulldozing their way into the sand, others sunk almost to the roof of their shells, with males holding fast to their prizes.

Walking a little farther, I realize there are *hundreds* of these animals, all intent on mating and laying eggs. This stretch of the bay must be a major nesting site.

Finding this mass arrival in the pull of the moon feels like stumbling upon a major secret. I reach for my cell phone and call a friend who I know would appreciate seeing all this.

In the act of coming shoreward to dig nests, the horseshoe crabs remind me a little bit of sea turtles, for which I hold affection. Anything that returns repeatedly, for long enough, can inspire feelings of reassurance.

Their rite is beyond reassuring: it's sacred. Nothing is more venerable than the act of creating new generations of living beings—or more vulner-

able. And that puts my heart on alert. Something in the pit of my stomach tells me that, after 450 million years, the only way to go from this feeling is down.

My friend Patricia arrives. She works at an aquarium where, among other things, she's a kind of horseshoe crab ambassador to school groups, showing students how, despite their weirdness and their spiky tails, the animals are interesting and harmless. But it's one thing to pull a horseshoe crab from a cooler in a classroom, or find one along a shore, and quite another to see this nocturnal ritual, to feel them keeping the ancient faith, to watch them gather like some secret clan, to find them in such numbers in the moonlight.

The scene and its magic immediately enchant her.

In a few hours the ebb will leave their eggs above high-tide line. They'll be somewhat vulnerable to birds, but out of reach of the carpeting snails that graze the bay floor and can more thoroughly relieve a nest of its contents than any birds. The next moon-aligned tides will rise high enough to fetch tiny hatchlings, who'll start their perilous bid for long life. Of course, only a small fraction will succeed. And if all goes as it's gone for the last few hundred million years, that should be enough.

But "enough" might be a concept better understood by horseshoe crabs than by humans.

The moonlight suddenly shrivels as high-beam headlights bounce onto the beach. Patricia and I stare like deer. I have a feeling I know what's coming.

The pickup stops and a man gets out. I hear him sloshing in the water, and soon I hear the thuds and bangs of horseshoe crabs hitting the bed of his truck.

The night, the spell—. The magic turns toxic, almost mocking. I begin to hate myself for having so enjoyed the scene. So naïve.

He moves his truck along, stops, gets back into the water, and we hear crabs hitting metal by the dozens.

I've known that baymen use horseshoe crabs for bait. But knowing is not the same as seeing an ancient rite turned wholesale into flying junk. My heart starts pounding with both rage and fear. In the inevitable confrontation I know is coming in the next minute, I'm afraid things may get out of hand.

He hasn't seen us yet.

Patricia charges into the water—with her cell phone in her pocket, I'm pretty sure—and now she, too, is jerking crabs from their nests. But instead of throwing them ashore she is flinging them as far out as she can, beyond reach of a man in boots.

The man—a guy in his twenties—notices her and yells, *"Hey! Stop!"* At first he doesn't realize she's doing this for the specific purpose of putting the crabs out of his reach. Then he gets it—and gets mad.

Patricia, waist-deep in chilly water and soaked to the neck, is likewise wound to a furious black anger. The more he yells at her to cut it out, the faster and more determinedly she works. Every crab is to him a living, to her a life. There is no chance of a meeting of the minds here. He speeds his truck to where I'm standing, hops out, and gets in my face.

He wants me to get her to stop. One might as well try to stop the tide from rising. He's clean-cut, athletically built, wearing hip boots and a light long-sleeve shirt. His brown hair makes a straight sweep across his forehead. He's angry, but his eyes suggest that he feels some combination of exasperation and worry; it's the look of someone already feeling besieged.

I see at least the opportunity to remain calm and prevent the situation from coming to blows.

He tells me that what he's doing is legal. I say I know it is. What Patricia is doing is legal, too. To oversimplify: she wants to take the horseshoe crabs from him; he wants to take them from her.

He wants to know how I'd feel if he came to my office and disrupted what I do for a living. I try saying that if you want to keep making a living, killing your animals while they're breeding seems a risky strategy. He says that's nonsense; his grandfather did this, too. They've been doing this for generations and *look*: the crabs are still here by the hundreds.

Yes—because taking a few for bait is one thing. Loading a pickup truck is another. Selling them out of state is yet another. Gold rushes have a way of crashing. His grandfather took crabs, but he didn't take *every* crab.

At stake for him is his self-identity, his family history. But his problems here go far, far beyond Patricia and me. It's a traditional way of life already eroded by overfishing, undermined by overreaching, overdevelopment, deteriorated eelgrass and a consequent crash of scallops, and a flood of linen-wearing outsiders who come to socialize while sipping wine in the sunset but don't really understand what this place is about. I empathize. Our worries largely overlap. The declines that threaten his interests also threaten mine. But at this moment, we have a significant difference of opinion.

He reaches into the cab to show me his license. Embarrassed by this, I tell him he doesn't need to do that. He says he's got a day job working for the town. He is pressing the point of his legitimacy. He is trying to show me that he's a respectable member of the community and that he's upholding a long-standing family fishing tradition. We're talking, not screaming—which is good—but we're talking past each other.

His job with the town indicates that you really can't be young and earn a full-time living as a bayman anymore. Not with the combined pressures of depletion, shrinking fishing options, out-of-sight real-estate prices, and soaring property taxes. I say we can't do what our great-grandfathers were doing. He points to his license again. I know, it's legal, I say again. But times change. What others did in the past limits our options now, because a lot of it was overdone. I just think he shouldn't be taking crabs at this rate—not filling trucks while they're laying eggs.

He says, earnestly, that he *can't* take every crab; they have a limit: "We're limited to five hundred a day."

"Five *hundred*? A *day*?" There aren't five hundred crabs here right now. That's the kind of limit that represents no limit. I tell him, Look, you can't just come and take every egg-laying female you can get your hands on and expect this to be here in a few years. *Five hundred* just seems excessive; that's how it strikes me, anyway. And even if he complies, who's checking what goes into other trucks?

Nearly four hundred people hold licenses to take horseshoe crabs from the waters of this state. In the old days, limits on catching horseshoes seemed unnecessary. But market demand for whelk and eels increased rapidly in the 1990s, and so did demand for crabs as trap bait for them.

In the year 2000 the state set its first quota: 366,000 crabs. That seems like a lot, but to fishermen, it seemed too little: they took 628,000 crabs, way over the limit. In 2004, due to widening concern about the crabs *and* about the shorebirds who use excess crab eggs as migration fuel, the state cut its quota to 150,000. The take actually dropped for a few years, then ballooned. In 2007, fishermen took 284,000 crabs—nearly double the quota.

Not only is no one watching, the state relies on the fishermen themselves to honestly and accurately report their numbers. It's unlikely they took *fewer* than they claim.

Another pair of headlights turns onto the beach, a death warrant for another five hundred horseshoe crabs if they can find them. There are two guys in that truck. This changes the dynamic. Patricia is down the shore, still grimly flinging crabs into deeper water. The guy I'm talking to drives over to consult with his buddies. I'm expecting a unified confrontation, but instead they decide to leave.

In the time it might take them to go have a beer, we're long gone. There is no one to call, because this is legal and the "limit" is so stratospheric there's no way they can exceed it, even by laying a hand on each and every crab they see.

In the morning the beach is laced and churned with tire tracks. They

came back, of course. Others came, too. There is something in man that
hates natural abundance, and something that clings to excess.

The Red Knot is a dove-sized shorebird with a straight, stout black bill
and, in breeding plumage, a pink or brick-red breast. In physique it merely
pleases, rather than impresses. But it is an athlete of almost incredible
accomplishment. It undertakes one of the world's longest migrations, its
twenty-thousand-mile annual round-trip spanning the hemispheric
landmass from the tip of South America (Tierra del Fuego) to the Canadian tundra.

For more than half the year, Red Knots are urgently on the move.
Even their destinations make no promise of reprieve. Once, in June, in
Canada's high Arctic at the northern tip of Baffin Island, I was stunned
to see a small group of Red Knots hunkered against a late snow squall
after enduring their incredible journey, weathering an unleashed wind
that could still lash and sting.

Typically for them, they'd gotten there anticipating two weeks of cold
weather. To carry them through weeks of scant sustenance, they'd brought
an emergency supply of fat—fat from horseshoe crab eggs. The fat gathered
by horseshoe crabs and garnered by the knots allowed them to survive,

court, mate, and lay eggs before insects became available in the short burst
of Arctic summer. So the crabs' eggs were both fuel and survival rations.

Back then (1986) nobody was terribly worried about Red Knots, merely
impressed by them. They were just one among a spectacular group of
shorebird species that *all* stopped for a few weeks each spring to fatten up
on horseshoe crab eggs before continuing long northbound flight treks.
They'd stop in many estuaries, but the epicenter of horseshoe crabs—and
the main fuel depot of North America's northbound shorebirds—was
across the New York Bight from here, on the shores of Delaware Bay. In
those years so many crabs jammed the bay's shores that they dug up one
another's nests. Billions of eggs drifted into windrows on the wave-lapped
shores. You could skim them up with your hands. Famished shorebirds by
the hundreds of thousands—officials estimated a million birds—swarmed
in clouds on the flats and beaches. I saw them. I saw knots there, too, during
those years.

Exceptionally nutritious, horseshoe crab eggs allow shorebirds to put on
weight faster than any other food. The birds can *double* their weight in
two to three weeks—if the eggs are there.

Delaware Bay's positioning, and its role as the horseshoe crabs' densest breeding ground, is not just perfect for the migrating birds—it is
crucial. To hit the Arctic on schedule for breeding in the short flare of
summer, the birds need to get their timing right. A significant decline in
the number of horseshoe crab eggs would make it impossible for many
of them to complete their journey to their breeding sites, or even survive.

Here's the math: after an arduous four-day nonstop flight from South
America, Red Knots arrive in Delaware Bay so depleted they weigh a
mere 90 grams—3 ounces. They *look* emaciated. They must eat and eat
until they recover from the depletion of the first part of their trek, then
pack on enough fat for the next. After more than doubling their weight,
they can safely depart weighing a plump and robust 200 grams.

If you took that crucial fueling stop out of their northward journey,
you might as well pull the plug; they'd go down the drain.

And they have. Between 1990 and 2005 horseshoe crab egg numbers
along Delaware Bay dropped 90 percent. Over that same time, eastern
Red Knot numbers (a western population migrates between Alaska and

Pacific Mexico) dropped 80 percent, from a high estimate of as many as 150,000 to about 30,000. During a study spanning 1992 to 2000, annual adult survival dropped from 85 percent to about 55 percent. And in a single year, 2005, the remaining population fell by half.

Knots have other problems besides crab depletion. Birds seem to be dying on their wintering grounds, and something is causing some birds to arrive along Delaware Bay a week or two late, and in poor condition. This makes it even more crucial that those birds that get to Delaware Bay find enough crab eggs to fuel them for the remaining eighteen hundred miles to their Arctic breeding grounds.

Red Knots must put on at least 6 grams per day at the horseshoe crab banquet so they don't fall short going toward the Arctic. In the late 1990s, the Red Knots could put on 8 grams per day. Ten years later, many couldn't gain more than 2. And when they launched the next push north, they starved. Researchers surveying parts of the Red Knots' vast Arctic breeding areas could no longer find any birds.

If recent trends continue, the eastern Red Knot will, by 2020, follow the Passenger Pigeon into the mists of memory. Like the Eskimo Curlew, which was once abundant enough to be shot by the wagonload, even its memory will fade. If the Red Knot comes undone, it will be just the first in an oncoming chain of shorebirds derailed in the crab-overfishing train wreck.

The government report on the Red Knot's status states: "The main identified threat to the population is the reduced availability of horseshoe crabs eggs in Delaware Bay arising from elevated harvest of adult crabs for bait in the conch [whelk] and eel fishing industries."

Fishers have long used egg-bearing females for eel bait. But in the mid-1990s, fishermen's take of crabs went from tens of thousands to over two million. Needless to say, that bent the horseshoe crab population downward. Newly maturing female crabs' numbers dropped nearly 90 percent just between 2001 and 2003. As usual, the first response by fisheries managers was cobbled together after an avoidable disaster was already entrenched. The crabs could recover; they have a history of doing so. Horseshoe crabs were once used for fertilizer. Horses drew wagonloads from the marshes.

Because of drastic—though necessary—limits on crab taking, recent counts suggest that Delaware Bay's breeding horseshoe crab population may have stabilized. Along Delaware Bay's New Jersey side, the heart of the shorebird stopover, the numbers of juvenile and male horseshoe crabs appear to be up slightly. To that extent, the plan is working.

But what the crabs need and what the birds need differ. The crabs need to lay *enough* eggs. The birds fatten up with *excess* eggs. The birds' abundance depends on egg overabundance. Because the crabs need about a decade to mature, even if fishermen stopped taking the crabs entirely, the crabs' recovery would require ten years or so. At recent trends, the Red Knot's eastern North America population may not have that kind of time.

The Red Knot is just the most imperiled, most studied shorebird reliant on horseshoe crabs. The Ruddy Turnstone, the little Sanderling, the littler Semipalmated Sandpiper, the Dunlin, and the rather long-billed Short-billed Dowitcher—they all depend on horseshoe crab eggs. And their numbers are down by more than half.

New Jersey, Delaware, and Virginia belatedly restricted the take of horseshoe crabs. New Jersey later banned it altogether. New Jersey also cleared debris from crab-nesting beaches and restricted access so birds could feed without constant disruption by people and their dogs.

That's all needed, but about 600,000 crabs are still killed annually for bait in Delaware, Maryland, Virginia, and New York. New York dropped the absurd "limit" of 500 per day to 200, then tightened it to 30 crabs per day—sometimes. At other times, it's still an excessive 250 per person per day.

Of course, those are just the rules. The law enforcement people tell me there's been a lot of poaching here on Long Island and elsewhere as prices quadrupled to over a dollar per crab.

Crabs and birds aren't the only things at risk in this. Your health is, too. It turns out that nearly every batch of injectable and intravenous drugs, as well as prosthetic devices such as heart valves and hip replacements, must, before they can go to market, be screened for bacterial contamination using a protein from horseshoe crab blood. For this purpose, laboratory suppliers continually collect blood from wild horseshoe crabs, which are then returned to the water. The same test is used to diagnose diseases like spinal meningitis. The people who tap their blood release the animals alive on the premise that they're too valuable to kill. Yet fishermen have lobbied successfully to keep killing hundreds of females annually for eel and whelk bait.

Long Island baymen can still take the crabs and sell them out of state. And so each May and June, on the full moon, the high-beam headlights bounce off the ends of roads and turn onto particular stretches of sandy beach. The people behind the wheel say they can't do without the income from the crabs. But when they take the last ones, they'll have to.

On the next full moon, in June, I ventured alone back to the bay during the nighttime high tide. This is the crabs' other peak month for breeding. But instead of the hundreds of animals of May, I counted seventeen males and just six females. The following night, I saw just three males, no females. One truck appeared briefly. The driver took a look and seemed to think it wasn't worth his while. On that, we agree.

JUNE

It's the time of spotted fawns, tiny cottontails, and fledglings. Already, newly fledged grackles loiter on lines at the edge of the marsh. When they move, their flight is sure and steady. The physical competence and mental acuity of three-week-old birds is surely one of the great inspirations of the world. And to them, all the world is new. Early rounds of robins are airborne too. The adults are back to singing, ready to do it again.

Box turtles, sometimes two or even three at a time, are coming daily for the cubes of melon I leave for them under the bird feeder. Anything they don't get by day, Raccoons scarf up by night.

Each morning I hear turkeys gobbling, and I still find it odd to see the toms in the salt marshes at dawn, giving hens the full-courtship treatment, with fanned tails and heads all blushed, out there where egrets usually preside. Ospreys have now become hardworking parents. Their eggs hatched in just the last few days of May; that's when I started noticing the adult offering food to chicks I can't yet see.

The toads' sundown tenor remains strong; they're still pumping out eggs. And even though the Garter and Hog-nosed Snakes stalk them, snakes, too, will depend on the success of a new toad generation. The future is always in the now. And because a predator relies on its prey, in the larger lens it is less an enemy than a dependent. The Fowler's Toads' "song" sounds like a muffled, distant coffee grinder being turned on and off every few seconds: *reeehhhhhh*. Multiply that by dozens. You might think that if you're going to be a toad, you'd at least get Pavarotti's voice. But there's no justice.

And reappearing as though from some deep hibernaculum: humans.

A few recreational boats have begun plying the water, joggers ply the sand, fishers plumb the depths, lovers walk hand in hand, and solitary beachcombers search for what they've dreamt—or never dreamt—of finding.

The first weekend after millions of New York's calendars, computers, and PDAs simultaneously displayed the word "June," coastal solitudes morph into the crowded summer Hamptons. At the town beach, where city acquaintances want to catch up on what happened over the winter with everyone's investments and candidates, the air smells of hot dogs and tanning lotion. Past the bikinis and up over the ocean an Osprey hovers, feints, hovers, then commits to a plummeting headfirst dive. In the last moment it swings those big feet out in front of its face, crashing a basket of claws through the ceiling of the surf. It latches a fish it cannot lift. This is pretty interesting. It struggles to get airborne—but succeeds only briefly; it's got a Striper. Then, just floating exhausted in the surf swells with wings splayed and that fish yanking, it seems to consider rowing its catch ashore. When that doesn't work, it decides that this is the big one it must let go.

In the morning when I round the bend where the pitch pines meet the tidelands, a pickup truck nearly cuts me off. The driver is honking and waving, and when I stop, he leaps out, and yes, it's me he wants.

As a marine biologist living in a small beach house, I sometimes feel a little like a country doctor; people I don't always recognize occasionally seek me out. But, it turns out, this is Dennis, who lives about a mile from me, and—as he's frantically telling me—from his porch he'd just noticed "a dolphin or whale, stranded on the bar."

A dolphin *or* a whale? That sounds odd.

He leads me a couple of miles down the road bordering the marsh; then he turns onto a dirt track to the shore of the wide, shallow bay.

The animal is about fifty yards from shore and stranded in calf-deep shallows on a broad sand flat. It is, in fact, a very large dolphin—*so* large and dark that at first I think it might be a young pilot whale.

It thrashes. Seeing for sure that it's alive, we're on our cell phones right away, calling family reinforcements. "Bring bedsheets and buckets." "Call the marine mammal rescue center."

Family members arrive minutes later; the rescue crew is more than an hour away. We wade to the stricken creature, whose dark gray back and scratched flanks are out in the drying air as the sun is climbing. The tide is still dropping.

It's a bottlenose dolphin and nearly twelve feet long. Much bigger than the bottlenoses usually seen along the beach and in bay channels. This is an Offshore Bottlenose, a different species. Its usual habitat is the edge of the continental shelf, which around here is about seventy-five miles from the beach.

I estimate its weight at around eight hundred pounds. No way can we move it, and there is nowhere, really, to move it to. The drill is to keep its skin wet until rescuers arrive. As we spread the first sheet over the dolphin, it thrashes out of fear, but only once. As soon as we start pouring water, it calms. Its eyes seem to convey understanding that we mean no harm, pose no threat. But that doesn't mean it's right on both points.

Patricia is here now, as well as Dennis's family and in-laws. We haven't seen these neighbors all winter and spring. Even on a tidal flat, tragedy brings out community. So here we are, getting caught up on news, maintaining this dolphin's life while awaiting added help.

For more than an hour we keep the sheets and towels wet with gently poured buckets of water. The dolphin scarcely moves. It keeps its left eye closed; the sun is on its left. Its right eye slowly swivels and watches as we splash water on its head by hand. It is taking about three breaths per minute—plosive, gasping-sounding breaths. In between, it keeps its blowhole shut against the sea, which drains farther away as the tide drops.

Bottlenose dolphins are intelligent, highly social animals capable of communicating, cooperating during hunting, and forming social alliances. Did this smart, rugged animal of the open ocean simply make a mistake? Or had it been ailing? And if so, did it specifically seek the calm, protected waters of this shallow bay to find refuge from sharks and other potential tormentors who might exploit its distress?

The marine mammal rescue people arrive. We know these four women too, but haven't seen them in months, either. They take one look at the animal and say we'll need more people to lift the stretcher or we'll never move the dolphin over the flat and into the rescue truck—a sort of animal ambulance—where it can get the aid it needs. So we start calling other friends and knocking on neighbors' doors. Tommy and Bo come with a pickup that can drive out onto the wet tidal flat. Then Diane arrives. Rebecca. Someone wakes the bar bouncer who's sleeping in a nearby beach house. Patricia recruits a guy who'd been fixing the road. We all get acquainted and figure out who knows whom.

What does the dolphin think of the commotion? Its eyes close slowly, seeming to declare a need to rest. Does it see its swift and sparkling life splashing before its eyes? It begins making barely audible clicking sounds. But whom is it calling out to, and with what message?

We've now gathered sufficient muscle power to move the dolphin. I'm feeling pretty good about this until the dolphin lifts its head from the sand for the first time, and opens its mouth. I see immediately that most of its normally sharp teeth are worn flat to the gum line. This dolphin is decades old.

My perspective of the dolphin shifts from unlucky victim to elder survivor at the end of a long and uncommonly successful life. How I wish it could share its stories from a long career of challenges, of dangers narrowly escaped, of borderless blues—of what it took to be so successful.

How I would love to know its impressions of humanity, its perceptions of fishing boats, its encounters with nets or hooks—and to hear a few stories about those interesting scars. Did it come here sensing somehow that it is time to let go?

When the lead rescuer notices the tiniest bit of bloody froth at the dolphin's blowhole, I suddenly know there can be no future for this old mariner. The best thing would be to euthanize it—now—without moving it from its resting place.

I also know that the rescuers won't do this. Not in front of a crowd. Now that we're assembled, we're committed to moving it first to the pickup, then off the flats to shore, then into the rescue truck.

But whose pain are we sparing: the dolphin's or ours? With much effort, we roll the animal enough to get the stretcher under it, then roll it the other way to position it on the stretcher. On the count of three we heave it up, then up again until it is even with the high tailgate; then we struggle as we attempt to load it into the truck. The animal starts thrashing. A whack from that tail could cause severe injury, so we let the stretcher down and step back, watching its pitiful efforts. On a second strenuous attempt, with much puffing and pushing, and pulling from people who've climbed into the truck bed, we succeed, barely.

We've rescued the dolphin.

But from what?

The next day I inquire. On the way to the rehabilitation center, the animal went into spasms. It was euthanized in the truck, and was dead on arrival.

We had reached across the species barrier with compassion in our hearts. But we'd gotten ourselves stranded in our commitment to do good, no matter what, and we'd carried that conviction too far.

There are worse ways to die than coming to a peaceful sand flat in a quiet bay in springtime and waiting for the tide to drain away.

When my time comes, I hope my gathered loved ones will remember that.

⇒

Solstice confers the longest day, the most northerly dawn—and true summer. Though the birds' dawn chorus thins as summer thickens, it suffices to call forth consciousness. Kenzie and I step into the morning and head down the beach path. The water is so calm, it seems your breath could fog its surface. Being out on a June morning that's this still requires either bug spray or a kayak. Bug spray will put the bugs at bay. The kayak will put me *on* the bay. Easy choice.

From under the kayak's tarp, several tiny toads, just past tadpolehood and limbering up their new limbs and lungs, hop away into the beach grass. It's so quiet that as I begin dragging the kayak toward the water, over the smooth beach pebbles, the sound—unnoticeable at midday—projects a resonant rumble.

I am concerned about our local colony of Least Terns. I've recently seen Great Black-backed Gulls landing in the tern colony and agitated groups of terns escorting them as they leave. Black-backs—the world's largest gull—can effortlessly penetrate a cloud of defending Least Terns, shrugging off their dive-bombing protests while searching for eggs and chicks. At other times and places, Black-backs kill ducks and swallow puffins whole. I fear gulls may have largely wiped out the terns' nesting efforts.

A few old-time fishermen still remember when Black-backs were new in these parts. Fishing boat discards and garbage keep the gulls subsidized and widespread, inflating their numbers and putting them in conflict with terns. Today I'll take no fishing rod or clam sack, just my old binoculars. The plan: paddle around the Least Terns' island and see what's up.

My paddle's blades enter silently. Along the hull gurgles the music of moving water. The alternating blades dip and pull, dip and pull, leaving whorled wakes and making the boat glide as if self-propelled. So meditative is the cadence, I almost forget I am the propelling self. The shore slides quickly by.

Kenzie is trotting along. She'll follow until the shore bends away. Then she'll finish her walk solo and work her way home. We've done this before, and I'll find her resting on the doorstep later.

The sun has not yet gathered sufficient determination to banish the mists that night has hung on the coastal hills like spiderwebs in dewy grass. On the water, the light remains glareless. The tide, briefly slack at low, sends no resisting current as I glide into the Cut. Roseate Terns wheel and dip over the shallows. The morning light shows their faintly peachy breast feathers.

The Least Terns nest on the sand-and-pebble island that lies just across the Cut. Through binoculars I scan the standing adults for signs of any chicks. Seeing none, I decide to land for a quick look. The terns are not pleased. They dive near my head, uttering warnings. I notice a lot of empty nest scrapes in the sand. That's a bad sign. But I begin finding a few nests with eggs, and tiny chicks lying prone in nests lined with shell fragments, and slightly larger ones hidden in the vegetation. Responding to the adults' alarm calls, the chicks freeze motionless. The number of juveniles seems reassuringly ample. The world just might go on, after all.

I walk out of the colony. The adults are already resettling as I shove off. A Piping Plover watches from the shoreline. Its tiny chicks, like cottonballs on toothpicks, stand still.

Twirling the kayak around, I press farther along the channel between the island and the main shore. A few scattered Bluefish and perhaps a small Striped Bass or two are rising. How to tell: Blues burst; Stripers slurp. A well-placed cast could prove it, but without fish-taking gear I'm freed to watch, speculate—and keep moving.

Rounding the bend, I see about a hundred Double-crested Cormorants strung in a ragged line, swimming toward shore like a beach seine made of birds, driving fish before them. At intervals most slip underwater together. As the cormorants go down, small fishes rise, and terns fall among them. Completing a geometry of appetites and ambush, several egrets line the shore, awaiting the small fish that will soon be darting for cover into the marsh grass at their feet.

I've been afloat just half an hour, but there's been life everywhere I turn my gaze. The rest of the world aside, this remains a remarkable place. It's taken four billion years to paint this morning, and the canvas remains wet. It's a work in progress, easily spoiled. I understand that there are smudges in the paint. Some neighbors remember when the bay was carpeted by lush eelgrass and at low tide you could walk out, plucking up scallop after scallop. They remember big oysters and skinny water bars thick with mussels. They remember—.

Suddenly filling my glasses—also silently, which astonishes me—a helicopter slides in low along the far shore. Only when it banks do I hear that ominous rotor chop. It is poisoning marsh mosquitoes. The county has fought mosquitoes since the 1930s. The main weapons have been

cutting ditches into the salt marshes and spraying pesticides. The ditch-
ing was to drain the marshes where mosquitoes breed—to destroy the
marshes, basically. The pesticides were quite hard on wildlife in the early
days, when workers sprayed the DDT and other long-lasting stuff that,
among many other things, wiped Ospreys clear out of the skies for
decades.

The county's new mosquito plan gives a sense of how successful its
administrators feel their strategy has been since the days of the Model
A Ford:

> The Long-Term Plan contains a "no new ditching" policy, and a policy
> of ditch reversion as opposed to ditch maintenance. . . . The Long-Term
> Plan also seeks to restore approximately 4,000 acres of tidal wetlands
> that were grid-ditched in the 1930s, and which now require routine
> larvicide applications by air. . . . [This] will reduce or eliminate the need
> for larvicide.

In other words, not to put too fine a point on it, they now believe that
everything they did was wrong. The "drainage" ditches they dug often
clogged, creating nice, deep mosquito-breeding pools. And because they
were breeding mosquitoes, they needed to spray. Compared to the era of
DDT and other wide-spectrum poisons that got concentrated as they
traveled up the food chain, the chemicals they're using nowadays are
greatly improved. But they still kill nontarget insects, including bees.
The county itself doesn't seem to like them. Their plan sets "an ambi-
tious target of a 75 percent reduction in acres treated with larvicide . . .
and seeks to further reduce use of adulticides."

What I get from this is that the authorities and I have come to a
meeting of the minds: it's better to leave the marshes intact, and it's also
better not to spray. Since there are still plenty of mosquitoes despite
decades of battling them, I believe the battleground is best relocated to
where it's needed: on my hat, cuffs, and neck. A little bug spray applied
to those places seems to work best. Let the swallows swallow as many
mosquitoes as the bats can't, and keep the screen door closed.

The mosquito-fighting office is called Vector Control, and the ratio-
nale is that it protects the public health from mosquito-borne diseases.

The county's helicopters would better improve health if they landed on the expressways and slowed traffic; that's our biggest killer. The county could save more human lives in a pen stroke by putting the speed limits back to where they were in the 1970s. Or, better, by banning cell-phone use while driving, because: 2 eleven-year-old boys who hadn't left our county came down with malaria acquired locally (that was in the early 1990s; they survived); mosquito-borne West Nile virus kills about 30 people a year across the whole country; mosquito-vectored eastern equine encephalitis causes an average of 5 cases of symptomatic human infection per year, nationwide (one-third fatal); and cell-phone-distracted drivers cause 2,600 traffic deaths and 330,000 accidents involving moderate or severe injuries annually (a cell-phone-using driver's likelihood of crashing equals that of a driver with a 0.08 percent blood-alcohol level, the legal threshold of intoxication).

I realize that's apples and oranges, but it's part of how we see the world. Age-old threats from nature, even minor threats, we are geared to tackle. New, enormous dangers, we can't even decide if they're a matter of public safety or individual freedom. It took us decades to decide that driving drunk is a serious public health hazard, and now that we have cell phone technology as dangerous, we still haven't transferred the general lesson that it's okay for the government to require safer behavior if it affects the greater public good. Though I often use a hands-free phone while driving, and am careful to be careful, the distraction and increased risk are obvious. I would rather know that the government is trying to protect me from teenage drivers sending text messages than hyping the risks from annoying insects that I can better deal with myself. We so easily change what we do—suddenly everyone started using cell phones while driving—but we can't seem to change how we *perceive* where danger really lies. We engulf new gadgets wholesale, but seem incapable of updating our concept of what does and does not actually threaten us. We act new and think old. Virtually no one questions spending millions fighting mosquitoes because the impulse comes naturally. Our main public policy toward mosquitoes is that they're dangerous rather than merely inconvenient, while the policy toward driving with cell phones is that they're more convenient than dangerous. We'll wage war on mosquitoes and in the process kill the birds and the bees, and wonder if it's saved any human lives. But virtually no one demands that we ban cell-phone use while driving (though most of us drove for years without phones) because we don't perceive the risks viscerally and we think it would be simply too *inconvenient* to stop causing 2,600 deaths and hundreds of thousands of injuries. In practice the national policy is to ignore those safety statistics. Anyway, back to the main topic: it is with gratitude and surprise, indeed—seasoned with a dash of cynicism—that I applaud the county for coming up with a more thoughtful mosquito plan. For that, at least, it's about time.

My paddle dips and pulls, dips, pulls, and the soothing rhythm returns in the stroke and glide. I slide through the narrow, knee-deep passage on the island's east side—my kayak could almost form a bridge across it—and am out in the Sound again. The shore here forms a right angle between a sandy peninsula to my right and the island's north side to my left. So I'm floating on a broad triangle of water.

The first school of baby Menhaden I've seen this year is right in the glassy surface, dimpling like rain. (Everyone here calls them bunkers, and these babies are "peanut bunkers.") A fish-processing factory whose chimney still stands on this little island is gone, and with it the vast Menhaden schools that supported it and others like it. But there must be some adults, because these crowds of babies appear in most years.

Two usually nocturnal Black Skimmers are still at work. Skimmers are the only birds whose lower bill extends past the upper. They precision-fly with that knife-blade bill slicing through the water, snapping up—instantly—any fish they contact. I've studied them at their nesting sites, but I've never been in the middle of a school of fish with a couple of orbiting skimmers slitting the water around me. And for the first time, I can *hear* the hiss of their bills as they shred water like shears cutting fabric.

Amazingly, they make many passes through the dimples without striking a fish. The birds usually hunt at night, remember; now their shadows are spooking these dense schools. The fish move and darken the water just ahead of the oncoming birds. The skimmers run the

length of the fish-dimpled patch, turn, run again. Finally one snaps its bill onto wriggling silver, and I hear their nasal *nyak, nyak* as they depart to a distant island across the Sound, retiring for the day. A sizable fish swirls. There is so much prey here now, the predators are camped out, lingering like herders monitoring their flocks.

The water is clear and I drift, scanning the bottom, prospecting for clams. I see several in the sand and stones, the rims of their partially buried shells showing among the seaweed here and there. This means there must be quite a few here, actually. I'm glad to know of another patch.

I strike out toward the open Sound where there is no horizon, only the mirror and the sky reflected—an Escher drawing with no end, enveloping yet dimensionless. The beauty of this morning has me feeling, in less than an hour's time, nourished and full, as though I've just had a good breakfast.

On many days I understand the world as a tragedy, a bad time for

things of great importance. Even with so fine a start to today, imper-
fections are evident. I know this, though: this morning, full of such
rich, deep, savage beauty, where predators and their prey perform their
rituals as they always have, indicates that there remain on Earth some
remnants of a long-lasting world, some yardstick.

For a bigger yardstick of what still works, and a look at a place where
everyone still has enough room to correct mistakes, I'm taking some of
this warm weather and heading north to Southeast. Southeast Alaska, a
place I've always wished to see.

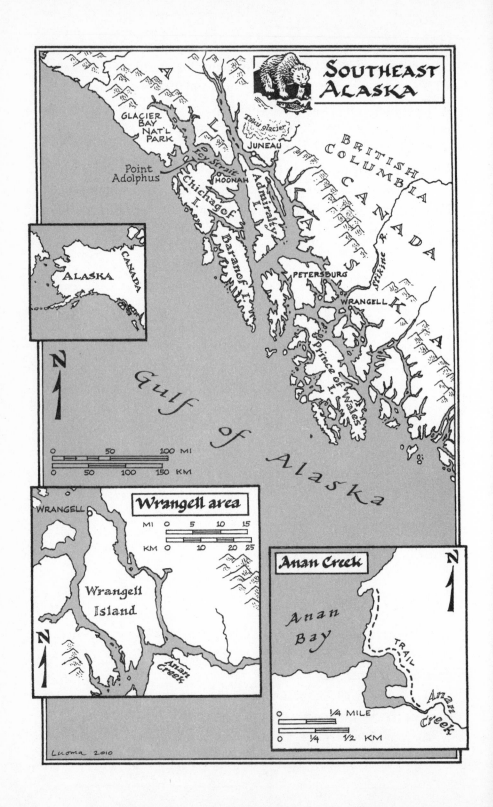

SOUTHEAST ALASKA

GLACIER BAY NAT'L PARK

JUNEAU

Taku glacier

Point Adolphus

HOONAH

Icy Strait

Chichagof I.

Admiralty I.

Baranof I.

BRITISH COLUMBIA

CANADA

ALASKA

CANADA

PETERSBURG

WRANGELL

Stikine River

Prince of Wales I.

Gulf of Alaska

0   50   100 MI

0   50   100   150 KM

Wrangell area

WRANGELL

Wrangell Island

MI 0   5   10   15

KM 0   10   20   25

Anan Creek

Anan Creek

Anan Bay

TRAIL

Anan Creek

0   1/4 MILE

0   1/4   1/2 KM

Luoma 2010

TRAVELS POLAR:
BEAR WITNESS—SOUTHEAST ALASKA

"That's gonna leave an ugly scar," says blond-haired Brenda Schwartz, a fourth-generation Alaskan commercial fisherman. She's gesturing to a recent clear-cut just outside of town, frowning. She knows that forests grow salmon.

Salmon also grow forests. Anan Creek runs through a forest—and we've heard that the salmon are in. From Wrangell, it's an hour's boat ride.

A few miles from town, those clear-cuts fade. Big spruces and tall cedars rise thick on steep slopes, each tree terminating in its own worshipful spire.

Brenda is telling me she tried living in several western states, "But after a while, you miss this wilderness. You think, 'Y'know, Alaska isn't such a bad place to raise a family.'" Now Brenda and her husband, John, are raising five kids, aged eight to eighteen. She's still a fisherman (as most commercial fisherwomen prefer being called) and is again spending more time fishing as her kids grow.

To the end of vision now, it's water, trees, sky. Slopes ascend into clouds, and clouds come cascading downslope as near-vertical streams.

We beach the boat near the mouth of Anan Creek and step into rainforest thick with undergrowth, swollen with ripe salmonberries and huckleberries, cushioned with mosses hanging from every branch and padding the forest floor. The chittering of circling eagles fills the air, dominating even the proclamations of gulls and croaking ravens.

The forest is as darkly near to enchanted as anything the imagination might conjure. That means a wild, dangerous place for those dwelling within—and perhaps more dangerous for those just visiting.

Brenda loads her rifle and we begin walking along a shoreside path.

The trail is stamped with bear tracks. "Let's keep talking," Brenda says, "to let the bears know we're coming. You don't want to surprise one." She's telling me stories of bears confronting people here, coming forward with ears laid down, and jaws snapping menacingly enough to generate warning shots near their feet. But no ugly contact—yet.

Brenda's committed to keeping it that way. "If a bear appears on the trail, *do not run*. They're like puppies; they'll chase you. Just stand facing them; they'll have to think about what to do next. Then it will be very important that you follow my instructions."

More than usually alert, I'm noticing that the place is *wet*. You couldn't sit without soaking your butt. To make a temperate rainforest you need: an ocean generating clouds and warmed sea air hitting cool air along mountains—thus felling the clouds as rain. Depending on where and how these uneven mountains tickle the clouds, parts of Southeast Alaska average over two hundred inches of rain a year.

The air is so sodden, it seems the humidity merges land and ocean. So where's the line dividing sea from land? Is it the high-tide line, the paths of salmon, the reach of ocean mists, the flight lines of fish-nourished eagles?

Deep, dark water is flowing through a thirty-foot-wide channel. Swift current. Any salmon entering Anan Creek must pass here, then enter a wide estuary whose sandbars are lined with Bald Eagles—dozens of white-headed adults and big, mottled juveniles. All here for the fish.

Farther up, those braided channels converge into one main knee-deep watercourse. Here the stream bottom appears to be made of black stones—but I suddenly realize: they're fish. Only right along the shore do they part enough to show light sand between them. I've seen a lot of fish, but this stream is, in places, packed with salmon—*stacked* with them. Pink Salmon, about five pounds each—thousands upon thousands.

We walk uphill beside a series of pools and riffles. At the lowest riffle, a Brown Bear is pulling a salmon between the clutch of its claws and the clench of its teeth.

Suddenly the vegetation explodes just ahead as a Black Bear bursts across the trail, loping toward the creek—and flooding me with adrenaline.

Anan, on the mainland, is one of the few places where Black Bears mix with Brown Bears. Black Bears justifiably fear the much larger Browns. On the islands of Southeast Alaska it's usually either Blacks or Browns (elsewhere called Grizzlies), not both. Although about seventeen thousand Black Bears and six to eight thousand Brown Bears roam "Southeast," Blacks (and wolves) are absent from Admiralty, Baranof, and Chichagof Islands, where Browns reign.

A few minutes farther upstream, two steep bouldery banks pinch the flow. The constriction blasts a frothing torrent over a series of low falls that impede the fishes' progress. To get through, a fish must wage prolonged propulsion. Water gushes the whole way. Any fish that manages to surmount the falls must keep its motor revved through a run of intense white rapids stretching about thirty yards. Above that, finally, is a calm pool that signifies success. But I see just one or two fish moving across that pool's light bottom. The majority find the falls a serious inhibitor.

Fish leap and fall back, leap and fall back, against the roaring blast of opposing water. Many get washed right back to the starting gate. Just below, salmon are traffic-jammed shoulder to shoulder. Salmon so densely throng the riffles below the falls that there seem to be more fish than water; they're slithering over one another's backs.

Pretty soon, two Black Bears emerge from between big boulders lining the opposite bank. Two others come from the woods behind us. Brenda and I watch from the tenuous safety of a low platform built specifically for viewing the bottleneck. In addition to these four Blacks, the large Brown Bear just downstream is stripping another salmon.

That seems like a lot of bears, until the Black Bears increase to seven adults. Two have jet-black cubs. One has cinnamon twins. A fourth has a single youngster. The mothers with cubs act uncomfortable around other, potentially dangerous bears; they tend to take a fish and disappear into the privacy of the forest primeval, their little ones following.

Bears come and go repeatedly from the shadows. Others keep squeez-ing through spaces in the jumbled boulders like muskrats in a stream bank. I lose track of who I've seen and who is new. Between their padded paws and the padded ground and the sound of falling water, we never hear them coming. At one point I am startled by a bear walking right past me.

There must once have been a great many places like this, wherever creeks swelled with salmon, down to California. Black Bears live all the way across the continent, and must have once crowded even East Coast tributaries where sturgeon, American Shad, Alewives, Striped Bass, Blue-back Herring, Rainbow Smelt, and Atlantic Salmon spawned in hordes. I try to imagine bears crowding pinched tributaries of the Hudson River in the spring of 1491. But what memory has recorded that; where in the rocks is it written?

Meanwhile, so many fish fill this stream that the bears hardly need to "catch" them. When a bear steps into the water, it has salmon swim-ming around its legs, under its belly. Bears just dunk their heads and clamp their jaws around a wagging fish. Bears too full to eat pluck

salmon from the throng, take a bite or two, and then release their grip. The urgent hunger is gone.

Bears and eagles benefit from many a salmon stopped short of the promised land. The salmon would seem to have a different agenda. But though the present interests of bears and eagles require that some salmon don't complete their task, the bears' and eagles' future, too, depends on enough salmon getting past them.

These bears are—for the moment—spoiled. These wealthy bears, in the fattest bear country of all, can afford to be wasteful, self-indulgent, and picky. Laughing all the way to the stream bank, they often drop a fish on the ground and press on it to see if eggs appear. If the salmon is a male or an unripe female (about three-quarters of what they catch), they simply leave it. If the fish is a ripe female, the bear usually eats just its fat-rich, energy-dense eggs. They boost their profits by giving themselves only the best, discarding the rest. Poor bears from inland areas would greedily eat any salmon they could find—if they could find any. Even among bears, the rich get richer and the poor take what they can.

These returning salmon originally hatched in this forest stream. The forests are, in a sense, the salmon source. Streams drawing from the mossy forest "sponge" flow more evenly, more dependably. Shade helps stabilize and cool stream temperatures. Fallen logs form eddies that break the current, giving rest and shelter to young fish and—when channels flow hard with swelling floods—protecting them from prematurely getting swept out to sea. Forests also produce insects that help feed young salmon.

The ocean clouds deliver rain. Everything then flows downhill. After all, gravity isn't just a good idea; it's the law. Nutrients in the form of fallen leaves and falling bugs, for instance, get into rivers and wash toward the sea. So salmon are here, in part, because of the trees.

Now, what if I told you that the trees are here, in part, because of salmon? That the trees that shelter and feed the fish are themselves built *by* fish? That's the biggest secret about the size of these forests.

Ocean nutrients traveling *uphill*? Against gravity and into the forest? It's never happened. At least, not in a way people really noticed. For a long while, no one thought to ask, "Hey, what about all these salmon?"

Defying gravity and all good sense, salmon flow uphill. From the heart of the ocean, salmon beat upstream and inland like flowing blood, until, lodged in a thin film of water in a tiny tributary, each is a corpuscle in a capillary. This upstream influx, this *invasion,* creates extraordinary effects. Salmon are energy. They are matériel. Follow that thought uphill: the trees are made largely of salmon.

Again a bear drops a fish, then turns back to the stream and nabs another. In this version of catch-and-release, the fish dies; what's released includes all the things the fish was: protein and fat and nitrogen and phosphorus and more. These forests are where the ocean comes to die— and be reborn as trees.

A fish grows by absorbing and superconcentrating the ocean. Salmon are the ocean incarnate. The salmon run becomes one long self-propelled infusion of ocean nutrients. Even before they hit freshwater, they have plenty of chances for reincarnation: feeding seabirds, seals, sea lions, porpoises, and Killer Whales. By the time they begin ascending streams, there is no turning back. They've ceased being mere fish and turned themselves into delivery packages of ultraconcentrated nourishment.

Bears, eagles, and other middlemen take hefty cuts before passing the goods along. Bears or no, these salmon will still die after spawning. Their carcasses will still draw gulls, crows, jays, and ravens. They'll still put smiles on the snouts of mink and martens and the four dozen birds and mammals—even mice, even deer—that nibble salmon.

But without bears, most salmon carcasses would just wash downstream. In some streams, bears move more than half of the salmon mass into the nearby forest. A bear might carry forty salmon from a stream in a day's work, leaving a couple hundred pounds of ocean flesh on the forest floor. Insects, slugs, and other invertebrates move in and lay eggs. Next, the ocean will transmogrify into insect-eating birds.

Plenty of forests stand where no salmon live or perish. But it's no coincidence that the world's densest salmon runs and the world's lushest rainforests go together. Bears bring so many salmon into forests that nitrogen and phosphorus concentrations near some Alaskan streams exceed recommended applications for commercial fertilizer. Up to 70 percent of the nitrogen in the leaves of nearby shrubs and trees is of ocean origin, brought by salmon, delivered by bears, drawn into the roots of plants. Sitka Spruce grow up to three times faster along streams that raise salmon compared to streams without salmon.

Salmon forests, it turns out, grow more wood—more living weight per acre—than any forests in the world. More than the Amazon; more than anywhere. Not tropical rainforests—*salmon* forests.

So why does this region harbor eighty bears for every *one* in interior areas far from salmon streams? Why do bears feeding on abundant salmon often have three cubs? Why is the Bald Eagle more abundant here than anywhere else in its cross-continental range? Why do these forests grow such massive trees? Now you know the answer: they are all salmon in disguise.

That's nice, but for all this to keep working, many of these salmon must attain the spawning reaches. For that, the fish must still vanquish the falls.

In late afternoon, something injects new motivation into the salmon. The whitewater thickens with leaping fish as many more assault the falling water.

Many find themselves in a sheet of foam falling over a big, slick-faced boulder. They skitter skyward against the pressure hose. Those gaining the first step face either a nearly impassable overhanging waterfall or a run over a boulder up a short, steep, blasting channel. They must choose quickly. Many get washed back into the roiling eddies. There, salmon are appearing and vanishing like dark rice grains in a rolling boil.

That a fish might conquer this ferocious challenge seems almost beyond reasonable striving. But nothing compels salmon to be reasonable.

I see a couple of fish get through. And now several are gliding gracefully over the light sand of the broad shallows above, their goal—spawning—nearly assured.

In the 1940s, fishery managers wanted bear populations across Alaska "culled." Why? Because salmon-eating bears inflict "economic damage" that could push Alaska into "financial and social collapse." But as we're seeing right in front of our eyes, salmon increase bear densities, and bears make forests more productive by planting them with salmon. Productive forests create salmon-friendly stream habitat and hatch insects that fall into streams, prompting young salmons' robust growth, boosting salmon survival—helping maintain strong salmon populations.

The fear had been that the number of bears limits the number of salmon. Turns out, the reverse is true; there are so many bears *because* there are so many salmon. And there are so many salmon, in part, because there are so many bears helping turn salmon into trees.

Just a few yards away, an adolescent bear ascends a hemlock, simply to rest. A little raccoon-sized cub of another bear decides to follow. When the adolescent swipes at it, the cub moves out onto a branch. From there, it can't get down. This isn't trivial; cubs can get killed when they find themselves alone with grouchy strangers.

Now we have a situation. The cub begins bawling. Mother comes running from the creek and bounds up the tree with astonishing speed. Now the edgy adolescent, seriously threatened, begins snapping its jaws, stomping the thick branch, then urinating and defecating on the angry mama below.

Complicating matters, Mama's second cub has climbed a nearby tree, gotten stuck *there,* and is also bawling. This sends the distraught mother running from tree to tree, with Brenda and me almost directly in the middle.

Mama calls the second cub down, and they *both* climb the tree containing the first cub and the adolescent stranger. Now four bears are in the same tree, twenty to thirty feet up. The mother wants the other bear away from her cubs. The other bear is highly conflicted. It wants to come down and flee, yet the angry mama continues trying to press the stranger higher. The more Mama presses, the more defensive the adolescent gets.

This standoff continues for half an hour, until the mother—with much snarling and jaw snapping and many lightning-fast bluffs that prove intimidating to the stranger (and to me)—forces the stranger higher. When she feels like she's achieved enough space, she turns her attention to getting her cubs down. Then she, too, climbs down, and the threat is defused.

When everything is back to normal—normal for here meaning the woods are crawling with bears and the creek swarming with fish and the sky infested with eagles—Brenda and I, too, feel it's safe (enough) to head back down the trail.

I tell Brenda how much I loved every moment of our adventure, and thank her for the privilege. Brenda is pleased, but she says, "More and more, I see people who say they like nature but, truly, it's not really that important to them. I call it the Discovery Channel mentality. And *I'm* seeing the people who actually want to come and see things like this. People today are so accustomed to manipulating every detail of their personal environment with the press of a button, they're very, *very* uncomfortable with a reality in which they aren't in charge. They don't like that humbling feeling you get in a place like this, where we're not in control. People are always asking me questions like 'What is the bear going to do?' and I'm like"—she shrugs—"'Whatever it wants.'"

⁓

Alaska's panhandle remains a place for people seeking to lose or find themselves. It's a place of transients, transplants, and deeply rooted native— Tlingit, Haida, and Tsimshian—peoples. Of ancient and varied origins, the islands of Southeast Alaska lie along the edge of the continent like geologic driftwood. Within the region—500 miles long and 120 miles wide (800 by 190 kilometers)—a thousand-plus islands create 18,000 miles of coastline. In the lower states, the longest stretch of undeveloped coast is about 30 miles.

I'm here to see a tinkered-with place that has saved all its parts, and to try to understand why it's still working. What will surprise me is that it's not so much virgin and pristine—though there's a lot of that, too—as recovered and recovering. It's a place where people have had the luxury of learning from their mistakes. And there's a reason for that, too.

Wade Loofbourrow guides the forty-two-foot *Legend* past Juneau's enormous cruise ships and holds southward. We've got Taku Glacier shining in pellucid summer light and, on our right, Admiralty Island, a vast stucco of epic peaks and snows.

Wade is a slender man in his sixties, with a steady hand on the wheel and a ready humor. He knows what he's doing but doesn't care who notices. He tells me he grew up all over western Oregon, adding, "And California, which I mostly detested." Why? "A big percentage of the land there is privately owned." Here, more than 90 percent is federal public land, including the Tongass National Forest (77 percent), Glacier Bay National Park (13 percent), Alaska Chilkat Bald Eagle Preserve, and other national assets.

After college, Wade fished. Abalone, Albacore, crab, drag boats, halibut, lobsters, rockfish, salmon, Swordfish. "On a good day you'd catch maybe three Swordfish, but they *averaged* well over three hundred pounds—back then. That was before the long-liners started catching all those babies." When his wife got offered a dental hygienist job in Juneau, they came for a look. "We went home to Oregon, packed up; that was that." All that was decades ago.

There were fewer people then. But there aren't many now, either. In this 34,000-square-mile region live about 75,000 people, half of them in Juneau; most others live in towns like Wrangell and Petersburg. The rest of the place lies lightly trod. "Most of our wild fish and other animal populations are reasonably healthy," Wade says brightly. "That's why I live here."

For ever-changing miles we move within one great panorama: pinnacles of rock, snow, and ice; a slow promenade of water, mountain, and sky. We're traveling inside something vast that shimmers.

In 1879, John Muir was perhaps the first person to venture here seeking to enrich only his spirit. "Never before this had I been embosomed in scenery so hopelessly beyond description," he wrote. "In these coast landscapes there is such indefinite, on-leading expansiveness, such a multitude of features without apparent redundance . . . that all penwork seems hopelessly unavailing."

Ocean swell doesn't penetrate these broad passages. The surface calms to a mirror dotted by raindrops. The green water is dark with dense pastures of single-celled planktonic plants thriving in nutrients washed off the land. In these straits, the land-sea embrace lingers before losing itself to the dilution of the open ocean.

Above forested slopes, ragged peaks of rock and ice rear forbiddingly into and out of clouds. Muir wrote wryly, "The marvelous wealth of forests, islands, and waterfalls, the cloud-wreathed heights, the many avalanche slopes and slips, the pearl-gray tones of the sky, the browns of the woods, their purple flower edges and mist fringes, the endless combinations of water and land and ever-shifting clouds—none of these greatly interest the tourists." He added, "Most people who travel look only at what they are directed to look at."

Wade points out the peaks and islands. I've got the map open and my binoculars out. The place feels new. These vast Sitka Spruce and Western Hemlock forests rooted only about seven thousand years ago, as ice sheets retreated. Muir wrote, "The mountains, wrapped in their snow and ice and clouds, seem never before to have been even looked at."

The forested slopes tune my mind to a more peaceful frequency. I am "rejoicing in the possession of so blessed a day," as Muir was moved to put it.

There still seems here *room enough* not just for people, but for human beings. We see them in their crab boats, or trolling for salmon, or just poking around, like us. It's not that the place is unpopulated. It's that it's multiply populated, by humans *and* by plants and animals that can take care of humans—and that can take care of themselves. Here, the web seems resilent, strong enough to regain a sense of future.

True, this region has issues. But the fact is, the place still works. It makes its own case for itself. You don't come here, look around, and ask, "How can this continue?" You just feel that it can.

But it wasn't always thus. The story of Alaska is the tale repeated wherever European faces appeared: calamity to natives, fevers over furs, insanity over gold, oil rush, depletion, conflict, and all the wretched rest. By the mid-1800s, hunting and trapping had so deeply depleted the fur-bearing wildlife that Alaska turned into a burden for Russia. The United States had been steadily taking land in its westward march, and it seemed only a matter of time before this country, in the name of Moneyfest Destiny, would take Alaska. So, for about $7 million, Russia washed its hands of the place. At the time, it wasn't universally viewed as a bargain. The deal was denounced as "folly" and a waste of public funds.

Alaska's land and wildlife management remain among the most successful in the world—if success is measured by saving all the working parts. Much of Alaska's wildlife is in better shape now than it was a century or two ago.

≈

Days later. Late afternoon. Heading north along Chichagof Island, our mood held effortlessly aloft by the continual spectacle of Admiralty Island's snowy peaks across Chatham Strait.

Off a big rocky point, the tide is turning slow pinwheels, with eddies collecting mats of giant rockweed called "popweed." Two scarlet-billed Black Oystercatchers and two Wandering Tattlers comb the nearby rocks. The tattlers deserve special mention. They will fly nonstop across much of the Pacific Ocean, to winter on tropic isles. How they even *find* those tiny specks in the ocean is astonishing.

Seeing a few salmon jumping in the rips, we slow to send them a message: "Please eat this herring." We mail our weighted lines to forty feet. We need a fish to save us from our frozen food. Trolling so slowly we're barely stemming the current, we slide along the tide, dreaming the boat toward the occasional leaping salmon. The salmon inflict an hour's humiliation as fish squirt from the sea.

Finally a rod comes alive, and soon I have the net around a gleaming Coho. Often called "Silvers," their jade, turquoise, and silver blend subtly, lightening beautifully from dark back to pearlescent belly.

Even for salmon, Coho show unusual determination in getting to spawning sites, fighting currents, and leaping falls that stop most others. Consequently, they spawn in twenty-four hundred locations in Southeast. Young Coho first taste saltwater several years after hatching, then stay at sea for about two years.

It is one thing to learn that some salmon are called Coho, some Pink, and others Sockeye, Chum, Chinook, or Steelhead. To further complicate matters, most have two English names: Pink are also called Humpback, Coho are Silver, Sockeye are Red, Chum can be called Dog, and Chinook are King. Steelhead, which are seagoing coastal Rainbow Trout, were once categorized in the same genus as Atlantic Salmon and are now lumped in the Pacific salmon genus.

They defy easy categorization because they're really all wet colors on evolution's palette. The tree of life's salmon branch splinters to a spray of hundreds of races and forms, adapted to specific rivers and specific times. Because streams vary widely in flow, length, grade, and the height of falls that must be overcome, salmon vary. Some rivers host different races of the same species in different seasons—"the spring run," "the winter run"—each tuned and timed to certain stream flow, temperature, distance to nesting reaches, and nesting conditions. Some races take months to reach their nesting areas. The young of some spend years in freshwater before going to sea.

The potential to know salmon is as infinite as the mysteries they inhabit. Some salmon range from the middle of the Pacific to the Continental Divide, finding their way across trackless ocean to the mouths of their birth streams, then accomplishing upstream spawning migrations of over a thousand miles *after* they hit freshwater—and they've stopped eating.

Depending on who they are, they may stay at sea from under one year (Pink) to seven years or so (Chinook). Those Pinks we saw at Anan Creek have the simplest life cycle. Soon after arriving in freshwater, they spawn in the lower reaches of streams. The young go to sea quickly after hatching. They're the most abundant salmon in Southeast. Chinook salmon spawn in the most challenging rivers—long or steep—and so live the longest and grow the largest. In Southeast, almost all Chinooks spawn in the big mainland rivers, the Alsek, Taku, and Stikine. They're called Kings because they sometimes attain sizes of over one hundred pounds. Pinks—like the ones at Anan—reach barely a twentieth of that.

This Coho I'm burying in ice is, I'd say, ten pounds. When you cut these fish into steaks, your hands could hardly be greasier if you'd rubbed them in butter. That fat is the fishes' rocket fuel, enough to propel their whole upstream run. That rich flesh is why, before Europeans arrived, the Pacific Northwest was the most heavily settled part of the Western Hemisphere.

Here, the situation with salmon is better than it's been.

In 1899, Jefferson Moser of the U.S. Fish Commission wrote that the Indians created rock corrals to concentrate fish for easier catching, but added, "The Indians appreciated the necessity of allowing the fish to ascend the streams to spawn, and therefore after obtaining their winter supply they opened the barricades."

In the late 1800s, new canneries deployed nets a mile long and erected permanent barricades that took every fish attempting to enter a stream. For them, there was no concept of "enough." Getting more was always better—until they got nothing. Same old story, from Lazy Point's little bunker factories to Alaska's big old salmon canneries; you see it everywhere. Because salmon return to the stream of their birth, barricades destroyed streams' entire lineages, leaving them fishless for many years to come.

Moser again, after speaking with Tlingit and Haida chiefs: "They cannot understand how those of a higher civilization should be less honorable—as they regard it—than their own savage kind. They claim that . . . their streams must soon become exhausted . . . and that starvation must follow."

In 1884 Congress issued a mandate stating that "Indians . . . shall not be disturbed in the possession of any lands actually in their use or occupation or now claimed by them."

Everyone ignored it.

Between 1906 and 1923, Congress attempted forty-two pieces of legislation to regulate the canneries. Cannery owners opposed each one; not a single bill passed. Tlingit and Haida ownership of salmon streams fell apart.

By 1924, sixty-five canneries were operating 351 immense salmon traps. That year, Congress finally passed a law requiring that half the salmon be allowed to spawn.

Everyone ignored it.

In 1947, canneries shipped a record 4.3 million *cases*. Afterward, output plummeted so drastically that in 1957, President Eisenhower declared Alaska's salmon a federal disaster.

In '59, Alaska gained statehood and banned the traps. Salmon began recovering. But by 1970, fishermen's numbers had doubled. And foreign boats were fishing just twelve miles offshore.

Salmon numbers plummeted again, sending shock waves. In 1972 the state created fishing permits and made them available only to individuals—not corporations. A series of measures pushed foreign boats out beyond two hundred miles (1976), ended high-seas drift-netting (1991), and dramatically cut foreign fishing on ocean-ranging salmon.

Salmon populations increased. From the 1970s to the 1990s, Southeast Alaska's catches grew from 25 million to over 180 million salmon, but fishing was closely regulated to make sure enough fish ascended the rivers. The increase was abetted by hatcheries managed to *enhance* wild runs, using mainly local fish as hatchery brood stock.

Contrast: In the Lower 48, salmon hatcheries had been established to *substitute* for wild runs—mainly to placate salmon fishermen while logging and damming ruined salmon habitat. The slogan "Salmon without rivers" encapsulated the delusion. Most hatcheries in the Lower 48 produce fish using brood stock from distant rivers. Ill-adapted for local conditions and pumped out in densities exceeding the stream's food supply, they compete with, and eventually eliminate, native salmon—then seldom sustain themselves. Now Washington, Oregon, and California have essentially no wild rivers—and essentially no salmon.

Alaska has done much better. Result: Alaskan boats catch 80 percent of the salmon taken by fisheries on the entire west coast of North America.

Alaska may be the world's best example of managing valuable wildlife to the benefit of regional jobs and prosperity. It stands as the world's last great producer of wild salmon. In recent years, annual catches by Alaska's commercial fishermen have averaged about 3 million Coho. Recreational fishers remove another 300,000. But the fish's numbers seem stable. That's because there's so much remaining natural habitat: five thousand streams in Southeast Alaska support salmon.

And *that's* because there are people—but not too many people. There are few enough people that they can make a reasonable living with reasonable regulations. The natural resources can go around without going down. And so you get good habitat, high numbers of animals, people working and earning livings—*resilience*.

Thoreau's dictum resonates again: "In wildness is the preservation of the world." Abundance begets abundance. And we don't even need to "protect" it—just to avoid wrecking it.

But south of Alaska, wrecking is more the rule. Dams have broken

the backs of once-supple rivers. Reckless logging has sent the great coni-
fer forests through the shredder, turning salmon streams to mud.

The widening salmon collapse is frosting Southeast Alaska's windows
with its breath. Just across the Canadian border, the *Yukon News* reports
that the Stikine River's King Salmon fell by half in the last few years; the
Sockeye run fell by half in a year. Most of the Stikine flows through British
Columbia, but its mouth opens in Southeast Alaska. Other west Canadian runs are reportedly down 80 percent in the last decade. Newspapers
bewail plummeting salmon runs in the mighty Fraser River. Canada's
west coast salmon farms—established mostly since 1990 to raise *Atlantic
Salmon*—produce parasitic sea lice that kill hordes of young wild salmon.
(Alaska strictly outlaws salmon farms.) Bears are going hungry on some
Canadian rivers. Salmon-eating Killer Whales are abandoning coastal
regions. After eagle numbers around Vancouver dropped by half in a year,
volunteers discovered hundreds of eagles at a garbage dump, scavenging
for anything edible.

Because streams deprived of the nutrients that had been brought by
millions of salmon can no longer support as many juvenile fish, salmon
decline becomes a death spiral. So, with typical "after it's gone" inanity,
some government agencies are trying artificial fertilizer "briquettes" or
actually bringing in dead salmon by helicopter and truck. They hope to
mimic what salmon brought so naturally, for free. Good luck.

Southeast Alaska remains a special place. But the parts of the Pacific
Northwest that lie south of here once had bigger forests, bigger rivers,
and even more salmon. Anything that can be loved can be lost.

The situation with logging here, too, is better than it's been.

In 1900, naval officer George T. Emmons described Southeast Alaska
to Theodore Roosevelt as "one immense forest of conifers."

Once upon a planet, the largest-treed, densest forests in the world
stood from northern California through Southeast Alaska, and they, perhaps more than anything, delineated the "Pacific Northwest." The world's
other temperate rainforests can quickly be summarized: a tiny bit on the
Black Sea (long gone), a tiny amount in Ireland and Scotland (long gone),
tiny areas in Iceland (oddly enough, and long gone), a little in Norway
(remnants remain), and western Patagonia (smaller). Temperate rain-

forests on the west coast of New Zealand and in Tasmania are shrunken and riddled with invasive species. Chile has significant tracts left, though their flora and fauna are very different. And that's it. British Columbia has been sliced to ribbons, and south of the Canadian border, saws have felled 95 percent of the original forests. Southeast Alaska holds half of the original Pacific Northwest forest area, and about a third of the world's remaining temperate rainforest.

But as we travel north of Tenakee Inlet, the clouds pull their skirts up on jaw-dropping clear-cuts spread along Admiralty Island's west coast. And Chichagof Island's plush and solemn forests give way to broad swaths of gray stumps and dirt running for miles along northern Chatham Strait. "Absolutely stripped," Wade sneers. "You see shit like this, and, well—this is what the Natives do to lands they got."

Native lands, yes, but not really owned by Natives. This is *corporate* logging. After years of fighting over encroachment on Native land, the Native Claims Settlement Act of 1971 awarded Alaska's original peoples about 12 percent of Alaska. But it canceled Native land titles and created Native corporations instead. Meaning: Native individuals own not land but shares of corporate stock. Like all other corporations, Native corporations "must" maximize profit. Turning trees into corporate cash greatly increased Natives' monetary wealth but radically changed their relationships with family, community, land, and wildlife. Native corporations own less than 5 percent of the land in Southeast, but they're responsible for half of the clear-cutting here.

The other half? After World War II, the U.S. Congress wanted to keep a rebuilding Japan away from the Soviet Union and lure it to Alaskan wood. So it guaranteed an immense quantity of timber to two pulp mills (one Japanese-owned), which monopolized the region's logging from the 1950s until the late 1990s. Massive taxpayer subsidies let them cut a centuries-old tree from public land for the price of a cheeseburger. Many trees were pulped to make cellophane, rayon, and throw-away diapers. "Right over there in Hoonah," says Wade, pointing, "for years and years there was always a Japanese ship loading whole logs, craneload after craneload after craneload. That's where this whole forest went."

Alarmed communities who didn't want their forests and salmon streams turned to mud finally banded together with conservation groups and went after the subsidies. They campaigned for years. In 1990, the Tongass Timber Reform Act killed the guaranteed timber cut and subsidy. It saved a million acres of prime forest and world-class fish streams (including Anan Creek, which was scheduled for clear-cutting); plus, it saved the bears, eagles, deer, hunting, fishing, *rational* logging, and everything else that comes with them.

Most of these clear-cuts we're looking at are ten to twenty years old, but the short summers here slow regrowth. John Muir counted the rings in a hemlock here that was only twenty inches in diameter—and 540 years old. Only 5 percent of the region has been clear-cut—but because of ice, rock, and quirks of drainage, only 4 percent of the Tongass is capable of supporting truly giant trees. Loggers cut: The biggest. The oldest. Those stands that were most important to wildlife.

The government still spends about $30 million annually auctioning federal timber to private loggers. Bids bring in about $750,000—a $29,250,000 loss to taxpayers. "Dividing that by 200 Tongass timber jobs," writes author Douglas H. Chadwick, "the government could pay each logger and mill worker $146,250 a year to stay home and let the rainforest be."

But hear this: the major clear-cutting is past. A *lot* of forest remains. At least for now. The corporations and the massive taxpayer-funded, congressionally pumped, market-distorting corporate subsidies have, like a threatening fever, largely run their course. Weakened by their own overreaching, they've given way to more rational practices. This region, seemingly so wild, has actually been *recovering* from massive logging and overfishing. I hope it can stay on track.

The region remains very much in transition toward "whatever will come next." And what's coming, mainly—is tourism. Nowadays, the 200 people employed by the region's thirteen sawmills make up less than 1 percent of Southeast's total employment. Meanwhile, gigantic cruise ships, each employing 1,000 workers, bring people who want to see forested slopes. In Ketchikan alone, population 8,000, cruise ships dislodge 800,000 passengers whose shopping sprees generate $120 million.

When I ask Wade where he sees the future headed, he says, "Juneau has transitioned to tourism. Wrangell has transitioned to fishing and tourism. Ketchikan is still carrying a grudge."

Some people don't want one more log taken out. But there's room for small operators. Some former clear-cuts have dense second growth, where thinning would benefit wildlife. These communities helped protect these forests. Now environmentalists should ask them, "What are your dreams for the future?"

~

Point Adolphus brings a sea change and a change of air. The mouth of Glacier Bay exhales chilly breath, wrapping the shores in a misty taffeta gown. Cloud-piercing peaks gleam in shafts of light. It's a dynamic, many-paneled sky, by turns somber and spectacular. Heavily timbered shores rise so steep they practically leap skyward. The place feels new again.

Icy Strait is mainly about absorbing injected energy from the nearby ocean. The chart warns that tidal currents "may attain velocities of 8 or 10 knots." Absolutely true; a manic tide is pushing roiling rivers of ocean water through the strait. Ocean-powered currents create lush plankton pastures, turning the water jade. Tiny zooplankton graze the single-celled, drifting grass. Swarms of small fishes reap the grazers. Whales, sea lions, and birds exploit the fish swarms. And we take it all in.

The main hot spot—well marked by seabirds—is a seafloor hill of gravelly rubble plowed into place when the glaciers of Glacier Bay extended this far. That hill is about half a mile wide and, underwater, runs out a couple of miles from shore.

With the tide forcing deep water over the drowned moraine, surface currents churn as if they're boiling. The squeeze concentrates everything, thickening the broth. If you think like a hungry fish, your thoughts take you to this soup kitchen.

Herring dimple the surface like raindrops. Even by Alaskan standards, this area seems supercharged with life. Flying birds crowd the air: Kittiwakes, Bonaparte's Gulls, yellow-legged Mew Gulls, scarlet-legged Pigeon Guillemots. Diving birds called Marbled Murrelets chase fishes by "flying" underwater. To get airborne, they leap up, then bounce off the water while whirring their wings. In California, Oregon, and Washington, where 95 percent of the original nesting forests were cut down, Marbled Murrelets declined 80 percent in twenty years. Their population from California through Washington dropped to around 18,000 adults. Their population in Southeast Alaska: 680,000. That's why they're everywhere I look.

Small, swimming shorebirds called Red-necked Phalaropes positively pepper the surface. When two predatory jaegers buzz in, the phalaropes rise in snaking lines that merge into smokelike clouds. I estimate—it's hard to see the end of the flocks—perhaps ten thousand phalaropes. Flocks I've seen elsewhere had about a dozen birds. The world's largest sea lions—Steller Sea Lions, elsewhere in trouble—proliferate here. Their jaws dwarf a Brown Bear's. One surfaces with a salmon, and a quick, skillful flip makes the fish vanish whole.

And soon we sight so many whales—Humpbacks—so close to shore that the sound of their breathing mingles with the chittering from eagles watching from towering trees. The whales' misty exhalations drift like little clouds against the forested slopes. In groups of six or eight, the herring-hounding whales plow through tide rips and along shoreline drop-offs. Gulls seeking injured fish fly around the whales and through their steamy spouts, dipping occasionally for a prize.

Fluke, fluke, fluke, fluke. Gliding shoulder to shoulder, the whales roll into their next dive and throw their tails skyward, the weight of their immense tailstocks driving them like pilings into the sea. For a few minutes, they vanish. John Muir: "Think of the hearts of these whales, beating warm against the sea, day and night, through dark and light, on and on for centuries; how the red blood must rush and gurgle in and out, bucketfuls, barrelfuls at a beat."

Blow, blow, blow, blow. Abruptly surfacing whales shoot dense jets of breath, roaring their steamy exhalations loud enough to echo from the rocks and higher silences. Strangely, one trumpets almost elephantlike whenever it blows.

For two hours we watch one dense herd of about fifteen Humpbacks surfacing in unison and plunging to hunt the unfathomable tons of small fish they need. The sonar screen shows flecking from 150 feet down to the bottom, at around 300. "Busted-up herring schools," Wade interprets. "This is a long time for feeding whales to stay pressed against one small stretch of shore. Those herring they've been working are probably shot to remnants."

Occasionally, a distant breaching whale detonates a great explosion, the sound taking as long as two seconds to report like muffled cannon fire. Wade's assessment: "Boy, this is some pile o' whales."

Whales aren't the only ones who have to eat. We drop a line with half a dozen shiny hooks—and in seconds several herring come over the rail. Wade moves us to a secret spot. We anchor on a hill just sixty feet deep and drop a couple of fresh-caught fish to the seafloor.

When we haven't had a bite in five minutes, Wade gets agitated. I'm thinking, "Wade, we're *fishing;* have patience."

Just five minutes later a fish comes knocking. Wade said this was a great spot for fish that are "the right size for dinner"—but he miscalculated. After a ten-minute struggle, we tie a seventy-pound halibut to our stern cleat.

In a world full of starving people, the herring themselves would have been sufficient blessing. Here, in a few minutes, we traded a quarter-pound herring for months' worth of beautiful fish meat. The thick fillets gleam with pearly translucence, delicious simply to look at. If you fig-ure, very conservatively, that only half the weight of the fish is muscle (and the rest is head, guts, bone, skin, fins), then we have 35 pounds of pure fillet—70 half-pound meals, 140 quarter-pound servings. Wade will be rich in fish all winter. Our biggest daily decision for the rest of the trip will be: Fresh salmon or fresh halibut, grilled, fried, or baked? Our halibut is the biggest Wade's ever seen from this spot. In most other places, the biggest fish were caught long ago. But like I said, this is a place that still works. Wade's assessment: "Boy, that's some heap o' meat."

❧

I'm spoiled. Smitten. It didn't take long to feel this place capturing my soul.

We anchor in a cozy, conifer-lined cove under a bowl of snow-draped peaks. I'm amazed to see so much snow in midsummer; but Wade's never seen so much bare rock up there. That's the value of having lived in a place: you have some idea of what's expected and what's unexpected.

From those peaks, streams pour down corrugated, nearly vertical slopes before plunging into dense forest. The icy fingers of meltwater serve a wide emerald marsh and a shallow, braided creek that runs to the tide-water.

The large island that our map calls "Admiralty" has a more apt Tlin-git name: Kootznoowoo—Fortress of the Bears. So when I get my first good scan of shore, this is what I see: A flock of crows picking through the tide-line rockweed, bent into their task like van Gogh's potato plant-ers. A Brown Bear lifts its head from the tall marsh grass. Suddenly, two. The second has cubs, so four. Another bear with two cubs strides into view along the forest border. So—seven Grizzlies.

This place bears Brown Bears at almost unimaginable densities: about one per square mile. The bears are so abundant because of beaches and mudflats full of shellfish, rivers that swell with salmon, and the gen-eral lushness the rain facilitates. Though the same species as Grizzlies, these Browns represent a distinct lineage believed to be descended from bears marooned between impenetrable ice sheets hundreds of thou-sands of years ago. Bigger than interior Grizzlies because of their salmon supplement and the longer foraging season, coastal Browns attain weights exceeding one thousand pounds.

I sleep with a headful of dancing bears.

Ursus arctos once ruled from the Mississippi to the Pacific and from Mexico to the Arctic tundra. They maintain their footing in parts of Russia and a tiny fraction of Europe and North America. (Though its visage stalks California's state flag, California's last Grizzly was shot in 1922.) Their final stronghold: Alaska. In Southeast they live largely on three big islands—Admiralty, Baranof, and Chichagof; the "ABC islands"—which harbor over four thousand bears.

Around the time of the last California Grizzly, the *Daily Alaska Empire* editorialized, "The brown bears ought to be exterminated—at once." Then John Holzworth's passionate 1930 book, *The Wild Grizzlies of Alaska,* sparked a national movement to protect Southeast Alaska's bears, and Admiralty's Browns appeared saved. But in 1968, loggers planned to cut down 95 percent of Admiralty's trees. Even at nine feet tall, the bears couldn't stand up for themselves. Litigation would decide whether the bear's fortress would fall. For a raging decade, lawsuits were lost, won, and appealed. In 1978, President Carter ended the debate by declaring Admiralty a national monument. Two years later, Congress designated most of Admiralty as the Kootznoowoo Wilderness. It took fifty years, but basically, the bears won. Whenever cooler heads prevail and something has been saved, time always confirms the value of salvation, and earns our thanks.

"Good morning; see any bears?" Wade's on deck with a face towel and his toothbrush.

Soon a dark Griz saunters onto the beach trailing *three* cubs past half a dozen loafing eagles. One cub, a runty little thing, endearingly pathetic, is likely doomed. More than half of Grizzly cubs die before their first birthday, and being the runt among siblings doesn't make for good odds.

One bear per square mile is Admiralty's *average* density. But at this time of the year, many bears move down to stalk salmon, making the lowland densities much higher. The bears have come but, unlike at Anan Creek, the salmon here are late, still sparse. That might mean hungry, edgy bruins.

This is a good, safe vantage. All of the most experienced people I've spoken to (and I'm talking about guides and biologists, people less afraid of bears than of traffic) have, at one time or another, felt the need to raise a loaded rifle at a threatening bear. We have no rifle. Nor could we have a better defense than the boat and binoculars.

But we decide—I cannot help feeling that this is foolish; I mean, there are a *lot* of bears with cubs—to go ashore.

A few days ago I declined to go ashore on a very pretty island when Wade mentioned that it was free of bears. No bears? What was the point? The on-edge feeling of being in bear country has become, well, I don't want to say "addictive." When I mentioned this later to a local, he *didn't* say something like "You're naïve; they're dangerous." He said, "Yeah, you want to know there are some bears around."

Well, yeah, that's what I want to know. And so—.

Into a light drizzle I'm carrying a heavy-duty can of pepper spray, my fly rod, and a lot of trepidation. Pepper spray isn't foolproof. (Nor are guns.) And because the canister costs about fifty bucks, we have no spares—so I've never practiced firing it.

All across the exposed tidal flats, I see little jets of water squirting; the flats are loaded with clams. At the mouth of the river, I notice small packs of newly arriving salmon—six to a few dozen fish in each—gliding in. This is a short stream, so these are Pinks. We walk past.

Griz tracks are everywhere in the sand. I soon notice that as a rose by any name smells sweet, this monumental island smells like bears. Their trail at the edge of the forest is well worn and wide. This is no vaguely visible "game trail." It's a bear *road*. Imagine a well-used horse-riding trail. That's how much bear shit.

The scat is full of blueberries, which grow luxuriantly to heights over our heads. There's a lot of close cover; a bear could appear from anywhere. Their trails network the whole forest. Brown Bears so thoroughly pervade the mists and shadows that the silence virtually hums with their presence. There's no need for Bigfoot. The Brown Bear is all the monster you could want.

I'm out of my element. Wade's the guy experienced in Brown Bear country. Sheepishly, I admit, "This seems a bit stupid." I await Wade's reassurance.

"Yeah," he says instead, "this is kinda on the ragged edge of that word."

I start calling, "Hey, bears! Hi-o."

Bears don't like surprises. But nothing guarantees that an alerted bear will choose to slink off. Some bears have pride. Others have cubs. Maybe a bear has just walked by but her cubs are fifty yards behind her when we show up between them.

"Hey, bears! Hi-o. Tasty white meat here." The thick wilderness silence quickly absorbs our calls. If anything can be simultaneously awe-inspiring and nerve-racking, this is.

Two planes and a helicopter suddenly overfly the creek, shattering the aura. Wade's radio informs us that they're searching for a floatplane missing since yesterday. A father and son—friends of Wade's. Fog soon suspends their search, and the sound of engines fades.

And when the aura of wilderness returns, it clamps down on me. This is no movie set. It's a big, primal place that can still swallow people whole, even people who come to penetrate with all the backup of modern civilization.

We walk in about a mile. Easy walk, mostly along the bank. But Wade is quiet now. I leave him to his thoughts and walk ahead, alone.

All along the shore, all since the last high tide: bear tracks. One set tells of a female with cubs, walking upstream this morning, just as I am. Her front prints dwarf my fist.

I look up frequently to call out my presence and scan around. The sedges in the estuary are tall enough to hide bears easily, but right now they're beaded with dew and bent into cowlicks. So my view—and the bears'—is pretty good here.

The main channel is only about fifty feet wide, with steep gravel sides and hairpin meanders. At a bend where a smaller creek enters the main stream, quite a few salmon are holding in the lazy current. An occasional fish leaps, probably just hyped on its own pent-up energy. If such fish harbor some deep inkling that the end is nigh, they don't show it. But what can they feel, and what can they know? You can get so close, sometimes, and still yearn for contact and a route in.

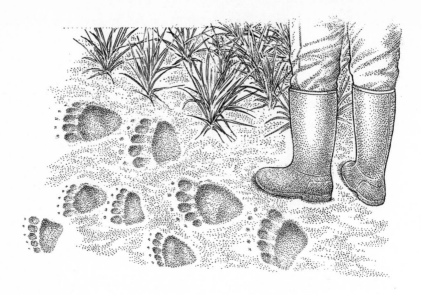

Lacking any superior way to plumb their inner depths, I resort some-what dumbly to the familiar. I strip some line and begin waving my fly rod in the air as I step into the water, then let the fly enter the flow. Certainly many fish see the drifting lure. Three casts. Five. I'm casting in front of, alongside, and amid dozens of fish. They entirely ignore my offerings. I cast again and again. I cast for over an hour; this is the most fish I never caught. Eating is not on their agenda. But if a salmon can point upstream without thinking much about it, so can a man cast.

I'm glancing around for bears when my hook snags something that pulses. A flank flashes. I put a bend in the rod and the fish shakes to rid itself of the prick. A male, it is changing into its courting costume, forming a conspicuous nuptial hump. It skitters upstream, splitting the current with the wedge of its enlarged back, its tail throwing water.

Seldom have I met a more determined fish. It knows, as nothing else, where it was meant to be. And it is determined—startlingly so—to stay right where it was. Its genes and biological clock have turned it into its own delivery package with a predetermined address. This late in its hegira, everything depends upon not wavering or being distracted. It has one right answer.

And so it acts toward the pressure from me as it acts toward the pressure from the stream: it opposes. Simply and completely. I certainly wasn't expecting that. Its main concern isn't the hook but staying in place, holding in the main channel. If I drop the pressure, it simply retakes its position, stemming the flow. If I reapply some pressure, I gain line only if the fish decides to turn around and charge briefly downstream, whereupon it again seeks the main flow.

I change tactics from trying to gingerly, almost surreptitiously lead the fish toward the bank (which clearly won't work) to applying significantly more persuasion. The fish resists, runs, thrashes, and leaps. The only way I figure I can finish the contest is to use my palm to brake the reel spool during one of its skittering arcs, when the fish's own momentum can propel it to the beach.

Whereupon I declare the fish the winner. It never gave up, never gave in, never stopped playing by its own rules. On its side, gasping now in inch-deep water, it shows me its black-dot pupil, its purpled cheek, and that swollen, sexual slope of shoulder. Its pea green, black-flecked back blends to rosy flanks, all under a fine crosshatch of dark-edged scales.

I pull the hook, and the fish shoots back through the looking glass.

I watch the current flowing and the many fish holding at the confluence. Perhaps they are waiting for the flooding tide to give them a shove up into the tributary. These fish are very much on the march, with miles to go before they spawn and then to death surrender. But right now, death is the very last thing on their minds.

Trouble with bears is often about mutual surprises. It's easy to get absorbed in something at the water's edge, especially when you've skidded down a steep gravel bank on a bear trail to watch fish. A friend of mine once hooked a salmon, got momentarily distracted, and when he refocused on the fish at the end of his line, it was in a bear's mouth. I keep telling myself that driving a car is more dangerous than standing here. But the danger of an unseen predator, in unfamiliar terrain—in *its* terrain—is more visceral and electric than knowing one risks a fender bender.

This region's combination of modernity and the primordial, facilitated by having enough room for people, seems ideal. We can't create this elsewhere, but we can value and retain it here. And we can take the lesson of it to any place where there's still contested space. Open space is never "unpopulated"; it's the room that people need, to keep the world and themselves intact.

Here among bear trails and pungent poop, I don't want trouble. Acknowledged, if I'd stayed on the boat, I'd be safer. For that matter, I'd be safer if I never left home. But we want to go places; we want to live. To live is to bear some risks—and to live here is to risk some bears.

Ravens croak and dong in the dark surround of forest, eagles whistle and chitter regal proclamations. The stream sings. An occasional salmon splashes. But the silence here is so big and enveloping and *resonant* that it casts a tone into the air, the way a silent room can have a tone. This place has a sky tone, a world tone, the music of the spheres.

I want to see another bear, but not just for a thrill. The animals don't seek thrills. They get more than their share, daily. When everything was real, thrills were cheap and attention was the price of living. Wild things pay *attention*. They try to avoid trouble, but they don't shirk life.

I try to avoid trouble, too. But the wild raises a level of alertness that feels alive inside me. It puts the bird back into my chest. What I really want, as always: a genuine moment, a shared glance, connection.

People came into a world like this, rich, natural, but not without danger. The prospects for real trouble here are low, but the prospects for feeling alive are guaranteed. Many people are shadowed most dangerously by beasts of their own imaginations. Being here is real. That's why this silence, coiled and charged, speaks volumes. Too often, we let fake things stalk us. Accept no substitutes for real experience, real friends, true love, and real bears. Either you set the bar high and keep striving or you create a danger greater than any Griz sneaking up on you: letting real life sneak away.

JULY

A false calm ensues. Lazy Point has some of its laziest days. The fishing slumps as we slide into sultry weather. Kenzie lies in patches of shade, her red tongue dangling. At the beaches, parents in folding chairs chat while keeping an eye on kids in the water.

But the birds always have their burners lit. The Ospreys' chicks, too big to brood, are sitting up in their great nests wearing speckled plumage. They're often dissatisfied with their parents' performance; I've frequently heard them calling for more food as I've walked past. But they don't know how good they've had it. It's been a good year for food and for chick survival, and it's looking like the salt-pond pair will fledge all three of their young. This morning the chicks are already full. And when Mom lands in the nest with another Bluefish, the already well-fed chicks accept her gentle beakful of sashimi almost diffidently.

Tern chicks are getting chunky and feathered out, and will soon start flying. I wish them a long life. And on a trip to the post office, I get confirmation that long life is possible. A letter informs me that just a week ago on the terns' main nesting ground, Great Gull Island, about ten miles north of Lazy Point, my old friend and colleague Helen Hays captured a tern I leg-tagged as a chick—get this—*twenty-five years ago*. And it's still a hardworking parent. When I search the Web for the U.S. Bird Banding Laboratory's longevity records, it turns out the listed record is twenty-five years. Quite a feat of survival. All those years living in every kind of weather, with no cover or shelter. All those long-distance migrations between here and South America. All those fish caught, all those mates, those broods raised—. This deepens the mystique of all the terns I see, and the secrets they carry of the vistas they've known.

Countervailing tides of life and time move in. The sun sets a little farther south each day, shortening the days even before summer seems to "peak." Likewise, even before mid-July, even while our local terns are still feeding their chicks, even as ocean temperatures continue warming, even before some of the warm-water fishes like Mahimahi and Yellowfin Tuna have arrived from the south for summer, the tide of migration has begun to turn.

Shorebirds that have bred in the Arctic are already southbound. Already perhaps a thousand (or two) miles south of where they raised their broods, they fly right past those local terns that are still carrying fish to chicks in nests. The Piping Plovers that have nested here lose their exclusivity, as Sanderlings back from high-latitude tundra resume a local presence, augmented by little bands of Semipalmated Sandpipers. On the bay and the Sound, dowitchers and tiny Least Sandpipers become briefly familiar, and a smattering of Spotted Sandpipers move through, easily recognized by that inexplicable body-bobbing gait. My globe-traveling companions the Ruddy Turnstones are filtering back from the far north, now, too. As I once resented back-to-school ads, I resent these early migrants for fast-forwarding my ever-accelerating sense of summer.

There is much more to it, of course. As always, they bring the exotic to the local. And there is the glorious energy of such tiny lives lived so large that to complete a year they require two continents.

The ringing, wilderness-evoking call of one or more Greater Yellowlegs is often the first thing that alerts me to those birds overhead as they sail past us on the way from central Canada to Central and South America. That call always strikes me as melancholy, as though it's somehow a remembrance of more crowded skies. Of the shorebirds I've mentioned seeing in little flocks and dribs and drabs here and there, early colonists of Nantucket—about eighty miles east of Lazy Point— described flocks so massive they appeared like smoke rising from horizon to horizon. It was said that the storm of wings drowned out the sound of surf.

A few people still alive remember fathers or grandfathers who shot shorebirds commercially for the markets of New York and Boston and other cities. They leveled flocks of almost unimaginable quantities, and no one has seen such numbers since. Of the Eskimo Curlew, once called "Cloud of Wonder" by Natives for their overwhelming abundance, as late as 1966 an old Inuk Native remembered, "They came suddenly, and fell upon us like heavy snow. . . . In my father's time they were so many on the tundra it was like clouds of mosquitoes." Shot relentlessly during migration, they were nearly gone by 1900. But they managed to hang on, and in 1963, on Barbados, one final confirmed Eskimo Curlew was shot. The Long-billed Curlew, now vanishingly rare, was once an abundant East Coast migrant that "decoyed readily . . . and the cries of a wounded bird would attract others which would circle until they too were killed." Wrote one sportsman in 1906, "The strong desire of shorebirds to succor any one of their kind which has been wounded is a fortunate thing indeed since it enables even a tyro hunter to kill as big a bag as he might wish." Hudsonian Curlews (Whimbrels) and Hudsonian Godwits were shot by the hundreds; individual hunters sometimes killed a thousand in a morning, often for sport. In the 1600s Samuel de Champlain described one spot along the St. Lawrence River having "such great numbers of plovers, curlews, snipes, woodcock and other kinds that there have been days when three or four sportsmen would kill more than three hundred dozen." He said, "I and a few others passed the time" hunting shorebirds, "of which more than twenty thousand were killed." An early trick: fire your harquebus at the ground next to the birds and the spraying sand and gravel could take out more of them than the shot itself. According to one Jesuit chronicler, one such well-placed shot could kill three hundred birds. (The skeptical, like me, perhaps simply can't envision flocks of such density. But numerous people writing after shotguns came into use repeatedly commented that even firing overhead could fell between fifty and one hundred birds at once.)

Before 1850 on Cape Cod, just a hundred miles or so from Lazy Point, migrating Red Knots, an observer wrote, "would collect in exceedingly large numbers, estimates of which were useless . . . as they rose up in clouds." On the mudflats at night, pairs of men, "one carrying a lighted lantern [to dazzle them], the other to seize the birds, bite their necks, and put them in a bag," killed them by the barrelfuls. "One hardly dares to estimate their numbers," another observer wrote of smaller sand-pipers, Piping Plovers and Sanderlings. Weighing just an ounce or two, "they were delicious eating." Dunlins came in flocks, according to Arthur Cleveland Bent, like "a large cloud of thick smoke . . . a very grand and interesting appearance. . . . As the showers of their companions fall, the whole [flock] often alight, till the sportsman is completely satiated with destruction." Of dowitchers, "Immense numbers were shot. . . . They have decreased very fast . . . and we now see them singly or in bunches not exceeding 10 or 12." Dr. Bent described yellowlegs as "absurdly tame" and so small that "many lives must be sacrificed to make a decent bag," but added, "gunning is not so much about . . . filling up the larder, but an excuse for getting out to enjoy the beauties of nature and the ways of its wild creatures." Wrote gentleman sportsman James A. Pringle, "I had no mercy on them and killed all I could, for a snipe once missed might never be seen again." (It apparently never occurred to him that a snipe once shot would never be seen again, either.) Between 1867 and 1887, he scrupulously recorded killing 69,087 Wilson's Snipe. In the 1920s Dr. Alexander Wetmore, visiting Argentina, described "migrant flocks, many of whose members offered sad evidence of inhospitable treatment . . . in the shape of broken or missing legs." Gunners shot them there, too. John James Audubon bore witness to migrating northbound Golden Plovers near New Orleans in 1821: "I several times saw a flock of a hundred or more reduced to a miserable remnant of five or six. . . . This sport was continued all day, and at sunset when I left . . . a man near where I was seated had killed 63 dozens. . . . And supposing each [gunner] to have shot only 20 dozens, 48,000 golden plovers would have fallen there that day." As late as the summer of 1863, Edward Forbush wrote, Eskimo Curlews and Golden Plovers descended on Nantucket "in such num-bers as to darken the sun," and were shot by the thousands. Here on Long Island in the 1860s, Robert Roosevelt described how thousands of Golden Plovers would "rise with a sounding roar, to which the united reports of our four barrels savagely respond."

When the flocks no longer came, some sportsmen said it had noth-ing to do with them; the birds had been scared away by the sounds of railroad engines. Arthur Cleveland Bent lamented the passing of abun-dance: "Those were glorious days we used to spend on Cape Cod . . . in the good old days when there were shorebirds to shoot, and we were allowed to shoot them. . . . It is a pity that the delightful days of bay-bird shooting . . . had to be restricted." Bent was at least honest about the "ruthless slaughter that has squandered our previous wealth of wild-life."

But why haven't they all returned in the century since they've been protected from shooting in the United States and Canada? Shooting continues throughout Central and South America, and for some birds, the beaches have people and dogs and it's hard for them to get the time to feed or a moment's rest. For others, farms have taken the marshes and plains where they nested or wintered.

Today, at Lazy Point, I hear a lot of noise from Willets and American Oystercatchers. Though our Willet was by 1900 "destined to disappear," it regained the East Coast in the mid-1900s and is now again common, including in the marshes right around here. The oystercatcher, "an easy mark to the spring gunners," is back, too, at least where the birds are not constantly disturbed by boaters and displaced by beach homes. Fortunately, there's room and respite for them here, on the sandy islands around Lazy Point.

The moon is two days past new, and the moon-aligned currents remain strong. Fish respond to tides and I respond to fish, so I budget my time to the tidal rhythm. Therefore: tonight is better for fishing than for working late.

With me is a friend I've known since I was ten years old. I have invited no one else. At forty-two, he's been struck by cancer, battling for his life. But tonight Matt just wants to catch his first "keeper" Striped Bass. The weather is good, the tide's right. Still, fishing is fishing; I'm not wholly in control.

Matt is a highly accomplished jazz musician. He was a true child prodigy. But like most jazz players in a non-jazz era, Matt's been compelled to take a lot of modestly paying commercial work. Now that his body is at war with itself, he hasn't worked in months. Struggling with the mortgage and the usual expenses of a family with a young child, he and his wife, who teaches kindergarten, are selling their house to raise cash for their debts. They'll be renting a smaller space. Next week his colleagues are planning to hold a benefit for him, twenty dollars at the door. Yet I'm pleased to see that he has sprung for a new rod and reel. As I pilot the boat out of the harbor, he fusses with and rearranges his lures like a kid, in high spirits. In fact, it's hard to imagine a happier person. He's right here, right now.

This is what's called quality time. But what does that slippery Q-word really mean? Like "love," "quality" seems a poorly charted term, too inexact for safe travel and precise landings. My boat's GPS can get me home in fog; language, however, still seems to sail in the Bronze Age, with a lookout in the crow's nest. A little linguistic miscalculation, and you're at dangerous risk of running aground on internal shoals or intimate harbors.

I look at the slouching red sun. It's three miles to the place I have in mind. The tide is already flowing hard, the way we need it to. Matt's got his mind set on a keeper of twenty-eight inches. I'm aiming to connect him with a much larger fish—a quality fish. But what is quality?

The GPS shows when I've reached my location. Agreed, it's an unfair advantage. One of many. We're about a mile offshore. I cruise a third of a mile farther into the tide, past where I want to start fishing. We need to bait up, and the tide is running fast. Underwater ridges deflect the currents, creating surface boils and lines of standing waves that will buck like black stallions after dark.

The Striped Bass's rise from depletion to abundance over the last twenty years is a triumph of fisheries management. Now, crazily, the bait—live eels purchased at the marina—presents a greater moral dilemma than the target catch. Because of overfishing, pollution, and dams, eel numbers are down as much as 99 percent from fifty years ago. And, they're caught in traps using horseshoe crabs for bait. Life is complicated enough without ethically challenging bait. Tonight I'm trading standards for expediency, a classic slippery slope: I've brought eels because they work like magic as bait for the biggest kind of bass. For catching big fish, they're high-quality bait. For your conscience, low-quality.

I inspect the knots to make sure they're neat and snug. Anything that looks "good enough" isn't. I sharpen each hook. I check the leaders, find a nick in one, shorten it to eliminate that weak spot.

I pierce two eels, and we stream them overboard. The sinkers strike bottom about forty feet down, telegraphing a little thud up the line. We set the reels' drag brakes. The tide sweeps our boat and our bait along.

This is a place of big fish and big water. The tide turns the near-shore ocean into a miles-wide river of streaming current. Fish position themselves along the ridges of long-drowned hills and behind boulders, hunkered down out of the full blast of the tidal wind, poised to ambush prey that gets swept up and over those ridgetops. Now two of those prey items carry our hooks.

The last glow of sundown dims away. Stars appear in the east. Night encloses us. The ocean seems to enlarge. When you're adrift at night, imagination and perception merge. They have to. You can't see as well, as far, as deep. You tie knots by muscle memory, and you operate your reel mostly by feel. Your boat drifts, your thoughts drift. You sense the sweep of tide and water, and the boat gets rocked in the turbulence just past each undersea ridgeline and boulder field. You visualize the fish stemming the dark current, gathering starlight with their special eyes, and scanning upward for vulnerable silhouettes. You, too, are looking up, searching constellations, dreaming. You feel again how flexible and expansive your mind can be when it's working right. And you slip your leash to explore the vast vault of sky and great interior spaces.

Because the boat is drifting fast, the sinker is constantly bouncing over rocks and mussel beds. So everything feels lively the whole time. People who've never done this before have difficulty getting used to all the little pulls and pauses as the tide sweeps their line along the rough

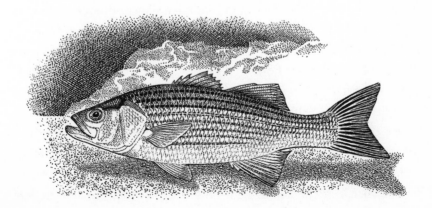

bottom. They always ask how they'll know if they get a bite. I tell them, Don't worry—you'll know.

All the while, I'm hoping my line gets arrested by a heavy fish. These fish come up on prey and in a lightning motion flare their gill covers and pop open their jaws; food simply gets sucked in. If that sucked-in prey happens to be your bait, you'll feel a sharp thump, a pause, and then a heavy surge as the fish turns and its weight comes against the line. But if a fish inhales the bait and realizes things don't feel right, it will eject it in a hurry. So you need to give a fish enough time to engulf, and hook it before it ejects. Elapsed time: under two seconds. Beginners with no feel for this can catch fish, but they miss a lot of strikes.

The tide is sweeping us along at almost three knots, like a brisk walk. I'm feeling my sinker hitting those rocks and mussels. Matt remains unsure of what to make of these taps and tugs. I tell him that if he's unsure, he should react as though it's a fish; lift the rod. Each time he lifts, his fishing rod stays straight.

It gets a little shallower, then a little deeper. Reel up a bit as it shallows; let out a little line as it deepens. Keep your bait near the bottom.

No fish.

Now the GPS shows the boat going over a spot on the chart marked "rocks." The surface responds with roils and boils in the current. Turbulence is good; eddies hold fish.

No fish.

Usually when I get past these rocks, I reel up and go back for another drift. But I've gotten a hot tip to stay on this drift after the rocks. So I do. I notice another boat downtide of us, doing the same thing. This is a chute between two sunken hills. On the sounder screen, though, I don't see any boulders or ridges where a fish might hide, just a few seafloor sand waves. I'm not expecting anything to happen here. For just that reason, I'm thinking, "Pay attention."

A minute later I feel a couple of light bumps that seem distinctly alive. I dip the rod tip, the line tightens, and when I lift, a heavy weight comes on and the rod bows to a respected opponent. A couple of deep throbs as the fish shakes its head; then the line goes slack. I reel in a bare hook.

Matt suddenly says, "Okay, here we go," and I turn to see his rod bounce sharply as he comes tight on a bucking fish. The rod arcs way down and his line zips off the reel into the dark current. The fish goes, goes, goes—deep and away—on a series of unusually long runs that deplete much of the line. And at the end of those runs, the fish is still hooked.

Matt is not practiced at getting the line back, but I don't care how long it takes him and I don't rush him. The hook stays in and the line and knots are holding. Those runs have tired the fish, and now Matt starts putting some line on the reel between shorter runs. Savoring the connection and each surge and pulse, Matt seems in heaven.

A few minutes later, looking into the black water, he says hopefully, "I think the fish must be near the boat." I check his depleted reel and tell him he's got a long way to go.

I'm not monitoring my watch, but I've never seen a Striped Bass on the line so long. Something like twenty minutes passes. It's a combination of the big fish's strength and Matt taking it slow even though he's so excited. "Just keep the line coming," I say. When Matt stops to rest his tired reeling hand on the side of the boat, I tell him he can stay at it slow and steady—but stay at it. Gain a little. Then gain a little more. The main thing is to keep ratcheting closer.

"This fish—" he says breathlessly. "It's almost—overwhelming." After various rounds of chemo and radiation over the last couple of years, Matt's stamina is compromised. Yet stacked against all the not-knowing, the bone-marrow transplant he faces in a couple of weeks, and the concerns for his wife and young son that have shadowed him for months, this whole evening is acquiring a sense of the transcendent. It seems that in the moment the only thing on his mind is the unseen fish somewhere in the dark, flowing water. Matt knows what he's up against in a way most of us don't. Still, the idea that his life is more at risk and his time more precious is only partly true. One thing you can learn from a serious illness is who your friends are. But we all have swords dangling over our heads and limited time. We're all terminal cases, and our stories all have plot twists and surprise endings. What Matt doesn't know at the moment is that, in a highly unlikely recovery, he will survive this illness; but through no one's fault, his marriage will not.

A long while after it had already seemed like a long while, I see by the line's angle that the fish is indeed, finally, close. I reach for the net. The fish looms into view in the shadowy water, swimming in an arc under the surface, then angling down and out of sight again on another run. This whole tug-of-war, with all its life-and-death implications in fact and metaphor, is starting to seem epic.

When Matt again conjures up the fish, she rolls a few feet down and her white belly shows. When she breaks the surface, my net engulfs her head and almost half her body, but the hook or something is hanging up. The fish begins sliding backward, so, fearing we'll lose her, I lean over the side, wrestling a little to prevent her from falling out, and shift the balance of her bulk inside the net.

I grab the net's hoop to avoid breaking its handle, and we haul the fish over the side. She thuds to the deck so exhausted she barely moves. The beautiful fish is indeed big. About forty-four inches long, about thirty-five pounds—and about fifteen years old.

For a moment, no one says a word. Matt is flabbergasted by the creature he's just caught. I switch on the deck light so he can run his hands over the fish's flanks and admire her pearly belly and the green back and the dashed-line stripes and the purple cast along her flanks.

The possibility of release occurs to me. The large fish are all females, and the bigger they are, the more valuable as breeders because every time they add a little growth they can lay a lot more eggs. Our legal limit would be four of these fish; that's excessive. But Matt's already talking about cooking techniques. I don't know what the rest of the night might bring, so—bird in hand—I put the fish in the ice and add a bucket of seawater. The fish sinks into the slurry, thrashes once, and goes still, chilled to final sleep.

That was our first drift. My GPS says we're nearly two-thirds of a mile from where I started the drift. My ideal for the evening had been a calm ocean, memorable sunset, starry sky, and big fish. It's turned out to be a high-quality evening. So that's it, rather simply; quality is the nearness of the actual to the ideal.

We're done. Catching another fish tonight would dilute perfection. I congratulate Matt on a fish of uncommon quality, start the engine, and turn the wheel toward home.

In the night kitchen with some Coltrane playing, I slice a few steaks from the thick forward end of the fish's translucent fillets, dip them in

olive oil, top with black sesames and basil, bake them a few quick minutes, and broil a browning onto them while their centers still blush pink.
Well after midnight we clink glasses, the fish becomes us, and we close
the evening.

＊

If quality is the nearness of the real to the ideal, then we can consider
not just the quality of our own time; we can also *evaluate* our relationship with the world. Early philosophers thought that if they could simply get human interactions right, they would have answered the primary
question. But when Socrates said, "We are discussing no small matter,
but how we ought to live," he had no idea what a hugely not-small
matter he'd begun to tug on. Considering all we've talked about—what
life is; how philosophers erected a firewall between us and nature; the
physical impossibility of infinite material growth; the need for a new
concept of development; and how we've become a new force of nature,
changing the world at scales and rates previously reserved for geological
processes—the quality of humanity's relationship with the world can
certainly be improved.

Quality is perhaps most easily judged in familiar terrain. But for
broader perspective, you need distance. The warm nights and warm waters
around Lazy Point are my idea of summer. Yet I'm leaving those familiar
qualities for a different kind of summer, in a different world where neither
land nor sea ever quite break the icy grip of winter. Even that world, however, is changing.

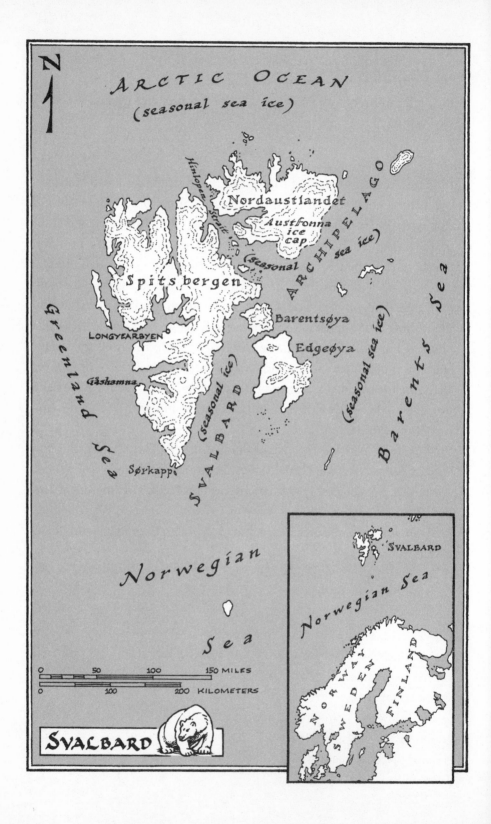

TRAVELS POLAR: SVALBARD

~ ~ ~

How would a biblical literalist count seven days and nights here? One day in Svalbard lasts four months, and the sun never sets; one night lasts four months, and the sun never rises. The other four months consist mainly of either long days with short nights or long nights with short days. Here the equinoxes—the two days annually with twelve hours each of daylight and darkness—really mean something. But what does "a day" mean here, and how many are there in a year?

The islands collectively called Svalbard rise from the sea so far north they seem to lie beyond human thought. The latitude is nearly 80° north, far beyond the Arctic Circle. Almost everywhere else in the world this far north, you'd be in the Arctic Ocean. Mainland Norway's northernmost tip is about five hundred miles south of us.

Many people have never heard of these islands; few would want to come. For those who have and who do, it's neither easy nor hospitable. The annual average temperature is 25° Fahrenheit (−4° C); the record low: −51° Fahrenheit (−46.3° C). Some 60 percent of the land is covered by glaciers and ice sheets; 27 percent is simply bare; less than 10 percent is vegetated. The nearest tree—or even shrub—is hundreds of miles behind us, on the European continent. Although Inuit people elsewhere learned to master sea ice and long crossings of the Arctic Ocean, no aboriginal people ever got this far.

But now I've come to the spare and elemental top of the world, into the music of vast silences and the heave and subsidence of a cold, dark sea. I hope to see creatures living to a different rhythm, a rhythm not of our time—though that pace, too, is changing. Partly, I came to this place beyond humanity to see where we're all headed.

Though it's mid-July, snow flurries greet my arrival. The bubble of civilization extends here, but barely. The two thousand residents live off coal mining. The main town, Longyearbyen, is named after the person who developed the mining, although with those four months of uninterrupted night, and temperatures dozens of degrees below zero, it must seem a "long year" indeed. The people here rely entirely on food imported from lands a thousand or more miles south. But that's not the only connection between local coal and distant places. Coal combustion is helping change the climate.

Cary Fowler is a curly-haired man who's come to this land without farming to save the future of agriculture. "It's a foregone conclusion that climate change will affect agriculture," Fowler is telling me. "The open question is: Will agriculture adapt?"

Adapting a plant variety to a new region—or a new climate—isn't easy or quick. Temperature limits the natural ranges of many species of plants and animals. To understand how profound this limitation is, think of it this way: at the edge of a species' range, each individual and each generation have the opportunity to expand just beyond the confines of their species' normal range. The rewards would certainly be great: more territory, less competition, more market share. Yet many species apparently cannot adapt to temperature regimes and climate conditions different from those to which they're already adapted. At the very least, such adaptation is not simple or certain. Just ask any dinosaur.

Through what looks a bit like a concrete-reinforced cellar door in a frozen mountain, we enter a nearly four-hundred-foot-long tunnel dug through solid rock. The tunnel connects a series of cavernous storage rooms maintained at 0° Fahrenheit (−18° C), and the whole space resembles a big multichambered cave. This is the Doomsday Vault, the world's cold-storage site for agriculture, a safety-deposit box for seeds. More formally it's called the Global Seed Vault, established in 2008 by the Global Crop Diversity Trust; its location was chosen for its insulation from conflict, floods, and fires. And the area deep beneath this mountain is expected to stay frozen for a long time, even under projected warming. Warming is why we're in so cold a place.

"Crop diversity is the biological foundation of future agriculture," Fowler asserts.

Agriculture is, and is not, very diversified. Out of about 300,000 named plant species, we get 90 percent of our food from 103 species, and we get 70 percent from just 3: wheat, corn, and rice. But between 200,000 and 400,000 varieties of rice exist in the world. Some grow on land, some under several feet of water. The roughly 60,000 kinds of beans include some that resist heat, others that resist bugs.

Collecting the world's seeds is a new work in progress. The vault currently holds over 300,000 samples, each with about 500 seeds, so 150 million seeds. It has sufficient capacity to store 4.5 million samples, 2.25 billion seeds. The seeds themselves—nondescript, methodically bagged, labeled, and racked—are a visual anticlimax. They're the least dramatic thing about the whole enterprise.

"Twenty years from now," Fowler says, "the climate in some countries won't be anything like it is now." He shows me a graph that plots growing-season temperatures in India for the past century and temperatures projected by the end of this century. During the growing season, the experienced and projected temperatures *do not overlap*. It won't just be on the warmer side of average; there'll be an entirely new range of temperatures. Concludes Fowler: "Agriculture has never seen the kind of climate that is coming."

That throws food forecasts into question. Economists project a 1 to 2 percent increase in corn production in South Africa. "That's because," Fowler explains, "they simply assume the increasing yields of the past will continue. They're looking in the rearview mirror." Corn needs rain. Forecasts for coming years predict worsening African droughts. And if a corn stalk's silk dries out, you get no corn.

"If you look ahead, and factor in climate," Fowler says, "you'd predict a thirty percent *decline* in corn in South Africa. That's total yield, not per person." You'd have to take the 30 percent lower total yield and divide that by the number of people expected due to population growth to really see how much less food per person is likely.

Corn's not the only concern. About half the world's population eats a bowl of rice every day. Rice pollination success is nearly 100 percent at roughly 95 degrees Fahrenheit (35°C). Rather stunningly, for every added 1 degree Celsius rise in nighttime temperature, rice yields drop *10 percent*. At night temperatures of about 105 degrees Fahrenheit (40°C), pollination fails almost entirely. Similarly, for each 1 degree Celsius rise in temperature, corn and wheat yields decline about 5 percent. The National Academy of Sciences says, "Temperature increases due to global warming will make it increasingly difficult to feed Earth's growing population."

"Is agriculture ready?" Fowler asks. "No. We've actually been losing seed diversity. It's as if, as we're facing a growing threat—we're dismantling our defenses.

"And where," Fowler continues, "will farmers get the drought- and heat-tolerant crop varieties they'll need? Not from inside their own countries; they'll have to get them from somewhere else." Somewhere else is this vault. Water requirements, light sensitivity, heat sensitivity, disease and insect resistance—all must be tuned, then fine-tuned. Even with genetic engineering, it takes about seven years to develop a new crop variety. This vault preserves those tunable traits from around the globe. Coded into seeds, these traits can be shipped anywhere to speed development of new varieties.

This vault is the sole global response to the crisis of shrinking crop varieties in a world with a changing climate. "We will need this seed bank," Fowler opines, "as long as we will need agriculture. This," he adds, waving at the spaces waiting to be filled with seed samples, "is a common heritage of humanity, a basic public good. Quite simply," he concludes, "there is no possibility of feeding ourselves without it."

❧

Critical as the vault is, it will store only agricultural seeds, not wild plant types. Not domestic animal breeds. And not, of course, the diversity of wild animals. To do the job right, Noah would need a bigger boat.

In that spirit, I board the *Endeavor*. Lindblad Expeditions has taken the ship off its eco-tour schedule explicitly to facilitate a more penetrating Arctic climate prognosis. Aboard are Julian Dowdeswell, a rather jovial ice expert who directs the Scott Polar Research Institute at the University of Cambridge and has done lots of fieldwork in this region;

climatologist Stefan Rahmstorf, who is a professor of oceanography at Potsdam University and an Arctic climate expert; and the good-natured, though at times intense Swedish naturalist Stefan Lundgren.

Hardly have we left the harbor when it becomes plain that we are slipping beyond the peopled planet, beyond the hospitable and humanly habitable. The sky is leaden. The mountainous landscape appears raw and forbidding, its bare rock like draped bolts of dark cloth, caked with snow.

But even this far north, seabirds *thrive*. Thick-billed murres and Little Auks (called Dovekies in North America), both abundant, look like flying penguins. Barnacle Geese gather in sparse flocks along the stark shoreline. Piratical Arctic Skuas chase Black-legged Kittiwakes until they drop their food. Stocky Northern Fulmars orbit us in hope of scraps. A train of Common Eiders is caboosed by one Long-tailed Duck. I see a few light-on-the-wing Arctic Terns; they'll spend the winter up to twelve thousand miles south, in the Antarctic. Along the shore floats a Red-throated Loon, its blush-feathered throat striking compared to the paler winter plumage they wear when visiting my home shores. Atlantic Puffins, the bright-billed comic relief of northern seas, fly in small groups. Those bills also add a bright splash of color in this place of grays and subdued hues.

The waterbirds all endure a long migration to get up here, but the most arduous trip must be for Svalbard's only land bird, the large sparrow called the Snow Bunting, for whom the five-hundred-mile-plus ocean crossing must be arduous beyond human reckoning.

Here at the outer limits of their summer ranges, these birds seem familiar; I know them from home. Even Ruddy Turnstones sometimes get this far. From their North American populations, these species all send delegates to waters near my beach house. The murres, auks, skuas, fulmars, the terns, the loons, the eiders and Long-tailed Ducks, of course, even the bunting—I've seen them *all* around Lazy Point. That's how small the world is and how big their lives are. Now, far from my own shores, they make me feel unexpectedly at home. Otherwise, this would seem utterly like the planet's cold shoulder.

Svalbard means, in fact, "cold coast." This is a hard-to-scale landscape. Along these many-fingered corridors of coastline, summit-cloaking clouds often obscure snow-frosted masses of bare land. Sea cliffs hundreds of feet high look small across distances difficult to judge. What appear like little piles of gravel on the shore are actually rock avalanches resting at the toes of buttes. Low clouds notwithstanding, the cold air seems dry and the view spans miles. Some valleys gleam in sun, some lie shrouded. The land rears back, imposing yet aloof, its head in those clouds, its shoulders arched up into the mists.

Unpeopled doesn't mean untouched. Willem Barents first cast a human gaze upon the Svalbard archipelago in 1596. He died a terrifying death from scurvy after his ship got trapped in ice, but he left his name written on these waters. Even the ends of the earth aren't too far to make a buck, and British and Dutch whalers were soon upon the place. Later, Arctic Foxes proved irresistible to Russian trappers. The whalers nearly exterminated their prey—primarily the Greenland Right, or Atlantic population of Bowhead Whales—by 1750. During the 1800s the wildlife further endured intense hunting and trapping. What the trappers weren't killing for fur, such as geese, eiders, and ptarmigan, they ate.

The economy no longer derives from blood. Now, 65 percent of Svalbard is officially protected for wildlife, and as much as 98 percent is de facto wilderness. But considering that the Arctic is warming about twice as fast as the rest of the globe, what place still really answers to the illusion of "untouched wilderness"?

A wall of ice two hundred feet high and about half a mile wide stands at the head of a place called Konowbreen Bay. Julian Dowdeswell, Stefan Rahmstorf, and I land on the adjacent gravel shore amid snow flurries. To gain perspective, we begin trudging toward the ridge, a steep seven hundred feet above us. From up there, we will have a grand view down upon the glacier-filled valley.

After a heart-poundingly steep assault up about five hundred feet of elevation over gravel and loose scree, the ground suddenly changes. Below us, it's 99 percent bare. Above, it's 99 percent vegetated with lichens and tiny cushions of Arctic flowers like yellow Arctic Cinquefoil, Reindeer Rose, lavender Moss Campion, varied saxifrages, and Svalbard Poppy, whose subtle exuberance helps cloak the chilly ground.

The sweeping view from up here shows that this abrupt transition from bare to vegetated forms an enormous bathtub ring along the bay's slopes, and runs up the valley above the glacier's edge.

Julian explains that a mere century ago the glacier reached—and scoured—the slopes to this height. In just the last hundred years, it has lost well over four hundred feet of its thickness. That's why the bathtub ring. The glacier's icy face has also retreated half a mile. But this *thinning* is impressive. Barents wrote the first description of the ice realm here. We may be helping compile the last.

Even with that crumbly face, what's left of the glacier remains very substantial, mostly about 450 feet thick, according to Julian. He's not guessing; it's been measured with radar from satellites and aircraft. The upper part of the glacier disappears into the mist and flurries of its wide valley.

Two Reindeer (same species as Caribou) stride jauntily over a rise, both carrying enormous racks swollen by their velvet growth sheaths. When they spot us, they immediately spook away.

Sea ice can melt all it wants to, but that won't raise sea levels. Because sea ice is already in the ocean, it's already displacing all the water its mass will ever displace. That's why a drink with ice in it doesn't overflow when the ice melts. Melting *land* ice, like this glacier, raises the sea. "That melted water," Julian says, "is decanted *into* the global ocean. And the vast majority of glaciers, worldwide, are melting." Sea level has risen about eight inches over the last hundred years. And the rate of rise is accelerating.

Rahmstorf adds. "There has been nothing like this rate of sea level rise in the last thousand years. If there had been, Roman-built wharves would be four meters underwater—and they're not."

Numerous icebergs calved from the glacier crowd this bay. While our sense of time makes the glacier appear fixed, its own inexorable movement, a few tens of yards annually, launches new armadas of ice daily.

Gaining the ridge earns us a view of the breathtaking plunge into the next valley, where another gleaming, corrugated glacier runs in still frames to the sea. I look back at our ship, anchored amid the bay's drifting bergs, shrunken by the ringing mountains, dwarfed by floating ice.

"Bear!"

At seven A.M.—not morning exactly, since it hasn't been dark in weeks—a fat Polar Bear stands on the beach. Facing us in sumo pose as we steam past, it looks like a yellowed patch of snow on high alert.

In Stefan Lundgren's Swedish accent, "Polar Bear" becomes an emphatic *POElah beah*. This planet's biggest land carnivore, males frequently reach one thousand pounds. Not far from here, someone once shot a Polar Bear weighing 1,760 pounds. They can stand twelve feet. Unlike other bears, which often eat plants, berries, and fish, Isbjörn—that's Norwegian for "ice bear"—eats big meat. Isbjörn specializes in hunting seals on sea ice. Bears forced ashore when the ice melts—like this one—can get hungry, dangerous.

From the beach it stares, and from the rail, we just stare back. It seems a missed opportunity that we don't have more to say, that the gulf between us is deeper than the fjord we're traveling.

To survive, Polar Bears need to get a good spring hunting season under their belts. Prime time is March, April, and May. Going into summer, fatter is healthier. In some places, the bears may have to live off that fat for months, losing hundreds of pounds. But with the ice now melting earlier, bears are coming ashore earlier, and with less fat.

With its feet planted in tundra mosses, this bear we're watching is, in fact, stranded far from the frozen ocean it needs for hunting. That's common in summer. "The other mammals, the birds, insects—they all love the summer," says Stefan. "No other animal in the Arctic hates summer like Polar Bears do."

Our bear walks about a hundred yards and lies down for a nap, looking bored. It must wait months to regain prime sea ice. Stefan says that anywhere we might choose to walk ashore, a sleeping Polar Bear can rise from a gully, suddenly reminded of its hunger. "If a Polar Bear stands up in front of you," Stefan says, "think about your next life."

I'll keep that in mind. Meanwhile, I imagine that the bear we're watching will dream of the liberation that comes with water freezing. Fade to white.

The beach at Gåshamna is strewn with the debris of old whalers, and the bigger-than-dinosaur-bones remains of the great whales.

We pick our footing carefully around the wood and iron, around the shacks. We must not damage the ruins. We walk around whale jaw-bones the size of building beams, skulls larger than people, improbable ribs, and vertebrae the size of hassocks. We examine in fine detail the weathering of the skeletons, and comment on how the pretty lichens and Arctic flowers grow more densely where the bones have leached their nutrients into the soil.

But let's not kid ourselves: it's a garden of death. It is bleak poverty to pick through what others discarded centuries ago, when the now-silent bay should be full of whales.

Imagine coming around a headland into a bay alive with leviathans. You can see that in the Baja bays where Gray Whales give birth and begin nursing their calves. And in Hawaii when Humpbacks are singing and being born. And in the waters of Alaska, and various places off California and New England, when the whales are in. Whales have begun recovering in some places, and the waters again carry the noise of their blows and their detonating breaches.

Not here. Here, what Herman Melville in *Moby-Dick* called "so reckless a havoc" still resonates as mere silence and calm water. And, in fact, these abandoned shacks are more thoroughly "protected" than the remaining whales in Norway's waters, since Norway is one of the few countries still hunting whales, in defiance of the global whaling ban. Further, Iceland has—after getting hit hard by the 2009 global recession— greatly expanded its commercial whaling, killing nearly 100 Fin Whales that year. Worldwide, whalers kill about 1,500 whales annually, with Japan's whale-meat market providing most of the incentive. The numbers of most large whales worldwide remain depressed from earlier whaling. And there's no humane way to kill a whale. Furthermore, with whale meat selling for roughly ten times the price of chicken, no one will starve if they can't get it. But it is true that the whaling Japan, Norway, and Iceland report is, probably, sustainable. It is also true that whaling seems to entail a willingness to break rules and to lie about how many and which species whalers have killed. Between 1948 and 1973, four

Soviet factory ships processed 48,477 Humpback Whales and reported only 2,710. (Humpbacks were supposedly protected by a global whaling ban begun in 1966.) In 1993, an air cargo handler in Oslo, Norway, uncovered 3.5 tons of whale meat—labeled as Norwegian shrimp—bound for South Korea. DNA tests have proved that packaged whale meat for sale in Japan often comes from species of whales and places in the ocean that are supposedly protected. The scientists who reported the DNA tests wrote, "These results demonstrate the inadequacy of the current system for verifying catch reports and trade records of commercial and scientific whaling. . . . Without an adequate system for monitoring and verifying catches . . . no species of whale can be considered safe." That's why the claims of sustainable whaling are always suspect. So can we kill whales sustainably? Apparently not. Then should we kill more whales? No.

Most of these bones are from Bowheads, the whales most adapted to life in ice water. The Bowhead has the most highly developed blubber layer among whales (a foot thick) and a complex blood-circulation mechanism for conserving heat. It's big, fifteen feet at birth, up to sixty-five feet at adulthood, weighing 200,000 pounds. Its huge head, which makes up one-third of the animal's overall length, can smash through ice up to six feet thick. The fibrous filtering plates that hang in the mouth from the top jaw, called baleen, reach extreme lengths of twelve to fifteen feet. With these the whale strains enough krill and fraction-of-an-inch-long copepods from the seawater to keep it swimming.

Bowheads ranged originally across most of the Canadian Arctic to Greenland, and from Greenland east across the Barents Sea to Novaya Zemlya, and off Alaska in the Bering, Chukchi, and Beaufort Seas, west to Russia and the Sea of Okhotsk.

Whalers got into this region in the 1600s, when the slow-swimming Bowhead was called the Greenland Right Whale because it was the "right" one to find in these waters. Whalers killed something like 60,000 Northern Right Whales (a different species) farther south; the Bowhead was just the next "right" one as the whale hunters ventured into the high Arctic. Between 1630 and 1635—1,825 days—tens of thousands of Bowheads lost their lives to humans.

Bowheads don't breed until age twenty-five and may have the greatest longevity of any mammal; they're known to live for two centuries. In 1993, two stone harpoon points were found inside an Alaskan Bowhead. It had been harpooned—probably in the 1800s—by hunters still living in the technological stone age. It was finally killed by industrial-age Inuit. In chemical analyses of several Alaskan Bowheads, the oldest whale was deemed 211 years old at the time of its death. That whale had been gliding through icy seas when Thomas Jefferson was president.

But now there are likely more of these great skulls on this one beach than there are in the heads of living Atlantic Bowheads in the whole ocean. They're all but extinct.

The first global oil wells were called whales, and the drills were called harpoons. People then thought only of themselves and the short term, and within a century they essentially ran out of oil and whale meat. Even in the places where whales are again common, they're at a fraction of their former abundance. Whaling for oil has ended; good riddance. Every time we sever a dirty—or immoral—source of energy, humanity improves.

The right and necessary things are not always decided solely on economic considerations. If ever energy came cheap, slavery was it. Slavery created jobs for slave catchers, a shipping industry built on the slave trade, and a plantation economy that could remain profitable only with slave labor. Slavery was necessary to "stay competitive." It was the lynchpin of the southern plantation economy. But no normal person today would argue that slavery is good for the economy. We've made at least that much progress.

Yet we hear—all the time—arguments defending dirty energy on economic grounds. Those arguments are as morally bankrupt as the ones defending slavery in its heyday. It isn't moral to force coming generations to deal with the consequences of our fossil-fuel orgy. It isn't moral to insist, in effect, on holding them captive to our present economy.

With the whales gone from here, we find the whalers' ruins and the bones interesting. We came all this way and encountered not waters roiled by spouts and blows, nor seas flagged by flukes. We got bones. They left us ... bones.

Among these ruins, I'd like to believe that we no longer think as the

whalers did. They, after all, weren't considering those of us who'd be here centuries later. They were simply after what they wanted, whatever the consequences.

Behind its cloudy veil, the sun never grazes the horizon, never alludes to night. Only a smudge of dusk marks the days. In the Arctic summer, one feels little need of sleep. So we sleep briefly. Before sleeping we rounded Sørkapp, the southern cape of Spitsbergen. We are south of the island of Edgeøya, in the Barents Sea, headed basically north.

It's a different realm, an ocean two-thirds ice. The rhythmic rocking and whoosh of water is replaced by the thud and grind of ice along the hull. The normal pattern of bright sky and dark water is inverted; under a pewter sky, we travel a sea bright with the reflective dazzle of broken pack ice stretching miles and miles.

Even here, in the harshness of Dante's ninth circle of hell, life abounds. A halo of kittiwakes and fulmars continue to seek some harvest from the furrow of our churning propellers. Guillemots, like ducks in tuxes, paddle between ice plates. An immaculate Ivory Gull comes floating into view, briefly ghosting by—and then is gone. One lone Walrus, a large male weighing perhaps three thousand pounds, is napping on a berg. His size and his astounding white daggers afford him peaceful sleep in the realm of the ice bear.

. . .

A crimson stain on distant ice. I raise my binoculars.

Like binary stars gripped in each other's gravity, two massive bears, burning white-hot in the vast freeze, attend their kill.

One engorged bear continues pulling listlessly at the well-worked wrack of bloody bones and bits. The other has just plopped down in satiated stupor a few paces away. His face looks dipped in crimson paint. Three hundred yards away, a third bear, much smaller, much whiter, rests on a blocky floe. It may also have smelled the kill from afar and come for scraps, waiting for the bigger and more dangerous bears to take their fill and—I'm sure—to leave.

The bear that has been pulling at the carcass decides to slip into the water and begins paddling away like an enormous white beaver. A small galaxy of orbiting Ivory and Glaucous Gulls waste not a moment squabbling onto the smear and frame that was a seal.

About 200,000 years ago off Siberia or Alaska, advancing ice sheets forced Brown Bears to venture far onto sea ice. They found Ringed Seals, and no competition. Killing Ringed Seals on a frozen ocean was an extreme new niche. And here is the resulting extreme new bear: *Ursus maritimus,* the "sea bear," in its true realm.

A Polar Bear is designed for two constants: hunting and heating. Its translucent white camouflage is merely its most obvious adaptation. Beneath their shaggy, hollow guard hairs, Polar Bears are insulated by

dense underwool. Under that fur, beneath their black skin, lies thick blubber. For pulling seals from ice holes, for swimming, and for stalking prey where there's nowhere to hide, the whole bear is elongated. Long neck. Flattened head. The big shoulder hump of other bears—gone. Their canine teeth are long, stabbing daggers, and their "molars" are sharpened for a diet that's almost 100 percent meat. Polar Bears' claws are sharply curved ice and seal hooks. Their large, hairy-soled feet afford nonskid ice walking.

The ice moves, the seals move, and the bears wander with them. Bears tracked by satellites in the Beaufort Sea north of Alaska logged annual average movements of 2,100 miles (3,400 kilometers). One traveled 3,850 miles (6,200 kilometers) in one year.

Through my binoculars, I watch the yellow-white swimming beaver-bear, at home immersed in water a mere degree above freezing, its muzzle waving left to right, its dark nose reading air like fingers decoding Braille.

Polar bears are astounding swimmers. Strong and slow, they just float while paddling their twelve-inch webbed paws. One Canadian bear, marked with the number 63 dyed into the fur on its back, swam seaward from shore, out across open water. Twenty-four hours later, the researcher studying it got a call from a colleague on a ship: "Do you know anything about a bear numbered 63? I'm watching it swimming." He was sixty miles out at sea.

The bear I'm watching moves so steadily that within minutes it has passed many slabs of ice. Following a dark channel between frozen plates of ocean, it's soon far from where it first slipped into the frigid water.

"I suspect a Polar Bear could swim two hundred miles in calm water," Stefan tells me, "but in storms, with waves and high winds, they can get exhausted. They can die." Since researchers began finding drowned Polar Bears in U.S. and Canadian waters, they've been increasingly worried about early ice breakup and receding sea ice forcing bears to swim long distances. In one day recently, researchers counting whales off Alaska's northwest coast spotted *nine* Polar Bears swimming in open water in the Chukchi Sea, fifteen to sixty-five miles offshore. The bears likely came off a patch of sea ice that had broken up northwest of Alaska's coast. Many were swimming north, away from land, apparently seeking pack ice. But satellite data showed that the main pack ice had receded to about four hundred miles offshore.

Two hundred yards away, the paddling bear latches its grappling hooks into a broad, jagged floe and hoists itself back into the Arctic air. It rolls itself dry and rubs its face in the snow, leaving several bloody shrouds, then yawns out its black tongue before it, too, conks out in a contented sprawl.

~

We would have gone up Hinlopen Strait but ice prevented it. Instead, we turned along the northeasternmost island of Nordausland, Svalbard's "cold corner" (which, in Svalbard, is saying something).

The shoreline curves toward a glacier that has been calving icebergs, which, under the pressure of many centuries, glow a translucent, neon blue. The point meets a flat gray sea with a flat gray gravel shore under a flat gray sky.

About fifty Walruses are lying on the gravelly point. Huge animals, Walruses reach forty-two hundred pounds. These are all males, of assorted ages. Females are farther north somewhere, tending pups on ice. While molting, as now, they shed all their hair at once. I listen to them snorting, and can almost feel them scratching themselves with that mittenlike flipper-hand. The insulation-compromised animals, like these, stay out of the frigid water for three weeks—so, no food. (Walruses' unique mouths can suck clams and scallops from their shells. They can eat a few *thousand* clams at a feeding.) They're huddling for warmth. The benefits apparently outweigh the tusks, but they continually jostle and poke one another with their ivory rakes. I'll bet they're capable of worse. One has a tusk broken off just a couple of inches from the gum. It's difficult to imagine the force of the blow required to crack it off like that.

Europeans, of course, were after those ivory tusks. From the hundreds of thousands of Walruses here when people first found them, perhaps one in a thousand escaped slaughter. Today a few thousand Walruses make up Svalbard's recovering population. Unlike seals, whose pups balloon in weight and are off the teat in a month or two, Walruses' shellfish diet translates to thin, low-fat milk, forcing them to suckle pups for over two years. Consequently, Walrus populations cannot rebuild rapidly.

Nordausland lies locked beneath a massive cap of perpetual ice that meets the sea as an enormous white palisade running as far as I can see. Attached to that wall of ice is shore-fast sea ice covering an area about five miles by two, ten square miles of frozen ocean. Foggy haze veils the farther distances, cocooning us into a kind of white dream.

Out on the sea ice lie about 150 Ringed Seals; they appear as subtle in the vastness as black poppy seeds scattered on a white dance floor. And for about every fifteen seals, a Polar Bear—an extraordinary accumulation of white terror.

Only about twenty-five thousand Polar Bears stalk the coasts and frozen ocean of the entire Arctic world. (Not the Antarctic; Polar Bears depicted consorting with penguins indicate an artist's geographic dyslexia.) About three out of five of the world's Polar Bears live in Canada. The population that ranges from Svalbard east across the entire Barents Sea to Novaya Zemlya numbers only about three thousand.

People with guns early on saw the white bears as fearless, deadly, having valuable fur, and worth shooting at every opportunity. Svalbard banned hunting in 1972. Stefan recounts, "It wasn't actually hunting. Baited gun traps, hanging bait on ships' rails for 'guaranteed kill' sport shoots, shooting from helicopters—it was just ridiculous."

People still hunt them elsewhere, though most Polar Bear populations are in trouble. Baffin Bay's population dropped almost a third between the late 1990s and 2008. Canadian scientists recommended limiting the hunting to sixty-four bears annually. Inuit tribal elders insisted that they were seeing far more bears than ever before. Scientists said that's because bears forced ashore by melting ice were venturing into settlements to eat garbage, unattended dog food, and dogs themselves. Scientists project statistics of decline and stress; Natives say Polar Bears are everywhere. The Inuit-controlled body that sets hunting limits upped the number from the scientists' recommended sixty-four bears—to 105. That Baffin bear population ranges between Canada's Nunavut Territory and Greenland, and Greenland added for its hunters another 68, for a total planned kill of 173 bears from that population. Reported the *Economist*, "Even without the rampant poaching that takes place in Greenland, 12 percent of the Baffin bears are set to be turned into blankets, mukluks and stews." James Qillaq of Canada's Nunavut Territory, who chairs the Kanngiqtugaapik Hunters and Trappers Organization, scoffed at the notion that hunting could be a problem. "Numbers are just numbers," he said. "We live here, so we know what's really going on. We can hunt anytime we want, anywhere we want, no matter what anybody says."

But more than hunting by humans, shrinking sea ice threatens the bears because without ice, the ice bear cannot hunt seals. Scientists expect Polar Bear numbers to decline about 1 percent each year. Where ice is melting faster, the bear is already having trouble; where temperatures remain cool, Polar Bears still do well. Stefan says sea ice near here has thinned a lot in the last few decades, but Svalbard is home to probably the healthiest Polar Bear population remaining on Earth.

The bears in view, widely scattered and, white on white, hard to see, become more visible through a telescope. Most rest. One sits at a seal's breathing hole, patiently attentive. One strides regally across distant ice looking very much the monarch of the realm. As people might bow their heads to royalty, the seals raise theirs.

Equal and opposite imperatives link these two animals: the Polar Bear's to hunt, catch, kill, and eat the Ringed Seal, and the seal's to avoid the foregoing. Named for its circle-marked fur, the Ringed Seal is the most abundant Arctic seal, and the smallest; adults weigh about 150 pounds.

Although it needs to forage in the sea and breathe air, the Ringed Seal has a way to live far into continuous sea ice, miles from open water. From below, it works continually with its strong foreflippers and well-developed claws to maintain three or four breathing holes in ice up to six feet thick. The Ringed Seal is the only Arctic seal that creates breathing holes. (The Antarctic Weddell Seal does, too.) You may find other seals breathing in wide cracks called "leads" and among broken floes or along the open-water edges of the ice. But the Ringed Seal can occupy expanses of solid ice—and the Polar Cod under it—that are simply unavailable to other seals.

Cat-and-mouse: A bear pads across the vast frozen sea. Eventually it finds a nearly invisible hole. It can smell whether the hole's been active. There it takes a number and sits, or lies down, completely still, its chin on the ice, waiting.

"But it's not so easy," says Stefan. Ringed Seals can stay underwater for up to half an hour. They often dive to 150 feet, occasionally to 500, foraging in the frigid dark. The seal's Achilles' heel is its need for air. It rises toward the light at the end of infinity. But it knows the danger. Before it bursts into air for that needed inspiration, it blows a bubble to clear any skim ice, trying to determine whether all's clear. If a bear makes a premature move as the water is disturbed, the seal swims to another hole. If the seal does not detect a bear, and there is, indeed, a bear, then the moment the seal's snout punctures the surface, the bear's teeth burst through its skull.

In spring, Ringed Seals dig dens into snowdrifts on the ice above their breathing holes. There, females give birth. The dens, designed to protect the seals from bears, can be rather elaborate and multichambered. Stefan believes that Polar Bears can smell seal-pupping lairs two miles away. If a polar bear smells or hears life in the lair, it rises up on its hind legs and, with its forepaws, smashes through the roof.

Over an average year, a polar bear kills about forty Ringed Seals. Nearly half are pups caught in their lairs during April and May. Another third are newly weaned pups taken in June and July. When the pups are weaned, they weigh fifty pounds. The naïve weaners give a Polar Bear its greatest opportunity to accumulate the fat necessary to carry it through the year.

If a Ringed Seal avoids bears for a couple of years, Stefan explains, "it becomes wise, and Polar Bears rarely get them." They can live for up to thirty years, though any that live that long must have some bear stories to tell. Despite the horrific risks and the hostile environment, many seals do survive, populating the ice.

In summer, Ringed Seals must lie on the ice next to their hole while molting. Even their best vigilance is not foolproof. Polar Bears have been known to swim under the ice and pop up *inside* the seal's own breathing hole.

• • •

If a Ringed Seal can be a meal, a Bearded Seal, at up to seven hundred pounds, is a banquet. A Polar Bear detecting a Bearded Seal sleeping at the ice edge may slide into the water. Within perhaps sixty yards it will slip under the surface, holding its breath while closing in. The seal will experience only the sudden white explosion as the bear erupts and bounds onto the ice. With the bear coming from the seal's only sanctuary, the seal may have no escape route. But even when pounced on by a firmly gripping thousand-pound bear, an adult Bearded Seal may splay its flippers and, with its nails dug into the ice, drag both itself and the bear into the water. If it succeeds in getting into its element, the seal can submerge, spin, and break the bear's grip. No encounter has a predetermined outcome. Polar Bears succeed in catching their prey an average of once out of every ten attempts. Usually, the seal escapes.

A bear can eat 150 pounds of blubber and meat in one meal. A female needs plenty of fat. Polar Bears mate in spring, but the fertilized egg does not implant and begin developing until autumn. That makes pregnancy rather provisional; if the bear fails to bulk on enough fat, her body is not heavily committed to the pregnancy and may abort and resorb the tiny fetuses. Males and nonbreeding females continue to roam and hunt in the months-long darkness. But around October or November, a pregnant female digs a cave in a deep snowdrift, usually on land. There she sleeps away most of her pregnancy and her delivery. She may also den in deep snow on sea ice. A bear who enters a drifting den may, with new cubs, emerge six hundred miles away. That's what it means to be an ocean bear.

Cubs are born in November and December, after only two months of true gestation. They weigh only about one pound, the size of a guinea pig. At a fraction of 1 percent of adult body weight, they're more like the semi-larval young of marsupials than the infants of most placental mammals.

During all her time in the den, the mother does not defecate or urinate. Her fat gets used—producing water in the process, letting her maintain her fluid levels—but her muscle mass remains constant. Meanwhile, she is excreting milk so rich it contains 30 percent fat, more like seal milk than the milk of other bears. By the time she emerges, around March, her cubs weigh about twenty pounds each. She has not had a good meal for six, perhaps eight months—the longest period of food deprivation of any mammal—and may have lost more than half her weight.

In March or April, with the temperatures well below zero Fahrenheit (−10°C) and the sun returning, the mother is pressed. Growing cubs make food a constant issue. But she can't just focus on hunting. She must also avoid males, who may kill her cubs. And when she is hunting, her cubs, lacking patience and the art of stalking, slow her down and spoil some of her opportunities.

She's got just a few months to recover from her depleted winter condition and to bulk up for the next summer. So she'll really need a good spring hunting season. In milder springs, ice that's shrunk by 30 to 40 percent makes seals much more concentrated on the remaining ice, and melted birthing lairs leave pups visibly exposed. Those times heavily favor the bears; they've been known to eat almost 100 percent of seal pups under such conditions.

But a pup eaten when it weighs ten pounds is not there to be eaten when it would weigh much more. A bear can get more than five times as much energy from a weaned pup than from a newborn. Heavy predation on newborn pups, as happens in milder springs, *lowers* the bears' overall energy intake. If the spring ice breaks up early, say, by June, the bears miss out on Ringed Seal weaners because they've eaten most of them as pups, and they miss out on the later influx of Harp, Hooded, Ribbon, Spotted, and Bearded Seals because there's too little ice for hunting. Polar Bears forced ashore in June face a nine-month fast. So in warmer years the body condition of bears, especially females nursing growing cubs, is much worse come winter—a severe challenge to survival.

In Hudson Bay, Canada, spring breakup has been happening about three weeks earlier in recent years. Lean, hungry bears forced ashore by early ice breakup come scavenging, and increasingly often get into conflict with people. Stefan says that around Hudson Bay during the last twenty years or so, pregnant females' average weight has dropped from 640 pounds to 500 pounds. To have a successful pregnancy, it's believed a female Polar Bear must weigh at least 430 pounds.

"In the other regions," Stefan says, "juvenile survival is dropping." In Alaska, females are increasingly emerging from birthing dens without any cubs. In the Beaufort Sea off Alaska, the number of cubs seen per hundred females has halved in just a decade.

So far, Svalbard's bears don't seem to be suffering these problems. About one in three cubs survives the two and a half years to independence. That may sound low, but it's stable.

But going into dens too skinny isn't the bears' only problem. Though many industrialized nations have banned PCBs (used worldwide in electrical transformers) and pesticides such as DDT, toxaphene, dieldrin, and chlordane, they persist in soil and water, especially the ocean. Traveling up each link in the food chain, from water to planktonic plants to planktonic animals to small fishes to larger ones, to seals to bears, these chemicals accumulate in each link. A Polar Bear's body has chemical concentrations billions of times greater than the seawater. During winter, when she loses weight, a female's pollutants become most concentrated. In her rich milk, she bequeaths those chemicals to her cubs. Mothers whose cubs die inside their dens have PCB concentrations three times higher than mothers whose cubs emerge. Cubs emerging from the den to get their first glimpse of the world are already among the world's most contaminated animals.

That's bad for their immune systems. PCB levels only one-fifth as high as in some Svalbard bears suppress immunity in captive seals. Svalbard Polar Bears exposed to flu virus cannot muster as many antibodies as Canadian bears carrying far less PCBs.

Contaminants also damage the bears' delicate sexual systems. Svalbard bears suffer altered testosterone and progesterone hormones, apparently causing them to stop breeding abnormally young. Of females with cubs here, only about one in ten are over fifteen years old, compared with one in two in Canada. And 3 percent of Svalbard bears show gross sexual abnormality, having both female and male genitalia.

"The good news," Stefan adds, "is the PCBs and DDT are declining." So is mercury, in Svalbard, at least. Danish researchers analyzing four hundred hair samples from bears killed over several centuries found that mercury contamination increased sharply starting in the 1890s to 1973, peaked during 1965–74 (at levels fourteen times higher than those in hair samples hundreds of years old), but by 2001 had declined 25 percent from the peak. Mercury comes mostly from burning coal. The researchers credited stricter European environmental standards for the decline. In parts of the Arctic subject to more fallout from Asia, mercury levels increased.

The bad news is newer chemicals. Polar Bears contain small amounts of compounds used in Teflon and formerly used in Scotchgard, as well as in flame retardants. Manufacturers put flame retardants in furniture, carpet padding, electronics, and plastics. Obviously, the intent is to keep people safe; no one thought these chemicals would poison wildlife and people. The most abundant flame retardant in Svalbard bears comes from a compound used in foam cushions. Flame retardants get magnified as they move from prey to predator; one compound was seventy times more concentrated in Polar Bears than in the Ringed Seals from which they'd gotten it.

Virtually every person tested on Earth now contains traces of flame retardants. After the milk of many U.S. women was found to carry concentrations approaching those that altered the brains of newborn lab mice, Europe and various U.S. states banned some of these chemicals. (They also disrupt thyroid function and sex hormones and impair motor skills, memory, and learning.) The rapid buildup in Arctic Ringed Seals stabilized soon after the ban, and, as a result, concentrations in seals and bears—and women—will probably decline. So there's hope.

As we're watching two distant bears moving across the seal-flecked ice, Stefan is telling me that the most difficult time for cubs is between the time they separate from their mother and the time they're about five years old. That smaller, whiter bear we'd seen the other day, waiting for those two to leave the remains of that seal, was probably in that category. Most young Polar Bears die from starvation. But a few survive to be thirty years old.

Isbjörn may be the monarch. But the monarch is not the realm. The ice bear requires ice. So do Ringed, Harp, Hooded, Bearded, Ribbon, and Spotted Seals. So do Ivory and Ross's Gulls, the Bowhead Whale, and the unicornlike Narwhal. The Walrus. That's just the beginning of a longer list of animals dependent on ice.

Consider the bear's main prey. Ringed Seals never come onto land.

When the ocean freezes, they live on and under the ice. When the ice vanishes, they stay in the ocean. Bears cannot attack them in the water. Does that mean that without ice, Ringed Seals would live safely at sea? Remember, Ringed Seals give birth in snow caves above sea ice. Other seals, too, give birth on sea ice. Already, the Harp Seals whose white pups have long been subjected to the controversial fur hunt are drowning by the hundreds of thousands as the ice melts from under them. An end to ice would mean an end to birth.

The bears and seals we're watching are playing their old game of chess on exactly the kind of habitat that is melting around the Arctic. The U.S. Geological Survey says, "Projected changes in future sea ice conditions, if realized, will result in loss of approximately two-thirds of the world's current polar bear population by the mid-twenty-first century." That prompted the *Anchorage Daily News* to observe, "Today's young bears may be part of the last generation in Alaska."

I'd like to think there's another way this all could go.

Julian joins us at the ship's rail. I ask him to read the region's fortune. "Just twenty years ago," he offers, "sea ice made it very difficult to get east of Svalbard, but last year there was no ice at all." Summer sea ice now covers about half the area it covered in 1970. Vast areas of bright, reflective ice have been replaced with dark water that absorbs more of the sun's warmth, accelerating the ice melting. Adds Julian, "*That's* why the Arctic is changing more rapidly than anywhere in the world." As I write, the world's average ocean temperature is the warmest ever measured, and Arctic water temperatures are up to ten degrees above average. This year, summer sea ice covers the second-smallest area ever recorded; last year it reached the lowest ever, so far.

On my map, Svalbard's north coast is marked with the words "Area of Permanent Ice." Satellites show that it now has open water. I guess the new meaning of "permanent" is: until it goes away.

～

A little farther down the coast, part of the ice cap meets the sea as a wall of white ice cliffs that run for more than 110 kilometers (70 miles), the longest ice cliffs in the Arctic outside Greenland. Julian says that the ice right here is about 100 meters (over 300 feet) thick, but much of it is underwater, resting on a gouge in the sea floor. At its thickest, the cap is 550 meters, a vertical third of a mile of ice. This ice cap, the biggest in the Eurasian Arctic, has a name: Austfonna. Covering 8,000 square kilometers (3,000 square miles), it's larger than Long Island and Rhode Island combined, roughly the size of Wales.

Water jets are spraying like firehoses through melt holes in the middle of the ice face. Waterfalls have cut grooves through the rim. Almost everywhere globally—Antarctica, the Arctic, Patagonia, the Himalayas, the Andes, and the mountains of Alaska—researchers and residents are seeing melting.

Twenty thousand years ago when the ice age froze an enormous quantity of Earth's water, the sea level was nearly 120 meters (400 feet) lower than it is today. Vast areas that are now seafloor were plains grazed by herds of animals. There's still enough land ice worldwide to raise the sea level another 73 meters (240 feet) if it melts.

The Greenland ice sheet is up to 3,200 meters (two miles) thick and a little smaller than Mexico. Melted, it would raise the global sea level by over 6 meters (20 feet). That would take centuries. But since 2000, some of Greenland's major glaciers—each draining enormous areas and already among the fastest-moving glaciers on Earth—have doubled their speed. Greenland's rate of ice loss tripled between 2001 and 2006, to about 200 cubic kilometers (50 cubic miles) a year. (The city of Los Angeles uses about 1 cubic kilometer of water per year.) It continues accelerating. Julian says Austfonna is also shrinking, losing an area about half the size of Manhattan and up to a cubic mile of volume annually.

Stefan Rahmstorf says, "The current change is extremely fast compared to past global change."

"The *acceleration* of the melting isn't factored into most models designed to predict sea level rise," Julian adds. "Our minimum prediction for sea level is a half-meter rise over the next hundred years," he says, "but many glaciologists think it will rise much higher than currently predicted in this century, at least a meter, maybe even a meter and a half."

One meter (three feet) of sea level rise would do little damage—on a calm day. But storm surges are a different story. In December 1992, when a nor'easter briefly raised the water surrounding New York City eight and a half feet above normal, saltwater poured into underground rail tunnels, causing the entire subway system to lose electrical power. Hundreds of passengers on stranded trains required rescue. Battery Tunnel held six feet of water. Parts of the system didn't work for a week and a half. If the sea level rises one meter, that kind of "once a century" flooding would be expected about once every three years.

Rahmstorf mentions implications for the Gulf Stream. Ironically, the Gulf Stream depends partly on seawater freezing in the Greenland and Norwegian Seas. As seawater turns to ice, it ejects salts. The nearby hyper-salty frigid water, about the densest water anywhere on the planet, sinks thousands of feet to the seafloor. Warm surface water from the south flows in to fill the hole made by this sinking water. That's a big part of what drives the Gulf Stream. The less sea ice forms, the less salty and dense the waters of the Arctic will be. Accelerated land-ice melting makes sea surface waters even fresher and even less dense. Less sinking water would mean less warm water flowing up from the south. The Gulf Stream could weaken.

Scientists recently decided that the chances of the Gulf Stream slowing significantly in this century are low, under 10 percent. But they could not confidently say the risk was under 5 percent. Says Rahmstorf, "About risking breakdown in a major ocean system and very severe consequences, a ten percent chance is, I think, not very reassuring. Ten percent, to me, that's too high."

AUGUST

Blue Crabs are in the bays, and my friend Pete has been among them in the moonlight, scooping up the beautiful swimmers, who soon find themselves conveyed from bucket to pot to the sauce of garden tomatoes and sweet basil, thence to their ultimate resting place between a mound of linguine and a round of baked clams. The aroma arouses Kenzie's interest, but she shows pretty good patience while she waits for dish scraps.

The first cool, dry winds—at the height of August—are autumn's way of whispering in our ear. The young Ospreys are all flying. They've had a year of good food and good luck. In some years, when food is low, winds high, or rains heavy, many chicks don't last this long. For the first time, the nests are empty in the midafternoon. And the sight of those empty nests foreshadows the loss and longing that will come as cooler winds prevail and so much life drains south like time running out. But for now this year's flying chicks and their parents still convene at their nests in the evenings, and the parents are still providing food. Their hunger will sharpen to daggers once they leave the nest site and the most dangerous period of their young lives breaks the idyll of being so lavishly cared for.

Monarch butterflies are already flitting down the beaches, along the bay shores, across the water, and over the ocean. Does anything look so frail and vulnerable as a migrating butterfly over open water, miles from shore? Headed from Canada to Mexico, they're easy to notice, and always difficult to believe. For beauty and the awesome mystery of evolution on our coast, nothing exceeds the epic complexity of the migrations of these big-winged bugs. Theirs is no simple north-south. It's a bizarre, multigenerational migration. Three generations go only north: one generation goes from Mexico to the southern United States; the next generation goes from the southern to the northern United States; the third generation hatches in the northern United States and finally reaches Canada. Only the fourth generation goes south, but *it* goes all the way from Canada to mass-wintering sites in central Mexico. (On the West Coast, some Monarchs winter in sites in California.) Northbound migrants live only about two months. Those making the southbound trip survive about nine months.

This raises questions much bigger than the butterflies themselves: How do they "know" what generation they're from and what they are supposed to do? And if their hatching latitude somehow determines their directional tendencies, we still have the question of how one generation is programmed to live so much longer. Scientists first realized the extent of their southerly migration in 1975, when tagged butterflies were discovered in a small number of sites in the mountains of Mexico. Those few sites harbored *millions* of butterflies.

These Monarchs passing our local dunes must travel up to twenty-five hundred miles in about a month, to a place none of them has ever been, and that their parents and grandparents never saw. Migrating Monarchs experimentally moved hundreds of miles off course can reorient using Earth's magnetic field, change their heading—and go to the right place. Each Monarch weighs one-fifth of one ounce. What they know is what they need to know.

What they don't know is that their Mexican destination is in danger. Logging is shrinking their winter sanctuaries. And the numbers of Monarchs are dwindling. Without their sheltering forest, they can die in cold weather. In one storm, 80 percent of the butterflies in one of their Mexican wintering sites died.

Egrets are moving—many one day, none the next. Cormorants are already pouring in from the north, heading south in large flocks, just the vanguard of months of travelers. And just to be contrary, or as a joke, Laughing Gulls are moving *north,* coming here from the south after breeding, as every year; they'll stay through the fall bonanza, when the Point becomes a two-month riot of migrant birds and fishes. For humans, August is high summer, vacation time. By contrast, my

hardworking *non*human neighbors always seem to be thinking and acting one step ahead.

❧

One hot day I was at the marina putting new line on some fishing reels,
replacing rusted shackles on my boat's anchor chain, and doing a few other
things I'd been putting off. Late in the afternoon, the sky gathered into a
dark knot of brooding anger. A wind came up and the clouds thickened
so dramatically that everyone left their boats and walked to the top of the
dock. The bar emptied, too. Weather is the subject of incessant commentary
at marinas, but this time most folks, many with drinks in hand, just stared.
We all just stood there, looking north as the sky charged down toward us.

Late-day thunderstorms aren't unusual in August. They're often dramatic, usually brief, and they cool the air nicely for sleeping. But this one
looked truly fierce. Everyone scattered before the first wave of rain hit,
running for their cars and houses. Except me. After so hot a day, I savored
the first cooling drops, the exhilaration of the lightning, and the thumping
thunder. But not for long. The big drops struck with a hail-like sting. The
rain gathered such vengeance that I, too, soon sprinted across a parking
lot sheeted with water. When I got into my car, I was already drenched.

The thick opaqueness of the sky and the sheer volume of falling
water cast everything in a deep shadow, like premature night. When I
started the ignition and the wipers began beating the windshield, my
headlights illuminated a shimmering bead curtain of raindrops dense
enough to veil the nearby boats. I slowly drove toward the inlet to watch
the storm sweep across the Sound. But halfway there, I had to pull off the
road. I couldn't see well enough to drive. In fact, I couldn't see through
the rain at all. That had never happened before. I did eventually get there,
and watched clouds carpet-bomb our harbor with rain.

After a few minutes it eased up. I got on the main road, headed home.
Soon another wave of rain came on, like someone pouring buckets of
nails on the car's roof. When I pulled off this time, I had plenty of company. The road's shoulder looked train-wrecked with blinded drivers. I
sat there, my windshield wipers rapidly pacing the confines of vision,
wiping away what began to seem like uncontrolled sobbing.

When I later approached home, less than seven miles away, I expected to see the marsh swollen over the roadway and my skylights weeping puddles onto my floor. Instead, the streets were dry. My neighbors the Badkins had worked their way through the same downpour. They've lived here for seven decades, and we agreed on two things: we were astonished that the storm had such a sharp edge to it that it could smite one town with a biblical downpour and leave the next town's roses thirsty after such a hot day. And: none of us had ever in our lives seen such rain.

I left it at that. But then I started hearing the same from other people—from other states; they talked about seeing rain so blinding that they'd had to pull off the road. A couple of months later, the Intergovernmental Panel on Climate Change noted, "The frequency of heavy precipitation events has increased over most land areas, consistent with warming and observed increases of atmospheric water vapor." The heat sends the sea into the sky, and the sky doth weep.

≈

August used to mean a lot of time spent far offshore. Who needed air-conditioning when you had the whole Atlantic? I believed that during summer you wasted a day if you untied a boat and planned to be back at the dock in under fifteen hours. And I did a lot of shark fishing.

In the mid-1990s, during a short spell of fine weather, I had the urge to go offshore but couldn't locate anyone who could join me on a weekday. I left the harbor in the dark, and the sun rose to find *First Light* already on the ocean, running southeast. About twelve miles offshore I noticed a change in the water color. Its greenish tint yielded suddenly to a clearer blue. The water temperature jumped several degrees in half a mile. This was a pretty distinct edge. The terns I'd seen inshore were now replaced by several shearwaters. The floating weeds were different here, too; drifting rockweed and eelgrass from the bays were replaced by a yellowish weed called sargassum that originates far offshore. I had crossed into new water. This drifting oceanic border was a reasonable place to look for sharks.

I cut the engine and set up, putting a perforated bucket full of ground-up fish over the side. Hoping for a mako, I baited a hook with a whole mackerel, attached a float, and drifted it out about 150 feet, letting the float bob in the blue swells. Then for a few hours I worked pleasurably on edits to a manuscript, drifting and dreaming.

• • •

During late morning I heard a splash, saw a swirl, and watched the line come tight and my rod lunge downward. I got to my feet as the line began slipping under the tight drag, and I struggled to wrestle the rod from its holder, snap my back harness to the reel, and follow the fish around the boat's stern.

Virtually no one goes shark fishing alone. A shark-fishing crew usually has three people: one for the rod, one to eventually grab and hold the leader, and one to gaff or release the shark. I had a plan to be all three: if I worked a fish to the boat, I'd put the rod in a holder, grab the leader with one hand, and deal with the fish with the other hand.

This plan might work well with sharks like medium-sized summer Blue Sharks, which always stay submerged and roll slowly, if at all, at boatside. But it could be trickier if this was a mako. Makos can be fast, erratic, liable to high-jump unpredictably (hooked makos have leapt into boats), and prone to rapid spinning at boatside. A wildly thrashing shark can throw a loop of leader wire around your hand—it's happened to me— and might pull you over. Things can happen out in big water with big fish. I would have preferred company.

Now I had company: on the other end of the line hissing through the surface.

The shark came up and thrashed. And I saw that cobalt back and those steely flanks; I saw the bullet snout and a stiff, strong tail and glimpsed a black pit of an eye. Mako.

To my mind the shark of all sharks, the Short-finned Mako is a sleek streak of sapphire, a gemstone cut from the sea itself. To say it is fearless and cunning seems like cheap anthropomorphism, so let's just say I have known excellent fishermen who consider the Short-finned Mako demonically clever. Even among sharks, it is big (the largest females exceed half a ton), unusually fast, and exceptionally aerial when hunting or hooked. It is the only known predator of adult Swordfish. It is warm-blooded. Also unusually among sharks, its flesh tastes delicious.

I always released all the sharks I caught, except that in those days I'd sometimes—once every two or three years—keep a mako for the grill. It had been seven years since I'd killed my first good-sized mako, a shark just over two hundred pounds. That was the last time I'd felt thoroughly excited

about a big fish, but even then I'd felt remorse afterward. That surge of buck
fever, that trembling adrenaline thrill I'd so often felt as a teenager and
even well into my twenties, was replaced with conflicting thoughts. These
big, dangerous animals had come to seem too vulnerable. In the interven-
ing years I'd caught and released a lot of sharks. I'd seen the Smooth
Hammerheads and Sandbar Sharks and Duskies and Tigers virtually disappear, and even the formerly abundant Blue Sharks decline, killed mainly
by commercial long-liners for their fins. I'd watched the makos grow
scarce, killed by both sport and commercial fishermen for meat. Each time
a happy crew in a victory mood hoisted a big mako or thresher onto the
marina's scales, I felt a sort of sadness.

But now, alone and with this shark hooked, I knew one thing: I
wanted this mako.

Finding a mako is difficult enough. Tempting it to bite isn't always
easy. Subduing and securing one is tricky even for experienced crews.
Most people wouldn't consider trying it alone, and can't imagine how it
could be managed. I knew that if I did all these things solo, there would
be congratulations and status at the marina. I would be respected as a
skilled fisherman. My ego was captaining this trip.

Understand, please, that I was the product of two cultures. I had
fished since I was three years old. Fishing had its rules and community
values. Anyone can understand why an athlete is thrilled to win, and
millions of sports spectators share that tense thrill of competition and
the honor and prestige that follow victory. Fishing is much more personal, but one facet is competitive, and prestige still accompanies big fish.
As a kid, I thought there could be no better compliment than for someone to gesture with their chin and whisper, "*He's* a good fisherman."

Now youth's wolf was howling me back to the pack. I was back to
wanting to *prove* something. I didn't ask why or intellectualize. This connection to the shark was direct and immediate. Adrenaline was returning me to my emotional roots—indeed, back to the emotional roots of
humanity, locked in battle with a large, dangerous beast. No witnesses or
referee presided, no photos could record a skilled release. I wanted this
animal for meat, and I wanted status as a skilled hunter. I wanted to drag
it into my village and have the other hunters dance around it.

We all do the same thing almost daily, of course. The corporate

climber seeks to be a tribal chief. The necktied, starch-shirted businessman seeks respect as a maker of killings. It's all the same: bring down
the quarry, tell the harrowing tale around the fire, howl in victory,
sleep off the full belly, and hunt again. The rawness is masked, the flesh
deodorized, but we still, simply for status, strive to excel among our
peers. Beneath the suits, the bulk of business consists of cave dwellers
on commuter trains.

All ashore was elaborate convention. Here was a truer enduring reality: a risky hunt, a struggle to capture food, the promise of praise. But if
I had thought of those things earlier, all thought now was narrowed to a
point. In the heat of the moment, the shark was neither allegory, nor
parable, nor metaphor. My knees were shaking. I wanted to kill this fish.

It was a hot, calm day, the August sun stabbing the sea to depth. The
shark went deep to fight in cooler shadows. Bowed over the arced rod, I
broke a sweat. I rocked and cranked. I raised the fish a few inches at a
time, so slowly, so sleightly, that the mako began to rise as if lulled, as if
it had gotten over its alarm.

Its glowing color appeared below, its body turned against the pressure, hanging hard and hardly moving.

I reached for my glove. I rehearsed the endgame in my mind: When
the ten-foot wire leader broke the surface, I'd unclip the harness from
the reel. When the leader reached the rod tip, I would put the rod in the
boat's rod holder. While grasping the leader—smoothly, so as not to
alarm the shark—I would lift the readied harpoon. I would delay the
thrust until the shark broke the water and hesitated. I would wait until I
had a clear shot to the wide part of its body behind the dorsal fin. Then
I would visualize darting the shaft clear through the other side and
would ram it with all the thrust one arm could muster.

The shark loomed up. It was tired and stayed calm. It seemed large. A
hundred and eighty pounds? All fish look bigger underwater. Pay attention. There's the leader. Unclip the harness. Here it is. Rod into holder.
Leader in hand. Be smooth. Harpoon seems heavy; arm's tired.

I had the weight of the fish on the leader in one hand, the weight of
the long wooden harpoon shaft overhead. A man with a spear, face to
face with a large, dangerous animal—an old, old scene.

I pressured the leader and the shark's bullet of a snout rose through the surface, pointing at me. Bad angle. The hesitation made my tired arm weaken.

I relaxed the leader a little and the shark rotated slowly onto its side and turned to dive.

I struck and the fish exploded, spinning crazily and diving, ripping the dart from its side and stripping line from my humming reel.

I had not lunged hard enough; my arm was too tired from the fight and from holding the heavy harpoon overhead.

Amazingly, the violence did not break the line or throw a weakening kink into the leader. In a few minutes I again drew the shark close. I decided that this time I would try for a shot through the gills. A gill shot is more decisive but riskier. The head, rather than the tail, swerves toward you, making it harder to place the securing tail rope, increasing the chance of the shark biting and perhaps severing the harpoon line, and—notably— raising the possibility that a sudden leap will propel the animal straight at you.

The mako came up again. I was ready. But when the shark presented the perfect shot, I hesitated.

The shark waited.

I looked deep into that black eye. Undefiant, matter-of-factly, the mako informed me that this was no game, not a "sport." That eye rolled forward just a bit, then back to me—and inquired, What next?

I reconsidered. Then I thrust.

The mako blurred into lashing froth and blood. I reached for the gaff and sank it and swept him toward me and cinched the tail rope.

Now I had my prize. Each subsequent thrash pumped a new pillow of blood into the water. For a few more minutes, the black eye queried: What next? Then the creature drained away into the sea, and all I had was a dead carcass tied to the boat, and myself. And something had gone from me in that same billowing blood that took the shark and left the carcass. I'd sought to prove my place among others. The shark taught me that everything has its place, and I had overstepped mine. I knew then it was the last time I would ever feel that trembling buck fever.

I had loved the sleek motion, the speed and agility, the gliding vitality and ocean-bursting power. And all these things, I had just destroyed. I had sought connection, but beyond connection, possession. And beyond possession, I had used the shark to prove something to others. That left my motives open to question. It is one thing to catch a fish and eat it. But there is in these equations a matter of scale, and such a thing as too much. And sometimes, why one does something is more important than what one does.

Now I'd have my steaks. Grills would sizzle. At the dock came the expected congratulations, the admiring onlookers male and female, the incredulous head shakes that I had conquered this fish *alone*. My name found its way into the weekly fishing columns. I had distinguished myself. Perhaps people would say, "*He's* a good fisherman." But with sharks declining, I could not duck the fact that I was still drawing blood from such magnificent creatures. And that made the sought-after admiration feel hollow.

A few days later I repeated the offshore solo venture and located another mako. This time, after its leaping fight subsided and I drew the creature close, I leaned overboard not with harpoon but with hook remover. In those days virtually no one released sizable makos. But at the dock no one who asked what I'd caught questioned my tale of solo catch and *solo release*—because I'd proven my prowess with the earlier carcass. Now I was proving—if only to myself—that the next step in prowess was to relinquish the prize. But as it turned out, I again made the fishing columns, this time as a kind of mako liberator.

Neptune pronounced this good and did what he could to encourage the publicity: I caught seven makos that season—more than twice my previous seasonal high. And except for that first, I released them all. Each release was duly noted in the weekly fishing news. People responded favorably; some suggested that I was setting an example. Maybe I *would* become a good fisherman after all.

People are hungry to make their mark in the world. Every shark would understand. Or would they? The shark has a hunter's attitude, but there's nothing social in its killing. It gains only nutrition, knows no pride. The shark does only what it needs, and needs only what it does. Of the burden of needing to make an impression, the shark is free. Yet we cause the whole world, even the sharks of the blue ocean, to bear the burden of our egos. Certainly I had.

We must all kill to live, and scarcely a vegetarian would deny it. Some measure of good resides in getting one's food from nature, for the connections it brings, the sense of place and the community it gathers. But two forks exist in the decision tree: One involves whether the killing is humane. The other, whether we can keep doing this. Shark hunting fails on both counts. If a course of action simply cannot last, we must admit to ourselves that it's wrong. I knew that whether I killed one mako shark a year or released them all would not decide the future of the species. I wasn't the problem, but we're all always only part of the problem. At some point one confronts the question of right and wrong in private, with the door closed. We can do the right thing. Right things maintain a community. I prefer a community that includes, among many things, sharks.

We each make our solo voyages to deep, expansive waters. Alone in our contest with the wider world, we test our mettle and seek our trophies, promotions, compliments, and accolades. We strive to be needed and to thereby know that there is a reason for us. We seek to be told we are good because we're too unsure of ourselves to know. Yet often we remain so focused on our neediness that we forget the creatures—human and otherwise—we're drawing into the vortex of our own passion play. All of us have compulsive loves we must forbear. We forget to see that we can engage the world without harming it. And although we fish for approval, the challenge is: to capture our prizes while bringing more to the world than we take.

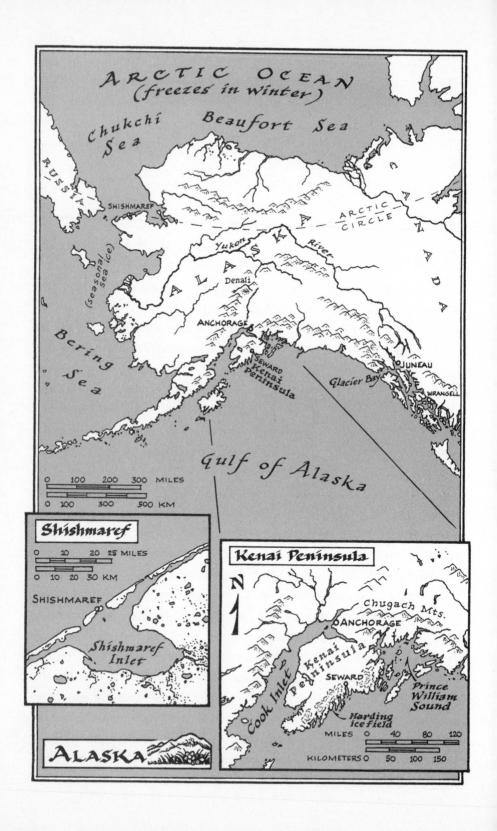

ARCTIC OCEAN
(freezes in winter)

Chukchi Sea

Beaufort Sea

RUSSIA

SHISHMAREF

(seasonal sea ice)

ARCTIC CIRCLE

CANADA

Yukon

River

ALASKA

Denali

ANCHORAGE

Bering Sea

SEWARD
Kenai Peninsula

JUNEAU

Glacier Bay

WRANGELL

0   100   200   300   MILES
0   100   300   500 KM

Gulf of Alaska

Shishmaref

0   10   20   25 MILES
0   10   20   30 KM

SHISHMAREF

Shishmaref Inlet

ALASKA

Kenai Peninsula

N

Chugach Mts.

ANCHORAGE

Cook Inlet

Kenai Peninsula

SEWARD

Prince William Sound

Harding ice field

MILES   0   40   80   120
KILOMETERS 0   50   100   150

TRAVELS POLAR:
BAKED ALASKA

❧ ❧ ❧

In the panhandle of Southeast Alaska, we saw a system working and recovering because enough was left to maintain its viability and resilience. Up in Svalbard, we saw how a changing Arctic climate can affect wildlife. In mainland Alaska, you can see how it affects people, too.

Belying its ferocious reputation as a deadly body of water, the Chukchi Sea is laid down flat like a lion among lambs, gently licking the shore-line. The air feels thin, the sun direct. I push up my sleeves, enjoying beach weather a stone's throw from the Arctic Circle.

The Inupiat Eskimo community of Shishmaref (population 600) stands upon a sandy island, three miles long but just a quarter mile wide. The mainland and its shimmering mountains lie five miles away. To say it is in Alaska, in the United States, is to obscure its history. These people have lived here for centuries. Located near where human foot-prints first marked a vast new world, this site has likely been used for millennia. The current residents say four thousand years. During all the long quotidian cavalcade of centuries, only in the last decade has their way of life seemed threatened.

Fluffy Arctic Cotton Grass nods in the breeze, acknowledging the faint melancholy of tundra summer. Long-tailed Jaegers and snowy Glau-cous Gulls drift overhead. Rock Sandpipers, Long- and Short-billed Dow-itchers, and Golden Plovers probe the marshes for food they will turn to jet fuel. The Goldens, once plumped, will launch another of the planet's most extreme migrations, crossing the trackless Pacific to somehow arrive, famished and exhausted, on little dots and atolls of land throughout Polynesia.

Over the sandy streets the sky is haphazardly crisscrossed with utility wires. Among the clustered wooden houses, snowmobiles, dogsleds, and all-terrain vehicles in repose and disrepair clutter the neighborhood. Everyone's got their own used-parts scrapyard. At the edge of town, canted oil drums and dead snow machines lurk in the weeds. There's no "away" to throw them.

One might see here an Arctic slum, but this community's sense of itself has withstood the twenty-four-hour nights of hundreds upon hundreds of winters. As Eskimos, their identity is as hunters, past and present. On the steps to one home, as I might temporarily place grocery bags on my own porch, lie two fresh Spotted Seals, their fine pied pelts stained crimson from gunshots to the head. The roofs sport caribou racks and whale bones. A Polar Bear skin, its fur impossibly deep and dense, dries outside. Numerous skulls and antlers, which elsewhere might be trophies, lie simply discarded.

Hunter economics still apply; meat gets shared. Many men support their immediate families plus needy extended-family members. There are some jobs in infrastructure and a little trade work. Sealskin handbags and carvings of Walrus ivory or bone are sold to shops in places like Anchorage. But for most people here, employment is as sporadic as berry picking.

In the school, virtues rim the gym walls: "Family," "Humility," "Respect for Others," "Loyalty," "Love for Children," "Domestic Skills," "Hunter Success." The gym also features an American flag and a large mural of frolicking Polar Bears (with a rifle-bearing hunter sneaking up from behind a floe so stealthily that I noticed him only when I reviewed my photographs days later).

Internet access notwithstanding, most talk revolves around hunting and the changing weather. Still heavily reliant on wild food, the people remain embedded in the cycle of seasons. But as the climate changes, they become not just dependent on nature but hostage to it.

Because sea ice buffers Shishmaref from winter storms, provides access to winter hunting, and brings Walruses and seals, ice loss threatens these people acutely. Eskimos rely on conditions that would kill Polynesians—or even New Yorkers. And vice versa, probably. But once people have adapted, change can destroy them.

Shishmaref is not about one unlucky community. It's about having a front-row seat to changes that will sweep the world. If a few Eskimos recently descended from a nomadic culture are finding the challenge of moving daunting, can our own entrenched energy, water, and agriculture systems adapt to accelerating changes? About how human beings respond to change, Shishmaref is oracle.

And Shishmaref's own local oracle is one Stanley Tocktoo, mayor, a man of medium build and copper skin. On a small bluff overlooking the sea, we talk over the growls of huge balloon-tired trucks delivering massive boulders to a crane; the crane is arranging the boulders into defensive beach armoring.

Earlier defenses—caged rocks and sea walls—the sea demolished. Now the folks are ratcheting up with boulders barged in from elsewhere. I'm told that this will cost $36 million. Thing is, nobody believes that it can fix the problem. Everyone understands this fact: Shishmaref is doomed.

"They tell us this place has nine to fifteen years left," Tocktoo relays. It would cost an estimated $180 to $200 million to move the town—houses, generators, schools, clinic, airstrip, infrastructure. The hope is, these boulders will buy the people enough time to abandon the place.

When asked if there is an Inupiat expression for climate change, Luci Eningowuk responds, "No. We're too busy fighting it." As Shishmaref's Erosion and Relocation Commitee chair, she doesn't have time for chitchat.

In times past, sea ice, and perpetually frozen ground called permafrost, constituted Shishmaref's natural armoring. Ice extending seaward from the shoreline prevented ferocious storm waves from approaching town. These days, there's often no ice.

Tocktoo says, "Without ice, we lose land. One storm, northwest, seventy-miles-an-hour wind, we lost fifty feet of land."

"A silent storm will do it too," adds Luci. She's referring to an exceptionally high tide, with no wind.

"We've seen the water rising up so far—. Every high tide like that, we lose part of our island. Never been like this before. Man, it's weird," says Tocktoo. A few paces away, a house lies newly shattered on the beach, toppled just days ago from the crumbling bluff. "There was eighteen homes here," Tocktoo adds. The ruins of only the last one remain visible between the newly collapsed bluff and the newly advancing surf. "One was my old house. Washed away. It can do that."

"In the 1950s we had three rows of rolling sand dunes out there," Luci tells me, waving beyond the rolling surf. Her mind must be painting a picture from memory, but her gestures carry my gaze only to open water.

"Used to be you could dig maybe five, six feet in summer to permafrost," Tocktoo explains. "Permafrost was our refrigerator. That's where we stored Walrus, seal meat, kept our seal oil—."

"It's gone," Luci emphasizes. "Even in the winter now, it's mushy."

Melting ice and melting permafrost drive a vicious cycle of "positive feedbacks" about which little is positive. Thawing permafrost exposes dead vegetation that was deep-frozen for millennia. Its rotting releases more methane and carbon dioxide, which trap more heat in the atmosphere. (Methane traps twenty times more heat than carbon dioxide and is currently at concentrations two and a half times higher than it was two hundred years ago. Methane comes from rotting and fermentation and natural gas. Most now emanates from gassy cows, pigs, and chickens; manure and sewage; and rice paddies.) There's a lot of carbon in Arctic soil, and its release hasn't been factored into most climate-change models.

Wind turbines at the edge of town lower Shishmaref's emissions. These people being swallowed by the swelling sea are doing their part but are suffering our consequences. To oversimplify: we took oil from the Natives and returned it in the form of heat, which is destroying their culture. Now it's a little as if, in order to placate the rising sea, we're offering as sacrifice the people of this town.

Arctic winter temperatures are up 4 to 7 degrees Fahrenheit (2° to 4° C) since the mid-twentieth century. The Arctic surface is mostly frozen ocean, which can all melt. As we saw in Svalbard, the more it melts, the faster the melting goes. That's because ice reflects 70 percent of sunlight striking it, but seawater reflects only 6 percent; the rest of the light gets absorbed and converted into heat. That's why the Arctic is warming about twice as fast as the rest of the planet. Consequently, the Arctic Ocean is melting faster than predicted. A few years ago, scientists predicted that the whole Arctic Ocean would be practically ice-free in summer by 2100; the latest analyses say before 2050. Where warming fueled partly by petroleum has helped melt the north, various nations are scrambling to claim the newly accessible Arctic seabed. They're hoping to find . . . petroleum. If we were nearing the end of the Stone Age, these are the people who would be stockpiling rocks.

"It's very sad, you know, to see our community wash away," Tocktoo says.

The sea level has been rising for millennia, though literally at a glacial pace. But now "glacial pace" is faster than it used to be, since nearly all the world's glaciers are melting, faster. And because seawater expands as it warms, warming compounds the oceans' rise. Since the last ice age, sea levels have risen four hundred feet. But during all of human *civilization,* neither the sea level nor the rate of its rise has ever been higher or faster than both are now.

Nearby, kids are swimming in the surf, something unthinkable just a few years ago. "The water's too warm to leave our salmon nets overnight," Luci complains. "The fish get soft and fall apart when you dry them. You have to check your net every few hours now." Elders were recently puzzled by a strange new fish washed up on the beach; it was the first skate anyone here had ever seen.

"Now you don't see freeze-up until January or February," Tocktoo says. "You don't see that thick ice, that blue ice, like when I was growing up. Sometimes, we have a quarter mile of slush." But because the people depend on Bearded Seals and Walruses, they must go hunting. Tocktoo hunts for his wife and kids, his father, and his father-in-law. "In spring," Tocktoo explains, "you gotta really recognize weak ice, thin ice—. It's very tricky because now we're getting big springtime snowfalls. Makes everything white; covers the weak ice. Very dangerous. People falling through the ice most years now." The community is mourning a young man whose snow machine recently fell through the ice while he was returning from hunting.

It's a major problem for animals, too. Bearded Seals, Ringed Seals, Walruses, various other mammals, and certain seabirds are all woven into the sea-ice system. For them, mere melting is a death sentence. Lean and hungry Polar Bears sometimes prowl into town. "Because we've got so many kids here," Tocktoo says, sounding apologetic, "we had to shoot three bears in just the last year."

He explains, "Used to have Walrus near the coast. Sometimes now we go sixty or eighty miles for Walrus, a hundred miles out for Bearded Seal. You gotta really read the weather that far at sea. We recognize mirages. We read the clouds. You need experience. Young people, sixty miles from shore, you tell them a storm is coming, they say, 'The weather looks nice.' When I'm out in the ocean, I'm always teaching my crew, 'Watch the clouds,' 'Watch this or that.'"

In summer the people go to the mainland, collecting eggs of water-birds, picking cloudberries and sour dock (a tricky plant that can be poisonous raw), and catching salmon. September is crowberry- and blueberry-picking time. Later in fall: duck, goose, Moose, and Caribou hunting.

"Facing having to leave all our food—it hurts," Stanley Tocktoo says sadly. "That is our grocery store out there." He sweeps his open hand as if stroking the landscape. "We've been here for four thousand years for one reason: easiest access to the food supply. We have good channels on each side of this island—access to the ocean, a lagoon behind the island for tomcod, whitefish, and access to the mainland. There is no other place like this on this whole coast. The other islands are surrounded by shallows. We picked out this place for survival purposes. If we make this just a hunting camp, we'd have to figure out how to get across the lagoon when the ice is bad."

Getting separated from the food supply isn't a problem limited to Shishmaref or to Inuit people—or to people. It's one of the great themes of the great decoupling effect of warming on what had been tight-linked ecosystems. Sea ice used to melt in spring, releasing nutrients to single-celled plankton, igniting the whole food chain. Now it melts weeks earlier, nutrients releasing when the days are still too short for plankton to grow or reproduce. (The short days lack sufficient sunlight for photo-synthesis.) No early plankton means scarce food for shellfish, which means starving sea ducks, Walruses searching too far afield from their hungry pups, and skinny Gray Whales migrating hundreds of extra miles yet still not finding enough to eat. In the North Sea, changing temperatures have shifted copepod populations north by about six hundred miles, taking them out of the range of cod larvae, helping push an intensely fished cod population into a steady decline. Elsewhere in the North Atlantic, similar shifts in copepods and northern krill have caused declines in salmon. It's happening globally. And now, like everything else in this community of life they belong to, the people of Shishmaref find their habitat changing, their food growing scarcer, and they are facing the need to move.

Until the late 1990s, I could travel from the Arctic Circle to the Antarctic Peninsula and along the tropics' coral coasts and hear little about global warming. There'd be the odd anecdote, and we always knew the sea level was rising because old-timers could tell of changes along the coast. But now, everywhere I go—or even if I stay home at Lazy Point—people have stories. The anecdotes form a mosaic of changes both subtle and widespread. For all the focus on spectacular events like crumbling ice shelves and open water at the North Pole, many small things are also happening. I hear that Arctic shorebirds are losing nesting habitat as bushes sprout across formerly open tundra. I've seen nesting sea turtles caught in the squeeze as home owners build seawalls to hold on to property that a rising ocean wants to repossess. I've visited atolls where the world's largest albatross populations—over a million adults—utterly depend on nesting sands just a few feet above sea level. I've learned about corals stressed by water getting too warm and acidic. I've seen melting ice affecting everything from Polar Bears and Walruses to, now, Eskimos, and I'll see it affecting people in the tropics and penguins in Antarctica.

Tocktoo pauses, chipping the ground with his shoe. "Gotta figure out something," he mumbles. "We've selected a place thirteen miles inland, called Tin Creek. It's one of our hunting areas. If we move into other communities, we'd have scary things for our kids, like drugs. That's a big worry for me. We're very happy that our culture is still with us, our heritage, our values—the Inupiat People, y'know?"

The pragmatic Luci says, "We want our kids to go to college and come back as surveyors, lawyers—. But they're afraid of our storms. They're settling elsewhere. Who'd want to come to a place that is so endangered?"

"We care about community," Tocktoo concludes. "When terrorists hit the twin towers on 9/11, we all got hurt. We didn't know the people, but we knew they had families. We got sad. We put our American flags outside."

Considering all we've taken from Alaska—minerals, timber, the oil, and the future of these people—and considering the billowing billions of dollars pumped from Alaska into the lower forty-eight states, $180 million to move the community would seem a reasonable cost of doing business.

Many other people around the world live in need, some whose islands are also washing away. But as Americans, we have a special compact here. And a bigger question looms: If it's so hard logistically and financially to move a small American community a few miles to an unoccupied place on uncontested ground, *what happens when it's time to move Bangladesh?* What will happen when tens of millions of poor people must abandon saltwater-flooded farms and ruined wells and move in on top of other poor people whose food and water supplies are barely adequate as it is? And coastal China, Africa, Southeast Asia—?

"When I was a kid we went to church every Sunday. But now, not so many people go," Tocktoo says as we stroll past the church cemetery, where departed Eskimos lie in graves marked by crosses. The minister, a white guy, is new. Luci says it's difficult to get a pastor. "Who'd want to come live in a place that's so endangered?" she repeats.

I'm invited into one house that displays prominent Christian iconography: a crucifix, paintings of Jesus. Edwin Weyiouanna has generously extended an invitation for a lunch of local delicacies. His mother, Flora, has spread the table with preserved black seal meat (from *Oogruk*, the Bearded Seal, dried for a month, then buried in a plastic pail of seal oil); seal intestine; dried seal jerky; *muktuk* (whale blubber with skin attached); boiled Caribou; smoked salmon; and boiled Arctic Char, a relative of trout that inhabits both sea- and freshwater and is the world's northernmost-ranging freshwater fish. I'm finding the Caribou especially tasty.

Chicken, pork, cereal, and the like are available here, and kids constantly suck sugar candies, so even grade-schoolers show rotten teeth. But these people aren't joking when they say they rely on hunting.

Flora, who still wields her *ulu* knife deftly enough to make short work of a thick chunk of pink Bowhead Whale blubber, says, "People with teeth like it. Dip it in this seal oil. It doesn't have much flavor, but you won't get hungry again soon."

The seal oil is clear, like fine olive oil. I've never tasted whale before. I'm told the people here don't kill whales but trade for whale meat with another village. Commercial whaling is corrupt and cruel. But under the circumstances, trying a bite seems permissible, and I concur with Flora on its lack of flavor and the effect on one's appetite.

On the question of whether Flora wants to make the move away from here, she deadpans in her elderly voice, "I want to go to Hollywood; that's where the money is."

На the flight from Shishmaref back to Anchorage I have my face in the window, soaking in the splendor of Denali and Alaska's unfathomable vastness. Compared to the white-bread blandness of the Great Plains and its straight-line, wrecked-angular, sod-busted subjugation, Alaska is a place of such depth your mind can founder. It's so seductive as to be positively menacing. I run my eyes over the landscape like fingers across a map before a great adventure, when the mind levitates with the elation of the unbounded possible. I know what it's like to get swallowed in wilderness, the euphoria—and the terror. Alaska just seems to be lying there, all undressed, winking at me.

I take off my sweatshirt outside the airport and a cabbie agrees that it's "too hot"—75 degrees Fahrenheit. "It was like this yesterday, too," he adds. His roses now bloom in October; that never used to happen. When I phone home I learn that a Magnificent Frigatebird, normally resident in the Caribbean, is being seen by birders near Lazy Point.

Driving toward Seward. The Chugach people lived around what's now called Prince William Sound, a name soiled and synonymous with

Exxon and Big Oil's long rap sheet against nature. But for scenery today I've got the Chugach Mountains and Chugach National Forest, five million wild acres.

Many of Alaska's locals resent the parks and national forests here because they object to federal involvement in "their" region (but they don't complain about getting our tax money; on a per-Alaskan basis, federal funds to this state run twenty-five times the national average). Like anti–"big government" folk in many places, such people are whining, selfish hypocrites. America has something for everyone, and those who want more development can move to Seattle, Denver, or Dallas. Meanwhile, Alaska itself has something for all of us: American public land. Call me patriotic, but *American* wilderness strikes me as among the most exquisite remaining untrammeled landscapes on Earth. Part of its beauty is in the way "wilderness" is an American concept. Part of its beauty is in the statesmanship and forethought that has, so far, kept some of these places wild and original. I thank those whose foresight passed the Alaska Lands Act. And thanks, everyone who has fought to keep Alaskan oil development where it was supposed to go and the Arctic National Wildlife Refuge where the Caribou are supposed to go. A deal's a deal.

In Turnagain Arm—a fjord where Captain Cook dead-ended, so turned again—the waters flow silty with fine "rock flour" ground by glaciers against stone. Several pods of Beluga Whales, dusky juveniles and ivory-white adults, roil the murky surface. To navigate and find fish, they use sonar. Seeing them is a treat, especially since this population has declined 75 percent in twenty years. The reasons—oil? other contaminants? native hunting?—remain debated. Probably all of the foregoing.

Here in Cook Inlet, the tide can swing an impressive thirty feet in six hours. It's North America's second-highest tidal fluctuation after the Bay of Fundy. We could harness some of that energy into clean electricity, perhaps without hurting wildlife. Someday, when the arguing over oil and global warming dies down in the face of inarguable realities, we probably will.

In a small stream, a marvel: Sockeye and Chum Salmon that are not just swimming upstream but actually spawning: courting, digging nests, laying and fertilizing eggs. Some are bright and vigorous. Others, spotted with fungus, their fins frayed, approach their final stroke. Courting males occasionally fight. One young "jack" male, returned from the sea a year ahead of schedule, orbits a courting pair, then streaks in, strafing sperm across newly laid eggs. He can't know the outcome of his daring act. So is his strange motivation just a sexual urge propelled by anticipation of intense pleasure?

Actually seeing their final drama play out in front of my eyes like this is quite something. A life of struggle comes full circle and becomes a death of service. It packs metaphorical power.

Salmon have another mysterious power: once they enter the human mind, they create a region's soul. Though Alaskans are a diverse and rowdy bunch, one thing they share is their love of salmon. Salmon are business; they are recreation and family; they are a highlight of summer where summer is the highlight of a year. In winter, they're what's for dinner. They are fish and they are icons.

Salmon do best at stream temperatures of about 42 to 55 degrees Fahrenheit (6 to 13°C). Warmer water poses problems. Above 55 degrees Fahrenheit, sperm and eggs get impaired; fertilization and hatching suffers. Temperatures above about 60 degrees Fahrenheit affect the delicate transformation from larvae to juvenile (from "fry" to "smolt") and inhibit internal changes that prepare smolts for migration from freshwater into seawater. In water between 66 and 75 degrees Fahrenheit, depending on the species, adult salmon stop migrating upstream. Around 77 degrees Fahrenheit (25°C), salmon begin dying.

Sue Mauger is a slender, soft-spoken woman with light brown hair and a gentle demeanor. Her small nonprofit outfit, Cook Inlet Keeper, has quixotically undertaken to "protect the Cook Inlet Basin and the life it contains"—an area the size of West Virginia.

Mauger's group is finding streams warming as air temperatures rise. In the summer of 2002, stream temperatures exceeded 55 degrees Fahrenheit for fifty days. Two years later, that was up to eighty days, with a week above 68 degrees. Some individual streams remained above 68 degrees for a month. Up in Yukon streams, warming favors a salmon parasite called *Ichthyophonus*. It turns salmon flesh so mushy that it can't be dried by the people there who've depended on it for winter food. So as usual, poor people suffer first.

"We were certainly surprised," Mauger says, "that the fish here are stressed in each phase of their life cycle."

Partly, the problem is less snow. Mauger explains that winter snow and ice are "like water batteries that need winter recharging if they are to power streams with cool meltwater in summer." But warmer winters mean potential snow falling as rain. Unlike the measured drip of snowmelt, rain just runs away. "So in summer, when we're counting on snowmelt for flow," Mauger continues, "streams have less water running." Low water warms faster. "I never thought I'd be worrying about warm streams in Alaska," Sue says, still incredulous.

Ripples: In California, where salmon, agriculture, and cities all rely on melting snowpack flowing from the Sierras, they're already competing for dwindling water. Snowpack was the year's water reserve. In some recent years, however, the snowpack's been half of normal. Precipitation that used to fall as snow now falls as rain that runs off so rapidly that even the state's extensive dams and reservoirs cannot hold it all for later use.

≈

Ed Burg, a somewhat shy, bearded biologist employed by the U.S. Fish and Wildlife Service, is a big-picture guy fascinated by how landscape and lifescape fit together; how ice, water, rock, sediment, vegetation, and animals weave their tapestry, do their dance.

We're in a roadside meadow dotted with trees, like a pretty Alaska postcard. When Burg drilled here, he found twenty feet of sphagnum peat, representing about fifteen thousand years of accumulation under very wet conditions. He didn't find any wood in those cores; trees did not grow here. When he cored growing trees, he found that the median age of the spruce in these meadows is about thirty years. The birches are just ten to fifteen years old. His main point is that the trees and shrubs are not only young; they're new. Until recently, all the emerald glades in view were wetlands. All these meadows, in other words, are drying out.

"It's a compelling climate story," Dr. Burg says. "But also, on the practical side, if the trees join across these meadows to form continuous forest with each side of these valleys, it would certainly make stopping fires harder."

We walk into deeper, older surrounding woodland. Burg leads. "It's hard working in these forests," he's telling me. "You spend all day climbing over fallen trunks."

But it's obvious that he loves it. All around us, however, trees are dying. His comment: "It gets much worse than this, I assure you."

At a smallish spruce, two feet in diameter, recently fallen, he kneels. "Spruce Bark Beetles have hit this. I'm going to peel off some of the bark and show you the galleries." Galleries—a nice word. "Normally, you can't peel the bark like this. But see this powder under the bark? It's called frass. Insect poop, basically. Beetles have eaten the inner bark layer, where sugar is concentrated, and filled the space with frass." If the attack is really heavy, he adds, they girdle the tree and it dies within a year.

This is about as small a tree as they'll hit. Bigger trees have more of that sugary inner bark. And smaller trees can better defend themselves. "Small trees have higher pitch pressure; they can cement the beetle right in, Mafia-style," adds Burg, relishing the thought.

Indeed, almost all of the surviving trees here are small. Most of the taller trees are already dead. The same temperature change that's drying the bog also stresses the trees; insufficient water impairs their ability to produce pitch, their best defense.

This is one of the largest infestations in North America. Why here? The beetles usually have a two-year life cycle. "Mom comes in spring and lays eggs," explains Burg. The larvae hatch, eat all summer, then spend winter in the tree. They continue eating the next year, change into adults, and spend their second winter in the tree. The *next* spring they come out and find new trees—normally. But when we have really warm summers," Burg says, "they can become adults in their first year." Then the beetles can do in a year what once took two. "You get a double dose."

The beetles have been here for at least 250 years. Only recently, however, have the infestations begun killing forests over a wide region.

"To have an outbreak, you need a loaded gun and a trigger," Burg explains. The gun is having mature trees, and the place was loaded, with trees several hundred years old. "Two warm summers in a row, where the temperature averages over fifty degrees Fahrenheit—that pulls the trigger."

In the past, warm periods were soon followed by cool periods that knocked the beetles back. But now warmth has prevailed for more than two decades. In Alaska alone, beetles are destroying spruces over vast swaths totaling perhaps three million acres. In the rest of the United States and Canada, the beetles are destroying *tens of millions* of forest acres. And while these bugs are hitting trees, in other parts of the world warming temperatures have aided the spread of insects and ticks vectoring malaria, Lyme disease, dengue fever, and other human diseases.

"This is the worst infestation around here; everything's been hit." Burg gives an appraising glance and comments, "They ate *all* the large spruce trees. The surrounding forests used to have trees one hundred and twenty-five feet tall, this big around." His arms indicate four-foot diameters. The average diameter now is six to eight inches.

Burg and his wife inhabited a log cabin in the forest. "It was just terrible to see those beautiful trees dying," he recalls. A dead standing forest is an extreme fire danger. So he felt compelled to cut and haul hundreds of trees. The adjacent landowner clear-cut 160 acres. "Cutting down all those old trees," he confides, "was an emotional shock."

From a small plane we gaze upon the remnants of a recent fire that burned fifty-five thousand acres and one hundred cabins. Below us stretch the spiky spindles of charred trees, then whole mountainsides of trees so recently killed they stand with their dried, highly flammable needles still attached. All these trees that had been soaking up carbon dioxide are now carbon emitters as they decompose or burn. This blaze started with an ill-tended campfire. It burned for weeks through beetle-ravaged lands. Then landowners logged heavily to suppress danger of further fires.

After the logging came roads, subdivisions, cabins, and an infestation of real-estate agents advertising "emerging view" properties. It had been wildlife habitat, some of it classified as wilderness.

Fire is advancing. Ice is shrinking. Portage Glacier is missing.

The famous frozen landmark has retreated around the corner. It's no longer visible from the visitor center. (If you want to see it, there's a tour boat.) The ranger who "interprets" for visitors says Portage Glacier is withdrawing at only twenty feet a year, so it ranks among the neighborhood's more stable glaciers. She reassures us that the weather's normally cooler.

That's another way of saying that it's abnormally warm. Rosy spins notwithstanding, in the 1980s the U.S. government predicted that the glacier would shrink out of view by 2020. Instead, it disappeared round the bend in under a decade. (Reality is outpacing predictions because most scientists are conservative.)

Undercurrents: Many cities were situated to take advantage of—so they now depend on—meltwater from glaciers and snowpack. But about 90 percent of the world's glaciers are shrinking. As South America's glaciers and snowpack shrivel, La Paz, Bogotá, Santiago—to where might these cities move? The summer weep of Himalayan glaciers feeds river water to 1.3 billion people, including 40 percent of the people from India to south China. Some 70 percent of the Ganges River's water comes from Gangotri Glacier, which will likely disappear in a few decades, making the sacred Ganges an intermittent, seasonal river for the nearly half billion people dependent on it. Glaciers also feed the Indus, Brahmaputra, and Mekong Rivers. Glaciers that feed both China's Yellow River (whose basin is home to 150 million people) and its Yangtze River (whose 370 million people rely heavily on river-irrigated rice) are shrinking at 7 percent annually.

Although Chinese spokespeople often downplay environmental problems. Chinese Academy of Sciences representative Yao Tandong had this assessment: "The full-scale glacier shrinkage in the plateau regions will eventually lead to an ecological catastrophe." With river flows already dropping, one Nepali farmer ventured, "Maybe God is unkind, and sends less water in the river."

Refugees displaced by environmental problems (drought, deforestation, sea level rise) now equal the number displaced by things like political oppression, religious persecution, and ethnic troubles: about 25 million a year. Predicted droughts and coastal flooding would displace around 200 million people.

If climate changes really do create hundreds of millions of refugees, how will people avoid widening havoc? Lord Nicholas Stern, the former chief economist and senior vice president of the World Bank, has expressed concern that failing to reduce greenhouse gas emissions could bring "an extended world war."

Life will go on; it's not the end of the world. But we're running high-stakes risks because, as I've mentioned, we're fundamentally messing with the stability that's prevailed during everything we call civilization.

Before Kenai Fjords National Park existed as such, a glacier occupied this now-forested valley and the road I'm on. Signs along the road follow the glacier's tracks. A sign at a glacier-deposited gravel pile marks the year 1815. Between 1815 and 1899, the glacier receded a short distance. Since then, the lengthening distance between signs demonstrates the glacier's increasingly hurried withdrawal.

Up in the mountains to my left the Harding Ice Field—thirty miles long, twenty miles wide, and something like three thousand feet thick—has thinned about seventy feet since 1950. Over thirty-two glaciers flow from it. Most are shrinking. McCarty Glacier receded fifteen miles between 1909 and 2004. Northwestern Glacier lost about nine.

Pursuing on foot now, I follow Exit Glacier past 1917, past 1951. Here, where just a few decades ago a high, grinding tongue of ice licked away the very rock, today the wind shivers a hint of autumn into a young alder forest. Walking uphill gains me commanding views of the slopes and sun-silvered braided streams running from the still-unseen glacier. At the 1995 moraine, a photograph taken then shows the glacier protruding gigantically into the frame, just a few yards from where I'm standing. I see the same rock formations that frame the photographed glacier, but no ice.

A few minutes later, I'm where the ice was in 2000. Then I'm at a rope placed here in 2004. "We put this here so visitors could stand safely behind this rope and simply reach out and touch the ice," explains the woman in the Smokey Bear uniform.

Really? A few seasons ago, this trail we're on was under tons of ice? Hundreds of yards up the valley, the now-visible ice is backed up like a treed bear. That image remains as I trudge uphill against the cool breath I finally feel the ice casting downvalley.

With candor every bit as refreshing as this breeze, the ranger says that 100 million people live within three feet of the present sea level, and that the scientific consensus is that the sea level will likely rise as much as three feet in this century. That would pretty much be the end of New Orleans and major chunks of a lot of other coastal towns and cities, she notes. No one expects the sea to stop rising at the end of this century, either. The ranger also says that sea level and other aspects of warming affect 90 percent of the more than 200 Native Alaskan villages. She adds that the Natives fear that the federal government will move them to Fairbanks, turning them into refugees. I know, I tell her, and we begin talking about what I saw and heard in Shishmaref.

At last, we meet our glacier face-to-face. Its blue ice, sculpted into deep creases and fins, stands dusted with the silt it has ground from the surrounding valley. As I'm composing a commemorative photo, the ranger adds, "We've lost two hundred feet so far this year."

SEPTEMBER

Tempus fugit, wrote Virgil. Time flees. Where has summer gone?

Seeing the first group of Black Scoters bobbing nonchalantly in the south side surf with terns flying overhead is as close as one can get to spanning summer and winter in the same glance. On the beach there's no sign of Piping Plovers; they're gone, like the summer lovers. I let Kenzie off the leash, and she lopes ahead.

The early migrants include some of my neighbors, whose cottages are mere summertime playhouses. When the calendar strikes nine they scramble out of them like hermit crabs moving to bigger shells. They're pulling their boats, wrapping them until next summer. I pity them for missing the best weather and the most energized time of the year, all coming up in the next couple of months. Summer has weeks left, but once the calendar displays the word "September," you'd think it was Latin for "evacuate."

Evacuation was on the minds of some as a hurricane was slotted to pass just east of here. Turns out it weakened and veered far out to sea, so we didn't get much weather from it. But for two days it lobbed ten-foot swells, which broke into the biggest kind of surf we see, dumping sand and seawater onto neighborhood streets. Most of us who went for a look soon fled. I'd barely gotten a glimpse when I was forced to scramble up a dune to higher ground. One older gentleman, having realized the beach was too hazardous, had turned back up the path to rejoin his family when a piston of surging water knocked him down from behind, immediately snatching his glasses and, thus, most of his eyesight. His children and grandchildren rushed to his aid, holding him by the arms as the water receded, preventing the wave from getting even more of him.

By the next evening, the manic swells were gone and the surf went back to snoring.

In the bays and the Sound, this has turned out to be a really big year for small fishes. Neighbors who've been here for decades, like the Badkins, say they've never seen so many baby bunkers and big silversides. Across the near-shore surface water, you can see them flipping circlets in the rich light of late afternoon; schools so big they look like rain.

This summer's fish bonanza has handed the terns an extremely successful breeding season. Many, many young are on the wing. They easily equal their parents in number—and in appetite. Over twenty thousand adults breed within ten miles of here, and now they've come to Lazy Point with all their flying children. For the adult terns, this means no more carrying fish all the way to distant nests. But adults are still feeding young birds that must continue developing the skill it takes to seize a tiny fish in a headlong plunge. Having left their breeding islands, terns are massing mightily along our shore.

Meanwhile, those fish swarms are beginning to move out into the Sound. And each evening this week, the dark schools have been shadowed by extraordinary tern flocks stretching more or less continuously for several miles, between Lazy Point and Cartwright Shoal. They wage intense aerial bombardment at the fluidly moving fish schools. They're stoking up for their next big transition. The ranks of terns born and bred here must now be augmented with migrants moving down from the Maritimes and New England. Through binoculars, against the setting sun, the terns look, at times, like smoke. In recent days several Ospreys have been among them, hovering high, hunting the bigger fish lurking around the small-fish swarms.

It's an extremely impressive display of life at the apogee of summer, the year's productivity mounded and piled past the angle of repose. It is a world lush with the living, a world that—despite the problems—still has what it takes to really *produce*.

Cormorants continue piling into the harbor daily. They're not going to miss out on fishing like this. Hundreds of the dark, sodden birds, swimming in line formations, continue driving herds of small fishes into panics that frenzy the attending terns. Black Terns from Canadian lakes and marshes have joined the Common, Least, and Roseate Terns. All these birds and the Bluefish and other fishes must rake off an incredible number of small fish daily, taking the profits of summer. Yet legions of the little ones still swim.

Again this afternoon, resting terns and their young by the thousands are gathered on various Lazy Point shores and bay bars, chattering and—.

A sudden, silenced takeoff of many hundreds of terns prompts the thought "Look for a falcon." Sure enough, on comes the falcon, high, the first southbound Peregrine of the year, the slow tilt toward autumn marked by this exclamation of life within its own parentheses of wings.

The falcon requires birds to make the bird it is. And several paths can lead to making a falcon: soil into plants into seeds into birds into falcon; or plants into insects into birds into falcon; or dissolved nutrients into plankton into fish into terns into falcon. The falcon heaps all this energy as tribute to its own bright burn.

It rises higher, higher. Someday this glowing ember called a falcon, this cloud-splitting crossbow, as startling as a pirate flag in a telescope, will be a pile of feathers and maggots in the rain. The way of all flesh. But this isn't that day.

Now out of sight, and now a speck in the binoculars, hiding in the heights, it determines its next taxpayer and calculates its trajectory. The falcon merely tilts its head; close parentheses, and the acceleration seems impossible. Fastest living thing. It is not that death comes so fast. It is that between the bookends of nothingness, we have this magnificent glowing life upon whose pages we can write book after book, or which we can leave blank. How many ways shall we make it count? How full or meager?

The chosen tern, cool in the face of imminent end, sidesteps like matador before meteor. Falcon misses, tail rudder twitches, and the momentum shoots it skyward. Now bereft of the element of surprise, it flies across the bay while close above it reel a blizzard of indignant terns. It angles along the marsh, then vanishes toward the ocean.

In coming days these tern flocks will rise high and circle the shores, and begin shrinking as though evaporating. They've got the urge for going. And they'll begin to go. This rich glimpse of death-defying life; this is the way it's supposed to be. And most astoundingly: this is the way it *is*. Terns' lives are shaped by real fish and real falcons. We shape our lives around things that aren't there, haunted by ghosts and demons; busily at work moving pieces of paper and screenfuls of black squiggles from one desk to another. And somehow in the process—we risk all there is.

It has been my great good fortune to live when I could experience some of the world's most thrilling wildlife. It has been our tragedy to see much of it ebb at our own doing. I'm not talking about little, obscure forms of life. I'm less concerned about the continued existence of tiny endangered remnants than I am about the accelerating decline of big wild populations and habitats. I know it's heresy on a slippery slope to say this, but I don't think conservation needs to focus on saving every nearly identical type of bird or lizard on every island. In one sense it's more important to prevent things from becoming endangered than it is to save endangered things from extinction. The conservation of large populations of abundant species matters at least as much as the conservation of rare species. How else could we maintain enough of nature to support a bearable amount of activities like logging and commercial fishing?

We live without what others took, and are poorer for it. But we can't blame earlier generations for most of the damage. We ourselves are causing the global deterioration of forests, rivers, reefs, and the rest. We are the ones altering the world's climate and the ocean's chemistry, straining the *process* of life.

There appears no assurance that in the times of our own grandchildren the world will contain viable populations of wild African Lions, Tigers, Polar Bears, Emperor Penguins, gorillas, or coral reefs and their millions of dependent species. These are the animals expectant parents paint on nursery room walls. Their implied wish: to welcome precious new life into a world endowed with the magnificence and delight and fright of companions we have traveled with since the beginning. Some people debate the "rights of the unborn" as though a human life begins at conception but we don't need to concern ourselves with its prospects after birth. Raging over the divine sanctity of anyone else's pregnancy is a little overwrought and a little too easy when nature itself terminates one out of four by the sixth week. There are much bigger, much more compassionate pro-life fish to fry. Passing along a world that can allow real children to flourish, and the cavalcade of generations to unfold, and the least to live in modest dignity would be the biggest pro-life enterprise we could undertake.

Children yet to come will be the cleanup crew to our festivities. Because we know they won't be coming to the ballroom until we've all waddled off, we've granted ourselves permission to party like there's no tomorrow. Our descended family is not at the table. They have no pulpit, no podium, no court of appeals. They cannot testify on their own behalf. But do they really need to be asked? There is enough to be heard in the pregnant silence of future generations. We know what their interests are and what is right. Of course, it's not as simple as this. And yet, of course, it is. There is so much left. But there is only so much left.

Think of the spirit behind our national parks, and envision that thinking applied to practical things like farmland, water, minerals, wildlife, an economy capable of functioning in the real world, and other things of value and necessity. The idea of explicitly saving and leaving things for coming generations is called "intergenerational equity." There's too little of it.

• • •

By mid-September the light has paled. Sunrise comes later, dusk earlier. The dawn bird chorus, so energizing in the spring and early summer, is gone. Only Blue Jays announce the day, their raucous calls ringing through the cooling mornings. No mockingbirds play minstrel to the dead of night, or issue their aubade. That's not to say the world has fallen silent. Insects fill the air with a deep-pile trill that carpets every corner of night, colors the dusk, and tints the morning. It is time for their cadenza.

The Virginia Creepers' green vines of summer are reddening. The red deer of summer are browning. Beach Plums are darkening. Is it a coincidence that the heaviest set of beach plums anyone can recall and the heaviest schools of small fishes both occurred this year? The plums are also truly sweet, sweeter than I've ever tasted.

Yesterday afternoon, rain came with clouds so dark I switched on a light in my office at four P.M. But overnight a strong, cool wind cleared the air of moisture. Dawn came bell-clear, like an authentic breath of autumn.

A cool and steady northwest wind like this lifts the tails of many migrants. Today it has Tree Swallows moving. They're riding that breeze across the water, coming on, headed south. You don't see them over the wide distances of the bays and the Sound—but they're there. You see them materialize as if from the breeze itself as they get within a few hundred yards of the shore. Their constant trickle adds up to thousands upon thousands.

My neighbor Georgia works in Manhattan and visits on weekends. She's standing on the beach with me, admiring water and sky. I point out the swallows making landfall overhead. They're crossing the threshold of shore at altitudes of thirty to fifty feet. Just the birds we can actually see are arriving at a rate of maybe twenty per minute. I have no reason to think this isn't happening along miles of our shoreline. Impressed by all the birds coming off the bay, Georgia brings her mother, Lee, out to see. When the swallows reach our marshes they'll mass up, feeding heavily on flying insects, then go to the ocean beach and turn right, down the coast. Occasionally, I've seen the beaches thronged with rivers of swallows, great snaking pulses of wings, in flocks of tens of thousands plus continuous volleys of smaller groups, actually taking hours to pass.

At this time of year all the birds' ranks are swollen by the season's many young on their first migration, energetically making their bid for survival. With the odds stacked so heavily against them, I wonder if they feel anything like the appropriate terror. All I see is them giving it all they've got.

Robins and jays are also crossing the marshes in visible flocks. Vireos, hummingbirds, tanagers, flycatchers; they're all passing now in the south-bound lane. Assorted warblers—American Redstarts, Northern Parulas, Magnolia, Pine, Chestnut-sided, Cerulean, Black-and-white, Prairie— their spring candy colors gone, slip by mostly unnoticed except by the most avid birders and the always avid hawks.

Two dark dove-sized falcons—Merlins—zip-line the edges of the marsh and the pines. There's much to hunt. I watch a few migrating drag-onflies catch mosquitoes with deft precision and almost untrackable speed. The Merlins sport after the dragonflies, and harry small birds in quick sprints or high-spiraling chases up into open sky, or relentless pur-suit over open water.

Riding the skies from the Arctic tundra, Black-bellied Plovers are again with us, some already in winter feather, some still bearing the outlines of their handsome breeding plumage. They still have a *long* way to go. Also from up north, those cosmopolitan travelers the Ruddy Turnstones—who've met and greeted me from the high Arctic to the trop-ics, from Europe to Alaska to the Caribbean—continue filtering through. Along the same shores where the birds' spring passage coincided with the sparse emerald shoots of new marsh plants, blooming Sea Lavender and Seaside Goldenrod now lace the luxuriant end-of-summer marshes with color and scent.

By the third week of September, the tern numbers have deflated from tens of thousands to a couple hundred. Some are gone; others have moved just a few miles to the Point, where the autumn scene is building as schools of anchovies are beginning to mass, and their predators are taking up their annual position for the autumn gauntlet known as "the blitz."

Between the North and South Forks, which form the "tail" of Long Island's vaguely fishy shape, the Peconic River enters saltwater at a place called Riverhead. There's a public aquarium there. And I've received an invitation from a couple of their fish keepers to join them on an expedition to catch tropical reef fish for their coral reef and warm-water exhibits. But the location isn't the Caribbean or the Coral Triangle of the western Pacific. I will board no aircraft. No palm trees will wave welcome. The collecting grounds are just a few miles from here, in the same bay system where I've often encountered a decidedly temperate contingent of sea robins, flounder, and squid. That's what I mean about the magic in the fluidity of water; you can stare at the "same" bay all summer, but under the surface, worlds change.

The winds of summer push warm surface water up the coast. Eddies break off the Gulf Stream and come whirling over the shelf and occasionally hit the beaches and inlets with startlingly blue, clear water. In that water ride the eggs and larvae of reef fishes from a thousand miles south. Thus do juveniles of tropical fishes of many kinds come to us in streaming tongues of warm water to live bathed in the solar-heated shallows of our late-summer bays. *But:* they're not equipped to migrate south. Having made a wrong turn or been caught in currents bound too far north, the tropicals, here by accident, are stranded. And soon, when the breath of autumn swings northerly and the frost is on the pumpkins, they'll have nothing to do but chill out and die. So rather than mount expensive expeditions to warm places to take fishes that could survive to adulthood and reproduce within their normal range, the aquarium guys—and some of their colleagues from other aquariums in the Northeast, inland as far as Wisconsin, and even from the South—now come here to grant doomed juveniles a long life in comfortable captivity. It's probably the only win-win in fishing.

We park on a dead end on the bay. Today the leader of our small band of hunter-gatherers is Todd Gardner. A local newspaper recently described him as having his "golden locks corralled into a ponytail," and it's obvious his coworkers aren't about to let him forget that description anytime soon.

We unload the buckets and coolers and battery-operated aerators. A T-shirt, swim trunks, and a pair of sneakers complete our uniform. Our main area today is a point about half a mile away. Most of the skill in this—as in all fishing—is knowing the best spots. For some reason, only a few places in this region seem to concentrate tropical fish near the shore. This is the best-known bay for it. I've heard about this for years and have seen the odd stray tropical, but I was never sure where most of them congregated. Todd knows particular spots that consistently produce.

Our main tool is a beach seine fifty feet long and maybe five feet high, with quarter-inch mesh. One person walks the net straight off the beach, while another holds the other end in the shallows. They drag it parallel to shore for a minute or two; then the person near the shore stops and the person on the deep side pivots the far end of the stretched net back to shore, whereupon the whole thing is pulled onto the sand. It basically sweeps fish onto the beach.

The water feels warm, all right, but it's anything except clear. Opaque with plankton, it's the forest green of late-summer baywater. Standing chest-deep, you can't see your feet. The murk makes it seem unlikely that we'll be seeing multicolored fishes of air-clear waters and crystalline reefs. Then again, the whole point is that they're misplaced here, out of their element.

The first pull brings the usual local grass shrimp, silversides, and killifish, half-buried in sea lettuce. We quickly rake through with our fingertips, as if panning for gold. What's this little yellow-and-blue thing? I wipe away some weed. It's a Bicolor Damselfish half the size of my thumb! Todd splatters over and opens his palm to reveal the black-and-yellow barring of a baby Sergeant Major. A few crabs abscond seaward and we quickly invert and rinse the net to release everything we don't want. One round bucket is now a little bit of the Caribbean Sea, circumnavigated by these tiny swimming jewels. It seems like a magic trick. The next pull brings a six-inch Blue-spotted Cornetfish that I can hardly believe and a crimson Short Bigeye. And soon our population of miniatures includes two Snowy Groupers, two Spotfin Butterflyfish, a Redfin Parrotfish, and a Pearly Razorfish. I find all this utterly delightful. Todd is pretty excited because the parrotfish are rare here and he's seen the razorfish up here only once, about ten years ago—and there are no other local records of its occurrence.

When I ask what else he's seen here, Todd says, "Scamp; Gag Grouper; Foureye, Spotfin, and Reef Butterflyfish; Blue Angelfish; Dwarf Goatfish; Planehead and Orange Filefish—. Lotsa other stuff." He adds, "Although, I have to say the most exciting thing for me is the night before a collecting trip, dreaming about what I might catch, and looking at maps and trying to find new, undiscovered spots and thinking up new techniques. It's hard to beat the excitement of pulling up something I've never seen before."

Todd adds, "We see a pretty big variation in species and abundance from year to year. We have great years and terrible years, but I don't see any long-term trend. I think the variation we see results mainly from spawning success of the populations in their native waters, how much Gulf Stream water actually reaches our area from wind and eddies, and how the timing of spawning coincides with a mass of water destined for our area." I would have found it interesting if he'd said he'd been finding more tropicals here, maybe linked to warming waters. But the lack of a trend comes as a bit of a relief, actually. It's comforting to hear that there are some ways in which the world *isn't* changing.

On the way back Todd decides to stop at some standing pilings he says are good for Lookdowns. Again, the intimate knowledge of local hunters pays off. Like pieces of pirate silver, the Lookdowns and several Permit go into our aerated plastic treasure chest. And Lookdowns like this cove because—? "That's one of the mysteries," Todd answers. "Why do we always find Flying Gurnards on one small stretch of beach but almost nowhere else, not even identical-looking habitats nearby? African Pompano—one tiny stretch of beach, year after year. Why do we find angelfish only at one dock, not at any of the other docks in the area?"

The net sodden, and the buckets and coolers heavy with water, we trudge to the truck bearing tropical treasure. These little fish, doomed until we caught them, will grow rapidly in captivity. Tens of thousands of aquarium-visiting families will enjoy the sight and motion of them. Parents will naturally explain to their kids that maybe someday they'll be lucky enough to go all the way to the tropics, to see these fish in the wild. Little will they suspect, but the local is always the exotic.

I'm scheduled to meet some acquaintances for a seventy-five-mile ride to the edge of the continental shelf. We're going to look for Yellowfin and Albacore Tuna, and that's how far you have to go, nowadays, to catch a few. I find the boat—my own boat doesn't have that kind of range—greet the people I know, meet those I don't, and climb aboard. Even with a trip to the edge like we're planning, nothing's guaranteed. There are a lot more Mahimahi this far north than ever before (partly because tuna aren't there to eat them when they're small). But as far as tuna, some boats return fishless.

The four-hour ride exhausts most conversation, and there is plenty of time to stare at water.

In 1985, my friends and I ventured my little eighteen-foot outboard boat fifteen miles south of Montauk to an area called the Butterfish Hole and anchored in 150 feet of water. When I was sure the anchor had caught, I secured the line and glanced at my watch. Six A.M.

My longtime friend John started throwing pieces of fish into the tide. I put a piece on a hook and instructed John's wife, Nancy, to strip sixteen arm lengths of line from the reel, letting the bait drift out of

sight, before engaging the reel's friction brake. I began baiting a second line. At the instant I heard her click the brake into position, the rod bent double and line started shrieking off the reel while Nancy gamely hung on. We all looked wild-eyed into one another's youthful faces. Could there really be *that* many tuna here?

Yes, there could.

By eight A.M., nine tuna ranging from thirty to a hundred pounds jammed our big coolers. Other tuna were coursing powerfully through the blue water behind the boat, eating every piece of fish we threw. We were now just hand-feeding wild Yellowfins, Albacore, and juvenile Bluefins. Having caught enough to make—as I now realize—a lifetime memory, we decided to haul anchor hours early, getting back to the dock in time for a late breakfast. By midafternoon my kitchen table was piled high with tuna steaks. Friends' cars were pulling up to the house as my outdoor grill heated up. We ate seared Yellowfin and raw Bluefin Tuna until we couldn't pop one more bite of sashimi.

As the submarginal size of my little boat for open-ocean fishing implies, we—not quite out of our twenties—were pretty new at tuna fishing. No matter. We went where everyone else went, and back then it never occurred to us that we'd ever need to go more than fifteen miles from shore. We thought that's where tuna lived because, well, that's where they lived. We had no way to foresee how much the world would change.

A year or two later, Japanese buyers arrived on the docks, and things indeed changed as the globalized market hit home and began eating our ocean empty. One morning offshore amid a dense fleet of boats slaughtering large numbers of Bluefin Tuna, I heard someone get on the radio to suggest that maybe we should all leave a few for tomorrow. Crackling through the speaker came this reply from a sport fisherman: "Hey, nobody left any buffalo for me."

In 1995, with a new and bigger boat, I slowed not fifteen miles but fifty miles from shore. Bluefin Tuna had become scarce, but word was of large numbers of Yellowfins. We stopped to drift at the edge of a wide group of boats, and I set out two baited lines while my friends started throwing into the sea handfuls of fresh silversides we'd seine-netted the night before. As I was setting out a third line, we suddenly hooked three tuna. Again I stacked my table with delicious fresh tuna steaks, friends converged, and the grill worked overtime.

But there's a big difference between having to go fifteen or fifty miles across open ocean. For that distance, my newer, bigger boat was as barely adequate as my older, smaller boat had been. The trend was clear. And there weren't many more days with so many fish. Soon the fish—scarcer, smaller—were mainly out of my new boat's range. It wasn't worth investing in yet a bigger boat to chase them. And so a thing that I had loved most in my life became a thing mainly of the past, the heart pounding and adrenaline reduced to memory, as if the road traveled was visible mainly in the rearview mirror. In the billion-year-plus history of life in the seas, two decades is a millisecond, but wow, how the world has changed.

Now the great tuna runs of the South Shore of Long Island are in the past. Autumn's "tuna fever" has broken, only no one feels better. You can still catch fish. But tuna fishing now is a long offshore shot, usually the seventy-five miles to the edge of the shelf or to even more distant canyons notched into the continental slope. It's about big boats, astronomical fuel budgets, long hours, and fewer, smaller fish.

Far from land and far from the days of plenty, the captain slows the boat. The lures go overboard and begin scratching across the ocean like a cat's claws.

OCTOBER

Early October brings new waves of migrants. But the southbound summer songbirds are now augmented by those who'll linger late with us, even through winter, like Ruby-crowned Kinglets, Cedar Waxwings, White-throated and Swamp Sparrows, chickadees, Tufted Titmice, and trunk-running Red-breasted Nuthatches and Brown Creepers. Troops of flickers also bound across the marsh and down the beach. Yellow-rumped Warblers have come in such droves for the waxy berries now festooning the Bayberry bushes that it can be hard to notice other small birds among them. These movements aren't just local; the birds move on a vast regional swath, embedded in the weather, and waves of songbirds in clear northwest winds can get noticed all the way west to Brooklyn. Another autumn first comes along with those cool Canadian winds: I can see my breath. Kenzie takes such momentous details in stride.

The Peregrine Falcon migration peaks now, the first week of October. For a rare falcon, "peak" is a relative term compared to, say, ten thousand swallows passing. Nearly wiped out by hard pesticides and for decades endangered, the Peregrine, triumphal and resurgent, is now quite evident—if you have the eye for them. And I do. For several days, I spot them three or four times a day. I see them along the bay, and while walking on the south side, and at the Point. I see them from the road. I see them from the ocean. I see one chasing starlings over the Long Island Expressway while I'm driving to New York City.

As a kid, I was infatuated with hawks for their looks and boldness, their rarity and mystique. I thrilled to anything written about falconry.

And in my teens, I taught myself how to trap and train hawks. "All in all, falconry is the perfect hobby," wrote Aldo Leopold in his great conservation classic. I agreed. And I disagreed with the law—which said I couldn't keep hawks. The birds' main problems were pesticides that caused their eggs to break—not teenagers. These same pesticides ran an Osprey eraser across most of the coast. It left Peregrine cliffs silent across the United States and Europe, their passage marked by chips of eggshell in the dirt of inaccessible ledges.

I had an innocent's hope that I could help. DDT and the other hard chemicals were banned when I was in high school, and an organization called the Peregrine Fund began breeding captive falcons to repopulate the wild. At twenty I got my dream job: summer assistant in the first releases of young captive-bred falcons. I'd be caretaker to a brood of three chicks as they grew. I'd take detailed notes as they learned to fly and taught themselves to hunt. To be plain, caretaker meant feeding them. Feeding growing falcons meant tending chickens, and killing a couple of chickens every day. But the setting! In a little shack on stilts on a private little salt-marsh island lost along the wilds of the southern Jersey shore, in a seldom-visited bay full of clams and sweet Blue Crabs, I was helping the recovery of my most passionately loved endangered creature (and, my nineteen-year-old girlfriend could come stay). Heaven.

Not long after that, I helped "monitor the recovery" of Arctic Peregrines. Alas, this did not involve traveling to the Arctic, as I longed to do (that would come later), but, rather, meant spending a month each fall catching and tagging with numbered leg bands the rare and occasional migrants bombing along the Long Island coast. Not a bad consolation prize. But Peregrines were still quite rare—still at their low point—when I started. Many days during the height of migration I'd sit tending my net, scanning the skies, seeing none. Sometimes I felt that people looking for UFOs might have better luck. On consecutive days, my notebook often showed a series of zeroes in the column titled "Peregrines."

There were plenty of other birds. They underlined the Peregrine's near absence. And I had plenty of company from friends. Behind a ten-foot-high, invisibly fine nylon net, I kept a pigeon tethered to a cord leading into the blind where we sat, hiding with a nice view up the beach. When we saw a hawk, I pulled the string, causing the pigeon to flutter like an injured easy meal, and the raptor—if hungry—would streak into the net and get pocketed. I'd dash and retrieve the bird. If it was large, I'd offer my toe as a talon pincushion while I folded its wings and got a grasp around its legs. While waiting for Godot we caught American Kestrels, Merlins, Northern Harriers, Sharp-shinned and Cooper's Hawks—all full of wild-eyed defiance and the urgent intensity of migration.

Every few days, a Peregrine would appear, usually much higher than any of the other raptors, and I could sometimes spot one through my binoculars before I saw it naked-eye, like a dot moving against the sky. Even at that distance, if I pulled the pigeon string, the moving dot usually stopped and began slowly getting wider. By the time such a bird arrived it was often streaking fast enough to blow a hole right through my net. (When that happened, the startled falcon would shoot skyward, swoop back, and usually get captured on its next pass.)

My dreams were often filled with fast-approaching birds, and I'd frequently wake several times in the middle of the night, too excited to sleep, hoping it was time for work. At the first gray hint of dawn I'd spring out of bed. It was never lost on me that friends took days off from their jobs (occasionally weeks) to come to "work" with me. High-pressure northwest fronts could bring a great wave of migrants. Once, before noon we'd released seventy-five hawks and counted passing hundreds—though not a single Peregrine.

I sat on their migration path for a month each fall, for a decade, and I did indeed monitor the Peregrines' return. By the end, we might see two dozen Peregrines—and have half of them come in for a leg band—before folding up the net for the day. It was a decade of terrific improvement. And nowadays, there are far more. In those days I missed a lot of great fall tuna fishing because I guessed the tuna would last and the falcons vanish. I guessed wrong; the tuna got demolished during the same span of time the Peregrines recovered.

Since some of the worst chemicals were banned, the hawks that were rarest when I was a kid—Peregrine Falcons, Ospreys, and Cooper's Hawks—have become among our most abundant. Those most abundant then—Kestrels and Sharp-shinned Hawks—are now far rarer, and no one really knows why, though it might have to do with the resurgence of larger raptors, or abandoned farms either reverting to thick woodland or converting to suburbs over a large region.

But autumn is still autumn, and numerous birds still come. Many other birds—not just hawks—cut south over the ocean across the gigantic coastal indentation called the New York Bight. Some that do, never make landfall.

I recently went thirty miles offshore with a shark researcher to try catching a Shortfin Mako or a Thresher Shark to tag with a satellite transmitter. While we waited for a rod to bend, I noticed a Yellow-shafted Flicker circling as though exhausted, perhaps disoriented. Flickers are not strong fliers, and I can only imagine what that woodpecker thought of a world that had turned into a circular blue wheel of moving water and haze. I also saw a Peregrine, looking almost at home. I know what a Peregrine thinks when it sees a bird flying in exhausted loops over the ocean. The flicker left us, headed toward a distant vessel. Over the radio, someone on that boat reported seeing a Peregrine snatch a smaller circling bird, and eat it while flying.

We never got a mako or Thresher on which to place a satellite tag. We caught six Blue Sharks, including one brute over ten feet long and about 350 pounds. Just as we were about to release it after a thirty-minute struggle, it straightened a very heavy new hook. How can a cartilage-jawed animal exert so much power? One of the sharks was wearing a hook from a previous capture. Another had the skin behind its head grown around a piece of protruding cord, as though it had long ago swum through a loop of the stuff. We cut the cord and pulled it out of the animal.

A squall blew up while we were fishing, and under drenching rain I noticed another bird, a songbird, circling the boat, looking for a place to land. The rain was so heavy I could not even clearly see the bird. I glanced out over the ocean, with its endless whitecaps and veils of rain, and thought that there must be thousands and thousands of birds out there getting slammed by this unexpected front, their promising tailwind turned into a deadly headwind full of pelting water. Looking at the ocean with them in mind, it seemed a lonely and terrible planet.

Later, on the way homeward, I saw yet another Peregrine, following us.

· · ·

The return of Peregrines. The decline of sharks. Who'd have thought people would bring about either of those trends? Maybe we'll live to see sharks recover. Right now, that seems as improbable as seeing all these falcons. Hope is the ability to see how things could be better. The world of human affairs has long been a shadowy place, but always backlit by the light of hope. Each person can add hope to the world. A resigned person subtracts hope. The more people strive, the more change becomes likely. Far better, then, that good people do the striving. Otherwise, as Yeats despaired in "The Second Coming,"

> Turning and turning in the widening gyre
> The falcon cannot hear the falconer;
> Things fall apart; the centre cannot hold;
> Mere anarchy is loosed upon the world,
> The blood-dimmed tide is loosed, and everywhere
> The ceremony of innocence is drowned;
> The best lack all conviction, while the worst
> Are full of passionate intensity.

> Surely some revelation is at hand.

The revelation is this: don't wait for some revelation. We make our own luck. It is by far preferable that the best people have conviction, and the worst get convicted.

As we click through the turnstiles and starting gates of catastrophes unimagined just a few years ago—the likelihood that hundreds of millions of people will be displaced, that the seas will dissolve their own coral reefs; fresh water scarcity, ocean depletion, flooding cities, gushing oil, and agricultural shortage—we can begin to see that it's no longer just about saving Polar Bears or the last wild places. What's gone around has come around. Problems of "the environment" are crucial matters of practical justice, peace, and morality. This is the second coming.

I used to think conservation was about saving falcons and sea turtles and tuna and forests. I thought that educating girls was a different cause. But the thing is, people matter to nature, and nature—it turns out—matters to people. Because educating girls simultaneously breaks poverty and reduces family size, it matters to people *and* nature. It's conservation and compassion combined. We can't heal the world without healing human-ity, and we can't heal humanity without healing the natural world. But reducing poverty, hunger, child and childbirth mortality, controlling diseases, and ensuring education "cannot be achieved," the United Nations has finally observed, "as long as most ecosystem services are being degraded." The U.N.'s Millennium Ecosystem Assessment notes in economic-sounding terms what has long been apparent to naturalists: "In effect the benefits reaped . . . have been achieved by running down natural capital assets. We are depleting assets at the expense of our children. . . . In many cases, it is literally a matter of living on borrowed time." And for those who still don't comprehend, the report adds, "The ability of the planet's ecosystems to sustain future generations can no longer be taken for granted." A blunter rephrasing: We are ruining the world for our children.

Hidden within those despairing phrases is the hope I see: when we can no longer run or sweep it under the rug, we'll have to look reality in the face. And the faces staring back at us will be our kids'. Nothing to date has awakened humanity to the realization that if we stay on the path we're taking, we'll end up where we're heading. If we don't get it, it will get us—then we'll get it. But a few alarm clocks are starting to buzz. We now have the chance to prove that we're as clever as we think.

We could just say that people in the future are on their own and they, too, will have to figure it out. But then we come bumping up against God, who, it turns out, is interested in the future. Or, at least, Scripture's scribes considered future children among the highest forms of good-ness: "A good person bequeaths to their children's children," says Prov-erbs 13:22. The Book of Deuteronomy (20:19–20) and the Koran teach that even in times of war, it is prohibited to destroy fruit trees. Our own disputes must not translate into our children's poverty. A teaching ascribed to Muhammad says that upon death, three types of good deeds con-tinue: a charitable fund, knowledge left for others' benefit, and a righ-teous child. Something like *four hundred* times in the Bible, God makes promises extending through generations, or speaks of covenants lasting into eternity. Religious people understand God as eternal, so to discount the future is to deny and cheapen God's eternal presence, a sin against both

God and the generations to come. Confucianism claims that the *prime goal* of society is the elevation of the next generation. The future has higher value than the present because the future is bigger than the present, with more lives at stake. So do we owe anything to people of the future? Don't take my word for it.

One of the reasons that saving and leaving things for coming generations—that idea of "intergenerational equity"—is so rare in practice is that many people basically embraced the notion that—in so few words—greedy is godly.

In one of Western civilization's most influential one-line mythologies, Adam Smith in *The Wealth of Nations* (1776) gave us the mightily convenient idea that an individual who "intends only his own gain," is "led by an invisible hand to promote . . . the society." This is not a fine point. Smith didn't say, "An individual who pursues only the public good is led by an invisible hand into a richly satisfying life." (Which, by the way, usually seems true.) There's a big difference.

I don't know about you, but I find the whole idea of trusting invisible hands a little creepy. I'd tell children, "If you can't see what someone's hands are doing, turn on the light and leave the room." In the early seventeenth century John Donne had at least the decency to ask permission and tell us what he was up to:

> License my roving hands, and let them go,
> Behind, before, above, between, below.
> O my America! my new-found-land . . .
> How blest am I in this discovering thee!
> To enter in these bonds, is to be free;
> Then where my hand is set, my seal shall be.

You know where you stand with Donne. But much colossally misplaced trust in "the market" stems from Adam Smith's busily invisible hand. Being "led by an invisible hand" evokes images of divine guidance, implying that God wants us to be rich, and he will use our pursuit of self-interest to serve the greater good. That interpretation aside, I perceive three problems with Smith's theory that those seeking "only [their] own gain" are "led to promote" the public interest. One, it's obviously bullshit. Two, its basic instruction is: Don't bother caring; magic will do the caring for you. In practice, since no magic applies to greed, people seeking only their own gain are a risk to themselves and a danger to society. Three, markets apply only lip service while the hand does whatever makes it feel best; there are no real rules, as we'll see.

Economic activities incur costs and confer benefits. If we cut a forest, that is a cost. If we pollute a river, that's a cost. The logger should pay for replacing the forest; the polluter, for cleaning up the pollution. If we take today what might have been taken in the future, that is a cost. We should pay the repairs before returning to future people what we've borrowed and used. All trade incurs these costs of business. Here the invisible hand becomes sleight of hand. Market prices almost never include these costs. Economists have simply declared that these costs—these fundamental, inherent, continual costs—lie "external" to market accounting. We trade what we manufacture, but because we don't trade the pollution or deforestation or other "externalities," we avert our gaze to keep prices low. Any budgetary system that does not factor in costs has a high chance of coming out in the black—but only on paper. The invisible hand of the market sticks the public—here, now, abroad, and in the future ("Behind, before, above, between, below")—for those costs.

But I'm just an ecologist, so for a second opinion, let me introduce the constitutional scholar and law professor Joel Bakan, who tells us, "All the bad things that happen to people and the environment as a result of corporations' relentless and legally compelled pursuit of self-interest are . . . neatly categorized by economists as externalities." His definition of externality is: "literally, other people's problems." The economist Milton Friedman's slightly more technical definition: "An externality is the effect of a transaction on a third party who has not consented." Bakan adds, "The corporation's built-in compulsion to externalize its costs is at the root of many of the world's social and environmental ills. That makes the corporation a profoundly dangerous institution."

Enron went bankrupt because it left costs off the books *and got caught*. Hiding costs is always attractive. That's why companies and economies get seduced into it. It's also what makes whole economies collapse. We have Earthron.

Many capitalists profess a faith based in markets. Many also claim to oppose socialism, but that's nonsense too, because the system they've created lets them continually privatize profits and socialize costs. And they are often quite comfortable interfering with markets. They tend to love (and make their lobbyists work like hell to get) subsidies, which are, by definition, market-distorting applications of money. And they applaud bailouts, which come like the deus ex machina of Greek tragedy, gods lowered from cranes to solve insolvable (and, in their case, insolvent) plot weaknesses. Want a war or to bail out criminally negligent banks? There's money. If corporations can profit, the market gets sidelined for the duration of a taxpayer-funded miracle. Repair Social Security or potholes, extend health care or boost schools? Sorry, we're broke. On matters in which the whole country would benefit—getting more money for those schools, for instance—well, public interest not-for-profit groups are generally prohibited from lobbying, and they certainly can't grease Congress's members. I'm not categorically against any subsidy or bail-out. But let's be honest: as far as faith in markets, many capitalists act like those people who say one thing in church, then do another. Many *are*.

The suggestion that a polluter must pay to pollute or a fisher must pay to catch fish from the public's waters is an attempt to price things more realistically so the market can work better. Of course, polluters and fishers balk. Why should *they* pay? They can make *us* pay.

Energy pricing is perhaps the worst. Consider the familiar: gasoline. The reality-checked costs of gasoline include: taxpayer subsidies and tax loopholes enjoyed by oil companies (they reap windfalls, then you pay *them*); military, diplomatic, and blood costs of protecting access to oil; health-care costs related to lung diseases caused by air pollution; administration and oversight of air pollution controls and regulations; and some of the costs of global warming. And most of oil's environmental calamities. Not one of these appears at the pump. These real costs would add roughly $12 per gallon (estimates vary depending on different assumptions). The price on the pump is meaningless. It reflects only the collusion of producers to fix prices low enough to keep us hooked. We do pay the other costs—in income taxes. (But rather than taxing people for working, wouldn't it make more sense to let people pay at the pump, so our choices matter? At-the-pump gasoline taxes in the United States are one-tenth what they are in Europe; that's one of the reasons Americans burn so much more gasoline, and one of the reasons Europeans get around much more easily on public transportation.) When people say that safe, clean, renewable energy "would cost too much," they don't realize that dirty energy looks cheap because the pricing doesn't reflect its costs—which we pay anyway. That's why global energy prices have been called "market failure on the greatest scale the world has ever seen."

Mainstream economists not only externalize costs but actually *discount* the future. Each year of the future is "worth less" than the previous year. The future quickly becomes worthless. Well, how *convenient*—since considering the future would put a crimp in our plans to lay waste to it. Really, what gets called "economics" is a game of make-up-the-rules-that-suit-you. When making important decisions the Iroquois famously considered seven generations. No economists there. To see how discounting the future has deeply infiltrated the Western mind, consider the scorn with which many folks dismiss predictions that environmental problems like groundwater depletion or sea level rise will become really serious sometime in the next century: "I'll be dead; why should I care?" Tomahawks notwithstanding, even the savage Iroquois understood: we need to be better than that.

Discounting would be fine if our own comfort didn't affect future people. While we are enjoying the party on our luxury liner, we are unaware that our food, our fine wine, and our white tablecloths are being provided by slaves belowdecks. The party is our way of celebrating ourselves. Those captives include the next few generations. When we discount the future, we're simply saying we don't want to care about people who will be stuck with the options we are currently shrinking. In "externalizing" the costs, we "externalize" anything and anyone not strongly positioned to complain about the very internalized pain they will feel.

But fancy evasions like "externalized costs" and "discounted futures" aside, we've almost always done it this way. Since the first human chipped the first stone tool, we've always kept what we liked and discarded what we didn't want. This was fine when our garbage was made up of stones and bones. But we are still using the same million-year-old system even though our leave-behinds are no longer stone shards. Now they're cancer-causing chemicals, eternal plastics sold for onetime use, empty oceans, stumps of thousand-year-old trees, melting polar ice, and mortgage defaults.

When we keep what we like and discard what we don't, we're privatizing gain and socializing pain. We make others pay for our mistakes. Now corporations demand, "Save my assets, buy my garbage." If they screw up—they still get paid. If you don't buy—you pay anyway. Here's what they learn (it's pretty different from what we learn): "If your failure and mismanagement are so colossal that your bankruptcy threatens the whole economy, we'll duck the fallout and you'll get the bailout." Fail. Bail. Repeat. We know what will happen as we create an expectation that destructive behavior gets rewarded. Don't we?

The failure of markets to realistically price the destruction of living systems and the fuels we use to run civilization makes it economically attractive to risk the entire planet. We've created markets unconscious of the single rock-hard truth of economics: the economy, as Timothy Wirth points out, is a wholly owned subsidiary of nature. On top of that, what is called "the market" is not really a free and honest market but actually a system that's been rigged to let certain individuals and corporations benefit by pulling strands out of the social and ecological fabric.

I don't think economists understand the choices our economic system is steering us into. Since we're running a deficit, eating into our principal, and liquidating our assets, economics should try to catch up to what we've learned about the workings of the world in the last couple of centuries, because the economy itself will be forced to comply, whether economists understand what's happening or not.

We're all wired into networks we have never understood: the shared air and water, our seas, and all the rest of nature. And now we all participate in a handy system that simply says we don't have to pay it back. Forests standing tall, we take. Air flowing pure, we taint. Water running clear, we tint. Oceans filled with fish, we strain. To food, land, and water we add chemicals, such that the very milk of mothers is a toxic asset that cannot be suckled unto our babes without worry. Our markets make us think we're "disposing" costs into the bigger, wider world—and now we find a finite world shrink-wrapping itself around the human venture.

When market economists and hard-nosed "pragmatists" speak of "the way the real world works," they almost never have a clue what they're talking about. The way we do business lags far behind, remains ignorant of modern and ongoing findings on how we are changing the present and the future, remains numb to how our changes affect others, ignores the depth and quality of human experience.

Markets alone won't get us all the way to being human, because marketers compete with us for control of the most meaningful and beautiful elements of life: our beliefs, values, dreams, and affections. Think about it. Though the human is a social, empathetic, altruistic creature, marketing disfigures human nature by trying to focus all our attention on desire. The barrage of shock-and-awe advertising works incessantly to transform thinking, evaluating beings into mere wanters, called "consumers." Community, relationships, the tone of work and family life, causes like peace or poverty or the environment, or just being happy being helpful—all lie unserved and largely abandoned by market economics. Those real things are hard for marketers to sell. They can't sell us simple satisfaction, so they market dissatisfaction. So we may get what marketers *can* sell and ignore what the soul needs.

Market economics falls on the wrong side of the moral divide in issues like slavery and equality because markets ask, "How much can I get?" while a human being must discern how to serve. Distinguishing good from bad and right from wrong are not profit-based decisions. But many economists view humans simply as consumers in a market, rather than moral agents. Religions—to their credit—do not make this mistake; they don't place ethics below profits. They seem to recognize that a person's human worth is different from their market price, and that people cannot just be put to whatever financial purpose they might promote. The generality may be simplistic, but the difference is enormous. It involves no less than whether humans exist in a business context or business will exist in a human context.

Yet, like a blind traffic controller, our medieval market accounting posts green lights at every intersection. If one country spends, say, 80 percent of its budget on police, the military, and prisons and another country spends the same 80 percent on education, parks, and arts, current economic measures cannot distinguish between these two countries. Their "gross national product" is identical. When coal is strip-mined, the value of the coal increases the "gross national product," but the loss of land and the resulting air pollution are not deducted (they're "external"), and when the pollution makes people sick, the cost of their medical care *increases* the GNP. The *Exxon Valdez* oil spill *increased* the GNP. As did the Gulf of Mexico blowout. The GNP can't differentiate between a balanced checking account and a reckless spending spree. (The gross national product's inventor, Simon Kuznets, understood this, writing to Congress in 1934, "The welfare of a nation can scarcely be inferred from a measure of national income.") But because we use GNP as a measure of economic "health," a country could exhaust its minerals, fell its forests, erode its soils, pollute its waters, extinguish its wildlife, empty its seas, and gasp for air—and its measured economy would look "robust" till the chaotic end. That is a gross product indeed.

In looking at how archaic and insensate our economy is, how ignorant of scientific understanding, and how full of distortions applied to rig and game the system, it's easy to see that price, value, and cost are three very different things. (And if cheap prices trump everything—think of toxic toys from China, for instance—then the lowest common denominator wins, and it's a race to the bottom.)

Thus, the "invisible hand" of the market pleasures itself by working with its eyes closed. It's an unsavory business that, in the end, cannot bear fruit. That knock on the door is from our externalized, exhausted lands, waters, air, our very bodies. Never has the word "external" been used to describe something so intimately internal.

Having received great gifts from the ages and the ancestors, we act as though we are a wall against which time suddenly stops.

~

Earlier in the week it was as humid, muggy, and summery as anything in autumn could be. I left the bedroom door wide open all night so I could listen to the crickets' shimmering singing, still going strong this late into Indian summer. Solidly into October, short-sleeve warmth remained.

Following a night of rain, an intense blast from the north has dropped the air temperature by twenty degrees, to 44 degrees Fahrenheit this morning. A few of yesterday's crickets continue calling, softly, fading like sunlight in the grass as the air of autumn cools. A sharp drop in ocean temperature—from the low 70s of summer to 57 degrees—kicks migrating fish into high gear. Catches of husky blackfish and big autumn porgies appear on the marina's cleaning tables. I untie the boat and leave the harbor to take autumn's pulse.

Bird flocks—Laughing Gulls, mostly—are working along every rip and shoal. Under most of them, a few stiff-tailed False Albacore streak through the surface. Badly named, oddly inedible, and generally enigmatic, the little tuna that dares not speak its name comes from no-one-knows-where. But from somewhere, it's here on schedule. Lucky for them, their unpalatable flesh has saved them much grief from fishermen. I'm seeing packs of them from the nearest shoal outside the harbor eastward to beyond the Point, an impressive six miles of nearly continuous activity.

Just off the lighthouse, *thousands* of gulls are hovering and dipping over rough patches of bronze-hued water. Anchovies. This year's extraordinary productivity is what's kept the immense numbers of gulls piling in since September. And despite the incalculable toll extracted by birds and larger fish, compounded daily, anchovy schools continue to pour though and remain astonishingly thick.

I move the boat in among the gulls. Because the water here is shallow, I have to be mindful of the surf and the boulders. So I don't get too close to shore, and I point the boat's bow seaward while I bob in the swell and the sweeping current. Suddenly, as though drawn to the surface in a vast net, a couple of acres of Striped Bass rise from under the anchovies. Packed shoulder to shoulder, the attacking Stripers shred their prey's tight defensive school like an egg slicer. Anchovies spraying into the air are beset by predators everywhere. The gulls go crazy—dipping and slurping little wagging anchovies—and as they concentrate wing tip to wing tip their calls merge into one *loud* sheet of sound. The surface froths as slapping bass tails also raise a roar, a white noise like applause at the opera. And when the Stripers conclude their assault and swim down, the tide carries thousands upon thousands of glittering anchovy scales.

"One hardly dares estimate their numbers," someone once wrote of the bygone shorebirds that formerly smoked these flyways. Let it be recorded that as recently as this very moment, I hardly dare estimate the numbers of bass, of gulls—. The anchovies, impossible to speculate.

More bass rise, several churning schools. Frustrated fishermen are repeatedly casting amid bass so stuffed they ignore the phony lures. I am not too interested in catching these fish. The bass are smallish, with many under ten pounds and below the legal size. I'd rather just take in the spectacle, the vitality and abundance, the deep reassurance. And the resilience: Striped Bass were once down for the count, so depleted by overfishing that there was talk of putting them on the endangered species list. Fishing was shut down for a while, and for a further decade remained tightly restricted. And now—well, just look at them. If we decided to, perhaps we could get the whole ocean back; maybe the whole world.

Bluefish schools are also massing up here in a feeding marathon that occupies most of the daylight hours, especially when the tides are moving. Like the anchovies and everything else, they too crowd in because the long, jutting east-west coast slows southbound movement like a traffic barricade. And because tidal currents collide with this shoreline, high-volume, high-velocity, nutrient-packed flows keep the food chain well provisioned and the prey dense. Southbound fish and the seabirds of autumn pause here for weeks, stoking, stoking.

That autumn fat they put on makes the Bluefish as delicious as they ever get. With thoughts of Thanksgiving, winter, and the holidays, I'd like a few of these fish for the smoker. So I move off to a long tide rip. Despite seeing swirling fish, I can't buy a strike. It's unlike them to be fussy. But a short while later the tide quickens and the birds become concentrated. I drift into another dense, screaming flock—and find the fish both eager and big. A new wave of Blues has come along the underwater ridge and shifted into feeding mode. These are seven to ten pounds and they pull so strong and sustained that they bend the rod for minutes on end. I get them alongside and grab the leader and swing them mightily into the waiting box.

Many regurgitate as they near the boat, their hard-won meals drifting away in the tide. One comes aboard with its belly bulging almost hideously, the contours of successful hunting. It's a brutal thing, this food chain. I am not without pity, nor without conflict. I take half a dozen; that's plenty. I leave them going at it.

On the drive home I turn down a sandy road to the beach just to see what's happening and because the adrenaline has me addicted to the energies of the season. Several people are coming off the sand here, carrying

Bluefish they caught in the surf. But one man is holding something else: a big lure hooked deeply into his hand. He is dripping blood onto the pavement. He says it's not hurting yet, and his friend comes and wraps it in a rag and makes a few calls to find a medical clinic where he might get attention—no small task at sundown on a Sunday, miles from town. Over the ocean, the curtain goes down on more frenzied birds silhouetted by the sinking sun.

❧

Gale warning. The wind came up early, intensified all day, and moaned all night. It blew away the memory of summer and dropped a chill upon us. It pinned the boats inside the harbor. It carried fall's first gannets, which swept over the spume-streaked ocean while almost all other seabirds seemed to vanish.

Summer's terns—long gone. The final few Ospreys of the year (I've seen two this week) are not our own. They lack intimate familiarity with our shoreline. Traveling only a straight, hurried track down the coast with a nippy breeze shoving, they quickly pass. Oystercatchers are going out with a bang; an astonishing twenty-seven of them at the Cut, along with a smattering of turnstones, are likely the last I'll see of each of these. The turnstones, busily probing the wet sand, are in their winter drabs now. Their chocolate-backed plumage contrasts utterly with their northbound costume as the harlequins of springtime.

Morning lights the first sizable lines of arriving scoters, moving along the ocean's lumpy horizon. A Marsh Hawk, tilting in the gusts, plows slow furrows in the air just a few feet over autumn-ambered grass. Half a dozen egrets are patiently working one end of the salt pond. Their immaculate whiteness, which for months had made them seem like perfectly set vases of lilies on the emerald tablecloths of summer, looks misplaced in the chill-rusted marsh.

Kenzie's gait is jaunty and invigorated. Even children can tell you, by the ripening pumpkins brightening in the fields and cramming the roadside stands, that it's finally fully fall.

On the south side, flocks of cormorants—which I'd thought nearly gone—are again writing lines across our skies. That's how a blast of cold air can loosen what's still stuck to the north. Their unending black scrawl, like a Dickens novel in longhand script, has now had its climax and must eventually resolve to an ending. These new generations of "sea crows" have no idea that their kind, too, was once laid low by DDT— but just look at *them*. Like those fishes and other birds that returned from death's door because people decided to change a few things, and like those others that simply remain strong despite it all, endurance belongs to them, and to all the living.

To my considerable surprise a Monarch butterfly comes fluttering along the dunes, beating its way toward Mexico. "You're late, Your Majesty," I'm thinking. "Your legions, your court and kin passed weeks ago; they're already hundreds of miles to the south. Some must by now have their wings folded restfully, their passports already stamped 'Mexico.'" Suddenly, the overdue Monarch simply collapses in midair and, still bright as a flame, falls at my feet, groping weakly in the sand, its epic wings now seeming a monstrous burden. Tragedy in minature. Icarus as insect. But the difference is only a matter of scale. Like a butterfly in a whirlwind, our lives feel the gusts of changing seasons, and eventually must also merge into the dunes of time.

The sun sinks farther south each day. We've watched the seasons and the weather change. We've seen some of the perils. Yet we also see the resilience of living things, not just around Lazy Point. We're about to leave Lazy Point again, to follow sundown halfway around the world. I'll miss the rhythm of the changing seasons, the migrants, and the intensifying energies of shortening days. One can travel quite enough right here, I think. But I want to continue exploring the odd fact that resilience belongs to the living; people are at the same time the most resilient and the most fragile of all.

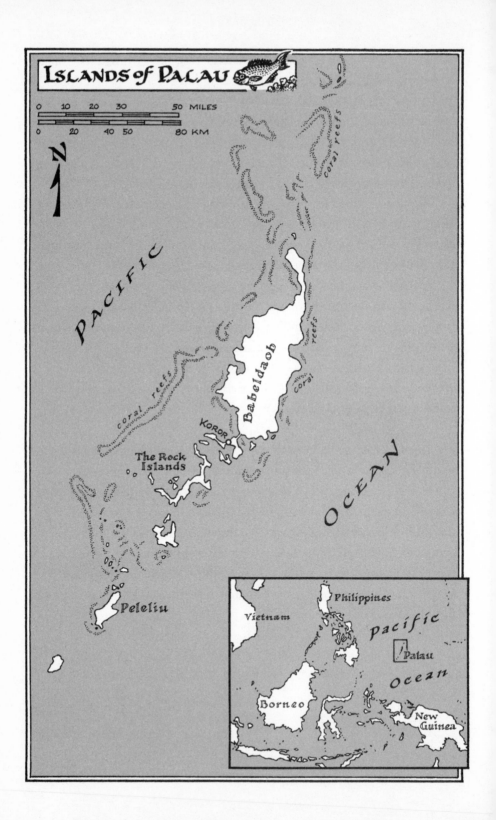

TRAVELS SOLAR:
RAINBOW'S END—PALAU

Parrotfish, damselfish, butterfly fishes in branching coral—and I'm not even in the water. I'm still standing on a concrete dock in Koror, the biggest town in Palau, the Pacific island nation five hundred miles east of the Philippines whose slogan is "Rainbow's End."

In the 1990s this place seemed like paradise, wild and beautiful to extremes. So when I got a chance to come back—I hesitated. "It is the better part of wisdom never to revisit a wilderness," Aldo Leopold warned, "for the more golden the lily, the more certain that someone has gilded it. To return not only spoils a trip, but tarnishes a memory." Good advice. But so far I'm not disappointed. As then, I'm watching rainbow-hued fishes darting among corals, even while I'm merely loading scuba tanks into a boat still tied to the wharf.

That doesn't mean Palau hasn't changed. After I was last here, ocean temperatures across the Pacific got hotter than ever recorded. Corals from the Indian Ocean to French Polynesia "bleached" white as their internal food-producing algae abandoned ship. In Palau, 95 percent of the corals died.

"The wind stopped. Everything stopped," remembers Noah Idechong, a robust Palauan fisherman and conservationist named by *Time* magazine as one of its "Heroes for the Planet"—and now Speaker of Palau's House of Delegates. "The water got so hot, it was actually uncomfortable to swim in. Even the oldest fishermen had never seen such a time. You can't imagine how sad it was, seeing all our reefs dying."

I've come back to see the reefs recovering.

• • •

Bob Steneck and Susie Arnold—with whom I traveled in Belize and
Bonaire—and I are joined by Peter Mumby, of the University of Exeter
in England, and Rob van Woesik, now at the Florida Institute of Technology. In the realm of reef research, these folks make a world-class
team.

We shove off, cross the channel, and are soon zooming among Palau's
famed Rock Islands. As Earth's Pacific Plate slides under the Philippine Plate, the massive remains of drowned reefs unimaginably old have
been wedged upward, forming this fabled maze of truly spectacular
islands. Thick vines dangle from vertical limestone cliffs rising hundreds of feet. Cinched at the waterline, some of the islands look whimsi-
cally designed and ready to topple. The water around each islet reflects
jungled slopes. Emerald, azure, turquoise, jade—.

Rob van Woesik gestures and says over the engine noise and wind,
"These islands—I never get enough." Van Woesik is tall, Australian-
born, late forties, with a soft, almost woofy voice. He's well-read outside
of science. He started as a commercial fisherman and followed his curiosity along a winding path that took him to academia. He spent eight years
as a professor in Japan, earning such respect from his colleagues that a
retiring professor bequeathed him his entire personal library, including
books two centuries old.

From behind the vines, yawning, partially hidden caves harbor
rusting remnants of Japanese cannons, relics of horrific fighting here
in World War II. When Japan disarmed, its strategy for conquest took
a new tack. Our boat displays a sticker announcing that it comes cour-
tesy of Japan. Computers in the lab proclaim, "Technological Cooperation from the Government of Japan." But there is a price: complicity.
Palau, which has never been involved in hunting whales, has joined
the International Whaling Commission at Japan's behest, where its
votes support Japan's festering whale hunts. It trades its votes for boats
but harms the world consensus. As the world gropes toward democratic agreement on the conserving of nature with bodies like the
International Whaling Commission and the Convention on International Trade in Endangered Species, Japan stacks the deck with jokers
and wild cards, countries paid to subvert the whole intent of these
bodies whose purpose is to debate and decide how much to use or to

conserve. Or, as it's done with tuna fishing, Japan votes on limits and then simply cheats; it has been been convicted of systematically over-fishing its quota of Southern Bluefin Tuna. Japan isn't the only country hunting whales. Iceland and Norway do, and even the United States permits some whale killing by Native people. Japan is just the only government that operates so dishonestly, undermining the broad con-sensus of the rest of the world and the other nations' ability to honestly debate the matter. The U.S. government was for years as dishonest and disruptive about climate change. At least the United States has improved on that issue.

We exit the Rock Islands, traveling across lime-green flats to a channel that takes us outside Palau's great ring of reef. The open Pacific Ocean seems surprised to find an atoll here, and does not so much greet the coast as attack it. A ragged line of snarling surf roars across the reef's crest.

We anchor in the swells. Our boat driver assesses how the hook is holding, then stuffs a new wad of betel nut into his cheek and relaxes. We splash in and descend. The water—*warm:* 82 degrees Fahrenheit (28° C).

I land almost on top of a sea cucumber that looks like a slow-crawling caterpillar the size of a loaf of French bread. Visibility out here is over one hundred feet. The crest we're on slopes to an abrupt vertical wall, plunging to true abyss. The current, insistent, pushy, makes this a tricky spot to dive. One moment you're over reef corals almost close enough to touch. One lick seaward and you're in open ocean, staring into blue-black water thousands of feet deep, silhouetted for any Tiger or Bull Sharks below like a roast pig at a banquet. It's intense.

The bewildering array of corals instantly overwhelms. And the thing is: ten years ago, this was devastation. Now—just look at it.

Corals shaped like finely filigreed tables, like sand castles—dozens of kinds. Many are much smaller than the corals that had been, but it's again a coral reef. The recovery looks better than I'd thought possible.

Embedded in bouldery corals, "small giant" clams—the size of my hand—pout psychedelic lips over the rims of their open shells. The color-crazed algae inside those lips turn the reef's solar power into the clams' food. Those wild lips are so sensitive that they twitch at my approaching shadow. At the wave of a hand, the shells close. I'm playing peekaboo with a clam.

The fishes—angels, parrots, surgeons, rabbitfishes, sweetlips, goatfishes, triggers, wrasses, breams, blennies, many more; clown fish, emperors, unicorn fish—different kinds of each. I recognize most groups, but the species are dizzying; this region has about fifteen hundred reef fish species.

Why on Earth so many? Can they really parse the habitat finely enough to give each kind a different job? Or do many perform redundant roles? Do the hundreds of different coral species here create such a palette of niches that only an explosion of specialists can exploit them all?

Diversity and color. I have dozens of fish *species* to view simultaneously: fish wearing pastels, wearing war paint, wearing spin art. Here Pablo Picasso meets Jackson Pollock. That yard-long cornetfish looks like a flute with fins. The shapes, colors, and patterns—the dots and dashes and stripes and hues—seem playful. The bold color patterns must have evolved along with the diversity, to help them sort out whom to mate with; I don't know another explanation that makes sense.

There are fish everywhere I look. Compared to what you'd find on land, the density and diversity of vertebrate animals is staggering.

Bob, Rob, and Peter all lay measuring tapes and swim along them, tallying what they see; Bob's absorbed with his crusting algae, van Woesik with corals; Peter swims with the fishes. Susie, meanwhile, checks terracotta plates she'd left here previously. Her tiles are clear of seaweeds. That's a *big* difference from most of the Caribbean. In fact, here I see no seaweed at all.

Seaweed-grazing fishes are much denser and diverse here. The Caribbean has only three species of surgeonfish; this region has about a dozen. The Caribbean has about a dozen parrotfishes; this region, about thirty. And the Pacific also adds different grazing groups, like rabbitfishes and others.

So many fish are doing so much grazing that they continually scour every surface. This coral garden is a harsh, harsh place for algae. Most "seaweed" never gets tall enough even to be called fuzz. It doesn't last as long as a daisy in a herd of goats.

Bob and Peter have analyzed video footage showing that the fish deliver up to one hundred bites *per square meter* of seafloor, *per hour*. Sitting here on a patch of sand under my bubbles, simply watching, is helping me see the intensity of a well-functioning coral reef.

Just off the wall, streamlined fusiliers and rainbow-hued *Anthias* positively swarm in the running current, as dazzling as fireworks. They part to accommodate a Whitetip Reef Shark—a pretty big one, at about six feet—that glides in serenely and effortlessly, poker-faced and confident. It reinforces the shark stereotype with its easy control, and betrays not a flicker of interest in me as it melds into the blue distance.

Along the drop-off, as if out for a stroll, comes a Napoleon Wrasse as big as my head and torso, displaying its blue-green body, its maze of fine markings, its curious eye and Nubian lips. It's an Alice-in-Wonderland fish. Boats engaged in the insatiable Chinese restaurant live-fish trade have scoured this fantasy with fins from reef after reef, coast after coast, country after country. Palau remains among the Napoleon Wrasse's last few strongholds—thanks entirely to Palau's fishing laws, which ban its export. Also banned: live export of any reef fish, export of crabs, lobsters, giant clams, and most sea cucumbers, and possession of groupers during spawning season.

The regulations are why this place still works. It works as few places do, as well or better than probably any other humanly inhabited reef region in the world.

Back aboard, Peter removes his mask, wipes his face, and says, "After doing my transects, I was just having a look around and thinking, 'This *has* to be the most incredible ecosystem on Earth. Absolutely.'"

Van Woesik says to me cheerfully, "It's nice to know it's not all gloomy, isn't it? Nice to see all this recovery going on."

Bob says something I've *never* heard him say: "There's very little seaweed here." And at other reefs around Palau, both inside its vast lagoons and out along its plunging ocean slopes, the story, happily, is the same.

"Here, in ten years," Rob van Woesik sums up, "it's recovered from near-zero live coral to about seventy percent of the reef covered in live corals. That's remarkable."

Two reasons: One, the fish. Two, the corals themselves. I ask van Woesik how many different kinds of hard corals live where we just dived. If anybody knows, he does.

"I don't know," he says. He consults his clipboard for an estimate, tallying thoughtfully, then, in his Aussie accent, gives me his total.

I ask him to confirm this: Did he say between eighteen and nineteen?

"No; between eight-*tee* and nine-*tee*. Eight-oh," he affirms.

"In other words," Bob says, "more kinds of corals live right here on this patch than in the entire Caribbean."

Van Woesik amplifies: "Actually, there are more species of hard corals growing on the concrete dock at the lab—I've actually counted—than in the whole Caribbean."

While the Caribbean has about sixty coral species, Palau has about sixty-five coral groups, called genera (single: genus), each with numerous species. For example, as I've mentioned, the great thicket builders of the Caribbean were Staghorn and Elkhorn Corals. They're closely related, so they're both in the genus *Acropora*. In that genus, the Caribbean has only those two species. The Indo-Pacific region has over 150 *Acropora* species.

While the whole Caribbean is about the size of New Guinea, the tropical region of the Indian and Pacific Oceans combined is truly vast. Big places have more species than small places and are more resilient to shocks. Over the contours and corners of this swath of the world, there lie so many coasts and islands that—over geologic timescales as sea levels have risen and fallen and climates changed—corals are continually getting isolated, evolving under new conditions, then spreading and evolving more as they interact and adjust to one another. It's the greatest evolutionary cauldron in the sea.

And here, some corals grow fast. *Acropora* begin reproducing when their diameter reaches about two inches (four centimeters). In the Caribbean, that might take ten years. Here: four months.

But that only explains rapid coral recovery here compared to the Caribbean. It doesn't explain rapid coral recovery here compared to other

places in the western Pacific with as many—or more—kinds of corals. The fish, at densities high enough to utterly suppress seaweed, explain it.

The fish are why seaweed didn't just spread like wildfire and take over the reefs here when almost all the coral bleached and died. The fish are why baby corals regained their foothold and have flourished. Because Palau decided not to let its fish get exported—and because its human population is small compared to their vast reefs—it now has: the fish, boatloads of paying tourists, and the highest coral-recovery rate ever recorded.

What I learned in Belize in the negative, I see here in the positive: reefs need enough fish to work overtime to suppress algae after something goes wrong for the corals.

Lessons: Diversity = resilience. Abundance = resilience. To survive catastrophe, you need a surplus, a reservoir, money under the mattress, food in the fridge. If you're already starving, you won't survive a famine. Take the world down to the bone and the only thing that flourishes are boneyards; the only thing that expands is collapse. For a reef to survive bad times, in good times it needs *more than enough* fish. Palau kept 'em, and now it has its reefs back.

So far, Palau has defended itself against distant export markets for its fish. Instead it draws a different distant market here: the tourism that lets Palau keep the goose and the golden eggs. But Palau is modernizing. Hotels serve foreigners the same kinds of reef fish that can't be exported to foreigners. There's pressure to build more hotels, bring more people, relax the rules—the usual story. I hope they don't overdo it. In one village, the rooms of the primary school are not numbered but are named after the different phases in the ripening of coconuts. Attention to detail, valuing what's local—that's usually the first casualty.

At one time in the yard of an old Palauan woman grew a magic tree. This tree had a big hollow branch, and through that branch came a continual stream of water and fish. The generous woman let anyone come, and a constant procession of people held their baskets under the tree, filling them with fish for their villages. But some envied the woman and coveted the tree. One night, they came with their adzes and chopped the tree down and took it to their own village. It never produced another fish. Turns out, that hollow branch had an underground connection to the sea. So don't mess with what works. Don't ruin a good thing. The greed of a few starves all.

A lot's at stake. Scientists have named over eight hundred species of reef-building corals globally, but on coral reefs live hundreds of thousands, perhaps up to two million, other species.

I hope Palauans don't wait till it's gone to realize what they've got. I visited one young Palauan at his home, which by U.S. middle-class standards would be considered poor. He told me he'd never considered Palau as anything special. It was all he'd ever known. But he'd recently returned from his first visit to the Philippines. "I was just shocked by the poverty there," he said. "I had never seen people living like that."

I have. I've seen Philippine markets offering piles of fish so small you'd expect to find them in a living room aquarium. Fried, they resemble potato chips. That's all they have left. That's the apocalypse, happening now.

"Want to see a really gorgeous little recruit?" asks Susie. To the naked eye, it's a dot on a slimed plate. Under the microscope, what comes into clarity is a tiny lattice of living structure, the tentacles of its baby polyps glowing neon blue.

She shows me that even here, corals prefer to settle on the same *Titanoderma* as do Caribbean corals. Incredibly, over a great swath of the world, one kind of nondescript crusting algae is superimportant for corals getting their start in life.

Here, because fish are grazing her plates clean of seaweed, Susie is averaging seven to ten new little corals per plate. In Belize, it's more like two.

But none of this makes the reefs immune from sudden temperature spikes. Bob reminds us, "It could happen again. We could be right back where we were, with hot water and ninety-five percent of the corals dead."

On the day I arrived here, the journal *Science* published a study of coral growth on Australia's Great Barrier Reef. It said: "Throughout the GBR, calcification [growth of corals' calcium-carbonate skeletons] has declined by 14.2% since 1990, predominantly because extension (linear growth) has declined." The reasons, the authors explained, are two: the seawater is getting too warm and, because of acidification, there's already too little carbonate for normal coral growth. They examined centuries-old corals for comparison. "Such a severe and sudden decline," the researchers wrote, is "unprecedented." The study's lead author said, "If this rate continues—which is accelerating—then the coral growth will hit zero round about 2050." Said Charlie Veron, former chief scientist of the Australian Institute of Marine Science, "There is no way out, no loopholes. The Great Barrier Reef will be over within 20 years or so." A few months after I left, scientists announced that the year set a new world's record high for ocean temperature.

Here in Palau, now, corals are doing great. But you never know when the rest of the world will intrude.

The world intrudes nightly on the four-channel TV in my little, low-rent hotel room. I can choose among such news sources as Catholic World Network, BBC World News, a Japanese news channel, or Japanese MTV. I tend to choose BBC News. But as I get the news I crave, I feel glad to be in a remote place, out of the mainstream, as news reports of horrors upon miseries around the globe continuously demonstrate that we the people haven't yet learned to distinguish justice from vengeance. Better to watch the sumo wrestling, an admirably straightforward and mercifully brief form of ritual combat.

Morning traffic snakes and crawls through Koror's main street. The first time I came here, there was not a single traffic light in the country. Then they tried them, but nobody paid attention when the light turned red. "It's like a machine telling people what to do," complained one person who gave me a lift. The lights came down. Now, again, the country has not one stoplight.

Palau is a country that can still feel like a small town. It has no pathologist. "If we really need a coroner," a government official assured me, "we can get him from Guam—but he's expensive." Okay, so no coroner unless we really need one. Palau is in the region called Micronesia, which also contains the Federated States of Micronesia (150,000 people), and the Marshall Islands. The Marshalls' 50,000 people include 30,000 on Majuro, an atoll of more than sixty islands with a combined landmass under four square miles. Parts of Majuro are so hair-thin, you can throw a rock from the lagoon side to the ocean. Its highest elevation: ten feet above sea level.

Into the Rock Island Café stroll Olai Polloi and Nyk Kloulubak, both around thirty. She's Palau's national climate-change coordinator; Nyk is the country's energy planner. A slight, shy young woman, Olai seems too innocent for bruising international politics.

In one sense, Palau is an innocent place. With only 22,000 people, the country's contribution to world carbon emissions is far smaller than that of my local university (which has 25,000 students). Yet just as "a rising tide floats all boats," a rising sea floods all shores, guilty and innocent alike.

We find a booth, and order. Nyk wears a printed shirt and a shell necklace. He's frustrated that Palau still has no official energy policy. He believes that's shockingly primitive in this day and age—and it is. It's also the situation we've always had in the United States.

I ask the climate coordinator if the weather has changed, and what she plans to do about it. "Extremes," she says. "When it's hot, it's extremely hot. And when it rains, it's extreme rain."

Just outside, the rain is falling so hard and heavy, daylight dims. This is the dry season.

Nyk says, "If we go all-solar and use all fluorescent lights—*if we emit no carbon dioxide at all*—will the sea level go down? That's what the elders ask, practical questions. And I cannot say, 'If you do this, you'll get your washed-away land back, or your house won't get flooded.' The people, they want results. I can talk about 'helping fight global warming.' But they ask, 'If I do this, will I save a hundred dollars?' Talking long-term—it doesn't get their attention."

Olai describes her experiences in international meetings, complaining, "Politics changed the whole science when I worked on the Intergovernmental Panel on Climate Change report. I was sitting *right there* in Brussels that day. In the morning, the report said, 'We are certain that a particular island will be flooded.' And by afternoon, the report said, 'We are uncertain . . .'" She looks at me wide-eyed, and nods to make sure I'm following. "I was sitting *right* there. This kind of thing was going on all day. It still *boggles* me that *politicians* can change a *scientific* report. They *totally* watered it down. I was so frustrated—and I could see how the scientists were so frustrated. I was thinking of places like Tuvalu, Kiribati, and atolls in Palau like Kayangel and Peleliu. I was thinking, 'While we are replacing words—these places are drowning.'

"Then I was standing in line for lunch," Olai continues. "And I meet the Saudi person. First time I met him. So he says, 'Where are you from?' I say, 'Palau.' I say, 'It's an island country.' He says, 'How many of you are there?' I say, 'About twenty-two thousand.' He says, 'Twenty-two thousand; that is nothing. Too bad for you.' Later he says, 'You will never convince me that oil is bad—because you need it; you want it. So don't try to tell me you think it is bad. Your need makes me produce it.'" She adds, "It's a hard day for me to forget." She stirs her tea, then says, "David used a sling and a rock. How should David fight Goliath now?" She brightens, smiles a shy island smile, and adds, "But the right change will come."

❧

The first century of the Industrial Revolution, the 1800s, was powered by coal, whale oil, and slaves. The twentieth was the century of petroleum (though 40 percent of U.S. train freight is still coal). World electricity generation is still two-thirds combustion (40 percent coal, 20 percent natural gas, 6 percent oil), plus 15 percent nuclear, 16 percent hydropower, and about 2 percent other renewables. That's how we get energy.

Here's a taste of how we waste it: In the United States, where tap water is safe, bottled water costs about one thousand times as much as tap water and consumes tens of millions of barrels of oil a year (I've seen estimates from seventeen to fifty million barrels); it's been likened to having each bottle of water one-quarter full of oil. It takes three times as much water to make the plastic bottle as the bottle contains. America's refrigerators use twice the electricity of the European average, and four times as much as the most efficient refrigerators currently available. Using the most efficient appliances, worldwide, would eliminate the need to build the fourteen hundred coal-fired power plants that are projected to be needed by 2020.

Cars. With nearly the least miles per gallon of gas and nearly the most miles driven per vehicle, U.S. drivers—who own more than a quarter of the world's cars—burn more gasoline than the next twenty countries *combined*, including Japan, Germany, China, Russia, and Brazil. If our average fuel efficiency merely equaled some of the better cars now on the market (forty miles per gallon), Americans would halve their gasoline use. Just like that. Going to plug-in hybrids would drop driving costs to the equivalent of one dollar per gallon; gasoline use would drop by 80 percent—without reducing the number of cars or miles driven. This isn't sacrifice; we're already sacrificing efficiency and wasting our money. Eventually, the electricity powering plug-in cars could come from wind or solar. Those are only some of the opportunities we're missing.

Henry Ford reputedly noted that if he'd asked people what they wanted, they'd have said "a faster horse." What else might we be missing? Every hour, enough sunlight strikes Earth to power our world economy for a year. The upper six miles of Earth's crust (people have drilled down seven miles) holds something like fifty thousand times as much energy as all the oil and gas. With an investment equaling the cost of one coal plant (about $1 billion) the United States could, by 2050, generate geothermal energy equal to 250 coal-burning plants. North Dakota, Kansas, and Texas have enough wind to supply not just all of the United States' electricity but all of its energy. (Denmark and parts of Germany already get 20 to 30 percent of their electricity from mere moving air.) On one windy quarter acre, a farmer can grow $300 worth of corn or allow a company to put up a wind turbine capable of generating $300,000 worth of electricity a year. If the company pays only 1 percent in royalties, the farmer still makes ten times as much by farming wind.

When ethanol made from corn pits people who need to eat in a bidding war against people who want to drive, drivers win. But some nonedible plants also produce oil. The seeds of *Jatropha curcas* are about one-third oil. Some algae yield up to thirty times more fuel than other energy crops. Airlines are already testing algae-based jet fuels. "The airplane performed perfectly," one test pilot said. "It was textbook."

These aren't even all the options. Compared to the possible oceans of improvements, humanity is still dog-paddling in the shallow end of the kiddie pool. Sometimes we seem determined to drown there just because we won't stand up.

Perpetua Tmetuchl goes by the nickname Tua. She's an upright elder, poised and calm. Her gray hair, pulled back and pinned, is adorned with a big flower. She wears a long floral skirt. Her face is relaxed, her gaze alert.

She's been farming taro in the same place since the early 1980s. It's the traditional staple, a starchy root so crucial to island survival for so long that it's still ubiquitous in ceremonies, revered and nearly sacred. Tua grows it commercially. Her main buyer comes from Guam.

As we are walking downhill to her taro patch, I tell her that her place, with its commanding views of the water and islands, scenic with coconut palms, fragrant with tropical blossoms, is like paradise.

"It *is* paradise," she corrects. But paradise is seldom trouble-free. She explains, "In 1996 my husband—he died a few years ago—he and I took a walk down to my taro patch, just like you and I are doing. But that evening, we were amazed. The high tide was coming inside, flooding the taro with saltwater. You know how water is; we couldn't do anything.

That was the first time. Then, it started coming every few months. Now, it's almost every full moon."

We walk down to her three acres of broad-leafed plants, bordered with ditches to direct freshwater. Taro needs to be seasonally wet, so it's grown near freshwater. But it also has to dry out. And it can't grow in seawater.

People have been growing taro for about five thousand years, and here some areas might trace an unbroken line of cultivation back fully three thousand years. Numerous varieties exist.

Growing it is guided by custom and taboo. Men are not allowed into the taro patch at the time of planting. Women do not sleep with their husbands the night before, for fear that they will wake late, in the wrong frame of mind for hard work.

Until the 1960s, most Palauans relied on local food for survival. Taro was the main source of calories. For older and poorer people, it still is. It's starchy and satisfying, like potatoes, but the flavor—quite good—is different.

Looking at the flooded portions and the yellowed leaves, Tua says, "All the villages close to the shoreline have this same problem. With the seawater coming up, and *so* much rain, the water doesn't drain." Tua has an explanation: "The Bible does not mention taro, but it says, 'Things you have not seen, you will be seeing in the end times.'"

"So," I ask, "you see this as a sign that the world is ending?"

"Ending." She nods with a smile. "Yes. And God says, 'I will protect the faithful ones.' So, I don't worry about it."

Others worry. "Rain. Rain, rain, rain," says Hilve Skang as we walk through a torrential downpour. A stout, bespectacled lady with short, curly hair, she's wearing flip-flops and a brightly printed dress. She's wielding a machete and chewing betel as she leads me down to her taro patch. And she's quite agitated. Two pigs squeal as we pass. Hilve sputters, "Last night, full moon, highest tide we ever seen. It was about a foot over the mark we made last time it was the highest we ever seen."

Her banana trees' leaves look like they're burning; who'd have thought seawater would scorch the earth? Her giant taro grows well above my head, to seven feet. But a big part of the taro patch is soggy and lifeless.

Hilve complains, "Every time I fix—the tide comes. New moon and full moon, the tide comes very high. All die. The lady over there"—she points her machete to a neighbor's bit of ground—"she already give up."

～

Getting to the seven-square-mile island of Peleliu entails an hour's boat ride from the main island of Babeldoab, across twenty wide miles of deep lagoon, toward lime-tinted clouds to the south. During the push to dislodge Japanese forces in World War II, Americans bombed and napalmed the lush island until it resembled a construction site. A few rusting tanks and bomb-pocked buildings remain. One large live bomb, too big to be detonated, sits to this day, merely cordoned off by tape. But otherwise the island is so quiet and sleepy, you feel you've stepped back a bit in time, even compared to the rest of Palau. Greeting me on the sandy shoreline: *a Ruddy Turnstone,* the Arctic-breeding bird that shadows me all over the world.

After the trauma of war, the specter of food shortage left a scar that remains. The five hundred people of the island live under a self-imposed ban on taro export, except for ceremonial purposes. During funerals, the bereaved family prepares food baskets for each attendee, with five or six pieces of taro. So prized is the yellow taro of Peleliu—it is said that the soil makes it distinctive—that a woman from Babeldoab confided, "I've gone to funerals when I didn't even know the person who died— just so I could come back with a basket of Peleliu taro."

Just a few years ago, the president's inauguration featured Peleliu taro. But at the most recent inauguration, there was none to be had.

Peleliu is much flatter than Palau's main island. That means more flooding. "Even people digging graves have begun hitting water," complains seventy-six-year-old Isor Kikuo, her lined face distressed. "Look," she says, her hands gesturing. "The water won't go down." Much of her own taro crop has died. She pulls up one plant and shows me the starchy root that has fed islanders for millennia. She demonstrates how she has to cut away rotting portions. "See—?" The root should be hard; it is mushy. It smells terrible. She carefully cuts the bad parts away. She cuts until she tosses the whole thing away in disgust, muttering, "This is all rotten. This is good for nothing.

"Taro and fishing," she continues. "The old people, we rely on that." She says that children with distant jobs are sending their aging parents money for rice. But Isor explains that the children's rents are high; sending money to feed their parents puts additional strain on them, and the price of rice has nearly doubled in the last year. She is careful to say that not all the taro is so badly affected. "Patches in the middle of the island"—she waves her machete inland—"they don't have any ocean in them."

Eriko Nalone, who has joined us, adds, "And I'll tell you what: this high water since the late 1990s, it has changed the time when the fish come to spawn. In April we go to the beach from three nights before till three nights after full moon, expecting the big trevally. No fish. Later, when you're not expecting them, *then* they come. The crabs used to come out on the road in March, April. No more. The *Trochus* snails used to come up on the reefs starting in May. This year they opened the season in June, but the snails didn't come until July. The tide is coming at, like, an hour from when we expect. Tide tables are no longer accurate. Sometimes they predict weak tides, but then it comes two feet higher. It's weird."

Like all problems, rising water hits poor people hardest. Over the bridge from Koror, in Malakal, the videographer Kassi Berg shares some unedited interviews she recently obtained from Falalop Island, part of Ulithi Atoll, of the Federated States of Micronesia. A woman named Tess comes on camera. She appears to be in her early twenties, with flowers in her hair and the kind of lips Gauguin traveled halfway round the world for. Gauguin, by the way, asked in one painting of Pacific Islanders, "Where do we come from? What are we? Where are we going?" That's what the islanders are asking. Tess is saying, "The island used to be so big. Now it's small. The water is really rising. For the children growing up now, the island will be, probably, gone. I don't know what will become of our children. They'll probably go to somebody else's place. They won't know of our island. They'll be eating food from the store. But that costs money, and not everybody has a job."

An older man, with a puffy, grizzled face and sad eyes, comes on camera, saying, "All the gardening areas on the windward side are gone. Five or six rows of coconut trees washed away. Already five hundred feet of land washed away. Our wells taste salty. The new road is already in the water. There is no way to control it. We're going to have trouble feeding all the people on this island. We have a very bad situation. And if there is a typhoon coming, we will be underwater." A chief adds, "I'm an old man now. I don't know what happened to the world. Maybe the scientists can fix the damage you have done to our atmosphere. Please be kind enough to solve the problem."

The world may try shirking off the problems of thousands of Pacific Islanders. But that won't be possible. While I'm in Palau, the Australian government issues this press release:

AUSTRALIA PROVIDES EMERGENCY ASSISTANCE

Australia will provide immediate emergency assistance to each of the Federated States of Micronesia and the Republic of the Marshall Islands, in response to tidal surges and storms that have inundated the low-lying Pacific Islands since early December . . . flooding the cities of Majuro and Ebeye in the Marshall Islands, destroying homes and submerging parts of the islands. The tidal surges left streets covered in rocks, coral and debris. . . . Groundwater and farming land has been contaminated with seawater. . . .

There's also this, from the U.S. government:

If the President of the Federated States of Micronesia determines that the emergency or disaster requires a greater response from the United States Government, the President of the Federated States of Micronesia may request that the President of the United States make a presidential disaster declaration.

That means money, folks. But why should we pay now? After all, we didn't pay at the pump; it wasn't on our electric bill—.

The first official sea-level-related relocations to higher land occurred in December 2005 in the Pacific island nation of Vanuatu. The Maldives, the Marshall Islands, Kiribati, Tuvalu—we're not talking about a few hundred people. Well over half a million people live in island countries whose average elevation above the sea is only six feet. (When people have trouble finding higher ground, many other creatures will simply perish. Seabirds that nest on low islands and atolls—millions of birds, of dozens of species, populating entire oceans—will lose their nesting grounds. They will not be able to move to high islands. All the high islands are taken by a peculiar new two-legged animal.)

On continents, the numbers of people are much more serious. The slow tsunami of rising sea will inexorably sweep millions to higher ground. Fifteen of the world's twenty biggest cities lie exposed to the sea, including Tokyo, Mumbai, and New York. Something approaching 100 million people live on land less than one meter—about three feet— above sea level. The sea level may rise three feet in this century.

The World Bank reminds us that as the sea level rises three feet, in Bangladesh alone 30 million people will have to squeeze inland, while half of Bangladesh's rice fields will be spoiled by saltwater. Already among the world's first climate refugees are 500,000 former inhabitants of Bhola Island in Bangladesh, left homeless after half of the island became permanently inundated in 2005.

～

Toward dusk, fruit bats the size of crows are commuting to the coast across a broad arc of sky. Leonard Basilius says there are two kinds, adding, "But you can hardly tell the difference unless you have them on your table."

I ask how well he likes eating fruit bats.

"I don't eat. But my wife and kids, they love it."

"We love it," his thirteen-year-old daughter affirms.

At Leonard's home, flowers scent the night air. The quiet neighborhood bears no sound of music, just murmuring voices, singing frogs, and an occasional dog's bark. Through the silhouettes of mangroves and coconut palms, the moon rises full and lovely.

But that moon pulls a pucker of sea around the world, and as the tide rises we watch Leonard's backyard disappear. Soon, he and his neighbors are sloshing around in shin-deep saltwater that rises up the wheels of parked cars and laps at front doors.

Leonard and his family—he and his brother and their wives and kids share a house—are making dinner outdoors, wading around in water that soon reaches almost to their knees. As they sit, their table stands in seawater. Benches become islands, dogs stand on cinder blocks, and fish are actually swimming around everyone's feet.

"I get very frustrated," Leonard admits. "After it started, for a few years it was once or twice a year. It happens every full and new moon now. But there is nothing we can do."

Inches higher, and it will be flooding the house interiors. "In a few years, we will have to move. Or maybe the government will assist us in raising the house. But the politicians see this problem only when they are campaigning for office, not after they get in." He pauses and looks at his family and their home. I glance at his flooded neighborhood. "Well," he says, "we'll have to find a way."

As I walk out from his neighborhood, I notice that seawater is coming uphill in the drainage ditches. A few days ago, this would have surprised me.

≈

From "Rainbow's End" to somewhere over the date line, fourteen time zones to home.

One of the densely inhabited islands just a few feet above sea level is Manhattan, where I'm having fantasies of the coming good news: Wall Street, underwater. But right now I'm headed toward the United Nations.

On a recent Friday, over fifty member states of the United Nations called on the U.N. Security Council to act on the "pernicious security implications of climate change for human beings worldwide." Palau's U.N. ambassador said frustratedly, "There is as great a threat from climate change as any bomb, poison, or terrorist." He added, "This is the first time in history that U.N. member states are faced with extinction—and the Security Council has been silent."

The Maldives has a population of 380,000 people; it averages a little over three feet above sea level. Its government is looking at property in Australia, should the whole country need to escape from itself. Kiribati is likewise in the market for land to which to relocate its country. Also in the news: dozens of families from the Solomon Islands are being permanently evacuated to Papua New Guinea as flooding turns several islands to wet rags.

A *Financial Times* article titled "Mass Relocation Planned as Seas Rise" reports that in Indonesia, "experts and the government fear that about 2,000 islands across the country will sink by 2040." In what sounds like comedy, Indonesia's maritime minister "asked the regional governments to keep an eye on the islands." But he also called it "the disaster that would affect the whole world."

Marlene Moses, whose business card identifies her as "U.N. Ambassador Extraordinary and Plenipotentiary Permanent Representative of the Republic of Nauru," is a large Polynesian whom you could imagine as a stone statue. But in conversation she's animated, articulate, and warm. Her whole tiny country has 14,000 people, but when you consider what it would take to relocate just 14,000, you begin to realize the enormity of the issue. During a hallway discussion about how sea level rise threatens her tiny island nation, she and her colleagues vow to defy the rising tide.

"We'll stay. There's no option," Moses insists. "No option. If we leave, Nauru would not exist as a nation."

Masao Nakayama, U.N. ambassador from the Federated States of Micronesia, adds, "We don't want to abandon our ancestors. That's a strong feeling. How can we just leave our ancestral place? It's unimaginable that climate change would cause a people to suffer extinction. It's very hard just to—"

"They use the word 'relocate' so easily," Moses says scornfully. "Relocate—for what? To become climate-change refugees?"

But Afelee Pita, the U.N. ambassador from Tuvalu (population 13,000), realizes that sands are running through the hourglass. Frustration is evident in his voice too, as he says, "Time and tide cannot wait for us to complete all these dialogues. At high tide, even with no wind now, water will just come onto the land. It's contaminating our wells and gardens."

Moses adds, "In Nauru now, we've had to move graves before they got washed away. In the olden days, each family had drinking wells; it was *fresh* water. Now it's not for drinking. Not anymore." She shakes her head. "It's pretty hard for our people to understand that these changes are being caused by, you know, industrialized countries so, so, so far away."

Nakayama adds, "Fish are a big source of meat for us. And we have traditional ways of conserving fisheries. But now our traditional ways may no longer work. If the fish are leaving because it's too warm for them, if the corals die because it's too acidic—how are we supposed to conserve?"

When I ask if it's true that New Zealand has offered asylum, Moses rolls her eyes and scoffs, "Oh, *please.* No. It's not an option. Why should we *lose our identity*"—she jabs a finger into the wall—"because of deeds committed by industrialized countries? It's a *justice* question, a *security* question, a human *rights* question—. Our whole country is just *one* island. If we sink, it's farewell to me."

I hit the streets of the Big Apple, thinking that Moses is wrong. It's not about her, or her people. Maybe she'd get further with her argument if she reframed it. The guy from Indonesia in that news article was closer to putting his finger on it when he said—what did he call it?—"the disaster that would affect the whole world"? When millions of people living along the continental coasts start moving to higher ground, they'll crowd right on top of poor, already crowded people already clinging to wafer-thin margins of life. One estimate of those at risk from rising sea level: over 70 million in China, nearly 30 million in Bangladesh, 12 million in Egypt, another 20 million in India, and over 30 million others elsewhere.

Australia's Defense Ministry warns that although Australia should ease suffering caused by global warming, if conflict erupts the country should use its military "to deal with any threats." The National Defense University, an educational institute overseen by the U.S. military in Washington, D.C., explored the potential impact of a destructive flood in Bangladesh that would send hundreds of thousands of refugees streaming into neighboring India. In real life, India is already racing to build a 2,100-mile-long fence. "It gets real complicated real quickly," said deputy assistant secretary of defense Amanda J. Dory, while helping the

Pentagon try to incorporate climate change into its national security planning. And the ensuing unrest will likely rise and widen, like the sea itself. It will cost us time and treasure and probably blood.

So ask not for whom the bell tolls. Recovering coral reefs threatened by warming and acidification and increasing human appetites, the rising waters and drowning lands—. Those warning gongs are for us all.

NOVEMBER

It's been a restless night; even Kenzie was up at one A.M., barking loudly at something. She's not much of a watchdog, and when I went outside to check, I encountered only silence, infinity, and the Milky Way, beauty-marked by a meteor. Peaceful images to take to bed, but I couldn't get back to sleep.

So, though I'd intended to check the beach early, at first light I'm awake but too tired to rouse. I wait half an hour, then soldier forth. That is to say, the south side beach is pretty light by the time I walk onto the sand. As I crest the dune, my first glimpse of the surf brings the sight not only of hundreds of gulls hovering over the breakers—good sign—but, to my surprise, dozens of foot-long adult Atlantic Menhaden, a.k.a. bunkers, flipping around on the wet beach. Something just drove them ashore. And I just missed a spectacular attack.

I make a couple of casts as the birds break up, and I curse my laziness for having missed the last half hour. Down the beach at the westward point, the air above the surf is thick with gulls. The point to my east holds a smaller flock, but it's closer. I walk briskly east into the gray morning behind my trotting Kenzie. Just ahead, a big sandbar extends from the main beach and then runs parallel to shore, creating a knee-deep trough about ten yards wide between the bar and the beach. The waves are breaking on that outer bar, and what's left of them rolls across the shallow trough and laps the beach. A quarter mile away, where the long sandbar ends, is the mouth of the trough; that's where the gulls are hovering and dipping.

A big Bluefish glides over the sand in the trough's green water. It looks trapped in that shallow, narrow chute, and I'm not expecting it to be thinking about food. But I lob a short cast, and as my big green lure begins wiggling back to me, a swirl rises behind it. I lose sight of it in the sea foam, but my line tightens and what comes thrashing to the surface is not the Blue but the sandy-beige back of a Striped Bass. It slides from the suds pearl-bellied and gleaming. I reach down with the pliers to free the hook, and pause to admire in this fine, soft light its suddenly light-green back, the iridescent violet on the shoulder and cheeks, its bold stripes drawn with alternating dots of dark chocolate and pale blue, and each scale etched just enough to suggest an almost imperceptibly fine fishnet veil.

As several bunkers come shooting along the shore in water that barely covers their backs, a Bluefish zooms in with its tail knifed out, ending one of the bunkers in a haze of blood. Half of another bunker bobs to the surface, and immediately vanishes under a frothy splash. So, it turns out the *bunkers* are trapped in the trough—and the bass and Blues crowded into here are very much on the hunt.

My bass is short of legal length, so I let the next wave reclaim it. I release several Bluefish, because my smoker is full of Bluefish fillets and working at this very moment. They're beautiful, though, fat and shining, and bearing the purpled flanks of the biggest kind of blues. Kenzie is increasingly excited over the magic of my conjuring ashore such big flopping creatures.

As predators rip along the curl of the lapping water, bunkers huddle in shallows so skinny that the next wave pushes a few of them high and dry.

With the sun climbing I decide to turn homeward from the morning's savage beauty. I whistle Kenzie back toward where we've come from, and she trots along, tail held high. Just past where the bar joins the beach, dozens of newly driven bunkers lie on sand amid gulls too gorged to care. Maybe there are bigger bass out in front of all these windrowed fish? The hypothesis becomes an excuse to unfurl one last cast before turning my back on the scene. Hardly has the lure splashed in when a fish grabs it and yanks my rod down hard while running seaward. It comes up frothing the surface, and when I see its wide broom of tail, I know I've got my keeper Striper. I head home anticipating a breakfast of warm Bluefish straight from the smoker and a good day of work ahead, feeling this morning's espresso of adrenaline more pleasantly than any caffeine.

A morning like this makes me feel happy. And I don't mind knowing that the feeling will be temporary. Happiness, like everything else in this rhythmic realm, comes and goes in waves, and it's good to savor it when the wave rises and, when the wave recedes, understand that another wave will come. Sometimes you ride the wave; sometimes you ride out the trough. A wave's height is measured by its depth, anyway.

My father, a schoolteacher who suffered from real depression, used to say, "Those who know they have enough are rich." I'm not sure he believed it. But I did. When I was young my friends and I would sit around with a fish on the grill and a beer in hand—very low-budget—and joke, "I wonder what the poor people are doing." A dry roof, a cold fridge, a hot shower, wheels, and climbing into any boat—even when the roof wasn't mine, nor the fridge, nor the shower, *nor* the boat—that's always felt like like incredible riches. I'm not knocking money, but it's got its limitations. It can make many things easier, but it doesn't guarantee that you'll choose the right things and ask the right questions, and a lot of people with money remain (or become) unhappy. Anyway, I've seen what real poverty looks like. So my middle-class life and my connection with the sea have always seemed amazing luck. I've never thought that having more stuff would solve all my problems or make me happier—and that's proven true.

Apparently, it's true for many. In the 1970s, Eric Fromm observed that the economic system's continuous push for increasing consumption (what many young people back then denounced as "materialism") sowed the seeds of alienation and passivity. Ivan Illich attacked the "ideas"—ideologies, really—that increasing affluence equals progress, and that commodities are "needs." Tibor Scitovsky was alarmed by consumerism's addictiveness—and its failure to satisfy.

To their insights, we can now add a little hindsight. Here we go: As real (adjusted) income in the United States more than doubled from the 1950s to about 2000, the fraction of Americans describing themselves as "very happy" stayed remarkably flat, at around one-third of the population. Though the United Kingdom's per-person gross domestic product

nearly doubled between about 1970 and 2000, the Brits' sense of satisfaction didn't change. In Japan between about 1960 and 1990 the gross
product rose by a factor of six—but people's sense of satisfaction didn't
change there, either. Take-home: People in developed countries express
a dramatic disconnect between the growth of the economy and their
satisfaction.

While the gross national product measures "how much," another
index asks, "How good?" This other index, called the Genuine Progress
Indicator, measures growth *and* costs. In other words, it's not just counting; it's actual accounting. It looks at productivity, at spending, puts a
value on housework, subtracts the costs of law enforcement, the costs of
pollution control, and the costs for depleting natural assets. The Genuine Progress Indicator also shows that while growth keeps growing,
past a certain point, well-being stalls. On a graph starting in the year
1950, for the United States, Austria, the Netherlands, Sweden, Germany,
and the United Kingdom, in each case the progress indicator rises
along with gross national product for a while. Then, in the 1960s, the
lines depart from each other as people's sense of well-being begins to
flatten while growth keeps growing.

In my personal map of life and time, I felt that the world reached
some kind of peak in the mid-1970s. But of course I would; I was traveling the country on my first true adventures, seeing vista upon new vista,
experiencing the exhilaration of wilderness, playing in rock bands, and
enjoying college's rarefied intellectual pretentions and genuine coed
dorms. And falling in love. I also thought the gains in civil rights, women's
rights, environmental legislation, and some very good music (I said
some) were all riding simultaneous peaks that, for a few too brief years,
seemed universally uplifting. After all, it was the Age of Aquarius.

And apparently, something *was* happening. According to the Genuine Progress Indicator's evaluation, people's sense of well-being *peaked*
in these years: United States, mid-1970s; United Kingdom, early '70s;
Germany, late '70s; Netherlands, late '70s; Austria, early '70s; Sweden,
late '70s. I find the timing interesting. While America's gross product
continued surging upward like an unmanned drone, human satisfaction got grounded. The gross national product really *is* too gross to detect

what's going on. What we *count* as progress includes some things that hinder real progress.

The data show what everyone claims to know: money doesn't buy happiness. But neither does poverty. And oppressive governments make people truly unhappy. Yet once a poor country achieves a per-person gross national product of merely $14,000, further growth doesn't improve people's sense of well-being. (Per-person GNP in the United States is about $44,000.) The point is not the dollar value. It's that once basic needs are met, happiness stays flat, even as the whole society gets "wealthier." (I put that in quotes because real wealth is something society can pass along. If we destroy the Northwest's forests or New England's cod, or coral reefs, some people might get rich, but we have not created wealth; we've created poverty.)

Interestingly, while growth in average wealth doesn't necessarily create happier people, people who are wealthier *relative* to their neighbors tend to be happier. In the naked city, the person with a hat is debonair. If you and your neighbor live in mud huts and your neighbor has one cow and you have two, you feel rich and happy. If your neighbor has a very big house and a new car and you have a big house and your car is six years old, well—. I first saw wireless Internet in the home of a billionaire. About a year later, people still working on their first million had it, and soon it became common among college students subsisting on coffee with sugar. How's a billionaire to stay happy?

America is a world power of expanding wealth and shrinking spirit, enlarged houses and broken homes, engorged executive pay and low worker morale, increased individualism and diminished civility, obesity and what Robert Lane calls "a kind of famine of warm interpersonal relations." We slave for prosperity but shirk purpose, cherish individual freedom but long for inclusion and meaning.

Simply put, more is better up to a point; after that, more is worse. When you're hungry, eating is good for you; when you're overweight, it isn't—but you want to eat more. The continuing appetite for more stuff, after emotional well-being stops increasing, is a psychic disease of the developed world. You can be right on track until you pass your destination; then—without changing course—you're headed in exactly the

wrong direction. What makes people happy: working on relationships. So maybe one stepping stone on the path to happiness has the word
"Enough" engraved into it.

❧

This morning I was pulling poison ivy. It looked like I was up against the
withering prospect of pulling more than a hundred individual plants.
But I found that if I dug my gloved finger to the root and gently tugged, I
could trace it through other roots and stems in my neglected garden,
then fairly easily zip out whole tracts of the stuff. Without pulling a single
individual plant, tugging up the root dislodged all the ones I could see
and a lot that I hadn't seen in the tangle of vegetation. When I was a teen
I yearned to travel America to see "how other people live." Now, basically, you can see how they live from wherever you happen to be. The
same advertising, the same chain stores, and the same TV, radio, and
print conglomerates have largely replaced America with the same
repeating road-stop strip mall, from sea to signing sea. Everyone's head
throbs with the same songs, and young people "relate to" the same handful of company logos and media characters. Corporate "news" reports
on how the actual people who play fictional characters are faring in their
reproduction and rehab. As I was freeing my American garden from
toxic infestation, my mind drifted to the image of chain stores along a
highway, each strip mall a sprig of leaves, connected by an unseen cable
of root. I imagined that I was driving cross-country on a big interstate
highway, pulling up chain stores as I went along, helping free up a land
strangling in a rash of sameness.

In my town, the Sou'wester Bookstore is no more, Rudy the druggist and
his wife are holding on by their fingernails, and the youngish couple
who've bought the hardware store are clearly worried. These are true
men and women in the best sense of the word "business." They are enterprising threads in the fabric of our community, not just commuters who
drive away in the morning and appear only behind their lawn mower and
their trash cans. When I enter a local store and the bell above the door
rings, I know I will be welcomed by name and the shopkeeper and I will
trade something valuable.

That's why for their sakes and mine, I do my shopping on this side of the tracks when I can. This gets increasingly difficult as the mall-and-chain drags real businesses and real people to exhaustion. By so dreadfully shrinking opportunities for people to go into business for themselves, the chains keep people acting as their stockboys and salesgirls well beyond the time they should have taken their place as adults in our communities. The middle-aged workers in the big-box stores seem like elderly teenagers, deprived of authority, creativity, responsibility, and pride. Mostly, they're nice people with a desire to be helpful. What could they have accomplished if given a chance? They may never understand who they are; they'll certainly never know who they might have been. Open on holidays, the chains undermine their employees' time for family. (Why anyone is actually shopping for TVs and washing machines on Thanksgiving is a question so large its answer eludes the wide, wide net of even my own cynicism.) Thus the chain stores threaten family more than any same-sex marriage, threaten Sunday more than Darwin ever could. Seeing my island in chains has driven me to the fringes, made me a castaway on my own native shores, a refugee inside my homeland. And for that I thank them. In that banal way, they helped me understand, at least, who I am not.

Though the shopping mall has largely driven Main Street out of business by usurping its commercial intercourse, it rejects Main Street's civic discourse. A friend reports that in his nearby megamall, people handing out anti-war leaflets were arrested. Free speech has no place on "private property"; it could distract those in the consumer caste from their main task and sole worth. Just keep that lite jazz playin'. A generation or so ago—one tends to forget—these same people were citizens in a democracy.

Is the end point of biological and cultural evolution really the isolation and anonymity of crowded noncommunities where the only place for youths to gather is a shopping mall filled with chain stores, where the people behind the counter are incapable of giving a knowing smile of recognition and we couldn't pick the owner out of a police lineup—because there is no owner?

Watch kids pacing enclosed shopping malls like veal calves, unable to get anywhere on their own, confined within rows of retail where they are force-fed like ducks gavaged for foie gras. And like ducklings that comically and pathetically follow the humans who've raised them, they seem not to know who and what they are. Searching for identity in a world purged of community and place, they bond to brands, confusing freedom to consume with freedom, and thinking satisfaction comes in bulk. More choice than ever brings ever more conformity. Our unifying purpose: to purchase. The cost: our freedom to imagine and to originate.

That might not seem like much to lose when there's so much stuff to get. But while we were shopping, corporations tiptoed in and hijacked our country. In much of the world, when people try to make government officials respond, they run up against a problem: government officials are corrupted by bribes. In the United States, on the other hand, bribes are called campaign contributions. It's not corruption because it's legal. But it's corruption. We can't really have free and fair elections. Money has radically reordered our country's priorities from the original idea of America.

If the social contract is that people voluntarily relinquish some libertarian liberties so that a citizen-run government can serve public interests, well, America has been largely turned inside out. We sold the truths that seemed self-evident. Government now largely serves corporate interests. This is government exactly backward. It's government of and buy the people. Those *in* government who say they "hate government" often seem to do their utmost to bend government into serving large corporations. They know where their bread is buttered—and who is really paying attention—so they abuse the trust they've been hired to keep. Between 1975 and 2005: corporate political-action-committee spending exploded fifteenfold, from about $15 million to $222 million. The number of multinational corporations ballooned from 7,000 to 65,000. About 35,000 lobbyists currently stalk the halls of Congress. They trudge back to their caves carrying big game: subsidies, tax dodges, low- or no-interest loans, dirt-cheap mining access, free access to ocean fish populations, forest giveaways, relaxed oversight of oil drilling, and laws limiting liability for oil spilled—the list must be 35,000 items long.

Meanwhile, remember, *public*-interest groups are *forbidden by law* from either making campaign contributions or spending significant time lobbying. If you don't represent a special interest trying to make money, you can't participate in democracy. If you're a not-for-profit organization representing a little of the public's interest—as government itself is supposed to do, anyway—you can't free-speak to your elected officials. This coup d'état is basically why government fundamentally fails to guide the economy toward the public good. It's basically why we've had such poor "leaders." In the United States, at least, government is supposed to be the system that immunizes the public interest from virulent personal greed. But, wow, how it's failed us. Because we let it.

In many important ways, it shows. The United States ranks behind more than forty countries in its citizens' life expectancy, behind twenty-eight in infant survival. The United States ranks 33rd out of 34 Western countries in the proportion of its populace who accept evolution (only Turkey ranks lower).

When the most powerful country in history so systematically fails the causes of community, equity, environment, social justice, and education, the public must sit up in its coffin, and lo, the politicians and corporate managers will be very afraid, and shrink back. Each revolution is inevitable—as is the one coming.

But when? In numerous revolts peoples have freed themselves from monarchs and despots, oppressors and dictators—only to find themselves repossessed by the new pharaoh. Deeply anti-democratic, highly corrupting forces have been at work against the ideal of America for a long time. "I consider the class of artificers [manufacturers] as the panders of vice and the instruments by which the liberties of a country are generally overturned," wrote Thomas Jefferson to John Jay in 1785. Walt Whitman, in the 1860s, admonished,

> Resist much, obey little . . .
> Once fully enslaved, no nation, state, city of this earth, ever afterward
>   resumes its liberty.

In 1961, that great hippie Republican, President Dwight D. Eisenhower, warned,

> We must guard against the acquisition of unwarranted influence by
> the military-industrial complex. The potential for the disastrous rise of

misplaced power exists and will persist. . . . The power of money is ever present and is gravely to be regarded.

Eisenhower's was probably the most honest and important speech delivered by any modern head of state. What the president feared, we live.

The 1960s counterculture attempted what we need now more than ever: a spirited culture of refusal, a counterlife. Compared to the days of rage of my youth—civil rights marchers facing police dogs, anti-war protesters facing riot gear and clubs—we seem as complacent as cattle. When people loosen their own grip on power, they will be relieved of the privilege.

As a patriot who loves this land and its ideal (if not the hard-heartedness of too many Americans), I take cheer. Although multinational corporations have made us believe that we are their slaves, in fact we are their masters. They, like all self-proclaimed masters, fear their subjects. They spend fortunes advertising to us because they'll die pretty quickly if we disconnect their feeding tubes, or simply ignore them. They know we'll destroy them if we wake up. And many of them are worried. Two-thirds of Americans want to see big corporations have smaller influence. Nearly 40 percent of Americans—a minority, but still—see big business as "the biggest threat to the future of this country."

The revolution is as simple as this: Don't buy the products by which they drain you and feed themselves. Listen to people trying to warn you, but don't vote for anyone trying to scare you. Resist! Do the unadvertised and the unauthorized. Comb someone's hair. Plant seeds. Reread. Practice safe sex until you get it right. Go to a museum, aquarium, or zoo. Be .org- and be commercial-free. Photograph someone you love with no clothes on. Not them—you. Walk a brisk mile to nowhere and back. Mark a child's height on a freshly painted wall. Climb into bed with the Arts or Science section of an actual newspaper and get a little newsprint on your fingers. Eat salad. Clean your old binoculars. Hoard your money until you get enough to make a difference to charity. Go to formal dinners in great-looking thrift-store clothing and brag about how much you paid. React badly to every ad and every exhortation about what you need, as though they are lying, as though they just came up from behind in the dark and said, "Give me your wallet." Scream when they come to rob you. You'll never go wrong. You won't miss anything worthwhile. The country needs your lack of cooperation.

People without plumbing or electricity wrote the U.S. Constitution and the Bill of Rights. Those documents stand among history's most magnificent achievements. You'd think that with toilets, fluorescent lights, fast cars, cold food, hot showers, jet planes, computers, antibiotics, cable news, and the Web, we might be smarter than people of the 1700s. Doesn't seem to work that way. The material world and the realm of the human spirit exist on different planes. "Stuff" doesn't seem to make people smarter or better. Rather, the contrary. We are not the products of four billion years of evolution just so we can have a cluttered garage.

Anyway, there's not enough stuff for so many people. As I mentioned, by midcentury we'd need another copy of Planet Earth to meet demand.

Where did *fall* go? Mid-November, and still no need to light the woodstove. Nearing Thanksgiving, nighttime temperatures back up into the low sixties still coax evening song from crickets that in years past would by now have been killed by a hard frost or buried under the first snowfall. Many trees still bear green. It used to be that fishing now would mean gloves and knit hats; an early-morning trip on the boat would start with a bucket of seawater on the deck to wash away the slippery frost. I admit, I enjoy the warmth. But usually, the run-up to Thanksgiving sees dense schools of big fish mobbing the Point and the beaches. Now the schools of just a week ago have vanished, replaced with a trickle of unseasonably small fish, and I wonder why they left early with the air so warm. Maybe the water's too warm for herring to come down from the north, and without that infusion of late-season food the big fish here felt pressed to move on? Maybe the herring are late because the giant trawling boats in the Gulf of Maine are into them again? I don't know.

Meanwhile, winter's scoters continue pouring down from the north in flocks of several hundred birds. I walk the beach watching lines of them flying single file over the ocean, undulating like the waves, more like express trains than sea ducks. Sanderlings are back too, in winter's numbers, a couple hundred running the south side sand, looking so at home they betray no hint that they've come thousands of miles and millions of years to be with us.

❧

Last night, I dreamt that I went to a place surrounded by tall-grown fields with scruffy hedgerows and soft edges, a landscape like corduroy and cotton, like English countryside, comfortable as old slippers. My destination there was a very large barn, like a big enclosed warehouse shed. I was "coming home," though I'd never seen the place. In the dream I was headed into the big barn because that's where some musicians, including me, had their instruments stored. I was pleasantly surprised that my editor, a man who has somehow managed to fit several lifetimes of spirit and wisdom into a mere eight decades, was staying in the barn. On a whim, Jack and I decided it would be fun to take a bulldozer and dig a big round hole, about as wide as an Olympic-sized pool is long, and maybe ten feet deep. Savoring an air of shared mischief, we got busy at one sandy end of the floorless warehouse. In Genesis, God never puts particular thought into creating the ocean; it's there upon creation of "the heaven and the earth." But in my dream we took some trouble to create ours. We decided to fill our fresh-dug basin with freshwater. Into it we placed two pond turtles. As we were enjoying watching the turtles swimming, I noticed other animals appearing in the water. Scallops, like swimming castanets—they puzzled me because this was freshwater. It didn't seem to matter to them; the scallops were happy as clams. A soft-shelled turtle—where had *it* come from? Out of nowhere, people began gathering, pointing into the water, marveling, happy. The atmosphere grew festive. One of the musicians rattled a piece of sheet metal like thunder, and everyone broke into applause and laughter. I dove into the water. It was refreshing and delicious in all ways possible. When real dawn came through my bedroom window, I awoke naturally. For just a few moments I lay in bed savoring a feeling of extraordinary well-being, trying to hold it a little longer before it ebbed in the light of day. As I lay there I realized my dream, so odd at first recollection, was of this planet and its life-giving complement of water, in which we may take purest delight.

• • •

Kenzie's anxious for her walk. But while the day's still early I call my mother to wish her a happy birthday. Even though its *her* birthday, she wonders how it is she's got a son so old. I get this every year. As always, turnabout is fair play on that remark.

The year, too, is finally giving up its youth, slowly, reluctantly, equivocally. Mockingbirds stand silenced by a low-angled sun and—at last—the chill of frost. They guard the introduced bittersweet and Multiflora Rose that let them live where winter formerly would have starved them. A recent gale finally stripped the leaves, and naked trunks stand shivering in bare woodlands as forest-floor autumnal gold ages to hibernal brown. The Ospreys' nests, now just stacks of sticks while their owners have gone to the tropics, provide an occasional lookout perch for our resident Red-tailed Hawks, who spend the winter unburdening the marsh of voles.

Late autumn now melds toward winter. The last cormorants straggle raggedly south in short-jotted phrases, a distinct style change from the lengthy, expansive script of the large flocks of earlier weeks. They're concluding their year's story not with any dramatic finale or surprise ending but with a drawn-out dribble. More and different ducks are cutting swift silhouettes across the bay. Great Blue Herons—a few—are back, stalking the tawny marshes, while along the marsh borders flit just-arrived juncos and White-throated Sparrows and more Red-breasted Nuthatches.

Loons that had drained away northward in May are now returning in force to our waters. Dark silhouettes—the slender Red-throateds and the sturdy Commons—dot the air above the bay and float along every stretch of surf. They're mostly silent but occasionally one remembers the haunting tremolo of love from longer days. I try to imagine passing night upon bobbing night in the cold surf, in calm and storm, but imagination fails me. And as though being a loon in winter isn't a hard enough life, dozens of loons—having come from a wide northern breeding region and concentrated along our shores—will drown in local fishermen's gill nets. That problem continues until the autumn migration of fish along the beaches ceases and the nets get stored. Kenzie and I and a few beach walkers will find some of their sleek loon corpses, discarded and washed up.

We make our lives in a world not of our making. We feel in a world that does not feel. Yet it's become a world in which our presence is felt.

What attitude might confront such a world? An attitude of curiosity, for the complex world? An attitude of admiration, for the beautiful world? An attitude of gratitude, for the improbable world? Of respect, for the elder world? Of awe, for the mystery? Of concern, for consequences? If these attitudes guide action, we may not always be certain which choice is right, but we may travel a path that is wise.

Early people, including writers of Scripture, saw in nature an awesome power that demanded respect or took retribution. The operating systems people invented to organize themselves into the defensive circle called civilization originated when we were tribes in the wilderness. Since then, of course, our knowledge-acquisition skills have exploded. Science and medicine change at the rate of discovery; look how far they've come at such an accelerating pace. You'd think our religious, moral, and economic institutions would limber up in the face of so much that's new. But they remain dogmatic, remarkably stuck. Some are just old; others, ancient. Maybe we should have noticed that their "use by" date expired centuries ago.

So, we're navigating a changing world with concepts that aren't up to the task, concepts that lack—or reject—modern comprehension of the world.

Yet maybe we need just a little more time to catch up. After all, only in the last few decades have we understood anything, really, about how the world actually works. Only since the late 1800s—and mostly since the 1900s—have we understood that all living things are related by ancestry and that sunlight powers life; that things like carbon, water, nitrogen, and nutrients flow in cycles through living systems; and a little of why plants and animals live where they do. We've learned that we can eliminate the most abundant herds and birds, and the fishes of even the deepest haunts; take groundwater out faster than it goes in; change the composition of the atmosphere and the chemistry of the ocean. Svante Arrhenius's 1906 claim that human-caused emissions of carbon dioxide could intensify the greenhouse effect and warm the planet—which he believed would be beneficial—was widely dismissed until about 1960 (and not widely accepted until after the new millennium). Starting just in the mid-twentieth century, we've created chemicals and plastics and nuclear material that will affect living things for centuries.

Consequently, most of civilization remains uninformed about the two great realities of our existence: all life is family, and the world is finite. That is why we keep making choices that threaten our own financial economy, the economy of nature, and the economy of time—otherwise known as the future of the world. What I'm saying, basically, is that in very consequential ways, our modes of conduct are so out of sync with reality that they're essentially irrational.

Return to the dream. I hope humanity survives and civilization develops. Just as we look back on the Dark Ages and shudder, people will look back at our time as dirty, crowded, superstitious, dangerous, and primitive. To get onward, we'd need to replace the no-accounting, throwaway, boomeranging, soot-powered economy with a clean, renewable, no-waste, recycling economy. We thank the thinkers and martyrs who gave their lives for Reason, that we might step into a few rays of sunshine. If our children, and most of our nonhuman co-voyagers, can get through the troubles of our time, there will be a brighter day. We can describe and measure what is needed, and show it in graphs and tables. The information is there. We don't lack information. We lack a new ethical relationship—and the new inspiration that is waiting.

Health, peace, humanity, creativity, life's grand and thriving journey, its epic enterprise, the miracles that float us, shimmering; these constitute the realm of the sacred. In this realm, the market analyst and the head of state find themselves beneath and behind the child, whose world and adventure it will be. And if, in an attempt to explain how simple it is to arrive at this realization, we must provide some translation harkening back to the primitive clutch of market economics, we can say that things have no price and but two values, right and wrong.

The values, called ethics, acted on as morals, answer the age-old question, "How ought we live?" No small matter, indeed. We are not just consumers but citizens, not just citizens but members of a living family, miracles of evolution, manifestations of the awesome mystery of creation, singularly able to perceive and consider the universe, our place in it, and our role. Our goal as human beings can be to elevate what is uniquely human; to see that meaning lies in relationships, that satisfaction comes from serving, that the creature who alone can consider and affect the future must alone maintain it; that science and all ethical, moral, and religious traditions that have come this far have converged in agreement: the place is ours to use but not ours to lose. All such traditions say we serve one another, the creation, and our children.

Why don't we? Can we? When will we?

If we could wipe the slate and say, "In the twenty-first century, here's what we know; now let's construct philosophies, faiths, and economics based on the way the world works," they would look very different from the anachronisms to which we keep ourselves yoked and saddled.

A member of a preliterate tribe might stumble on a book and see it useful only to start a fire. In our use of the world, we are just beginning to learn the first ABC's while rifling through the encyclopedia of life and muttering, "What good is it?"

We are just awakening to the fundamentals of who and what we are, insights denied to humanity until Copernicus, Galileo, Darwin, Leopold, Hardin and his "Tragedy of the Commons," and a handful of other towering, courageous minds. From a few great pearls of insight, pried from the wisdom of centuries, we know at last that the universe does not revolve around us, that we are citizens in a living community where our membership implies stewardship, and that—contrary to Adam Smith's invisible-hand nonsense—those in pursuit of self bring suffering to many.

To this we add a new insight under the sun: just our usual way of doing business can harm the world. By driving the processes of land and atmosphere, by throttling the flow of rivers, by turning nearly half the sunshine to our own purposes, by changing the very chemistry of the air and the seas, by all these things, we have made Earth ours. We are no longer voyagers. We are proprietors. We have put our name on time itself, changed the marquee, and declared, in lights: THE ANTHROPO-CENE ERA, STARRING HOMO SAPIENS. The world belongs to us, the wise ones, we declare. The claim is nothing new; philosophers and the writers of Scripture began making much the same claim millennia ago. But it's no longer just rhetoric; there's a lot at stake now. Will we be pirates or captains, slumlords or godparents of time? Will we burn the furniture for heat or be good tenants? That remains to be seen. But so far, the odds seem against our getting back our security deposit.

DECEMBER

With all this winter coming on, there's time for one final fishing excursion. Word is out: herring are in. Finally. This is no time for fair-weather friends, so Pete and I leave the harbor well-bundled and adequately gloved. Our objective is to get enough herring to fill a shelf's worth of pickling jars.

We go just a few hundred yards outside the harbor jetties, to where the bottom, sloping from about thirty to sixty feet, gives fish a cold shoulder to school up against. I hunt the sonar and, yup—look at all those green dots. Our weighted rigs each bear six tiny, shiny lures. We drop them to the bottom and jiggle the rod tip.

In under a minute I feel a couple of taps; then one gets hooked and I feel it wiggling. I wait. I feel another hit, and the rod dips a little more. When the trembling line pulls the rod a bit more heavily, I begin gingerly reeling up.

Two ten-inch herring and a mackerel come up into the air, and all three go down into a bucket. The mackerel is a sweet, fusiform miniature cousin of a tuna, brightly silver-sided, its blue back marked with wavy black lines. The herrings' pearlescent bellies grade to iridescent backs that, as you slowly change the angle of the light, gleam with luminous hues of blue, green, and lavender.

Herring scales give that pearl shimmer to things like nail polish and lipstick, leading one Web commentator to report, "Global herring production is threatened by overfishing, raising the specter of a world full of nonshimmering lips." That's how deep some see the stakes. But here is a person who connects, my friend John, who was for twenty years a commercial lobsterman (in the late 1990s the lobsters in his area died, apparently stressed by warming water, putting him and dozens of others out of business): "I used to get totes full of fresh herring for bait at this time of year. They looked so beautiful it would make me dizzy." That's how he felt about his *bait*. And that's why we've been friends since we met at age fourteen.

Pursuing the southbound herring, Northern Gannets have returned in force. Over a big school they gather by the hundreds on six-foot wing spans, until their white bodies form a dense cloud of birds. When the fish rise into range, the gannets begin streaking into the sea behind that water-splitting warhead bill, sending geysers of spray.

More herring come into our bucket. It's fun to catch these little fish. They're easy and—for now at least—they're abundant. They're low on the food chain, so they're pretty low in toxic chemicals, and they're high in healthy Omega-3's and all that. Good brain food. The herring include not only Atlantics but also a few Bluebacks and one Hickory Shad. They've been feeding on baby squid as long as my thumbtip. Catching them several at a time makes me feel rich. We take about sixty fish. This population had been heavily depleted in the past and recovered, and though they are again targeted by enormous boats in New England, they remain sufficiently numerous that for now I think it'd be okay even if we'd taken twice as many. We'll pickle these guys in wine vinegar, allspice, and bay leaves, and their luscious fillets will serve proudly on holiday tables alongside our smoked Bluefish, helping keep us fed through winter.

Pete and I decide to bring our bucket of fish to the tide rips and ring the doorbell on whatever bass have hung around for this last session. We select two herring for bait. The bass are here but, with the water down to 51 degrees Fahrenheit, they're slow on the take—and sluggish. In two passes, we find two fish that have lost the dash and surge of even a few weeks ago. One fish has, stuck in its belly, a small stainless-steel hook with a few inches of line trailing; it's been here since the October blitz when the surface schools were so thick, fish often got snagged. With these two final bass for the table, I turn the bow homeward. It's good to see there're still plenty of fish here. This late into the year, and this late into the story of life on the planet, it is still possible to catch, in one tide, enough to feed a family all through the winter.

No sooner do I tie up to the dock than my friend Bob rings my cell phone. He'd been hunting fish in the surf all day, checking spots along forty miles of beach. Nothing. But on the dunes just a couple of miles from my house, he saw a Snowy Owl. "A female, *very* nicely barred; and probably the biggest Snowy Owl I've ever seen."

❧

With a real frost in the air and a mad-dog bite to the wind, winter is no longer just a concept. A new moon has the tide kicked way up. Waves acting like winners at a poker table greedily pull piles of beach into their lap. On the south side, waterfront home owners are finding the water much closer. Many have lost up to a staggering twenty feet of land this autumn, and in places, sloping dunes that once led gently toward the beach have become ten-foot-high bluffs. Swept-away beach stairs and walkways have gotten hurled back at the crumbled dunes up and down the beach. And it's not even officially winter yet; such has been the strange tantrum of a mostly warm autumn.

A clear, crisp night with the Milky Way spilled across the sky. Looking up at stars overhead, or when drifting on dark waters, I often feel connected to something larger, infinite. Mystery beyond knowing. The word is "spiritual."

I don't mean the realm of disembodied conscious entities—angels, gods, and demons, or the spirits in trees and brooks—that many believe exist. I mean the mystery in and about us, that wondrous result of whatever it is that we are, this thing inside humanity that moves. This is spirit as much as anything I believe exists. It is not outer, not other. It is our unique amalgam of animal, culture, and yearning. It's the strange creative synergy between emotion and intellect. It's the—let's say it—the magic of common human genius. If it was simply neurons firing, we'd be subservient to squid, who posess the largest nerve cells but arguably less spirit than we. It is as hard to pin down as any imagined angel, but when Abraham Lincoln called upon "the better angels of our nature," he alluded both to the loftiness and the intangibility of this—the human spirit.

And the horror and darkness we're capable of—they're also part of the human spirit. Atrocities have also connected people to something that feels larger, like nationalism, race, and religion. Good impulses and bad are two sides of the imperfectly minted coin of human nature. Compassion is what keeps the coin toss loaded toward "heads."

For us to be straining the cables of our planet's life-support systems despite clear warnings may constitute mere foolishness. But the unborn, who did not choose this path, will arrive saddled with all conceivable consequences. The poor likewise did not choose it, nor the other living creatures that, like us, strive to live and raise their young, yet find their world besieged. "Justice" means to render what is deserved. And because we've created a situation that is not merely unsustainable but *unjust*, it becomes a moral matter. To have these things revealed and then choose to revert to blindness is, dare I say, sin and sacrilege.

The grandiose language of Scripture makes apt metaphor for the true grandeur of life, for the towering magnificence we can sense whenever our usual numbness abates. But scriptural metaphor notwithstanding, I am secular. The suffering of innocents and the faithful is simply too inconsistent with God as advertised. I sense that we're very much on our own, with no one watching over us, no cosmic righteousness to check our folly, no just reward postmortem, solely responsible for our content and the consequences.

I believe in the universal power of the golden rule. "Do unto others," indeed. Some see "sin" as contravening religious teachings. I see sin as contravening ethical teachings. Some see "sacred" as worthy of religious veneration. I see as sacred all that is worthy of reverence, all that is deep and true.

The sacred does not require the divine. If God exists, he doesn't need to hear it from us. The sacred are the values we hold highest. Let's seek to fulfill the ideal, to satisfy the idea. If we guide and ground our actions in these values, the pang subsides, and something nourishing to the human essence—to our soul, in that sense—fills its place.

If a mere book can be considered holy, can we fail to consider as sacred all of creation? If there is a God, then all things natural are miraculous. If there's no God, then all things natural are miraculous. That's quite a coincidence, and ought to give people holding different beliefs a lot to talk about. People who see the world as God's and people who sense an accident of cosmic chemistry can both perceive the sacred. Let's not be afraid to say, to explain—and, if necessary, to rage—that we hold the uniqueness of this Earth sacred, that the whole living enterprise is sacred. And that what depletes the living enterprise always proves to be, even in purely practical terms, a mistake.

Technology has carried people beyond our planet. But what can keep us here on Earth? Science, technology, and the right values each provide only part of what we need. Science without ethics is blind, and ethics without science is prone to errors.

I'd always thought science was amoral because it's committed to finding and accepting the truth, whatever the answer turns out to be. What I never realized—a religious person actually pointed this out to me recently—is that science's commitment to truth makes it a fundamentally moral endeavor. Businesspeople may succeed by sacrificing some truth while pursuing profits. Lawyers may succeed by ignoring aspects of justice in defense of clients. Economics isn't concerned with either truth or justice. Religion thinks it has the truth and can't walk its dogma too far from the curb. Science accepts only evidence that can be repeated, witnessed by skeptics, and shared. This doesn't mean science is "true," necessarily. There always remains the possibility that new findings might sweep away older beliefs. That doesn't mean science is weak. Rather, that's its strength. It means scientists grow better as scientists the more devoted they are to finding the truth, and the more open to recognizing it. Of course, some scientists (and some atheists) are dogmatic and act more like fundamentalists. Some religious people constantly seek better understanding, acting more, in their open curiosity, like scientists. Because it's humanity's best truth-seeking endeavor, science is completely compatible with freedom. It is completely at home in a free-speech democracy. It cannot progress under repression, dictatorship, or religiously dominated political systems. Things that embrace truth support science because science deepens the pool of known truth. Things that repress truth are threatened by science. It's that simple. It's that powerful.

The relationship between science and religion is important because about 85 percent of the world's people belong to, and largely take their values from, a religion. If the immense power of science can be harnessed to values, if values can be powered by facts, civilization might avert the pain upon which it's poised.

It's not that I see science and faith as natural allies. It's that I don't see them as natural enemies. Many scientists share a sense of wonder and a moral imperative so profound that their sense of purpose and their emotional experience widely overlap those of religious people, and might, in their devotion and consistency, be called religious in the broad sense. Some scientists have traditional religious faith, just as some people of faith have scientific curiosity. More to the point, regardless of whether the world originated through chemistry or divine providence, the same present confronts us all. We all breathe, drink, and rely on animals, plants, and the march of seasons for our survival. Cosmic origins and afterlife destinies aside, in *this* world, life is what we have and what we are. With so much at risk, all we can afford is to put differences aside. If we sink the ark everyone on it goes down, regardless of what they believed.

And so paths converge: what serves the continuity of life is sacred. And what serves the future serves us, too. In a world of accelerating changes, these thoughts often accompany me to many a faraway place, and back to Lazy Point.

This morning, all is calm, all is bright. On the bay, my favorite saltwater ducks—"our" Long-tailed Ducks—are back in force, beautifully painted in their crisp sepia tones, bills pink in the gold of morning. Their calls ring clearly across hundreds of yards of sounding surface. *Ah—oh-da-leep*. Those calls, so imbued with a sense of being home in winter, help cinch the circle of the year, tying the end of last winter to the start of this, completing a cycle of the ducks, one of the dozens of circles that make a Lazy Point year.

In the mirror that is the bay, a first: the water is so calm that when a duck dives I can track its progress by its rising bubbles, as though it is using scuba gear. I would have thought they held their breath, but perhaps they exhale so they can expend less effort diving. Or is air getting squeezed from their feathers?

The big waves of yesterday's great blow have taken away much. The south side beach is reduced to a shockingly slender ribbon. One person's planked walkway now extends about ten feet from the lip of the new bluff, ending in midair. Another section of that same walkway fell to the sweeping sea.

But yesterday's big waves have also given a little in return, and Kenzie and I are here in the morning's angled light to accept their modest gift. For about a hundred yards of beach, right where I'd been catching fish six weeks ago, the sea has yielded dozens of big Surf Clams. I test the shells first with my foot because such shells are usually empty by the time they're cast ashore. These are full. I bend to heft one. Yes, it's not just filled with sand; it's an intact clam, slightly agape. Finally, I tap it, and in the cold it sluggishly closes its fortress gates—it's alive. I go to get a sack and return. I leave dozens of the smaller clams for the gulls, who, just down the beach, sit looking bored, so fat are they. And in a few minutes I have easily ten pounds of clams to tote home—nice! In the season that welcomes hot chowders I walk off the beach again feeling rich, again looking forward to savoring the connection between sea and table.

To the extent that connections have been severed, ligaments cut, and our understanding thus hobbled, the coming endeavor must be one of reconnection, religation. *Religare* means to retie, or to gather to bind, as with a sense of obligation. Thus "religation"—reconnection—is one root of the word "religion." Here again worlds converge. Ecology, family, community, religion—these words all grope toward the same need: connection, belonging, purpose.

Albert Einstein said our task is to "widen our circle of compassion to embrace all living creatures and the whole of nature in its beauty." I get a little hit of that in talking with my neighbors along our shifting shore, in the buoyancy of birds, in the sinking weight of reading the newest entry on the roster of threatened beings, in stories of refugees from places that have killed their reefs, their grass, or their neighbors.

Unity of need becomes unity of purpose. To deflect disaster, this is where we must be headed next.

So I guess what I'm trying to say is that, though I'm a secular person and a scientist, I believe that our relationship with the living world must be mainly religious. But I don't mean theological. I mean religious in the sense of reverent, revolutionary, spiritual, and inspired. Reverent because the world is unique, thus holy. Revolutionary in making a break with the drift and downdraft of outdated, maladaptive modes of thought. Spiritual in seeking attainment of a higher realm of human being. Inspired in the aspiration to connect crucial truths with wider communities. Religious in precisely this way: connection, with a sense of purpose.

If you don't like the word "religion," I understand. Think of it this way: it's imperative to have something to believe in that both centers and expands your life. Call it what you will, or call it nothing and pursue it.

This kind of spirituality feels like thirst for human potential, and finding it comes like rain on the tongue; a little makes a big difference. Is belief in the power of guiding principles—like reverence, devotion, compassion, and hope—ever less than "spiritual"? Is striving toward ideals, working toward a larger purpose, ever less than religious? It's often more.

Think again of Einstein's radiating circle of compassion. And if you'd like to know what's in it for you, Confucius is credited with saying, "He who wishes to secure the good of others has already secured his own." Albert Schweitzer observed, "One thing I do know: the only ones among you who will be really happy are those who have sought and found how to serve." Let Adam Smith reel in his grave.

A blanketing snow has come to add its white weight to the beaches and woodlands for one lovely, silent night. Upon the lighthouse hangs an enormous wreath, part of the annual aspiration to a world of peace. The foghorn blows its warning to a wet morning. The drizzle puts a slick ice plating on the shoreline rocks, making the footing hazardous.

I've come to see whether the Point's great annual winter duck conflation has returned. But the long swells roll to the Point sparsely populated. So wide a sea so void of ducks makes me question why I rose predawn to subject myself to an iced drizzle. Kenzie looks like she's questioning my judgment, too.

One Common Loon, one Red-throated, bob near shore, then lean into the sea and vanish. A smattering of gannets gleam white in the slanting dawn. I see only a few dozen ducks, strung in the tide like a frond of kelp, waving in the undulating swell. I find none of the rarities: no King Eiders, no Razorbills, no Dovekies.

But in the time it takes me to scan, the surf begins to stock Common Eiders. A glance offshore reveals long scarves of scoters flying into the rips by the hundreds, and soon the bobbing dozens become thousands. Black, Surf, and White-winged Scoters, a few Red-breasted Mergansers.

I've often wondered how they spend the long winter nights. Now the answer arrives in an icy dawn drizzle: they drift for hours on the tide, and by first light they're miles away. Here they come, trains of commuters starting their workday.

I never regret pushing out of bed early; it's satisfying to have learned something with so much of the day left. By eight A.M., when it's time to go find a hot cup of liquid and start the holiday, the sea ducks are still piling in, by the hundreds.

❧

Four days till New Year's, and in the Cut several fish rise and swirl. I've never seen that kind of activity this late. Then again, it's usually not this warm. But what are they? Small bass? Sea robins? The winter morning retains time and mildness sufficient for a comfortable walk, and Kenzie and I intend to use it well. The Cut holds Long-tails and several uncommon Common Goldeneyes.

Baymen are taking their fish-trap poles home from the boat-launching ramp. Several piles of their discarded netting have been lying in heaps there for the last few years. Our public ramp is their dump. It's just the way they've always done it. But considering their determined reluctance to return a wave from a stranger, it's hard not to infer a passive-aggressive, resentful sense of place. Deep family roots don't count for much when outsiders and the price of fish conspire to push the cost of homes beyond reach of their children. Walled off in a dying tradition, their surliness is understandable.

With our season marching into winter, it's time for me to visit a place just coming into summer on the other end of the world.

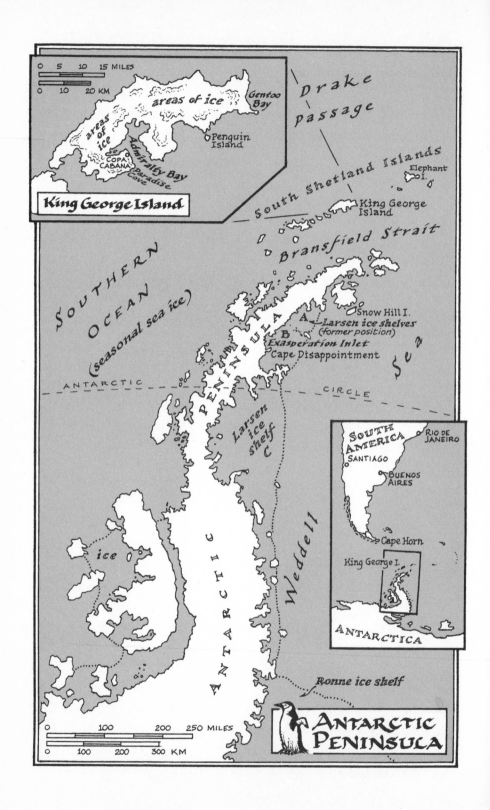

King George Island

0 5 10 15 MILES
0 10 20 KM

areas of ice

Gentoo Bay

areas of ice

Penguin Island

COPA CABANA

Admiralty Bay

Paradise Cove

Drake passage

South Shetland Islands

Elephant I.

King George Island

Bransfield Strait

SOUTHERN OCEAN (seasonal sea ice)

PENINSULA

Snow Hill I.

A *Larsen ice shelves* (former position)

B

Exasperation Inlet

Cape Disappointment

ANTARCTIC — — — CIRCLE

Larsen ice shelf C

Weddell Sea

ice

ANTARCTIC

SOUTH AMERICA

RIO DE JANEIRO

SANTIAGO

BUENOS AIRES

Cape Horn

King George I.

ANTARCTICA

Ronne ice shelf

100 200 250 MILES
0 100 200 300 KM

ANTARCTIC PENINSULA

TRAVELS POLAR:
COPA CABANA—ANTARCTICA

≈ ≈ ≈

"We haven't seen a weather map like this for a long time," a passing officer tells me with word-to-the-wise conviction. "It will be a rock-and-roll
party—trust me. Once you get your stuff tied down, try hard to stay in
your bunk."

From an already spray-drenched deck in an already howling wind, I
watch a Wandering Albatross, its wings ten feet across, disappear into
the darkening maze of mountainous waves; then I head for the stairwell.
At ten P.M. crew members distribute anti-nausea pills throughout the
ship and hang seasickness bags from all interior handrails.

The Drake Passage lies squeezed between two oceans and two continents. Serving too many masters, this unquiet stretch pinches and intensifies the winds that come screaming around the bottom of the globe,
making it the world's most punishing crossing.

I stuff duffels under one edge of my mattress and pull the other edge
partway up the wall. The goal is to make a mattress taco, be the stuffing—
and stay there. This is not about sleeping. It's about taking cover in a
padded way.

All night, the ship rides up the mountains, falls off the tops of waves,
and shudders into deep troughs. Destination: a fractured arm of rock
and ice called the South Shetland Islands, Antarctica.

Morning. My head . . . foggy. The wind continues a dull roar over the
still-rocking ship. The vessel plods slowly toward a long, sloping coast
where crystal mountains rise in crystal air.

We enter a large bay where pods of penguins porpoise along like tuna, seemingly neither fish nor fowl. Unbirdlike birds. Across the bay, black cliffs plunge to freezing water and surf blasts rock with cruel, elemental energy.

Weeks of gear and three people crowd into two Zodiacs. We zoom to a gently curving beach nearly a mile long, bounded by two rocky headlands.

Wayne Trivelpiece, his wife, Sue, and I splash ashore on King George Island as a wave swamps our boat and dozens of cans of food break through sodden cardboard. Wayne looks up and down the shoreline and says, "Ah. Home."

Penguins line the beach and speckle the slopes. Up from the dark sand stands a long plywood hut, green-painted, tin-roofed. Whale spinal disks as wide as stepping stones line the path to the hut door. A whale rib hangs over the central window. Sue, gesturing *ta-da!,* says cheerfully, "Welcome to Copa Cabana."

The hut is tight and spartan. Its four rooms include a mudroom, two small bedrooms, and a kitchen doubling as office and radio room. The unpainted plywood walls bear maps, penguin pictures, a Minnie Mouse clock, a dartboard—all brought thousands of miles.

We'll hang our parkas on pegs; boots go on a rack. Pots, pans, and dishes are in those boxes. Shortwave radios, computers, a CD player, and stacked notebooks crowd the kitchen shelves. Out there—that's an outhouse without the house. It's called "the Box."

Wayne is a large man, just this side of stocky, with slightly graying hair and a neat grizzled beard. Sue is slight, bright, of medium build, and keeps her dark hair longish. They met at a conference, got married a year and a half later, and started coming to Antarctica for half the year. The kids stay with Grandma. Before starting in the Antarctic, they both did research on the effects of oil on gulls—in Svalbard. Small world. "Under no circumstances would I have done this without Sue," Wayne says. "It is way too abnormal a life."

This station's "refrigerator" is the air outside. Want an egg, or leftovers? Just reach out the window; they're on the shelf. That wouldn't work in the Arctic, but Antarctica has no bears, no foxes, no four-footed animals. We will sweep no spider webs, contend with neither moths nor mosquitoes; there won't be rats or mice to trouble the food stores, nor maggots in the meat. Just keep those eggs covered, or skuas will take them.

The hut stands between the curving shoreline and a curving mountain. Gentoo Penguins—their markings suggest white earmuffs—occupy about a third of the open ground. Adélie Penguins, prefering high slopes, stand along the mountain's ridges. The temperature hovers around the freezing point and the windchill approximates 5 degrees Fahrenheit (–15° C)—but the penguins are eating snow to stay cool. Some sit on their heels with their webbed feet splayed to dissipate heat, like Hawaiian albatrosses. Everything's relative.

Wayne has documented deep penguin population declines, down roughly half since 1980. Far more worrisome: in that same time, the regional populations of their main prey, shrimplike krill, have shriveled—down nearly 80 percent. Penguins can still catch full loads and care for their chicks, but it takes them a lot longer and they must work harder.

At three-thirty in the morning, venturing outside to pee, I hear what I think is a Black-bellied Storm-Petrel's single high note, a thin spare whistle, elemental and lovely. The sun's already glowing like a red ember at the horizon. The Adélie Penguins' workday has already started; long columns of commuters are coming down the slopes. Every few feet, another well-worn penguin on-ramp merges to the coast highway. Penguins walk bumper to bumper along the beach.

They disappear two-thirds of a mile away, where the shoreline bends. Always reluctant to enter water, Adélies would walk to the feeding grounds if they could. Large groups mass along the shore, no individual wanting to go first. Eventually, they take the plunge in large groups. Their fear: Leopard Seals.

It is pleasant to be near the Adélies, their subtle head crest suggesting that the interest is mutual. The Adélies are black-backed, white-bellied, with a short reddish bill. The white around their black pupils gives them a stuffed-toy appearance, like sewn-on eyes that jiggle. The three penguins in the region—Adélie, Gentoo, and the elegant Chinstrap—all

build pebble nests. With an exaggerated bow and much ceremony, a penguin delivers a stone to its mate. If a nest is unguarded, a neighbor may walk over to steal stones from it. As that neighbor walks over, *its* neighbor starts stealing stones. And so on, down the line.

We all know that penguins dress in tuxedos and waddle like plump nuns. Granted, they're charming, but real penguins are creatures of fearsome durability and endurance. Even the shy Gentoos dive to depths of around five hundred feet. (Emperor Penguins reach fifteen hundred feet.) An animal capable of routinely diving to crushing, numbing depths that would instantly kill any human, living day and night in these waters, and bobbing up for breath in hurricane-force winds is no cartoon. These represent an extreme in the evolution of "bird."

The morning's throngs enter the sea, leaping toward the distance.

In late morning, I scan the bay but see little sign of those leaping penguin herds. They've traveled beyond sight. By late afternoon a forty-knot wind is driving rain sideways in billowing curtains like smoke. Yet in a bay full of spume I see penguins again, undaunted. The water seems alive with them, porpoising shoreward.

They come bursting through the fangs of waves along the beach, streaking the shallows, riding panes of water on their bellies, their feet churning for purchase as the retreating wave tries to rake them back toward the sea. New birds squirt out of each wave, walking up beyond the wiping water.

Wayne pioneered penguin tracking, and he's found that penguins don't go any farther than they must to find krill in sufficient numbers. As the season progresses, krill begin moving inshore, penguin foraging trips get shorter, and the krill get bigger. Earlier in the season, foraging trips last twenty-four to thirty-six hours; now, twelve to eighteen hours.

Hundreds of penguins, paused by their exertions, line the beach, preening, rewaterproofing their feathers. Then up they go, in long defiles, waddling and hopping up slippery gravel slopes to their improbably high nests and their big, hungrily waiting chicks.

Meanwhile, at nesting sites, noise! The penguins' various calls sound like rusty sheep, braying donkeys, growling puppies. Chicks squeal. Adults waving flippers point skyward, trumpeting like cranes, saying, "I'm back; this is mine." When fights erupt, adults batter each other, their stiff flipper-wings slapping and smacking. It's a rich vocabulary for so spare a place.

A chick rattles its bill against its parent's. The parent leans over and opens its mouth. The chick buries its head up to its eyeballs into the adult's gullet, jackhammering back and forth, chugging food. I see two large siblings curled against each other after feeding, resting peacefully.

I absorb the Rousseauian peaceability of the place. But I know better.

At the highest penguin colony, I can gaze upon the sloping grandeur of timeless valleys, and upon every breeding penguin here—like any good predator. I watch giant petrels glide the ridges. My eyes fill with distant ice fields, the bay, the strait beyond. I savor the activity, the noise, the vital stink of it.

One chick, just fed, chases its parent halfway down the slope, begging for more, before it finally gives up and the parent continues hurriedly to the sea. About fifty yards from its peers, the chick turns to trudge back uphill, toward group safety. For a young penguin, the known world ends at the edge of the guano-stained ground.

A giant petrel with a seven-foot wingspan flies over, checks its glide, and spirals down. The two-way defile of adults stops as though the giant petrel is a traffic light that's just turned red. The chick is in the middle of the intersection.

When the chick attempts a left turn, the petrel locks its hooked bill into the young penguin's plump, soft, just-fed belly. With its wings half open and its feet firmly in place, the petrel yanks backward while the penguin, frantically trying to pull away, hastens its own catastrophe. With a few quick jerks the petrel massively opens the chick's abdomen. The doomed chick, still struggling, breaks free. The lumbering petrel grabs it again, and in moments the chick collapses and goes limp. The petrel glances around, its face drenched red.

Soon several giant petrels, including a pure white one, land. But it's a fat season and none of them seem very hungry. Eventually a couple of them peaceably share the carcass.

As I head back, a large group of Adélie chicks, about forty of them, cluster tightly near a rock outcrop. Peering over the rocks with them, my gaze is returned by another big, bloody-faced giant petrel huddled over another large, freshly killed Adélie chick. A dozen other giant petrels also stare back.

Seeing giant petrels killing penguins was gruesome, I tell Sue and Wayne—as we sit down to a pork dinner. Each evening we take turns cooking, washing dishes, and sweeping. Each night at nine comes the radio call: Palmer Station, the main U.S. base in the region, checking in with the other bases to make sure all is well. Poland, the United States, Ecuador, Brazil, Uruguay, Korea, China, Argentina, and Chile all have bases nearby. Some of the bases here amount to little more than territorial claims marked just for the sake of it. Where dogs would hoist a leg, men hoist flags.

The calls bring news, weather comparisons, scientific questions, discussions of penguins and krill, menu comparisons, and spirited debates such as whether gumbo without okra is really gumbo. In Antarctica, food commands uncommon attention, even reverence. And when Wayne decides to do some baking, I pray aloud, "Give us this day our Adélie bread."

Breakfast. Outside, it's one degree above freezing. In a moaning gale, snow flying horizontally is coming thick enough to obliterate the bay.

On such fierce mornings we all engage in a silent waiting game. On wide-open ground a mere fifty paces from the hut stands the Box. Even that is too grandiose a description for the stark reality of an utterly exposed Antarctic potty seat (outhouses blow away in hundred-mile-an-hour winds). Here's the system: You put on the big red parka near the door so you are plenty visible. Make sure it's got a roll of toilet paper in the pocket. Then just walk up to the box and mount the throne. What privacy there is—and this stretches the concept wafer-thin—comes from the cover of the parka itself. Privacy aside, nothing softens the hard fact that it's cold work to put your bare ass on that seat first thing in the morning. And sitting there while your underwear fills with snow is one thing, but the Box is worst in heavy rain. If this morning's temperature drops a couple of degrees, moreover, the first person will have to melt a glaze of ice. Consequently, the morning's cheeky waiting game: Who'll be the first seat warmer?

Today we'll put flipper tags on five hundred Adélie chicks. We halt where a group of dark chicks in fluffy charcoal down stand together in a group called a crèche. We spread a thirty-foot-wide net and gently herd young penguins toward the barricade.

As fair warning, Wayne shows me his hands, the backs of which are crisscrossed with faded half-inch scars made by penguins.

With the chicks corralled, Sue demonstrates: "See, you just lift the bird by its flippers, then sling it between your knees so that its back legs are well behind yours." (A penguin chick is a loaded weapon; despite our attempts to keep their back ends pointed away from us, our slickers are soon caked with guano.) "Then put the tag around the left flipper, and close it with the pliers." The tag is a bit like a flattened ring, with a serial number that identifies individuals.

"Okay," I say to Sue, "I could use a penguin right about now." She hands one to me and I sling it between my legs like an old hand. The chicks are so downy, handling them seems like a cross between bird banding and sheep shearing. With the dust from the down and the smell of guano thick on the breeze, the place is a bit rank, but without the stench it'd be a lesser place. When I'm sure that the tag is closed smoothly, will stay in place, and won't chafe, Wayne nods; the bird waddles off in an excited hurry. We trudge up rocky slopes to higher colonies with names such as Tortilla Flats, Trojan Plains, and Funky Town. The penguins like places with the best views. Hours later, when we apply the five hundredth flipper tag, we have moved about a mile and gained three hundred feet of elevation.

Marking individuals is the only way to understand how long they're living—or how fast they're dying. Wayne and Sue have found that survival rates are dropping. Up through the 1980s, the chances of a young Adélie surviving its first years at sea were about four out of ten. Since 1990 it has been more like one out of ten.

That's about the time the winter sea ice started rapidly shrinking. Suspected: something about the penguins' food is changing. That's what Wayne and Sue are trying to figure out.

꩜

Each evening now in the Adélie villages, there's a graduating class of seven-week-old youngsters. Along the shore, they come down to the beach a dozen or two at a time. Their graduation attire: alabaster white and glossy black, with a downy brown cap. At the shore, they halt. Any adult entering the sea, they study with intense fascination. Hours pass.

I watch a youngster vigorously flapping its flippers while leaping into the air, as though its fledgling hormones have triggered its brain to run some ancestral shadow memory of flight. Like any adolescent confronted by a wild new experience of youth, young Adélies facing their first swim seem both afraid and very excited. Finally, one gets brave and goes—and this wad of young penguins all spill into the water.

Unlike the nonmigratory Gentoo chicks, who come and go comfortably from little exploratory swims, for the Adélies water is a once-and-for-all deal. They won't return to land for several years, so it's a very abrupt life-changing event—and they can't swim.

The Adélies hit the sea crazed and panicky, flapping and flailing, thrashing and splashing as though trying to stay off the water, seemingly afraid they'll sink and drown. When the furious flipper flapping starts to tire them and they realize they actually float, they seem quite surprised by the whole thing. Sitting unpenguinlike, with heads up high like ducks, they begin uttering honking calls as they paddle seaward.

With the true courage of the fearful, they go straight toward their odyssey to the unknown, and never waver.

But subtle, they're not. The noise carries.

One of the trailing fledgers suddenly goes end over end in a spray of red-and-white water. For a Leopard Seal, picking a fledger from the surface must be about as easy as picking tomatoes.

A spreading oil slick immediately draws several giant petrels, a couple of gulls, and a dozen little Wilson's Storm-Petrels. These daintily dipping robin-sized birds are world travelers capable of routinely riding out the harshest ocean weather on the planet. One of the world's most abundant birds, they migrate all the way from the Antarctic throughout the Atlantic, Indian, and South Pacific Oceans, a vast swath of world. Since childhood I've seen them, sometimes by the hundreds, in waters off Long Island and New England.

The Leopard spends several minutes on the surface, thrashing the penguin from its skin. It returns at leisure to the carcass, and its elongated, reptilian-looking head shakes off the next bite.

While the seal is occupied, penguins pass at safe distances, and even swim though the slick. When all returns to quiet, the bay is as full of porpoising penguins as ever.

Ten minutes later, fifty yards away: another splash, another spreading slick.

≺

The weather delays our day's plans, and for hours we sit in the kitchen reorganizing equipment, getting caught up on data, and working on cameras.

Eventually, though, we suit up—heavy insulated boots, waterproof pants, parka over layered clothing, fleece hat, gloves—for the walk to Paradise.

Wayne and Sue need to get samples of food from Chinstrap Penguins nesting across the island near a place called Paradise Cove. They warn me: it can be a challenging hike.

The first leg is a long coast walk. At every stretch of open gravel and every partly sheltered cove, ribs, skulls, and the great curving arcs of whales' mandibles lie embedded in the beach. In the twentieth century, industrial whalers took something like a *million* whales from the Antarctic. Though the Antarctic is the greatest whale habitat on Earth, Leviathan remains rare in its realm—and still stalked by Japanese ships.

Here in Antarctica, as in the Arctic, what remains abundant about whales is their bones. In one stretch, you can walk three hundred yards on whales' bones without stepping on the beach. The bones lie like felled trunks. One nearly intact skull—this must be from a Blue Whale—measures about twelve feet across its width, eye to eye. Lengthwise, from tip of jaw to base of skull, it paces out at twenty-seven boot lengths. The lower jawbone is so thick that, though lying on the beach, it comes up past my knees.

About a mile and a half from Copa, we round a headland called "the Sphinx" and start across a stark, wide bowl of land bounded by mountains and the sea. Deep snowfields lie up against the mountains, pierced by occasional spires of rock.

"This landscape has changed so much," Wayne says. "Before, there was a hundred-foot-thick snowbank. Now, every bit of this snow will disappear before we leave."

He points, saying, "That one peak was sticking out of this glacier when I first came here, but now you see about a hundred feet more of it. That's how much it's thinned." Almost to himself he adds, "Look at all these exposed slopes and peaks—"

Pushed here by a sheet of ice not long ago, the ground remains desolate to the distant hills. It's the moon, with wind.

But how wrong that impression is; Wayne reaches into the seemingly lifeless scree beneath our feet, hands me an odd-shaped rock, and says, "Petrified wood."

There was a forest here? We soon find a remnant of a tree stump nearly two feet in diameter. Its growth rings lie wide, suggesting long growing seasons. Similar beech trees still grow in Patagonia. In a rock that looks like fired clay, Wayne finds a fossil seed head of a small reed. All these rocks, jumbled together by the glacier, are travelers in time and space.

This landscape, as spare and exposed as a stripped-down bed, bares not only the impressions of a changing climate but also the imprint of climates past.

Now Wayne points to the coast. He says, "That used to be the toe of the glacier." It's receded about three-quarters of a mile uphill from there, where it now melts into a new lake.

"Getting around here has really become a pain because of all the running water," Sue tells me. "On the glacier more crevasses are opening. So we keep having to learn new routes."

We cut straight up a little ravine with running rivulets and come out alongside the gleaming, mile-wide glacier. After pausing for half a chocolate bar each, we step up onto the ice.

With no tufts of grass to bend over, no flowers to bow, no leaves to rustle, nothing on the land reveals the fierce wind that greets us. The wind rampaging down these slopes is gusting to at least fifty miles per hour. Wayne once came over a ridge with three colleagues and all four people blew down like bowling pins. I'm leaning so far into this wind that when I look straight forward, I'm staring at the ground. Overhead, dark clouds hurtle along at a startling pace.

Suddenly the wind drops out—complete calm—as though taking a deep breath. And now—*wow*—that wind blasts down the valley, snapping our coats, slapping our hoods against our heads. Ice is what Antarctica uses to freeze you; wind is what it uses to burn you.

Ragged, broken, crenellated, corrugated—the glacier is a wild white-water river in stop-frame slow motion. My companions, they're used to the exertion and the distances. Having unzipped everything, I'm huffing as we trudge across the glacier's jagged surface. Even with my hat in my bare hand, my scalp is damp with sweat. We're like toy action figures on a hyperenlarged landscape.

The sheer scale of this place is vaguely frightening. The danger, however, is real. Crevasses can be disguised, roofed over with snow. On one step, I drop just up to my thighs, but it's quite enough to stop my heart.

Sue wheels, and reinforces. "Don't walk on snow—step on the ice, there. You might want to just walk in our footsteps." She doesn't need to tell me again.

We walk ridges with yawning blue cracks up to twenty feet deep on each side of us. Far more dangerous are deep crevasses that lie thinly iced over, like pitfall traps.

All along the ice surface, dips and divots and undulations reflect light differently, here like blue shadow, there white satin, now sparkling diamonds. In the edges of the cracks are tiny spires. At eye level, minute towers, turrets, and minarets form endless little ice kingdoms. Almost every step crunches some miniature realm.

A mountainlike rock—about half a mile long and two hundred feet high—cleaves the glacier, letting us perceive the motion we cannot see. Glacial ice piles high against its uphill end like water colliding with a ship's bow. This ship splits the glacier in two, leaving a muddied tailrace, with the glacier streaming off on either side in enormous wakes.

As the walking flattens out and eases, my heart rate returns to near normal, and I stop overheating, glad to feel cool in Antarctica. Getting off the glacier, we stop for clear water so cold we have to pause between gulps. I turn and look back. So far, so good.

On open ground not far from the ice, a skua drops to the ground only to be met and chased off by several dozen suddenly rising nesting terns. They wheel overhead, their elegantly attenuated wings and forked tails lifting them on the breeze. In Svalbard I'd seen Arctic Terns. These nearly identical polar opposites are *Antarctic* Terns. They're all close relatives of the terns at Lazy Point, and sound and act in ways that help me understand that these seemingly different worlds are really just one. The unity of opposites. The unity, indeed, of everything.

Sue finds a nest with two tern eggs in it. Their warmth in a land where warmth is rare makes me ponder the path of that energy from sun to sea to flesh of bird and the excess heat that flesh affords this egg. If all things are not miraculous, "miracle" means nothing.

We need to end up on the other side of a mountain. As we're cresting a saddle sloped across the ridgeline, a fresh blast of sea wind makes me zip my coat closed again. The landscape before us is polished bare by wind, the soil frost-heaved to a spongy texture. Trudging across this extraordinary soft bare ground earns us the commanding brink of cliffs whose jumbled ledges fall away to pounding green sea foam.

The scale is enormous in a way that landscape in peopled areas never can be. Cloud shadows continually change the distant snowfields, and the sky itself begins to look like moving ice.

"I'm glad I shall never be young," wrote Aldo Leopold, "without wild country to be young in." A canvas this open is a Refresh button for a spirit of any age, not just wildness to feel young in but a place to feel wild in.

We turn and head down toward the notch called Paradise Cove. We have been walking now for about three and a half hours. One end of Paradise Cove has a well-sheltered black-sand beach. Nearby lies a wallow with over a hundred bellowing behemoths packed together like logs in a raft: elephant seals. These logs wriggle over one another and snort. They have heads like enormous bowling balls, and lazily open their huge pink mouths to threaten us. Here is a comely cow, her face full of snot, inhaling the wallow's acrid, urine-scented air with one nostril dilated round, the other closed tight. The muscles that operate that mighty nostril can shut the schnoz tight against the sea. Elephant seals dive to the unimaginable depth of four thousand feet. I imagine them surfacing far from land, after a descent to crushing pressure in frigid darkness, to take a deep breath in twenty-foot seas with freezing winds whipping so much spume across the surface that it's hard to tell where the sea ends and the air begins.

Stark though it is, the sheltered cove is wonderfully pleasant. We unpack a couple of oranges, a couple of apples, raisins and peanuts, smoked oysters, kippered herring, grilled sausages bartered from the Polish research station—even some wine. These folks know how to rough it! We've brought a little firewood, too, and the exotic scent of smoke smells delightful in the Antarctic air. Around the fire, we sit on whale vertebrae the size of tree stumps, enjoying the lush life of scientists.

One imperfection in the provisions: the crackers are stale. Sue says they're probably a couple of years old. "How come when bread goes stale it gets hard and when crackers go stale they get soft?" she asks. Ah, the imponderables. In Antarctica the spirit of inquiry ranges as wide and unbounded as the landscape.

We stroll to a high spot where Sue wants to show me the Chinstrap colony, and she suddenly says, "Wow. That's unbelievable. They're gone!" On several flat-topped ledges, there's a lot of guano and the ground is well trod—but no penguins.

From where we cannot see, we hear the remnants of this colony. Down to the right, around a little bend, we see some Chinstrap Penguins on a rock.

Sue, still flabbergasted, says, "Fifteen years ago, this was all Chin-straps. They nested all along these rocks, all the way down and all the way across to those few penguins over there."

As we start toward them, a sudden whoosh next to my head precedes a blur. Skuas have a nest nearby. Both mates zoom past us again and shoot upwind in perfect unison. With the bodies of gulls and the bearing of eagles, they can strike like a two-pound sack of sand going forty miles an hour, and people working with Wayne and Sue have been cold-cocked. One look at that dark body speeding toward my head tells me I don't need to know how it feels.

Across a bare, broad plain stands a rocky headland still plentiful with penguins. Birds coming up from the sea walk to the nest area with the undersides of their flippers blushed pink from exertion, blood flowing through translucent skin beneath translucent feathers.

Wayne says, "Look at the belly on that krill-swilling Chinny there." A quarter of its whole body weight is krill intended for chicks. Good for that one; it's nice to see such thriving success. May its chicks be many.

Fluffy gray-and-white chicks three-quarters of the adults' height look like downy Buddhas, their center of gravity so low they couldn't possibly fall over.

Penguins look as tough as footballs, and when you see them trying to claw their way up a wet cliff in the breakers and getting bounced around, you understand that they actually are that tough. Their feathering is so densely packed, you'd have difficulty working a small finger in to find out how thick it is. It's thick. They can take a pounding. And they can give it. Wing bones as flat as blades can slap hard, and a bite can raise a palm-sized bruise. Wayne tells of prying open the beak of a penguin that was biting Sue, only to have it clamp on him. Then Sue prying it off, only to have it bite her. Like peanut butter, with jaws.

Wayne and Sue need food samples from five penguins. We select a volunteer from the incoming adults. No one likes this part. Wayne inserts the soft rounded end of a clear plastic hose down the gullet of our detained penguin. The tube must go carefully past the bird's tongue and palate—which bristle with krill-holding backward-pointed barbs—and behind the trachea's airway.

The tube is connected to a warm-water bag; with Wayne raising the bag and Sue holding the penguin upright, water flows into the penguin by gravity. When the penguin gargles a little, Sue inverts it, one hand around its legs and the other supporting its body. Sue massages it, saying, "Hey, buddy, don't look so sad. Give it up easy and you're on your way home." Then with the aid of Sue's finger, the penguin's precious krill spills in a big gushing rush into a white plastic pan.

Wayne says, "It is not pretty, but in the old days, people killed them to get food samples. That was awful."

As soon as we've got our five samples, the temperature drops sharply. A gray sky, pregnant with snow, begins shedding flecks. I raise my hood,

then fumble to get my gloves on in a hurry. Wind gusts are suddenly raising white tornadoes of water that shatter in the air. The weather decides
for us: time to go.

After the day's rugged round-trip, I feel wiped out, but a round of "barley
sandwiches" (read: home-brewed beer) and some brownies from the oven
fortify us to start processing the krill samples. On the kitchen table, Wayne
and Sue weigh the whole sample from each bird. The stomach contents
average about 600 to 800 grams—roughly a pound and a half—and are
almost all krill. With incense burning to mask the scent, and music
playing, the hut smells and sounds like a college dorm. Next, we measure
the length of fifty krill from each stomach. The krill, of several species,
are nearly all mature creatures, and you can see the little orange dot in
the midsection that says most are female. These are spawners.

These older krill can store enough energy in summer to survive a
winter without food. But young krill require a winter food supply, or
most won't survive the season. They get their winter food by grazing
single-celled algae off the underside of sea ice. Where there's no ice—
there's no winter food.

Two years ago, the krill averaged 35 to 40 millimeters (about an inch
and a half). Last year they were mostly 42 to 45 millimeters. This year
they're two-inchers, 45 to over 50 millimeters. Wayne explains, "We are
seeing just the survivors of the krill born in the last good ice year."

"They're growing up and maturing," Sue adds. "But there's almost no
younger krill coming in behind them. In recent, relatively iceless winters,
there are almost no young krill surviving."

"In the 1980s," Wayne continues, "on our way down here in a heavy
ice year, we would hit ice two hundred miles north of these islands. In
years when we had to push through heavy ice to get here, Adélie numbers
were way up compared to the year before. Younger birds had abundant
food, and more of them returned to breed. You need at least one heavy
ice year every few years to replenish at least one strong generation of
krill." The more frequent the years of heavy winter sea ice, the more krill.
"But recent years, with little ice," Wayne says. "It's really knocked the
krill down."

• • •

The winter air of the Antarctic Peninsula is warming several times faster than the global average. When mean air temperature in the winter months (between May and September) was about 27 degrees Fahrenheit (−3°C) or colder, extensive pack ice formed. Warmer than that, it didn't. Satellite photos show that until the early 1970s, this region had extensive ice four out of every five years. In 1979, ice lasted about three months longer than it did in 2009.

"Air temperatures here," Wayne says, "have risen about ten degrees Fahrenheit in the last forty years." Starting a few years ago, daily high temperatures in *winter* began averaging above freezing. "As it's gotten warmer," Wayne continues, "it's been, like, two good years of ice, three years of almost no ice, two good years of ice, three, four, five years of almost no ice."

"Krill can live up to around seven years," Sue says, "so it took a while for them to really crash." Eventually, almost no ice means no krill.

That starves penguins. Chinstraps and Adélies' numbers are both down by more than half in this region since the 1970s.

"The drop in penguin numbers coincided with very dramatic krill declines," Sue explains. "Fewer young penguins are surviving their first years." In earlier years of their studies, about 40 percent of young Chinstraps and Adélies survived long enough to return and breed. Recently, it's been 10 percent.

"After whales were reduced by ninety percent," adds Wayne, "people in the fishing industry were saying, 'There's enough krill out here to double the total output of the world's fisheries.' Well, things have certainly changed."

Things have always changed. Twenty-five million years ago, over a hundred species of penguins—including one six feet tall—drilled through the ocean. Now a dozen and a half species remain. That wasn't our fault. But we can reasonably ask if rushing some of the remaining penguins off the stage is something we want on humanity's résumé. Two-thirds of the world's penguin species are declining sharply. Northern Rockhopper Penguins have dropped 90 percent since the 1950s, a loss of a couple million birds, equivalent to losing one hundred birds daily for the last half century. African Penguins have declined from about 150,000 pairs around 1960 to 25,000 pairs today. Magellanic Penguins are declining 1 percent per year. Even the magnificent Emperors are down as much as half in the last fifty years, with extinction in this century a possibility.

I'd like to think that the bottom of the world is far enough from tail-pipes and smokestacks that the animals can live unbothered by us. But I know better. And tonight's radio call with Palmer Station brings news from a Russian oceanographic ship: an iceberg estimated at a staggering 170 miles long and 25 miles wide—nearly the size of Connecticut—is breaking free from the mainland and will soon be adrift.

JANUARY

Pop.

  Pop pop.

  Pop pop pop.

  Weekend gunners keep a constant banter ringing in from various bearings. During extended stretches of time they allow scarcely a silent minute.

  As ducks come slipping gracefully to settle among their companions for the safety in numbers, the guns explode. The lovely ducks' bones shatter, and they stumble, crumble, and tumble, splashing wounded among the deceiving decoys. In the reeds are people having fun with this.

  But, okay; I used to hunt rabbits with trained hawks. Some of my friends hunt. I understand that some duck hunters support conservation groups because they want more ducks, duck hunting, and the marshes and all that goes with them. And fishing is just hunting in the water. So it's not that I oppose hunting. (Admittedly, fishing doesn't send all nearby fish fleeing. It doesn't disturb the peace of people in bed on a Sunday morning. You can release a fish you don't want. But still, I'm not categorically against hunting.)

  When a cease-fire ensues at midday, I walk to the Cut. A couple hundred yards distant on the opposite shore, three hunters—two fat middle-aged men and a younger guy, all dressed in camo—are gathering up decoys and rolling up their fancy store-bought blind. One of the fat guys is standing with two fistfuls of our Long-tails, dangling by their feet, limp necks swaying. He walks into the dunes and flings the ducks into the grass. The younger guy picks up a few more birds, and he, too, throws them into the grass. Then they leave.

If they killed the ducks and ate them, I wouldn't object. But for all the years I've lived here, slob hunters have left ducks (and plastic shotgun cartridges) scattered on the beach. I have a neighbor—nice guy otherwise—who says his annual donation to a conservation group makes up for his wasting ducks he doesn't like to eat but likes to shoot anyway.

No gloss will adhere to that mind-set. Turning our wildlife into garbage invalidates any feeble justification. Every ethical tradition, each religion, has long deplored wastefulness. Who still fails to see the sin?

These guys are phonies. They're playacting—like Elvis impersonators or Civil War reenactors—only they're spilling real blood. These hunters act out a ritual that once had meaning but has been hollowed out by changing times and their own hollow heads. Now it's just meaningless and mean.

Innocents have always to fear. Not just death, not just predation, not just being kicked a rung up the food chain; but also people who inflict pain simply because they can. Waste is one symptom of a world with a death wish.

Weeks later, when I notice a nice flock of Goldeneyes and Long-tails in good light and walk toward the Cut for a better look, they flee in panic. I hate to see them interrupt their feeding and waste valuable energy, but I think, "Good for them"; trust is a killer.

❧

As a species evolving, we entrain a frightening combination of animal passion and unique mind. From atom to opera, malice to medicine, we are by far the most magnificent, menacing creature of all time. On Earth, at least. Jeopardies to nature are a matter of great concern, but civilization itself seems even more vulnerable. Consider: our economic accounting is illusory, our cultural balances tenuous, our ideals elusive, our achievements fragile, our anger too real.

Human awareness stands on the threshold of something we've never really considered before: our place in time. The "tragedy of the commons" exists beyond the mere breadth of the grazing meadows; it's a tragedy across time, too. We can take our neighbor's grass—or our children's. This capacity to heap up not just riches but time itself now characterizes the human venture. We occupy more than our fair share of space, and more still: we occupy a bigger-than-life chunk of time. By toxin and carbon, by chainsaw and fishing net, by appetite and sheer force of numbers, we survive by being way overleveraged on loans from generations yet to come, loans for which we the borrowers—not the lenders—dictate the terms. The downside exposure is so enormous, it threatens not just the civilization bubble we've created but Life, incorporated. The future, indeed, isn't what it used to be.

When the wind holds its breath, calm days in winter can feel soft and soothing. This one feels worth a walk at the lighthouse.

In astonishing swarms, sea ducks are, once again, stringing dark necklaces across the gray horizon and peppering the coastal view. They're mostly scoters—all three species—and Common Eiders. Gathering over mussel-crusted ridges and boulder bottoms, as usual, they throng the near-shore ocean in flocks totaling tens of thousands. An e-mailed birders' alert says, "The huge scoter and eider flock was estimated to contain 10,000 White-winged Scoters, 7,000 Surf Scoters, 2,000 Black Scoters and 5,000 Common Eiders."

Swept along in the tide, diving to feed, then flying back to where they started, they work the place as vigorously as ever. They're most concentrated about half a mile from shore, but they're all over. Those actually in the surf pour themselves into the curling faces of big breaking waves to avoid getting tumbled. They are obvious yet mysterious, and their numbers provide deep comfort, especially in the short daylight of winter.

Several loons, grebes, and Red-breasted Mergansers also swim the surf. Winter's gulls are likewise arriving. I see the common Bonaparte's, and scan for the rarer Glaucous, Iceland, Lesser Black-backed, and Black-headed Gulls.

The birds know somehow where they've been and where they're

going. When the stable weather changes, they move, and will move again. For twelve thousand years or so, humanity has lived in a period of very stable climate. That stability has been the climate envelope for all of civilization so far. Now we are committed to leaving that stable period for points unknown. It's humanity's most hazardous journey yet. And unlike the journeys of these birds, unlike even our voyage to the moon and back, this time we don't know where we are going. We've been running like a wheel out of round, and the wobble, barely detectable at the Sermon on the Mount, the signing of the Declaration of Independence, and the publication of *On the Origin of Species,* now threatens to rattle the world hard enough to shake hundreds of millions of people from their homes, their histories, and their futures.

Currents roil the surface. The duck flocks' epicenter is a place that people in fishing boats call the Elbow. Not far away, over a long seafloor ridge in about forty feet of water, the tide creates a long line of rough water called Pollock Rip. I've never heard of a Pollock coming out of there in all the years I've known the place, though older captains have told me they used to catch a lot of big Pollock until the early 1970s.

Formerly the season's influx included winter's fish as well as fowl: "King Cod" and his court—Pollock, Haddock, and the like, all so depleted now that their tattered remnants scarcely wave a flag of surrender. The bulk of them return as oral history: "Yesterday we got a few but, *boy*—we ran for three hours. When I was a kid, we never went more than a couple of miles. We'd catch them right outside the inlet. You never had to look for good bottom. You never had to chum. You just cut the engine and drifted." Thanks for the fillets, Bob, and the memories.

Stories make a mighty coarse net for capturing memories. Most eventually get away. Older people may bemoan the poverty of codless winters and places named for creatures that no longer come. Or the asphalting of wild lands they were young in. Or the closing in of room to roam—and room to breathe. For young people, this new poverty is simply normal. A cooped chicken doesn't realize that its ancestors were wild birds. Most young people don't know what isn't there, don't sense their inheritance plucked from them. They don't even think about it; bullhorns and billboards call their attentions elsewhere.

And where would they turn, anyway, for a sense of how it's supposed to be? We can consult classical philosophy and religion for advice on how to behave toward each other, but not for how we should behave toward the changing world. Economists can tell us how to value currency, but not how to value the only known life. Or even our own life. These institutions were never equipped to consider that the world changes, much less that we are changing it.

I hope that one day our time will be remembered as wasteful, impoverished, and primitive. And after that, I hope that the memory of our violent times and anti-Reason ideologies and dirty engines will be forgotten, too, or at least seem as distant as the Black Plague and the Inquisition.

Nature keeps trying. This winter, far offshore, there's a surprising influx of cod. In fishing communities this has produced both a rush to catch them and political turmoil over whether to protect them. We know that life's resilience makes recovery possible. We see it when and where it's allowed to happen. Maybe we'll get through this after all. Maybe, in so many necessary ways, we'll get through this.

A lot that should be here is missing. And some things that were missing are back. Ospreys. Peregrine Falcons. The Stripers we love to catch and love to eat. That we can regain what we have abused not only matters, it instructs. It inspires. When I was a kid, seeing a seal swimming in these waters was rare and remarkable. After centuries of persecution, in 1972 the Marine Mammal Protection Act made killing seals illegal in the United States. Now when walking our winter beach, it's not unusual to see a seal watching from just beyond the surf. One morning, when the bay froze, I sat up in bed and saw several seals hauled out along the ice's edge. Seeing seals without getting out of bed was a new experience. It seemed fitting to literally wake up to renewed abundance; it's my recurring dream.

But it's no small matter to go from letting birds and bass and seals recover to taking the giant steps required to rechill the poles, regrow forests, refill the seas with fish, save the tropics' reefs, stabilize the ocean's chemistry, secure agriculture, quench the fire, tame growth, recognize the finite possibilities, lighten up, and calm down.

The world is changing because we're changing it. And that makes me understand, at least, what kind of person I'd like to be. A person can seek ways, whether big or small, to heal the world. That, to me, is spirituality and one's "soul." Not some disembodied eternal wishfulness but a way of being that, most days, I can work on. Life is like walking with a flashlight on a dark night. You can't see your destination, but each step illuminates the next few steps, and, taking one after another, you can get where you need to go. Only now, we'll need to quicken our pace if we are to avoid major upheaval in this century. It's up to us not just as individuals but as citizens of nations and of the world.

Kenzie lopes ahead toward the Cut. I throw a pebble into the Sound. My mind sees the ripples spreading from where a first small pebble of realization strikes until those ripples touch all shores. And in the circles rippling outward I see a kind of geometry of compassion. Many lives are spent right where each of us first splashes in, inside the first circle. Most religions tread mainly within the perimeter of the second circle, which widens enough to encompass humanity. If we get to ride in the widest expanding circle, we call our name and hear it echo across the span of deep time, and all Life answers, through the whole dance of birth and death and birth traveling out of the past and blurring into the far future. That rippling, ever-widening circle—that's where we need to be.

Albert Einstein said, "The intuitive mind is a sacred gift and the rational mind is a faithful servant. We have created a society that honors the servant and has forgotten the gift." Our inventiveness must serve, not enslave. Air, water, land, and skies: healing is possible. Great new innovators are plotting a course that could let factories mimic the efficiency of biological systems, cycling essentially without waste, generating renewable flows rather than liquidating nature, creating products, buildings, even cities that enter the life process itself. We can harness energy without setting fire to the world. The moral must guide the technical. Better we be threads that strengthen the fabric, rather than that we pull the rug from those who will come next. The mere existence of the human mind enhances the universe; our human presence should not diminish it. And if we alone, of all creatures, can best think ahead—then we should.

The music becomes new when the rhythm changes. We may yet hear a different drummer. We must understand three things formerly unknown:

that Life is a fully networked community; that because expanding knowledge suggests remaining ignorance, we ought to act with humility, reverence, and caution; and that the story we write with our lives affects those living near and far, and not just now but in the near and distant futures.

The moral must guide the technical—but whose morals? We have the benefit of some hard work by others. "Love your enemies," said Jesus. Honor the stranger. We have been formed into tribes and nations, the Koran says, that we may come to know each other. Our responsibility to heal the world is central to Judaism. Compassion is what brings Jews, Christians, and Muslims to what they call God; it's what the Buddha says will bring you to Nirvana. Confucius propounded the golden rule five centuries before Christ. The ability to feel along with another is the minimum standard of religiosity, "because in compassion," says the former nun and author Karen Armstrong, "we dethrone ourselves from the center of our world." In science, much the same. Remember, we've got Copernicus's deduction—truly astounding when you fathom how counterintuitive—that the sun and the universe do not revolve around us; Darwin's perception of the totality of our relatedness; and Aldo Leopold's insight that our true community is not just people but the community of Life and all that supports it. Jesus, Copernicus, Darwin, Leopold—and the other giants. One central theme: one widening circle. This is the story of all we have learned. Simple, right?

Yet we've fought bitterly each step of the way toward saying, simply, that all men are created equal; and not just white men; and not just men. The struggle for democracy, the emancipation movement, the civil rights movement, the women's movement, and the environmental movement collectively give the modern world a glimpse at what an end to humanity's brute stage would look like. No group of individuals who have ever demanded their freedom and their human dignity—slaves, ethnic minorities, persecuted religious sects, women, gay people—has been shown by history to have been on the wrong side. Every oppressing or bigoted group has. Each time we've expanded the circle, the test of time has proven it absolutely the right thing.

Around these various struggles runs that one gathering thread: whenever we take the focus off ourselves and move it outward, we benefit.

Life's most fortunate ironies are that what's best for the long run is best now, and selflessness serves our interests far better than selfishness. The wider our circle of considerations, the more stable we make the world—and the better the prospects for human experience and for all we might wish. The core message of each successive widening: we are one. The geometry of the human voyage is not linear; it's those ripples whose circles expand to encompass self, other, community, Life, and time.

Temperatures haven't nudged the thaw point in many days and nights. What was fluid is solid. Stand resolutely in the same place, and the view changes anyway. But once the freeze is in and the bay locks up, any change will mean a thaw. The great thing about hard times is: when things change, they can only improve.

Though the land and ponds are hardened with ice and deep in winter, we've turned the corner on the length of days. That and a layer of snow bring a brightening. Life knows the beat of this tune, though the dance steps can be subtle. Where dead branches poke the winter sky stand the silhouettes of Red-tails in love. After shooting hawks for fun went out of style, Red-tailed Hawks recovered. Now they're as common as they should be. Their hormones anticipate nest building and all it implies, and for a brief honeymoon in late winter before the real work begins, you see these eagles of the suburban woodlots perched closely in pairs, silently anticipating spring. One morning I hear a descending *deeee-deeee*. Chickadees—or at least one—are switching from their winter *chick-a-dee* contact call ("Where's everybody?") to their breeding song ("Here am I"). Their roaming flocks, formed for winter safety, will disband as the birds reassert property claims in the pines. They feel the world changing, and they change their tune.

Can we do less? "A change in the weather is sufficient to recreate the world and ourselves," said Marcel Proust. We must make a new song, tell the new story that there has arisen a need to consider the future in ways that seldom burdened generations past. Our new story, so much better informed this time, ought to feel newly inspired.

Our year's journeying has brought us glimpses of next horizons and unprecedented urgencies. By the dimming lights of our outdated philosophical, ethical, and economic traditions, we are sailing in uncharted waters. To navigate safely, we'll need to be less heavily freighted, more nimble in steering. To orient ourselves, we'll need a new compass whose poles are dispassion and compassion. A "compass of compassion" would be a formidable navigator. But still we'll need to decide where we want to go. Perhaps we'll describe the place where we'd hope to find our children living. Compassion can begin to plot the course.

Even an accurate compass can put you on the rocks if no one's monitoring the obstacles. We need good navigating instruments, a destination; we also need to have our eyes open. We need to avoid the rocks and the ideological shallows, keep the world's vitality brimming—and stay afloat.

You can see the origins of human traits in the behavior of other animals: their drive to survive; their passion to defend and reproduce; curiosity; and even, among a few, glimmers of caring. (This summer my neighbor J.P. had been hand-feeding a gull that landed on his roof each morning, and one day it arrived with a billful of fine grass and other nesting material, and delivered it into his hand.) Uniquely among animals, though, our minds are gifted with a capacity for extension, reflection, and far-ranging compassion.

Compassion doesn't simply mean caring for poor people or putting band-aids on need. It seeks to remedy *sources* of suffering. It means we require a clear, peaceful way of providing what the world can bear—and knowing when enough is too much. In part, it means realizing that far fewer people would mean far less suffering.

In the 1830s, Charles Lyell's book *Principles of Geology* sent tremors by demonstrating that the workings of the past, visible now, are still shaping the workings of the present. The idea impressed a young and observant Charles Darwin and changed our way of seeing—indeed, our way of searching. What we now need to realize is that the workings of the future, too, are visible in the workings of today. For better or worse, we shape the future in the present. Because we can love our children, we have a twin stake: in this place and in its prospect.

To advance compassion and yet survive in a world of appetites—that is our challenge. Where any weakness is crushed or exploited, empathy must be load-bearing. Yet compassion may be the lightest, strongest concept yet devised. Century upon century, it wages a widening peace.

The compass of compassion asks not "What is good for me?" but "What is good?" Not what is best for me but what is best. Not what is right for me, but what is right. Not "How much can we take?" but "How much ought we leave?" and "How much might we give?" Not what is easy but what is worthy. Not what is practical but what is moral. With each action we decide whether to sow the grapes of wrath or the seeds of peace.

The compass of compassion suggests that very few things, each simple, are needed. We shouldn't hate people for the group they were born into, or because we hold conflicting beliefs about things that cannot be proven, seen, or measured. We can't infinitely take more from—or infinitely add more people to—a finite planet. While living in a world endowed with self-renewing energy, we can't run civilization on energy that diminishes the world. If we can get these simple things under control, I think we could be okay. Simple does not mean easy. Yet more than ever before in history, we can now understand what's needed. But nations need to act boldly and soon. Time runs short at an accelerating pace.

We are self-assembled stardust aware of the universe and the future. Energy that had been headed across the eternal, infinite vacuum of space is at this moment running the thought machine that is the breathing you. We are one knot in a great web of being, building out of the vast past and (with luck) continuing billions of years into the future, until the sun dies, the last of its energy reaches Earth, and our local light goes out. The most appropriate response to the world is to realize, with awe, the ferocious mystery of being alive in it. And act accordingly. The worst thing anyone should be able to say about their life is also the greatest thing anyone can say: "I tried my best."

The harshness of deep winter continues driving ducks, crossbills, siskins, and Snowy Owls south into our region. Yet even as they are still arriving from the north, the first grackles and robins, inspired by February's lengthening days, are already returning from the south.

So the year curls around on itself, nuzzling its nose in its tail.

And in the morning, a Red-winged Blackbird, singing, returns the world. We end at the new beginning.

REFERENCES

COAST OF CHARACTERS

Cooking in evolution: Wrangham, R. 2009. *Catching Fire: How Cooking Made Us Human*. Basic Books.

40 percent of land's productivity used by people: Vitousek, P. M., et al. 1986. "Human Appropriation of Products of Photosynthesis." *BioScience* 36:368–73. **That quantity is similarly estimated at over 30 percent overall but much higher locally by:** Imhoff, M. L., et al. 2004. "Global Patterns in Human Consumption of Net Primary Production." *Nature* 429:870–73. **For coastal shelves the estimate is similar; see:** Pauly, D., and V. Christensen. 1995. "Primary Production Required to Sustain Global Fisheries." *Nature* 374:255.

Half a percent of the animal mass: Imhoff, M. L., et al. 2004. "Global Patterns in Human Consumption of Net Primary Production." *Nature* 429:870–73.

Vertebrate populations down 30 percent since 1970: *WWF Living Planet Report: Living Planet Index,* available online.

Forests are shrinking: FAO. 2006. *Global Forest Resource Assessment 2005.* Rome: United Nations Food and Agriculture Organization. **See also:** *Millennium Ecosystem Assessment,* available online.

Dead zones: Nellemann, C., et al. 2008. *In Dead Water: Merging of Climate Change with Pollution, Over-Harvest, and Infestations in the World's Fishing Grounds.* United Nations Environment Programme.

Convention on Biological Diversity shortcomings: United Nations Secretariat of the Convention on Biodiversity. 2006. "Global Biodiversity Outlook 2." www.cbd.int/gbo2/.

Two Planet Earths: Kitzes, et al. 2008. "Shrink and Share: Humanity's Present and Future Ecological Footprint." *Philosophical Transactions of the Royal Society B* 363:467–75.

Luca Pacioli and accounting: Lanchester, J. 2009. "It's Finished." *London Review of Books*, May 28, 2009, p. 3.

Eiders: Pearson, T. G., editor. 1940. *Birds of America.* Garden City Publishing.

Nicolas Denys: quoted in Mowat, F. 1986. *Sea of Slaughter*, pp. 52–74. Bantam.

Forbush, on sea duck palatability and decline: Pearson, T. G., editor. 1940. *Birds of America.* Garden City Publishing.

FEBRUARY

Harold Morowitz as quoted in: Des Jardins, J. R. 2000. *Environmental Ethics.* 3rd ed., p. 219. Wadsworth/Thompson Learning.

MARCH: IN LIKE A LION

Eating myrtle berries: http://elibrary.unm.edu/sora/Auk/v109n02/p0334-p0345.html. **See also:** https://drum.umd.edu/dspace/bitstream/1903/2181/1/umi-umd-2170.pdf.

A fifth of the world can't see the Milky Way: "Dark Sky Park in Ohio Takes Long View." *USA Today*, February 26, 2009.

Aristotle, Aquinas, Bacon, Descartes, and Kant quoted in: Des Jardins, J. R. *Environmental Ethics*, 3rd ed., pp. 219, 95–96. Wadsworth/Thompson Learning. **Also:** Freud, S. 1927. *The Future of an Illusion.* Norton, 1979.

Emerson quoted from his *Nature*, 1836. **Thoreau quoted from** *Walden*, 1854.

Charles Darwin quoted from closing of *On the Origin of Species*, 1859.

George Perkins Marsh's 1865 book was *Man and Nature.* **Pinchot:** quoted from his 1914 book, *The Training of a Forester*, J. B. Lippincott Co.

MARCH: OUT LIKE A LAMB

About 2,500 of 6,000 amphibians threatened: iucnredlist.org/amphibians. **Including Yellowstone:** McMenamin, S. K., et al. 2008. "Climatic Change and Wetland Desiccation Cause Amphibian Decline in World's Oldest National Park." *Proceedings of the National Academy of Sciences* 105:16988–93. **Various causes of amphibian declines:** Stuart, S., et al. 2004. "Status and Trends of Amphibian Declines and Extinctions Worldwide." *Science*

306:1783–86. **Atrazine:** Hayes, T. B., et al. 2002. "Hermaphroditic, Demasculinized Frogs After Exposure to the Herbicide Atrazine at Low Ecologically Relevant Doses." *Proceedings of the National Academy of Sciences* 99:5476–80.

"Remoteness" of future people: http://gadfly.igc.org/papers/orfg.htm.

John James Audubon quote regarding Passenger Pigeons from: Matthiessen, P. 1989. *Wildlife in America.* Viking. **"Where a tremendous slaughter took place," plus other history and speculation on disappearance:** Fischer, M. 1913. "A Vanished Race." *Bird Lore* March–April, available online. **Passenger Pigeons also in:** Cokinos, C. 2001. *Hope Is the Thing with Feathers.* Grand Central Publishing. **And in:** Pearson, T. G., editor. 1940. *Birds of America.* Garden City Publishing.

Aldo Leopold's 1949 classic book is *A Sand County Almanac,* Oxford University Press.

Charles Darwin from his 1871 book, *The Descent of Man, and Selection in Relation to Sex.*

"As much and as good": Locke quoted in Des Jardins, J. R. 2000. *Environmental Ethics.* 3rd ed., p. 62. Wadsworth/Thompson Learning.

"The Tragedy of the Commons": Hardin, G. 1968. "The Tragedy of the Commons." *Science* 162:1243–48.

TRAVELS SOLAR: CORAL GARDENS OF GOOD AND EVIL—
BELIZE AND BONAIRE

Certain pollutants: Kline, D. I., et al. 2006. "Role of Elevated Organic Carbon Levels and Microbial Activity in Coral Mortality." *Marine Ecology Progress Series* 314:119–25. **And:** Bruno, J. F. 2003. "Nutrient Enrichment Can Increase the Severity of Coral Diseases." *Ecology Letters* 6:1056–61. **Also:** Voss, J. D., et al. 2006. "Nutrient Enrichment Enhances Black Band Disease Progression in Corals." *Coral Reefs* 25:569–76.

Algae obliterate light that baby corals need: Lee, S. C. 2006. "Habitat Complexity and Consumer-Mediated Positive Feedbacks on a Caribbean Coral Reef." *Oikos: A Journal of Ecology* 112:442–47. **See also:** Box, S. J., and P. J. Mumby. 2007. "Effect of Macroalgal Competition on Growth and Survival of Juvenile Caribbean Corals." *Marine Ecology Progress Series* 342:139–49. **Seaweeds transfer harmful bacteria to corals:** Smith, J. E., et al. 2006. "Indirect Effects of Algae on Coral: Algae-Mediated, Microbe-Induced Coral Mortality." *Ecology Letters* 9:835–45.

Parrotfish are important for the corals: Mumby, P. J., et al. 2006. "Fishing, Trophic Cascades, and the Process of Grazing on Coral Reefs." *Science* 311:98–101.

Roger Revelle and Hans Suess: Doney, S. C. 2006. "The Dangers of Ocean Acidification." *Scientific American*, March 2009.

There's a third more carbon dioxide: Intergovernmental Panel on Climate Change. 2001. *The Scientific Basis: Contribution of Working Group I to the Third Assessment Report of the Intergovernmental Panel on Climate Change.* Cambridge University Press. **One hundred times faster:** Fabry, V. J., et al. 2008. "Impacts of Ocean Acidification on Marine Fauna and Ecosystem Processes." *International Council for the Exploration of the Sea Journal of Marine Science* 65:414–32. **Also:** Royal Society. 2005. *Ocean Acidification Due to Increasing Atmospheric Carbon Dioxide.* Policy Document 12/05. **We've reversed a long natural cooling:** Kaufman, D. S., et al. 2009. "Recent Warming Reverses Long-Term Arctic Cooling." *Science* 236–39. **Stabilizing climate requires that:** Stern, N. 2007. *The Economics of Climate Change.* Cambridge University Press. **A warming of five degrees Fahrenheit and the doubling by midcentury:** Sachs, J. 2009. *Common Wealth: Economics for a Crowded Planet*, pp. 91–93. Penguin Group. **A different planet:** Hansen, J., et al. 2007. "Dangerous Human-Made Interference with Climate: A Giss Model." *Atmospheric Chemistry and Physics* 7:2287–312.

The North Atlantic is absorbing: Sabine, C. L., et al. 2004. "The Oceanic Sink for Anthropogenic CO_2." *Science* 305:367–71.

Changes in pH and a review of climate effects: Brierley, A., and M. Kingsford. 2009. "Impacts of Climate Change on Marine Organisms and Ecosystems." *Current Biology* 19:R602–14.

Carbonate concentrations: Orr, J. C., et al. 2005. "Anthropogenic Ocean Acidification over the Twenty-First Century and Its Impact on Calcifying Organisms." *Nature* 437:681–86.

Ocean surface has 30 percent more hydrogen ions: Feely, R. A., et al. 2004. "Impact of Anthropogenic CO_2 on the $CaCO_3$ System in the Oceans." *Science* 305:362. **And:** Feely, R. A., et al. 2008. "Evidence for Upwelling of Corrosive 'Acidified' Water onto the Continental Shelf." *Science* 320:1490–92; published online May 22, 2008. **And:** Orr, J. C. et al. 2005. "Anthropogenic Ocean Acidification over the Twenty-First Century and Its Impact on Calcifying Organisms." *Nature* 437:4095.

How changing carbon dioxide concentrations will affect the ocean's

calcium carbonate concentrations: Hoegh-Guldberg, O., et al. 2007. "Coral Reefs Under Rapid Climate Change and Ocean Acidification." *Science* 318:1737. **See also:** Kleypas, J. A., et al. 1999. "Geochemical Consequences of Increased Atmospheric Carbon Dioxide on Coral Reefs." *Science* 284:118–20.

Carbon dioxide expected to reach 550 ppm after midcentury: Rogelj, J., et al. 2009. "Halfway to Copenhagen, No Way to 2°C." *Nature Reports*. Published online: June 11, 2009, doi:10.1038/climate.2009.57. **See also:** Silverman, J., et al. 2009. "Coral Reefs May Start Dissolving When Atmospheric CO_2 Doubles." *Geophysical Research Letters* 36:L05606.

Foraminifera shells: Moy, A. D., et al. 2009. "Reduced Calcification in Modern Southern Ocean Planktonic Foraminifera." *Nature Geoscience* 2:276–80. **Experiments with clams, oysters, mussels:** Fabry, V. J., et al. 2008. "Impacts of Ocean Acidification on Marine Fauna and Ecosystem Processes." *International Council for the Exploration of the Sea Journal of Marine Science* 65:414–32. **But see:** Iglesias-Rodriguez, M. D., et al. 2008. "Phytoplankton Calcification in a High-CO_2 World." *Science* 320:336–40.

Corals able to survive "by going naked": Fine, M., and D. Tchernov. 2007. "Scleractinian Coral Species Survive and Recover from Decalcification." *Science* 315:1811. **Hundreds of millions depend heavily on reefs:** Cinner, J. E., et al. 2009. "Linking Social and Ecological Systems to Sustain Coral Reef Fisheries." *Current Biology* 19:206–12. **See also:** Hoegh-Guldberg, O. 2005. "Low Coral Cover in a High-CO_2 World." *Journal of Geophysical Research* 110:C09S06, doi:10.1029/2004JC002528. **Also:** Pandolfi, J. M., et al. 2003. "Global Trajectories of the Long-Term Decline of Coral Reef Ecosystems." *Science* 301:955–58. **And also:** Donner, S. D., et al. 2005. "Global Assessment of Coral Bleaching and Required Rates of Adaptation Under Climate Change." *Global Change Biology* 11:2251–65.

60,000 small-scale fishers and heavy fishing pressure from: Nenadovic, M. 2007. In: "A Report on the Status of Coral Reefs of Bonaire in 2007 with Results from Monitoring 2003–2007." R. Steneck, et al., pp. 71–80. Informally published.

FAREWELL, WHOLE NEW TIME

In 2007 the United States consumed as much oil: U.S. Energy Information Administration at: http://tonto.eia.doe.gov/country/index.cfm?view=consumption. **Also:** *Millennium Ecosystem Assessment* (available online). **And:** Worldwatch Institute's annual *State of the World* (Norton) contains statistics on resource use. **Resources since 1950s:** Speth, G. 2008. *The Bridge at the End of the World*, pp. 1–3. Yale University Press. **See also:** *Millennium Ecosystem Assessment.*

The Anthropocene: Crutzen, P. J., and E. F. Stoermer. 2000. "The Anthropocene." *Global Change Newsletter* 41:12–13. **See also:** Zalasiewicz, J., et al. 2008. "Are We Now Living in the Anthropocene?" *Geological Society of America Today*, available online.

Gannets and trawler discards: Grémillet, D., et al. 2008. "A Junk-Food Hypothesis for Gannets Feeding on Fishery Waste." *Proceedings of the Royal Society B*, doi:10.1098/rspb.2007.1763.

Using resources 25 percent faster than the world can replace them: WWF *Living Planet Report: Humanity's Footprint*, available online.

Mill: John Stuart Mill. 1848. "The Art of Living." *Principles of Political Economy*, book IV, chapter VI, section II.

Number of people the world could support: Brown, L. 2008. *Plan B 3.0*, p. 188. Norton. **Chinese refrigerators and China's resource consumption:** *Plan B 3.0*, p. 219, and elsewhere. **Forests largely gone by around 2025:** *Plan B 3.0*, p. 88. **See also:** FAO. 2006. *Global Forest Resource Assessment 2005*. Rome: United Nations Food and Agriculture Organization.

Comparisons of Americans with other nationalities: Pearce, F. 2009. "Consumption Dwarfs Population as Main Environmental Threat." *Yale Environment 360*. April 13, 2009, available online.

4 billion people live on less than $2 per day: Lierowitz, A., et al. 2005. "Sustainability, Attitudes, Values, and Behaviors: A Review of Multinational and Global Trends." *Annual Review of Environment and Resources* 31:413. **Inadequate caloric intake and two and a half Earths:** *Millennium Ecosystem Assessment*, available online. **See also:** "Number of World's Hungry Tops a Billion." United Nations World Food Programme, 2009, available online.

Grain harvests tripled since 1950: Brown, L. 2008. *Plan B 3.0*, p. 176. Norton. **Nitrogen:** Fryzuk, M. D. 2004. "Ammonia Transformed." *Nature* 427:498–99.

Groundwater and grain: Brown, L. 2008. *Plan B 3.0*, pp. 68–69, 71, 82. Norton.

Demand for water: Pearce, F. 2004. "Asian Farmers Sucking the Continent Dry." *New Scientist*, August 18, 2004. **See also:** Pearce, F. 2006. "The Parched Planet." *New Scientist*, February 26, 2006.

"When the balloon bursts": Pearce, F. 2004. "Asian Farmers Sucking the Continent Dry." *New Scientist*, August 28, 2004.

Water tables dropping: Brown, L. 2008. *Plan B 3.0*, pp. 72, 74. Norton. **See also:** Brown, L. R. 2008. "Could Food Shortages Bring Down Civilization?" *Scientific American*, May 2008, available online.

Water in Asia: Pearce, F. 2004. "Asian Farmers Sucking the Continent Dry." *New Scientist*, August, 28, 2004.

Two-thirds of all people will suffer water scarcity: U.N. Thematic Initiatives. 2006. "Coping with Water Scarcity: A Strategic Issue and Priority for System-Wide Action," available online. **Water:** United Nations Web site waterforlifedecade.org. **See also:** Globalfootprint.org.

Grain a proxy for rain: Pearce, F. "Water Scarcity: The Real Food Crisis." *Yale Environment 360*, available online. **See also:** Myers, N. 2002. "Environmental Refugees: A Growing Phenomenon of the 21st Century." *Philosophical Transactions of the Royal Society B* 357:609–13. **And see:** Sachs, J. D. 2007. "Climate Change Refugees." *Scientific American*, June 2007, available online.

Africa populations, relation to Nile water, population projections and tensions, and Rwanda: Brown, L. 2008. *Plan B 3.0*, pp. 117–19. Norton. **See also:** Brainard, L., et al., eds. 2007. *Too Poor for Peace?* Brookings Institution Press.

Education and reduction in fertility: Brown, L. 2008. *Plan B 3.0*, pp. 109, 134. Norton.

Getting worse at a slower rate: Longman, P. 2006. "The Depopulation Bomb." *Conservation in Practice* 7:40–41. **Fifty countries will likely have fewer people:** Lierowitz, A., et al. 2005. "Sustainability, Attitudes, Values, and Behaviors: A Review of Multinational and Global Trends." *Annual Review of Environment and Resources* 31:413.

FDR quote on conservation as basis for peace: Pinchot, G. 1947. *Breaking New Ground*. Harcourt, Brace.

How we think of problems: See Lovins, A. 1991. "Technology Is the Answer (but What Was the Question?)." In *Environmental Science*, ed. G. Tyler Miller, pp. 56–57. Wadsworth.

APRIL

Last time our planet was free of polar ice: Barrett, P. 2003. "Cooling a Continent." *Nature* 421:221–23. **Also:** Zachos, J., et al. 2001. "Trends, Rhythms, and Aberrations in Global Climate 65 Ma to Present." *Science* 292:686–93.

Václav Havel: editorial, "Stalin's Legacy of Filth," *New York Times*, February 7, 1990.

Shell out $700 in subsidies and "The world taxes itself" from: De Moor, A., and P. Calamai. 1997. "Subsidizing Unsustainable Development: Undermining the Earth with Public Funds." The Earth Council, available online.

Quotations from Thomas Jefferson: http://etext.virginia.edu/jefferson/quotations/jeff1320.htm.

History of corporations in the United States: http://www.reclaimdemocracy.org/corporate_accountability/history_corporations_us.html.

"The most fundamental redesign": Mander, J. 1996. *The Case Against the Global Economy*. Random House. **See also:** Speth, G. 2008. *The Bridge at the End of the World*, pp. 166–68. Yale University Press. **195 countries:** http://www.infoplease.com/ipa/A0932875.html.

Supreme Court of Michigan in 1919 and what a corporation is for: See the history of Ford vs. Dodge at: http://everything2.com/node/1768159.

Twentieth century growth numbers and amount of "annual stuff" consumed: McNeill, J. R. 2000. *Something New Under the Sun*. Norton.

Fully half the transformation of earthly materials: Turner, B. L., et al. 1990. *The Earth as Transformed by Human Action*. Cambridge University Press.

"It is impossible for the world economy to grow": Daly, H. E. 1993. "Sustainable Growth: An Impossibility Theorem." In *Valuing the Earth*, ed. H. E. Daly and K. Townsend, Massachusetts Institute of Technology Press. **See also:** Simm, A. "Does Growth Really Help the Poor? *New Scientist*, October 15, 2008.

MAY

Ben Franklin quotes: *The Autobiography of Benjamin Franklin*, available online.

Tern foraging ecology: Safina, C. 1990. "Bluefish Mediation of Foraging Competition Between Roseate and Common Terns." *Ecology* 71:1804–9. **And:** Safina, C. 1990. "Foraging Habitat Partitioning in Roseate and Common Terns." *The Auk: A Quarterly Journal of Ornithology* 107:351–58. **Also:** Safina, C., and J. Burger. 1988. "Prey Dynamics and the Breeding Phenology of Common Terns." *The Auk: A Quarterly Journal of Ornithology* 105:720–26. **And:** Safina, C., and J. Burger. 1988. "Ecological Dynamics Among Prey Fish, Bluefish and Foraging Common Terns in a Coastal Atlantic System." In *Seabirds and Other Marine Vertebrates:*

Competition, Predation, and Other Interactions, ed. J. Burger, pp. 95–173. Columbia University Press. **Also:** Safina, C., and J. Burger. 1985. "Common Tern Foraging: Seasonal Trends in Prey Fish Densities, and Competition with Bluefish." *Ecology* 66:1457–63.

Horseshoe crabs 450 million years old: Rudkin, D. M., et al. 2008. "The Oldest Horseshoe Crab: A New Xiphosurid from Late Ordovician Konservat-Lagerstätten Deposits, Manitoba, Canada." *Paleontology* 51:1–9. **American horseshoe crab eggs poisonous to humans:** Iverson, E. S., and R. H. Skinner. 2006. *Dangerous Sea Animals*. Pineapple Press. **Horseshoe crab commerce:** Angier, N. 2008. "Tallying the Toll on an Elder of the Sea." *New York Times*, June 10, 2008. **Number of people licensed to take horseshoe crabs in New York and horseshoe crab prices going over a dollar:** Wacker, T. 2008. "Restrictions Reduce Horseshoe Crab Fishing." *New York Times*, June 10, 2008, and Long Island Weekly Section, p. 5. **Red Knots:** *Red Knot and Shorebird Facts: Imperiled Shorebirds on Delaware Bay.* Pamphlet by New Jersey Department of Environmental Protection, available online. **Also:** Niles, L., et al. 2007. *Status of the Red Knot (Calidris Canutus Rufa) in the Western Hemisphere.* New Jersey Department of Environmental Protection, Division of Fish and Wildlife. **Horseshoe crabs and shorebirds including the Red Knot:** *Red Knot: An Imperiled Migratory Shorebird in New Jersey.* New Jersey Department of Environmental Protection. **Newly maturing female crabs dropped nearly 90 percent:** Eilperin, J. 2005. "Horseshoe Crabs' Decline Further Imperils Shorebirds." *Washington Post*, June 10, 2005. **Crabs appear to be up slightly:** "Horseshoe Crab Population on the Rise." Reuters, May 29, 2008.

JUNE

Plosive, gasping breaths: photos of the dolphin and a recording of its breathing are on YouTube as "Dolphin's Last Dance."

Mosquito Plan: http://www.suffolkmosquitocontrolplan.org. **Malaria in Suffolk County:** http://www.cdc.gov. **Malaria and encephalitis in New York City and State:** www.health.state.ny.us/nysdoh/. **Encephalitis:** www.cdc.gov/ncidod/dvbid/arbor/eeefact.htm.

Cell phone driving accidents: Richtel, M. 2009. "Driven to Distraction: U.S. Withheld Data on Risks of Distracted Driving." *New York Times*, July 19, 2009, p. A1.

TRAVELS POLAR: BEAR WITNESS—SOUTHEAST ALASKA

"Hey, what about all these salmon?" and information about salmon carcasses washing downstream, and a bear carrying forty salmon and Sitka Spruce growth: Gende, S., and T. P. Quinn. 2006. "The Fish and the Forest." *Scientific American*, July 2006. **Bears move more than half of the salmon:** Reimchen, T. E. 2000. "Some Ecological and Evolutionary Aspects of Bear–Salmon Interactions in Coastal British Columbia." *Canadian Journal of Zoology* 78:448–57. **Bears feeding on abundant salmon often have three cubs:** Gende, S. M., et al. 2002. "Pacific Salmon in Aquatic and Terrestrial Ecosystems." *BioScience* 52:917. **Bears threatening financial and social collapse:** see "The Fish and the Forest," above.

John Muir: Muir, J. 1993. *Travels in Alaska*, Penguin.

Jefferson Moser of the U.S. Fish Commission: Moser, J. 1899. "The Salmon and Salmon Fisheries of Alaska: Report of the Operations of the United States Fish Commission Steamer *Albatross* for the Year Ending June 30, 1898." *U.S. Fish Commission Bulletin for 1898.* Government Printing Office. **See also:** Moser, J. 1902. "The Salmon and Salmon Fisheries of Alaska: Report of the Alaska Salmon Investigations of the United States Fish Commission Steamer *Albatross* in 1900 and 1901." *U.S. Fish Commission Bulletin for 1901.* Government Printing Office.

Southeast region physical statistics and canneries history, and history of salmon fishing in Alaska: Schoen, John, and Erin Dovichin, eds. 2007. *A Conservation Assessment and Resource Synthesis for the Coastal Forests and Mountain Ecoregion of Southeastern Alaska and the Tongass National Forest*, chapter 9.5. Available online at: conserveonline.org/workspaces/akcfm. **Alaskan boats catch 80 percent of the salmon:** Schoen and Dovichin, chapter 8.1. **Five thousand streams in Southeast Alaska support salmon:** Schoen and Dovichin, chapter 8.4.

Problems with Canadian Kings: Hopper, Tristin. 2008. "So Long and Thanks for All the Fish." *Yukon News,* September 3, 2008. **Canadian salmon down 80 percent:** www.stateofthesalmon.org/iucn/. **Chronic mismanagement of Canada's salmon:** Hume, M. 2008. "Bureaucracy's Bad Decisions Share Guilt for Depleting Wild Salmon." *Globe and Mail*, May 19, 2008. **Stocks are in wide decline; bears are starving:** Hume, M. 2008. "We're Killing Too Many Salmon, and It's Time to Take the Blame." *Globe and Mail*, September 3, 2008. **Eagles eating garbage:** Rolfsen, C. 2008. "Bald Eagle Count Lowest Since 1990; Shortage Blamed on Lack of Salmon in Area Rivers." *Vancouver Sun*, January 7, 2008. **What salmon brought so naturally, for free:** Gende, S. M., et al. 2002. "Pacific Salmon in Aquatic and Terrestrial Ecosystems." *BioScience* 52:917.

Summary of world temperate rainforests: Kellogg, E. L., ed. 1995. "The Rain Forests of Home: An Atlas of People and Place." *Ecotrust*, available online.

Cutting a tree for the price of a cheeseburger; only 4 percent of the Tongass is capable of supporting giant trees; and the region's thirteen mills: Servid, C., and D. Snow, eds. 1999. *The Book of the Tongass*. Milkweed. **Tongass Timber Reform Act history:** Bart Koehler, personal communication. **Tongass logging history and tourism in Southeast Alaska:** Chadwick, D. H. 2007. "The Truth About the Tongass." *National Geographic*, July 2007. **A third of the remaining big-tree forests are unprotected:** Schoen and Dovichin, cited above, chapters 2 and 3.

Brown Bear densities: O'Clair, R. M., et al. 1997. *The Nature of Southeast Alaska*. Alaska Northwest Books. **Bear population of the ABC islands and Congress designating most of Admiralty as the Kootznoowoo Wilderness:** Schoen and Dovichin, cited above, chapters 6, 2.

JULY

Eskimo Curlew and killing of other shorebirds: Mowat, F. 1986. *Sea of Slaughter*, pp. 52–74. Bantam. Mowat quotes much from A. C. Bent's *Life Histories of North American Shore Birds, Parts One and Two*, 1922 and 1929, Smithsonian Institution.

TRAVELS POLAR: SVALBARD

Yield declines in grain: Peng, S., et al. 2004. "Rice Yields Decline with Higher Night Temperature from Global Warming." *Proceedings of the National Academy of Sciences* 27:9971–75. **"Difficult to feed Earth's growing population":** National Academy of Sciences. 2004. "Warmer Evening Temperatures Lower Rice Yields." *Proceedings of the National Academy of Sciences News Archive*, June 28–July 2, 2004. **Reduced corn and soybean yields with increasing temperatures:** Lobell, D. B., and G. P. Asner. 2003. "Climate and Management Contributions to Recent Trends in U.S. Agricultural Yields." *Science* 299:1032. **Sorghum seeds viable up to 20,000 years:**

"Arctic 'Doomsday' Seed Vault Opens Doors for 100 Million Seeds." *ScienceDaily*, February 27, 2008; available online.

These results demonstrate: Baker, C. S., and S. R. Palumbi. 1994. "Which Whales are Hunted?" *Science* 265:1538.

Bowhead Whale: Norwegian Polar Institute, http://npweb.npolar.no/english/ arter/gronlandshval. **Stone harpoons and age of bowhead:** http://www.gi. alaska.edu/ScienceForum/ASF15/1529.html. **Walrus, Bowhead, and other marine mammal facts:** Folkens, P. A., et al. 2002. *Guide to Marine Mammals of the World.* Knopf. **Bear hunting in Nunavut and Greenland:** "Unbearable Pursuits: Saving Canada's Polar Bears." *Economist,* November 22, 2008.

Polar Bear movements, denning and fasting, breeding, and other aspects of their biology: Amstrup, S. C. "The Polar Bear, *Ursus Maritimus:* Biology, Management, and Conservation," polarbearsinternational.org/polar-bears-in-depth/denning/.

Polar Bears' hunting success rates, weight of pregnant bears versus those with cubs, Ringed Seal pup growth rate, Ringed Seal density in years of ice shrinkage: Rosing-Asvid, A. 2006. "The Influence of Climate Variability on Polar Bear (*Ursus maritimus*) and Ringed Seal (*Pusa hispida*) Population Dynamics." *Canadian Journal of Zoology* 84:357–64. **Also:** Gjertz, I., and L. Christian. 2007. "Polar Bear Predation on Ringed Seals in the Fast-Ice of Hornsund, Svalbard." *Polar Research* 4:65–68. **And:** Angier, N. 2004. "Built for the Arctic: A Species' Splendid Adaptations." *New York Times,* January 17, 2004.

Polar Bears forced to swim: Joling, D. 2008. "Observers Spot 9 Polar Bears in Open Ocean." Associated Press, August 21, 2008. **And:** O'Carroll, E. 2008. "Polar Bears Spotted Swimming in Open Seas." *Christian Science Monitor,* August 22, 2008.

PCBs and DDT: Cone, M. 2003. "Of Polar Bears and Pollution." *Los Angeles Times,* June 19, 2003. **And:** Cone, M. 2006. "Polar Bears Face New Toxic Threat: Flame Retardants." *Los Angeles Times,* January 9, 2006. **Contaminants and Polar Bears:** Dietz, R., et al. 2006. "Trends in Mercury in Hair of Greenlandic Polar Bears (*Ursus maritimus*) During 1892–2001." *Environmental Science & Technology* 40:1120–25. **Svalbard polar bears exposed to a flu virus and PCBs:** Lie, E., et al. 2004. "Does High Organochlorine (OC) Exposure Impair the Resistance to Infection in Polar Bears (*Ursus maritimus*)? Part I: Effect of OCs on the Humoral Immunity." *Journal of Toxicology and Environmental Health, Part A* 67:555–82.

U.S. Geological Survey and *Anchorage Daily News* **quoted in:** Knicker-bocker, B. 2007. "Charismatic Bears on Thin Ice." *Christian Science Monitor,* September 13, 2007.

Ocean temperature warmest measured: Borenstein, S. 2009. "World Sets Record for Ocean Temperature." *Boston Globe,* August 20, 2009. **Sea ice extent:** National Snow and Ice Data Center, at nsidc.org/arcticseaicenews/.

Svalbard ice cap melting: Dowdeswell, J. A., et al. 2008. "Iceberg Calving Flux and Mass Balance of the Austfonna Ice Cap on Nordaustlandet, Svalbard." *Journal of Geophysical Research* 113:F03022, available online. **Greenland ice melting:** Dowdeswell, J. A. 2006. "The Greenland Ice Sheet and Global Sea-Level Rise." *Science* 311:963–64. **Greenland melting rate change and Los Angeles uses one cubic kilometer of water:** Rincon, P. 2006. "Greenland Ice Swells Ocean Rise." BBC News, February 16, 2006, online. **Between 2001 and 2006 Greenland's ice sheet tripled its rate of loss:** Reach, J. 2006. "Greenland Ice Sheet Is Melting Faster, Study Says." *National Geographic News,* August 10, 2006, available online. **Also:** Howat, I. M. 2007. "Rapid Changes in Ice Discharge from Greenland Outlet Glaciers." *Science* 315:1559–61; published online February 8, 2007.

Storm flooding in New York City: http://stormy.msrc.sunysb.edu/. **See also:** Bowman, M. J., et al. 2005. "Hydrologic Feasibility of Storm Surge Barriers to Protect the Metropolitan New York–New Jersey Region," p. 5, available online.

AUGUST

Monarch Butterflies: www.fs.fed.us/monarchbutterfly/biology/index.shtml.

TRAVELS POLAR: BAKED ALASKA

Arctic Ocean will be practically ice-free in summer: Wang, M., and J. E. Overland. 2009. "A Sea Ice Free Summer Arctic Within 30 Years?" *Geophysical Research Letters* 36, available online.

Since the last ice age, sea levels have risen: Bindoff, N. L., et al. 2007. "Observations: Oceanic Climate Change and Sea Level." In *Climate Change 2007: The Physical Science Basis. Contribution of Working Group I to the Fourth Assessment Report of the Intergovernmental Panel on Climate Change,* ed. S. D. Solomon, et al. Cambridge University Press. Available at: http://ipcc-wg1.ucar.edu/wg1/wg1-report.html.

Great decoupling: Grebmeier, J. M., et al. 2006. "A Major Ecosystem Shift in the Northern Bering Sea." *Science* 311:1461–64. **Also:** Beaugrand, G., and P. C. Reid. 2003. "Long-Term Changes in Phytoplankton, Zooplankton and Salmon Related to Climate." *Global Change Biology* 9:801–17. **Also:** Lovvorn, J. R., et al. 2005. "Organic Matter Pathways to Zooplankton and Benthos Under Pack Ice in Late Winter and Open Water in Late Summer in the North-Central Bering Sea." *Marine Ecology Progress Series* 291:135–50. **Starving ducks:** Lovvorn, J. R., et al. 2003. "Diet and Body Condition of Spectacled Eiders Wintering in Pack Ice of the Bering Sea." *Polar Biology* 26:259–67. **Lost and abandoned Walrus pups:** Dawicki, S. 2006. "Lost Walrus Calves Stranded by Melting Ice." Woods Hole Oceanographic Institution, April 13, 2006, available online. **Also:** Perryman, W., et al. 2002. "Gray Whale Calf Production, 1994–2000: Are Observed Fluctuations Related to Changes in Seasonal Ice Cover?" *Marine Mammal Science* 18:121–44. **Also:** Koeller, P., et al. 2009. "Basin-Scale Coherence in Phenology of Shrimps and Phytoplankton in the North Atlantic Ocean." *Science* 324:791–93. **Also:** Moore, S. 2007. "What Is Happening to Whales in the Bering Sea?" Alaska Fisheries Science Center, NOAA. Available online. **For North Sea cod:** Beaugrand, G., et al. 2003. "Plankton Effect on Cod Recruitment in the North Sea." *Nature* 426:661–64. **Copepod shifts in Atlantic:** Beaugrand, G., et al. 2002. "Reorganization of North Atlantic Marine Copepod Biodiversity and Climate." *Science* 296:1692–95. **And more generally:** Parmesan, C., and C. Yohe. 2003. "A Globally Coherent Fingerprint of Climate Change Impacts Across Natural Systems." *Nature* 421:37–42. **And:** Root, T. L., et al. 2003. "Fingerprints of Global Warming on Wild Animals and Plants." *Nature* 421:57–60.

Federal funds to Alaska run twenty-five times the national average: usatoday.com/news/opinion/editorials/2005-05-17-alaska-edit_x.htm.

Salmon and temperature: Richter, A., and S. A. Kolmes. 2005. "Maximum Temperature Limits for Chinook, Coho, and Chum Salmon, and Steelhead Trout in the Pacific Northwest." *Reviews in Fisheries Science* 13:23–49. *Ichthyophonus:* Weiss, K. 2008. "Alaska Salmon May Bear Scars of Global Warming," *Los Angeles Times,* June 15, 2008.

Water shortage due to lack of snow: Martin, G. 2007. "Snow Pack in Sierra Is Way Low." *San Francisco Chronicle*, March 29, 2007, available online.

Beetles are destroying tens of millions of acres: Fox, D. 2007. "Back to the No-Analog Future." *Science* 316:823.

Number of people dependent on Himalayan glaciers: Brown, L. 2008. *Plan*

B 3.0, p. 54. Norton. **"Full-scale glacier shrinkage":** G. Lean. 2006. "Ice-Capped Roof of World Turns to Desert; Scientists Warn of Ecological Catastrophe Across Asia as Glaciers Melt and Continent's Great Rivers Dry Up." *Independent,* May 7, 2006. **"Maybe God is unkind":** Sugita Katyal. 2005. "Water Crisis Looms as Himalayan Glaciers Melt." Reuters U.K., September 2, 2005.

Global warming could displace 200 million people: Myers, N. 2002. "Environmental Refugees: A Growing Phenomenon of the 21st Century." *Philosophical Transactions of the Royal Society B* 357:609–13.

OCTOBER

Reducing poverty . . . "cannot be achieved": "Ecosystems and Human Well-Being: Synthesis." *Millennium Ecosystem Assessment, 2005.* Island Press; also available online. **Also:** "The Ability of the Planet's Ecosystems." *Millenium Ecosystem Assessment 2005.* **And:** "Living Beyond Our Means: Natural Assets and Human Well-Being." *Millenium Ecosystem Assessment 2005.*

Something like four hundred times in the Bible: Various authors. 2002. *Ethics for a Small Planet,* pp. 65–66. Biodiversity Project.

"All the bad things that happen" and Milton Friedman quote: Bakan, J. 2005. *The Corporation.* Constable.

Real cost of gasoline: International Center for Technology Assessment. 1998. *The Real Cost of Gasoline.* International Center for Technology Assessment. **Taxing gas and autos:** Brown, L. 2008. *Plan B 3.0,* p. 270. Norton. **"Market failure on the greatest scale":** The economist Lord Nicholas Stern in remarks associated with release of his *Review on the Economics of Climate Change,* a 700-page report for the British government released in 2006; available online.

The economy is a wholly owned subsidiary: Timothy E. Wirth, under secretary of state for democracy and global affairs, Department of State, from a speech entitled "Our Global Future: Climate Change," September 15, 1997; available online.

Distinguishing good from bad: See Sagoff, M. 1990. *The Economy of the Earth.* Cambridge University Press.

Economic measures cannot distinguish: Based on Speth, G. 2008. *The Bridge at the End of the World,* p. 138. Yale University Press. **Its measured economy would look "robust":** Based on Repetto, R., et al. 1989. *Wasting*

Assets: Natural Resources in the National Accounts. World Resources Institute.

TRAVELS SOLAR: RAINBOW'S END—PALAU

Dishonesty in whaling: Baker, C. S., and S. R. Palumbi. 1994. "Which Whales Are Hunted? A Molecular Genetic Approach to Monitoring Whaling." *Science* 265:1538–39.

Lack of resilience of stressed reefs to bleaching: See Carilli, J. E., et al. 2009. "Local Stressors Reduce Coral Resilience to Bleaching." *PLoS ONE* 4:e6324, available online. **More grazing fish mean less leafy algae:** Newman, M. J. H., et al. 2006. "Structure of Caribbean Coral Reef Communities Across a Large Gradient of Fish Biomass." *Ecology Letters* 9:1216–27.

Species numbers on coral reefs: Reaka-Kudla, M. L. 1997. "The Global Bio-diversity of Coral Reefs: A Comparison with Rainforests." In *Biodiversity II: Understanding and Protecting Our Natural Resources,* ed. M. L. Reaka-Kudla, et al., pp. 83–108. National Academy Press.

Calcification has declined 14.2%: De'ath, G., et al. 2009. "Declining Coral Calcification on the Great Barrier Reef." *Science* 323:116–19. **Charlie Veron quoted in:** "Scientists Say World's Coral Reefs Doomed." United Press International, July 7, 2009. **Ocean temperature warmest measured:** Borenstein, S. 2009. "World Sets Record for Ocean Temperature." *Boston Globe,* August 20, 2009.

40 percent of U.S. train freight is coal: Brown, L. 2008. *Plan B 3.0,* p. 260. Norton. **Bottled water; more water to make the plastic bottle; oil in the bottle:** Azios, T. 2008. "The Battle over Bottled vs. Tap Water." *Christian Science Monitor,* January 17, 2008, available online. **Fossil fuel use and appliance efficiencies:** Brown, *Plan B 3.0,* pp. 214–31.

Auto and gasoline statistics and auto efficiency: Brown, L. 2008. *Plan B 3.0,* pp. 228, 244. Norton. **Power of sunlight and Earth's crust compared to energy needs and oil and gas:** Brown, *Plan B 3.0,* p. 252. **Wind potential of central U.S. states:** Brown, *Plan B 3.0,* pp. 237–40.

Ethanol's food trade-offs: Brown, L. R. 2009. "Could Food Shortages Bring Down Civilization?" *Scientific American,* May 2009, available online. **Algae as fuel:** "First Flight of Algae-Fuelled Jet." BBC News, January 8, 2009.

Announcements of aid by Australia and the United States to Micronesia: available online.

Climate refugees: Friedman, L. 2009. "How Will Climate Refugees Impact

National Security?" *Scientific American,* March 23, 2009. **Sinking Indo-nesian islands:** "Mass Relocation Planned as Seas Rise." *Financial Times,* November 1, 2008; available online.

Well over half a million: Barnett, J., and W. N. Adger. 2003. "Climate Dangers and Atoll Countries." *Climatic Change* 61:321–37. **Something approaching 100 million:** Brooks, N., et al. 2006. *Sea Level Rise: Coastal Impacts and Responses.* German Advisory Council on Climate Change; available online. **Cities exposed to the sea:** German Advisory Council on Global Change. 2006. *The Future Ocean: Warming Up, Rising High, Turning Sour.* German Advisory Council on Global Change; available online. **30 million in Bangladesh:** Chopra, A. 2009. "Salt Surge Puts Crops in Peril." *National;* available online.

Pernicious security implications: See, for example, the press release by Islands First, October 31, 2008; available online.

At risk from rising sea-level: Myers, N. 2002. "Environmental Refugees: A Growing Phenomenon of the 21st Century." *Philosophical Transactions of the Royal Society B* 357:609–13. **India is building a fence:** Friedman, L. 2009. "How Will Climate Refugees Impact National Security?" *Scientific American,* March 23, 2009. **"It gets real complicated":** Broder, J. M. 2009. "Climate Change Seen as Threat to U.S. Security." *New York Times,* August 9, 2009.

NOVEMBER

Fromm, Illich, Shitovsky: Summarized in Jackson, T. 2005. "Live Better by Consuming Less? Is There a 'Double Dividend' to Sustainable Consumption?" *Journal of Industrial Ecology* 9:19–25. **See also:** Speth, G. 2008. *The Bridge at the End of the World.* Yale University Press.

Indices of social health and social progress: Summarized in Speth, G. 2008. *The Bridge at the End of the World.* Yale University Press, pp. 134–40. **Also:** Jackson, T., and S. Stymne. 1996. "Sustainable Welfare in Sweden." Stockholm Environment Institute; available at www.sei.se. **Also:** Venetoulis, J., and C. Cobb. 2004. "The Genuine Progress Indicator, 1950 to 2002," available at www.rprogress.org. **Also:** Miringoff, M. L., and S. Opdycke. 2007. *America's Social Health.* M. E. Sharpe. **See also** the New Economics Foundation's happyplanetindex.org.

Well-being literature reviewed: Diener, E., and M. Seligman. 2004. "Beyond Money: Toward an Economy of Well-Being." *Psychological Science in the*

Public Interest 5:1. **Also:** Lierowitz, A., et al. 2005. "Sustainability, Attitudes, Values, and Behaviors: A Review of Multinational and Global Trends." *Annual Review of Environment and Resources* 31:413.

Per-person GNP in the United States: See Earthtrends. WRI.org/text/economics-business/variable-638.html.

Expanding wealth and shrinking spirit: Myers, D. G. 2000. *The American Paradox: Spiritual Hunger in an Age of Plenty.* Yale University Press. **"Famine of warm interpersonal relations":** Lane, R. 2001. *The Loss of Happiness in Market Democracies.* Yale University Press.

Number of lobbyists and corporations, plus related statistic: Summarized in Speth, G. 2008. *The Bridge at the End of the World*, pp. 168–70. Yale University Press.

Thomas Jefferson to John Hay: In Foley, J. P. 1900. *The Jeffersonian Cyclopedia*, p. 57. Funk and Wagnalls.

Walt Whitman: First published in the 1860 edition of *Leaves of Grass* as "Walt Whitman's Caution," a title he later changed to "To the States."

A spirited culture of refusal, a counterlife: I've taken this phrase from White, C. 2007. *The Spirit of Disobedience.* PoliPoint Press.

Two-thirds of Americans and "the biggest threat." Esty, D. C., and A. S. Winston. 2006. *Green to Gold.* Yale University Press.

TRAVELS POLAR: COPA CABANA—ANTARCTICA

How many whales were killed: http://news-service.stanford.edu/news/2003/august6/whales-86.html. **Also:** Reeves, R. R., and T. D. Smith. 2003. *A Taxonomy of World Whaling: Operations, Eras, and Data Sources.* Northeast Fisheries Science Center Reference Document 03-12, available online.

Pack ice and plankton changes: Montes-Hugo, M., et al. 2009. "Recent Changes in Phytoplankton Communities Associated with Rapid Regional Climate Change Along the Western Antarctic Peninsula." *Science* 323:1470–73. **Chinstraps and Adélies are both down by more than half:** Trivelpiece, W., et al. "Chinstrap Penguins: Vulnerable Monitors of Ecosystem Changes in the Scotia Sea Region of Antarctica." Unpublished manuscript.

Various penguin declines: Agence France-Presse. 2009. "African Penguin Numbers in Sharp Decline," May 20, 2009. **Also:** Dean, C. 2008. "A New Twist in Penguins' Already Uncertain Future." *New York Times,* July 1, 2008. **And:** MSNBC. 2009. "Penguin Species Nears Extinction." MSNBC.com. **See also:** Jenouvriers., et al. 2009. "Demographic Models and IPCC

Climate Projections Predict the Decline of an Emperor Penguin Population." *Proceedings of the National Academy of Sciences* 106:1844–47.

JANUARY

Our factories could mimic: Hawken, P., et al. 1999. *Natural Capitalism.* Little, Brown. **Enter the life process itself:** Adams, W. M., and S. J. Jeanrenaud. 2008. *Transition to Sustainability: Towards a Humane and Diverse World.* IUCN.

ACKNOWLEDGMENTS

Many generous people supported parts of this work. They include the David and Lucile Packard Foundation; the Wallace Research Foundation; anonymous homeland generosity; Julie Packard; Marjie Findlay and Geoffrey Freeman, Repass-Rodgers Family Foundation, West Marine; Eric Gilchrist; Angus Gilchrist; Marshall Gilchrist; Andrew Sabin; Yvon Chouinard; the Curtis and Edith Munson Foundation; Shari Sant Plummer and Dan Plummer; the Code Blue Foundation; the Claneil Foundation; Patagonia; Vicki Sant and Roger Sant; the Summit Fund of Washington; Royal Caribbean; Chantecaille cosmetics and the Chantecaille family; the Moore Charitable Foundation; the Vital Spark Foundation; Swiss Re America; Lindblad Expeditions; the National Geographic Society; the Susan A. and Donald P. Babson Charitable Foundation; the Vervane Foundation; the R. K. Mellon Family Foundation; the Community Service Society; Bob Campbell; Henry Jordan; Michael Freedman; Leo Hindery; Rose Safina; Patrick Martin; Jeffrey Miller; Paula Cooper; Joanne Prager; Gale Mead; Patrick Luke; Catherine Rasenberger, Dimitri Sevastopoulo; Birgit and Robert Bateman; Mercedes Lee; Mark Glimcher; Stony Brook University's School of Marine and Atmospheric Sciences; the National Science Foundation's Antarctic Artists and Writers Program; the Avalon Park and Preserve; many others—and Furthermore, a program of the J. M. Kaplan Fund. I thank you deeply.

For very insightful comments on drafts, I thank John Angier, Gary Soucie, Cynthia Tuthill, Steve Dishart, and Lorna Salzman. For sage counsel in fields of Arctic cotton, Peter Raven. For faith that clarity would come, Jean Naggar. And for floating this vessel, the unsinkable Jack Macrae.

My neighbors John, Marilyn, Linda, and Robbie Badkin, Janice Elze, and Dennis Curles provided clams, anchors, bonfires, wine, driftwood, and whales.

For keepin' it all together, Myra Sarli. Megan Smith more than ably assisted with research and all manner of logistical grace. Special thanks, also, to Todd Gardner and Chris Paparo and the Atlantis Marine World aquarium in Riverhead, Long Island. For varied assistance: Flora Lichtman, Eric Salzman, Peter Osswald, John DeBellas, Bob Leonti, John DeCuevas, Ken Mades, Augie Brown, Matthew Milmerstadt, Chris Miller of Westlake Marina in Montauk, Alan Duckworth, and Kate McLaughlin. My copyeditor, Bonnie Thompson, was great as always. Jon Luoma of Alna, Maine, did the maps. Trudy Nicholson of Maryland rendered the equisite drawings.

I thank Bob Steneck for painting the big picture of tropical reefs and, with Susie Arnold, for terrific camaraderie in Belize, Bonaire, and Palau. I greatly thank the Smithsonian Institution for facilitating my visit to the Carrie Bow Cay research station in Belize. Researchers Nikki Fogarty and Raf Ritson-Williams provided my coral sex ed. In Palau, I learned loads from the world-class reef experts Rob van Woesik and (secret agent) Peter Mumby. I thank Palau's visionary conservationist (and 'cuda chaser) the Hon. Noah Idechong, along with Yimnang Golbuu and the staff of the Palau International Coral Reef Center, and also Ron Leidich of Planet Blue Sea Kayak Tours, Mesikt Idechong, Perpetua Tmetuchl, Takashi Mita, Leonard Basilius, Olai Polloi, Nyk Kloulubak, Hilve Skang, Baudista Sato, Sunny Ngirmang, Isor Kikuo, Umiich Sengebau, Bernie Ngiralmau, Jordan Ewadel, and Kassi Berg.

Regarding Svalbard, I thank Julian Dowdeswell, Stefan Rahmstorf, and Stefan Lundgren for coloring in the white spaces, Chevy Chase for Waltz for Debby, and Sylvia Earle for being Sylvia Earle. And for inviting me and arranging travel, Mary Jo Viederman, Amy Cadge, the outstanding staff of Lindblad Expeditions, and the unique vision and astounding commitment of Sven Lindblad.

For facilitating my visit to mainland Alaska, I thank the Center for Health and the Global Environment at Harvard Medical School. For ecological interpretation, I thank Carmen Field, Sue Mauger, and Ed Burg.

My visit to Southeast Alaska would not have been possible without the thoughtful consideration of the photographer Amy Gulick and her publisher Mountaineers Books. Part of that chapter, some terrific writing by other authors, and Amy's marvelous photos of the one-of-a-kind region are in Amy's book *Salmon in the Trees: Life in the Tongass Rainforest,* published by Mountaineers Books–Braided River in 2010. Chris Gulick, a.k.a. the Prince of Heat, taught me Dolly Varden's secret handshake and performed magic upon the grill that made our time delicious. Wade Loofbourrow was simply the best possible captain for that trip; *Legend* was the perfect boat. I also thank Matt Kirchoff for generously sharing time and space during his surveys of murrelets, and Bart Koehler for his unique and gentle wisdom and hard-earned insights into Southeast Alaskan logging politics and reform.

Wayne and Sue Trivelpiece made Antarctica feel warm and were superb facilitators, guides, brewmasters, and krill gurus. I thank also Shiway Wang and Laina Shill. And the penguins.

As always, I thank Patricia and Alexandra for creating my harbor, and for leaving my cage door open and my wings intact. Our parrots, happy though they are, have it only half as good.

One note on style: There are many kinds of white-throated sparrows, but only one is the White-throated Sparrow. So for clarity, and to acknowledge their uniqueness, I capitalize the full common names of species. Since copy editors demand that "Dumpster" be capitalized because it's a "product," I insist on capitalizing Yellow-rumped Warbler and Blue-spotted Salamander. There are products, and then there are products. Fair's fair.

In memory of Kenzie.

INDEX

Arnold, Susie, 63–67, 75–76, 280, 282, 286–87
Arrhenius, Svante, 315
arthropods, 131
"Art of Living, The" (Mill), 87
Atlantic Ocean
  North, 72, 237
  South, 25–26
atmosphere, 13, 14, 315, 317. *See also* carbon dioxide; greenhouse effect; ozone layer
Audubon, John James, 18, 49–50, 186
auks, 199
  Little (Dovekies), 199, 326
Australia, 90, 287, 295, 297, 299–300
Austria, 304
automobiles, 88, 104, 150–51, 290–91

Bacon, Francis, 35, 52
Badkin, Marilyn, 21
Baffin Bay, 210, 211
Baja California, 203
Bakan, Joel, 268
Bangladesh, 90, 238, 296, 299–300
Barents, Willem, 200, 201
Barents Sea, 204, 206, 210
Barracuda, Great, 76–77
Basilius, Leonard, 296–97
Bass, Striped, 25, 109, 117, 143, 148, 158, 274–75, 302–3, 319, 351
  crash and recovery of, 115, 188, 275
  night fishing for, 187–93
bats, fruit, 296
bayberry. *See* Wax Myrtle
beaches, 9–10
  coral sand, 65
  erosion of, 96–98, 102, 233–35, 320, 324
  as nesting ground, 25, 102, 120, 134–41
bears, 172
  Black, 157–59
  Brown (Grizzly), 156–57, 176–79, 181–82, 207

Polar, 202, 207–18, *207*, 232, 236–37, 252
  salmon and, 156–62, 170
bees, 121, 151
Beetles, Spruce Bark, 243–44
Belgium, 14–15
Belize, *60*, 62, *63*, 78, 124, 280, 285
Bent, Arthur Cleveland, 186–87
Berg, Kassi, 294
Beston, Henry, 5
Bhola Island, 296
Bible, 266, 312
Bigeye, Short, 256
Birds of America, The (Audubon), 18
Birds of America (Forbush), 18–19
birds. *See also* sea and shorebirds; *and other specific types*
  decline of, 36, 41, 128, 151
  fledgling, 142
  forests and, 88
  migrations of, 25–26, 31, 128
  skill in looking for, 21
  songs of, 106, 128
bittersweet, 313
blackbirds, 102
  Red-wing, 23–27, 29, 38, *103*, 356, *357*
blackfish, 25, 274
blennies, 282
blueberries, 178, 236
Bluefish, 1, 25, 114–18, *117*, 122–25, 148, 183, 250, 275–76, 301–2, 319
Bobwhite, 129
Boesky, Ivan, 101
Bogotá, 245
Bonaire, *60*, 74, 75–79, 280
Brahmaputra River, 245
Brazil, 290, 334
breams, 282
British Columbia, 170–71
brittle stars, 67
Bruno, Giordano, 52
bryozoans, 67

ABOUT THE AUTHOR

CARL SAFINA is a MacArthur Prize winner and was named by *Audubon* magazine among the leading one hundred conservationists of the twentieth century. He's been profiled by the *New York Times,* on *Nightline,* and by Bill Moyers. His books and articles have also won him a Pew Fellowship, a Lannan Literary Award, a Guggenheim Fellowship, the George B. Rabb Medal, and the John Burroughs Medal, among other distinctions. He is an adjunct professor at Stony Brook University and the founder of Blue Ocean Institute.